WE THE STUDENTS

SUPREME COURT CASES FOR AND ABOUT STUDENTS

THIRD EDITION

Jamin B. Raskin

Professor, American University
Washington College of Law

Member, Maryland State Senate

COSPONSORED BY THE SUPREME COURT HISTORICAL SOCIETY

CQ PRESS

A Division of SAGE
Washington, D.C.

CQ Press
2300 N Street, NW, Suite 800
Washington, DC 20037

Phone: 202-729-1900; toll-free, 1-866-4CQ-PRESS (1-866-427-7737)

Web: www.cqpress.com

Some of the content of Chapter 5 originally appeared in *Youth Justice in America* (CQ Press, 2005). The content, which appears in adapted form, begins with the heading "Strip Searches" and ends with Exercise 5.13.

The table in Chapter 1 originally appeared in *Constitutional Law for a Changing America* (CQ Press, 2007).

Cover design: Naylor Design Inc.
Cover photos: AP Images
Composition: Auburn Associates, Inc.

⊗ The paper used in this publication exceeds the requirements of the American National Standard for Information Sciences—Permanence of Paper for Printed Library Materials, ANSI Z39.48-1992.

Printed and bound in the United States of America

12 11 10 09 08   1 2 3 4 5

Library of Congress Cataloging-in-Publication Data

Raskin, Jamin B.
    We the students : Supreme Court cases for and about students / Jamin B. Raskin.—3rd ed.
        p. cm.
Includes bibliographical references and index.
    ISBN 978-0-87289-760-1 (alk. paper)—ISBN 978-0-87289-761-8 (alk. paper)
    1. Students—Legal status, laws, etc.—United States—Cases. 2. Students—Civil rights—United States—Cases. 3. Educational law and legislation—United States—Cases. I. Title.
    KF4150.A7R37 2008
    344.73'079—dc22
                                                                        2008023743

CONTENTS

Preface / ix

Foreword by Mary Beth Tinker / xvii

1 **"WE THE PEOPLE": OUR CONSTITUTION AND COURTS / 1**

Why a Constitution? / 1

The American Constitution: What Is It? / 2

The Constitution: Whose Is It? / 2

The Constitution: What Does It Mean? / 4

Federalism: How the States Share the Power / 6

The Incorporation of the Bill of Rights / 6

The State Action Requirement / 8

Judicial Architecture: How Our Court System Works / 8

Majority and Dissenting Opinions / 10

How to Brief a Case / 11

2 **VOICES AND CHOICES: THE FIRST AMENDMENT AND STUDENT SPEECH / 13**

Expressive Conduct and the Right Not to Speak / 14

- *West Virginia State Board of Education v. Barnette* / 16

The Right to Speak Freely and Protest (but Not to Disrupt) / 22

- *Tinker v. Des Moines Independent Community School District* / 23

The Confederate Flag and Other Racially Provocative Symbols / 30

Hirsute Lawsuit: Do Boys Have the Right to Wear Long Hair? / 33

- *Karr v. Schmidt* / 34

Double Entendres and Double Standards: Lewd and Suggestive Language
in a Student Government Campaign Speech / 36

- *Bethel School District No. 403 v. Fraser* / 37

Coed Naked Civil Liberties / 41

"BONG HiTS 4 JESUS": Testing the Limits of Free Speech / 43

- *Morse v. Frederick* / 44

Thought Control or Quality Control? The Problem of Library Book Removal / 53

Viewpoint Neutrality and Religious Speech: Good News for the
Free Speech Rights of Religious Americans / 56

- *Good News Club v. Milford Central School* / 57

3 FREEDOM OF THE STUDENT PRESS: ALL THE NEWS THE SCHOOL SEES FIT TO PRINT / 63

Freedom of the Student Press in Official School-Sponsored Activities / 64

- *Hazelwood School District v. Kuhlmeier* / 65

Squelching Debate: A Different Sort of Blair Witch-Hunt / 70

Cyber Censors: Rising Conflicts over Internet Homepages / 72

- *Killion v. Franklin Regional School District* / 74

4 THE WALL OF SEPARATION BETWEEN CHURCH AND SCHOOL / 78

Freedom from Establishment of Religion at School / 80

- *Engel v. Vitale* / 81

Graduating from Invocation and Benediction / 86

- *Lee v. Weisman* / 87
- *Santa Fe Independent School District v. Doe* / 94

Government Aid to Private Religious Schools: When Does It Cross the Line? / 100

- *Everson v. Board of Education of the Township of Ewing* / 100

School Vouchers: Making Education Redeemable in Secular or Religious Schools / 102

- *Zelman v. Simmons-Harris* / 104

The First Amendment and the Ten Commandments / 107

- *Stone v. Graham* / 108

Season's Greetings! The Court's Agonizing Ambivalence over Christmas Nativity Displays / 111

One Nation, under Canada, with Constitutional Controversy for All:
New Conflict over the Pledge of Allegiance / 114

- *Newdow v. U.S. Congress* / 115

The Supreme Court's Curious Response to *Newdow v. U.S. Congress* / 118

The Free Exercise Rights of Religious Americans / 119

- *Wisconsin v. Yoder* / 120

The Theory of Evolution and the Story of Creation: An Ongoing Duel in the Classroom / 126

5 THE FOURTH AMENDMENT: SEARCHING THE STUDENT BODY / 130

Reduced Privacy Rights at School / 132

- *New Jersey v. T. L. O.* / 132

A Fluid Analysis of the Fourth Amendment: Drug Tests and Extracurricular Activities / 139

- *Board of Education of Independent School District No. 92 of Pottawatomie County v. Earls* / 140

Strip Searches / 149

- *Doe v. Renfrow* / 149

Locker Searches and Drug-Sniffing Dogs / 152

- *Commonwealth of Pennsylvania v. Cass* / 153

Metal Detectors and the Constitution / 155

- *In Re Latasha W.* / 155

6 **THE CONSTITUTION AND STUDENT DISCIPLINE: "DUE PROCESS" AND "CRUEL AND UNUSUAL PUNISHMENT" AT SCHOOL / 158**

Due Process / 159

- *Goss v. Lopez* / 160

The Crime of Hanging Out with Gang Members: "Loitering with No Apparent Purpose" in Chicago and the Due Process Clause / 164

- *City of Chicago v. Morales* / 165

Corporal Punishment / 169

- *Ingraham v. Wright* / 169

Corporal Punishment in the Aftermath of *Ingraham v. Wright* / 174

7 **EQUAL PROTECTION AGAINST RACE DISCRIMINATION: FROM SEGREGATION TO MULTICULTURAL DEMOCRACY / 176**

The Persistent Legacy of Slavery and Racism / 178

- *Brown v. Board of Education of Topeka* / 180

Two Steps Forward, One Step Back: "Massive Resistance" and the Reaction to *Brown* / 183

- *Cooper v. Aaron* / 184
- *Griffin v. County School Board of Prince Edward County* / 185

The Right to Love / 189

Can Public Schools Deliberately Integrate Students Today? / 189

- *Parents Involved in Community Schools v. Seattle School Dist. No. 1* / 191

Race and Ethnicity in College and Graduate School Admissions: Affirmative Action or "Reverse Discrimination"? / 197

- *Jennifer Gratz and Patrick Hamacher, Petitioners v. Lee Bollinger et al.* / 199
- *Barbara Grutter, Petitioner v. Lee Bollinger et al.* / 203

8 THE OTHER LINES WE DRAW AT SCHOOL: WEALTH, GENDER, CITIZENSHIP, AND SEXUAL ORIENTATION / 214

Rich Schools, Poor Schools: The Court's Treatment of "Separate but Equal" School Financing / 217

"Suspect" Classes and Gender-Based Segregation / 220

Boys and Girls Equal: Title IX / 223

• *Roderick Jackson, Petitioner v. Birmingham Board of Education* / 225

Separating Citizens from Noncitizens under the Law / 227

• *Plyler v. Doe* / 228

Discrimination against Gays and Lesbians / 235

• *Boy Scouts of America v. Dale* / 236

9 HARASSMENT IN THE HALLWAYS: SEXUAL HARASSMENT, BULLYING, AND THE LAW / 243

When Teachers Harass Students / 245

• *Gebser v. Lago Vista Independent School District* / 245

When Students Harass Students / 248

• *Davis v. Monroe County Board of Education* / 249

The Rights of Gay and Lesbian Students against Harassment / 257

10 A HEALTHY STUDENT BODY: DISABILITY, PRIVACY, PREGNANCY, AND SEXUALITY / 260

The Rights of the "Differently Abled" under the Individuals with Disabilities Education Act / 261

• *Cedar Rapids Community School District v. Garret F.* / 262

Peer Grading and the Right to Privacy / 265

• *Owasso Independent School Dist. No. I-011 v. Falvo* / 266

Three Trimesters: Pregnant at School / 269

• *Pfeiffer v. Marion Center Area School District* / 270

• *Curtis v. School Committee of Falmouth* / 273

Abortion and the Privacy Rights of Teenagers / 275

• *Planned Parenthood of Southeastern Pennsylvania v. Casey* / 277

Appendix A: Supreme Court Confirmation Exercise: You Be the Judge / 283

Appendix B: Constitution of the United States / 287

Appendix C: Glossary / 305

Appendix D: Bibliography / 315

Appendix E: Marshall-Brennan Constitutional Literacy Project / 320

Photo Credits / 323

Index / 325

PREFACE

"In our system, state-operated schools may not be enclaves of totalitarianism. School officials do not possess absolute authority over their students. Students in school as well as out of school are 'persons' under our Constitution. They are possessed of fundamental rights which the State must respect, just as they themselves must respect their obligations to the State."   JUSTICE ABE FORTAS, *TINKER V. DES MOINES INDEPENDENT COMMUNITY SCHOOL DISTRICT* (1969)

The great educator John Dewey once observed that students learn at school from both the "formal" curriculum and the "informal" curriculum.

The *formal* curriculum is the subject matter of our classes: algebra and history, chemistry and ceramics, Spanish and Shakespeare. These are the things students are tested and graded on. The *informal* curriculum is everything else that students learn from the experience of being at school. This might include what happens to students when they get in trouble; how rules are enforced; the way principals treat teachers when everyone is watching; how teachers treat students in the absence of other adults; how boys treat girls and vice versa; what the school board addresses; the social lives of students; how students of different racial and ethnic backgrounds interact; the content of the school paper and who controls it; whether athletes are treated differently from everyone else; the amount of money spent on boys' and girls' sports; who gets tested for drugs; how a school teaches students about sex and birth control (or does not); and the quality of the library and what books are on the shelves. These and many other issues make a difference in the emotional and intellectual growth of students but appear nowhere on a syllabus or final exam.

I have always believed that the informal curriculum is as important as the formal one; indeed, it is usually more influential in creating the lasting lessons that will stay with students after they graduate.

We the Students tries to introduce the informal curriculum of school life into the formal curriculum of classes on law, government, and American history. It invites students to ask what they are learning at school when they are not studying. It focuses on the kinds of conflicts that occur at school every day and how the Supreme Court has interpreted the U.S. Constitution to define the rights and responsibilities of students. It is also about the difference students can make in the communities where they live and go to school.

In high school, students can form the habits of critical thinking and participation that make them effective citizens. In fact, many high school students (and even some younger students) have stood up for their beliefs and their rights in such a dramatic way that they have changed forever the way the Supreme Court has interpreted the Constitution and the rights of all Americans. By standing their ground, a number of young people in the twentieth century became constitutional heroes. *We the Students* introduces such remarkable young people as the following:

- Mary Beth Tinker, a thirteen-year-old who defended her right to protest the Vietnam War by wearing a black armband to school and changed the way the Supreme Court analyzes the First Amendment rights of students;
- Linda Brown, age seven, of Topeka, Kansas, and Spottswood Bolling, age twelve, of Washington, D.C., whose families resisted racially segregated schools and helped move the Supreme Court to abandon the doctrine of "separate but equal";
- LaShonda Davis, age ten, whose family insisted (and won the court's agreement) that schools are responsible for protecting students against peer sexual harassment;
- The Barnette children, Jehovah's Witnesses whose family defended their right not to recite the Pledge of Allegiance because of their religious convictions; and
- Deborah Weisman, a fourteen-year-old from Rhode Island whose family's opposition to the inclusion of religious prayers at her middle school graduation led to a Supreme Court ruling requiring that commencement ceremonies be secular.

Of course, most of the students who have objected to official practices—especially locker searches and drug tests—have *lost* their cases. There are many heroes among them, too, and their stories are included as well. Winning is great, but it isn't everything, and there are different ways to win. Before the Barnette family won the right not to salute the flag, other Jehovah's Witnesses had lost the same case just two years prior. With their effort, they readied the ground for the Barnette decision.

The Supreme Court seesaws, however, and recent Courts have tended to turn a cold shoulder to student rights. Even with respect to the First Amendment and equal protection, areas in which the Court has traditionally been most open to hearing student voices, the

Stanford Law School's class of 1952. Future Supreme Court justice Sandra Day O'Connor is in the first row, second from left; future chief justice William Rehnquist is at far left in the back row.

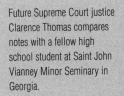

Future Supreme Court justice Clarence Thomas compares notes with a fellow high school student at Saint John Vianney Minor Seminary in Georgia.

Court's majority has been cutting back on student rights. Every case and problem in *We the Students* is thus the source of fascinating study and lively debate. There are few objectively right answers but endless possibilities for creative thinking.

We the Students invites each reader to be a framer and reframer of the Constitution and American democracy in the twenty-first century. The spirit of liberty lives not primarily in the government but in the hearts and minds of an active people. Thomas Jefferson insisted that "the earth belongs … to the living; that the dead have neither powers nor rights over it." He wanted to avoid the mistakes that come from adopting an attitude of "sanctimonious reverence" for the Framers of the Constitution. Rather than assuming that the Founders always knew best, we must, Jefferson wrote, "avail ourselves of our reason and experience to correct the crude essays of our first and inexperienced councils."

In other words, people should think for themselves and avoid getting stuck in the past. Ironically, being faithful to the Framers of our Constitution, means following Jefferson's democratic sentiments and looking at them as mortals, as people both inspired in their love of country but sometimes flawed in their vision. They are honored most through improvement on their work. The people honor the Framers best by acting like Framers themselves.

The brilliant Jefferson himself provides a fine example of how this process works. In the Declaration of Independence, he expressed the crucial sentiment that "all men are created equal," but he owned many slaves and depended on them for his livelihood. Unlike some of his contemporaries, such as Benjamin Franklin and Thomas Paine, Jefferson never challenged the essential legitimacy of slavery as an institution. Yet, later generations of great

Future Supreme Court justice Ruth Bader Ginsburg in her high school yearbook in 1950.

Americans, including people such as Frederick Douglass, Abraham Lincoln, Wendell Phillips, Thaddeus Stevens, and Sojourner Truth, would rekindle the meaning of Jefferson's beautiful Declaration and work to transcend his personal limitations by opposing slavery and abolishing it with the Thirteenth Amendment to the Constitution.

It is my hope that readers will finish this book with the following state of mind: a profound appreciation for the United States' constitutional journey and a passionate commitment to create a future of justice, freedom, and democracy that past generations could only imagine.

Constitutional Knowledge, Critical Thinking, Persuasive Argument, and Values Clarification

To approach these cases with an inquiring mind, students must first learn the basics of what the Constitution is and how the legal system works. They can participate in debates about how particular cases were decided or ought to be decided. Why does the Court resolve a case one way rather than the other? Who has the better argument in a Supreme Court decision, the majority or the dissenters, and why? What makes an argument relevant or irrelevant? How does the Supreme Court go about the business of interpreting words? Is it always consistent? Should it be? Is constitutional law about facts, rules, and values or about some complex interaction of all three? Why does law change over time, and what makes it change?

Pretty soon students will discover that there are few right answers when it comes to interpreting difficult questions of constitutional meaning. This ambiguity requires that persuasive arguments be made based on the various methods of interpretation. As students practice arguing and writing about the Constitution, they will improve their verbal and written communication skills, including clarity, cogency, and the use of evidence and analogy to make points.

Every great legal conflict has at its heart a clash over values and principles. Learning the Constitution in this way helps students clarify their own values and work with other people to shape the rules of their society.

It is hoped that students will come away from this text with a love and appreciation for a document that has held the United States together for more than two centuries. As Chief Justice John Marshall wrote in *McCulloch v. Maryland* (1819), "We must never forget that it is a constitution we are expounding." It belongs to everyone.

Becoming a Democratic Citizen: Rights and Responsibilities

This book was written with one driving conviction: One cannot be an effective citizen without knowing the Constitution. Learning about the Constitution is not only a birthright, but a rite of passage that should be as important to a transition to adulthood as learning about the economy, learning to drive a car, or registering to vote.

It is a splendid thing to learn one's rights as a citizen, but democratic rights exist only in the context of a community where all assume corresponding responsibilities. Just as every person has a legal right to speak and be heard, each has a parallel obligation to listen in a respectful way. Just as citizens and residents have a right to insist that government not violate their rights as individuals, government has the right to insist that each person respect the rights of others. It is this tension between rights and responsibilities that creates much of the excitement of this text.

The young readers of this book are mature enough to handle its sensitive and complex themes. Nothing here is a license for irresponsibility or recklessness; rather, the material serves as a challenge for fulfilling the highest calling of democracy—to be an active, engaged, educated, and responsible participant in it. Thinking seriously about the problems and cases raised in this book will fine-tune students' moral and political sensibilities as members of their community or citizens of the United States. Who knows? Perhaps, even now, this book is in the hands of a future U.S. president or Supreme Court justice.

The Marshall-Brennan Constitutional Literacy Project

We the Students was born of the Marshall-Brennan Constitutional Literacy Project. The project takes law students from across the United States into public high schools each day to teach the Constitution and Bill of Rights to students.

Students in the fall 2007 Marshall-Brennan class at Cardozo High School in Washington, D.C., gather at the Supreme Court before attending an oral argument. They are accompanied by their four Marshall-Brennan teachers from American University Washington College of Law.

American University's Washington College of Law launched the project in fall 1999, when twenty-five law students began teaching in the public high schools of Washington, D.C. They were cheered on by Mrs. Thurgood Marshall and the late Mrs. William J. Brennan Jr., the widows of two great Supreme Court justices who championed constitutional education for all young Americans.

Today, the Marshall-Brennan program thrives from coast to coast with programs affiliated with the law schools at Arizona State University; Drexel University; Northeastern University; Rutgers University; Southern University in Baton Rouge; the University of California, Berkeley; the University of Louisville in Kentucky; the University of Pennsylvania; and others. In all these projects, the law student fellows have found that the best way to learn something is to teach it to someone else; many fellows go on to splendid teaching careers in law schools, colleges, or high schools. Through a passionate commitment to their students, to public schools, and to their communities, the fellows are helping young people wake up to their intellectual potential, their citizenship, and their ability to go to college and succeed in life.

For more information on the Marshall-Brennan Constitutional Literacy Project, please see Appendix E. To bring the program to your community, please contact me at raskin@wcl.american.edu or Gwen Stern at gstern@drexel.edu. Visit our Web site at www.wcl.american.edu/marshallbrennan.

How to Use This Book

Read *We the Students* along with the Bill of Rights, located in Appendix B at page 297 as part of the Constitution. Each chapter invites you to examine a new amendment and a different set of rights to see how they translate into the school environment. If any words are unfamiliar, look them up in the glossary, which can be found in Appendix C, or in a dictionary.

The text is organized around Supreme Court decisions. Read the majority (or plurality) opinion first to see how the Court actually decided. The decisions have been shortened to remove as much procedural jargon as possible and to allow you to see clearly the facts of the case, the Court's framing of the relevant legal issues, and its analysis and judgment in the case.

Next read excerpts from the opinions of dissenting justices, which are summarized and explained in the "Dissenting Voices" sections. Compare the reasoning of justices in the majority with the reasoning of the justices in the minority. Ask which decisions better capture and resolve the true conflicts in the case.

After that, do the exercises, working on your own or with a small group. These exercises are meant to strengthen and test your grasp of the constitutional principles at work by applying them to new factual contexts. Do not get frustrated if the implications of a decision seem uncertain, ambiguous, or arguable; this is what makes the law exciting and unpredictable, and it is what enables lawyers to make a living! The suggested readings and Web sites at the end of the chapters and at the end of the book direct you to readings that delve more deeply into the history of particular cases and fields of law.

Work with your teacher and classmates to do class exercises. When in the role of a lawyer, a Supreme Court justice, or a reporter, stay in your role and try to speak in the appropriate voice. You will be amazed by how quickly you develop the skills of an advocate.

If you are interested in participating in the National High School Moot Court Competition or the Marshall-Brennan Constitutional Literacy Competition, please e-mail Tabitha Acosta at tacosta@wcl.american.edu.

Acknowledgments

This book is a labor of love that is part of a broader movement to raise constitutional literacy in the United States. I wish to thank the hundreds of dedicated Marshall-Brennan fellows who over the past five years have road tested, developed, refined, and improved these materials in the Arizona, California, Louisiana, Maryland, Massachusetts, New Jersey, Oregon, Pennsylvania, and Washington, D.C., public schools; Mrs. Thurgood Marshall and the late Mrs. William J. Brennan Jr. for their generous support from the first day we walked this path; the magnificent agitator for peace and justice Mary Beth Tinker, a living American hero whose name can be mentioned in the same breath as that of Rosa Parks and who is a cherished friend of the Marshall-Brennan program; Maryam Ahranjani, a former fellow who transformed the program with her vision, creativity, and equanimity as our academic coordinator; the staff of the Supreme Court Historical Society, including consulting editor Jennifer Lowe, publications committee chair E. Barrett Prettyman, and sensational managing editor Clare Cushman, who gave invaluable editorial suggestions on the first edition; my cherished colleague and codirector Steve Wermiel, who has been instrumental at every turn in this project; the playwright and scholar Paula Caplan, whose passionate support has been immeasurably important; Amelia Duroska, Tabitha Acosta, and Chasantia Preer; and Doug Goldenberg-Hart, Andrew Boney, and Emily Bakely, my fine editors at CQ Press.

On a personal note, I would like to thank my dear mother, Barbara Raskin (1935–1999); my beloved father, Marcus Raskin; my brother, Noah Raskin; my brothers-in-law, Keith Littlewood and Kenneth Bloom; my sisters, Eden Raskin and Erika Raskin Littlewood; and my sisters-in-law, Abby Meiselman and Heather Maurer; my three naughty and wonderful children, Hannah Grace, Thomas Bloom, and Tabitha Claire, whose precocious (and compulsory) readings of this book have given me infinite satisfaction; my beloved nieces and nephews, Emily Blair, Zachary Gaylin, Maggie Ryan, Mariah Sophia, Phoebe Rose, and Boman Grant; my stepmother Lynn Raskin; and my ubiquitous mother- and father-in-law, Arlene and Herbert Bloom.

This book is dedicated to my wife, Sarah Bloom Raskin, the beautiful and mysterious woman who sat across from me in Professor Laurence Tribe's constitutional law class at Harvard in Langdell North in fall 1986. It still seems like yesterday.

For Further Information

If you have further questions about the cases presented here or about the larger constitutional issues they raise, consult your school librarian or a law librarian at a nearby law school or university. Bibliographies and suggestions for other contacts conclude each chapter of *We the Students* and others can be found at the back of the book. You may also call the Student Press Law Center at 703-807-1904 if your question relates to the free speech or free press rights of students. You may e-mail me at raskin@wcl.american.edu, and I will get back to you with an answer as soon as possible.

Remember, it's your Constitution, and it's up to you to learn it, to teach it, to quote it, to change it, to defend it through thick and thin.

Jamin B. Raskin
Professor of Law
Washington College of Law
American University
Washington, D.C.

Member, Maryland State Senate
Annapolis, Maryland

FOREWORD

This is a book for students everywhere, especially if you have ever looked at our world, as I have, and said, "There must be a better way!" *We the Students* is full of true stories of young people just like you who used the Bill of Rights and the Constitution to stand up for their rights and change history.

If you think the Constitution and the Bill of Rights are dull and boring, you are in for a big surprise! Do you think you have a right to say something in class that your teacher disagrees with? Do you have the right to talk about sex in school? Do you have the right to wear a shirt that says "No war in Iraq" or one with a picture of Malcolm X? What about a shirt with a Confederate flag? Can you hold up a sign that says "Bong Hits for Jesus"? Can you be searched in school? Can you have a religious club in school? A gay club? Can you be forced to give a urine sample if you are a student athlete? A blood sample? Do you have the right to write about controversial things in your school paper, or even to have a school paper at all? Can your school system take into account the race of students in order to integrate schools and classes?

You will learn about all of these things and more as you study the constitutional law cases in this book. They are about students like you who wanted the right to be treated fairly.

When I was thirteen years old, in 1968, I didn't know anything about my rights. But I knew something was wrong with the world. When I came home from school every night, I saw on the TV news stories about the civil rights movement and the war in Vietnam. When we saw pictures of African Americans being attacked with water hoses for trying to vote, my parents went to Mississippi to try to help. They didn't think it was right.

The 1960s followed a decade in which people were afraid to dissent. In the 1950s a senator named Joseph McCarthy claimed to be patriotic, and accused everyone who didn't agree with him of being unpatriotic Communists. Workers in labor unions—or people working for racial equality and peace—were accused. No one was safe. McCarthy's friends in the FBI accused even Martin Luther King Jr. of being a Communist. All over the country people lost their jobs, and families and communities were destroyed.

Even as a child in Iowa, I was affected by this intolerance. My father tried to integrate the all-white swimming pool in our small town. That was considered too controversial; we had to move out of town. Later, the effects of McCarthyism continued.

In the 1960s, when I saw pictures on TV of Vietnamese kids getting bombed by the United States with napalm, I didn't think that was right, and it mobilized me to action. The napalm would burn the kids like gasoline, but it was sticky and they couldn't get it off. It was chemical warfare. Kids in our neighborhood were being sent to the war. Robert Kennedy, the brother of President John F. Kennedy, called for a Christmas truce. My brother and a group of our friends thought we should do something to support the truce. We decided to wear black armbands to school.

The school officials said we didn't have a right to do that. They suspended me. As you will see, they turned out to be wrong. In this book you will learn about the constitutional case that was fought and the First Amendment victory that was won for students everywhere when the U.S. Supreme Court ruled in our favor. But it was not an easy victory. When we wore the armbands for peace to school, some people thought we weren't being patriotic and threw red paint at our house to suggest that we must be "reds." One woman even threatened to kill me. Many people did, however, support us.

If you are shocked, as I am, at the news on TV or if you feel outraged or sad at the way the world is, you are not alone. When you read about the law cases in this book, you will see that there have always been ordinary people who felt the same way. When ordinary people take a stand against things that make them outraged or sad, history is made. It may not be popular, and it is never easy. But if there was ever a time when ordinary people need to take a stand, it is now. And if there was ever a time when students need to stand up for their rights, it is now.

It's hard to remember another time when young people were blamed so much, so unfairly, for the problems of adult society. By teaching about real constitutional cases involving public school students, *We the Students* is a powerful tool to help you stand up to injustice. It will also help inform adults who want you to be able to accomplish change. You will learn about the Constitution, which is necessary not only so you can pass a test or write a paper but also so you will know how to use it to change the world.

Thurgood Marshall was the first black justice on the Supreme Court, and he was one of the greatest. He used the Constitution to end segregation in public schools. William J. Brennan Jr. also was a Supreme Court justice known for his rock-solid integrity and commitment to justice. To honor these men, their widows helped Jamin Raskin, the author of this book, start the Marshall-Brennan law project so that high school students could learn and use the Constitution in their own lives. The Marshall-Brennan projects—from Boston to Louisville to Berkeley—are showing young Americans that from our past we can learn the traditions of constant education and social reform. As you read this book, you can feel fortunate to follow in the tradition of these two great Supreme Court justices, who cared about young people and wanted you to have everything you need to become active, respected citizens.

When I was little, I read a story titled *The Emperor's New Clothes*. It was about a stupid, selfish emperor who spent all of the kingdom's wealth on an invisible robe for himself. When he strolled down the road naked, no one dared to say anything, except a little boy who cried out: "The emperor is naked!" At last, all the people had the courage to say what they really thought. They all yelled out: "The emperor is naked, the emperor is naked!" and the world was changed forever.

I always liked that story because it's about the power of a child. That story and the book you are holding in your hands have much in common. They are both about young people like you and the power you have, if you will only dare to use it. The cases reviewed have one thing in common: hope. Join us and lead us with your youthful energy and creativity in this lifelong struggle for justice and democracy. That is *our* hope. You will never regret it!

Mary Beth Tinker
January 25, 2008

1

"WE THE PEOPLE":
Our Constitution and Courts

"A people who mean to be their own governors must arm themselves with the power which knowledge gives." JAMES MADISON (1822)

This is a casebook about the Supreme Court decisions that affect students at school in the United States: cases about drug testing and censorship of student newspapers, desegregation and affirmative action, prayer in the classroom and discrimination against girls' sports teams, and a myriad of other issues that students and their families face in the public school system.

But before you sink your teeth into these cases, there is some basic information you need to have about our Constitution, our courts, and our legal process.

Why a Constitution?

Many high school students read William Golding's novel *Lord of the Flies* (1954). It tells the story of a group of shipwrecked English boys making their way alone on a desert island.

The boys create a fragile community with simple rules. They work together to find food and to keep the fire going. Whoever holds the conch seashell has the floor, and everyone listens when he speaks.

But one tough kid, Jack, has contempt for the community's ethics. He wants to lead a pack of "hunters" to go kill wild pigs. He ruthlessly teases an overweight cerebral boy named Piggy, who clings to the conch and to the embattled leader of the community, Ralph.

By the end of this riveting story, things have fallen apart. Jack's hunting crew turns savage and murderous. Chanting, "Kill the pig, cut its throat, spill its blood," they steal Piggy's glasses and make war on their classmates.

These boys never had a written constitution—only an informal verbal understanding, which could not restrain the selfish and violent impulses that destroyed the bonds of the group.

In democracies, citizens write constitutions to prevent power from being concentrated in one person, such as a king or a dictator, or a single faction, such as a political party, a church, or the military. A constitution tries to provide that conflicts will be resolved through law and that political change will take place nonviolently. An effective constitution secures essential rights to the individual.

Of course, the existence of a constitution is no guarantee of freedom, peace, or justice. Slavery, with all of its violence and horrors, defined life for millions of people in the United States for nearly a century under our Constitution (and for centuries before it was written). Nor did the Constitution succeed in ending slavery or the controversy over it. It took the Civil War, America's bloodiest conflict, which left hundreds of thousands of people dead on our soil, to abolish the "peculiar institution," and change the Constitution. The mere existence of a constitution does not prevent oppression.

We can fairly say that a democratic and rights-protecting constitution is a *necessary* condition in modern life for political justice and stability, but it is not a *sufficient* one. The other necessary conditions are a decent level of provision for everyone in society to prevent a breakdown in order, political checks against total fear and a psychology of war, and an enduring loyalty to the constitution and rule of law in the hearts of the people.

The American Constitution: What Is It?

The U.S. Constitution sets forth our nation's governing structure, establishing both the powers of government and the basic rights of the people. The modern world's first written constitution, it is the glue that has held the nation together through civil war, recession, depression, world wars, the al-Qaida attacks of September 11, 2001, and profound social, economic, political, racial, sectional, and cultural conflict.

When the delegates to the Constitutional Convention in Philadelphia approved the Constitution on September 17, 1787, its provisions principally concerned structural issues—namely, the separation of powers, which refers to the distribution of powers among the legislative, executive, and judicial branches of the national government, and federalism, or the allocation of powers between the national government and the states.

Three years later, in 1791, freedom was addressed by the Constitution. In that year the states ratified the first ten amendments, called the Bill of Rights, which defined the rights of the American people. The Bill of Rights had been championed by Anti-Federalists, who feared a tyrannical central government. Under these amendments, Congress could not establish a church or deny free exercise of religion, deny the right to assemble and petition for a redress of grievances, violate free speech or free press, conduct unreasonable or warrantless searches and seizures, or punish people twice for the same offense (double jeopardy).

Read through the Constitution and Bill of Rights in the Appendix. Ask yourself, What values were most important to our Founders? What would our Constitution be like without the Bill of Rights and later amendments? Do you agree with Thomas Jefferson that "no just government should refuse" a Bill of Rights?

The Constitution: Whose Is It?

The Constitution begins "We the People." These may be the three most important words in the document. They establish that, in America, the people are sovereign and the government works for us. Our Constitution embodied the ideas of John Locke, Jean-Jacques Rousseau, and Thomas Paine, Enlightenment thinkers who argued that all people have inalienable rights and that we create governments to secure those rights and promote the common good. In the Declaration of Independence, Thomas Jefferson wrote that govern-

The Constitution defined the structure and powers of the national government and, in short order, set forth a Bill of Rights for the people. Here the Founders take turns signing their names.

ments derive "their just Powers from the Consent of the Governed," implicitly contrasting the monarchical idea that governmental power flows from God.

President Abraham Lincoln invoked the democratic principle in his Gettysburg Address, perhaps the greatest speech of American history, when he poetically proclaimed that "government of the people by the people for the people shall not perish from the earth." It was the Civil War and the resulting Thirteenth, Fourteenth, and Fifteenth Amendments that ended slavery and launched the American people on a path toward equality for all.

Congress and the people of the states have the power to amend the Constitution on "great and extraordinary occasions," as urged by James Madison in *Federalist* No. 49. Americans have exercised this power only seventeen times since the Bill of Rights was ratified (fifteen if you exclude our experiment with Prohibition and the amendment repealing it), almost always to expand our political rights or to try to perfect our vexed presidential election process. But if the people are the ongoing authors of the document, it is the Supreme Court that is the final *interpreter* of the meaning of constitutional language. At its best, the Supreme Court—along with the lower federal courts and state courts—acts as the guardian of our civil rights by striking down unconstitutional laws. This is the power of *judicial review,* by which the courts may declare "unconstitutional" and invalid any federal or state law or policy that violates rights, rules, or principles set forth in the Constitution.

The principle and practice of judicial review were established in the great case of *Marbury v. Madison* (1803), where the chief justice of the United States, John Marshall, declared, "[I]t is emphatically the province and duty of the judicial department to say what the law is." The Supreme Court announced its own constitutional power to strike down laws—even laws passed by an overwhelming majority in Congress or the state legislatures. In your opinion, does this make judicial review undemocratic? Or does it enrich our understanding of democracy by incorporating irrevocable commitments that we have made as a people to protect basic rights?

The Constitution: What Does It Mean?

In some places, the Constitution seems very clear and specific, such as where it states that citizens must be thirty-five years old to become president. In other places, the Constitution speaks in broad, majestic generalities, such as where it says that states may not deprive persons of "equal protection of the laws" or abridge the "freedom of speech."

How exactly the Supreme Court and other courts should interpret broad constitutional terms is an issue of enduring and fascinating controversy. To interpret the Constitution, the Supreme Court draws on

- the text of the Constitution itself;
- *precedent,* or rulings from factually similar cases that illuminate the Constitution's meaning;
- the intentions of the Framers;
- the history of the nation and its institutions;
- the general structure of the constitutional design based on the division of national, state, and local powers through federalism and the separation of powers among the legislative, executive, and judicial branches at the national level;
- the spirit and values of the Constitution embodied in the Bill of Rights; and
- practical concerns and requirements.

The Constitution does not enforce itself, nor do judges go out searching for violations. If people think that their constitutional rights are being violated and want judicial help, they must summon the courage and resources to bring a case to court themselves.

Under the Constitution's case-or-controversy requirement, which is set out in Article III, the federal courts may take only those cases brought by people who have a live controversy involving an actual injury. Our courts are not permitted to issue an "advisory opinion," which is an abstract statement of how the court would rule on a legal matter that has not actually come before it. The "ripeness" doctrine says that a case or controversy must be present and "ripe" for deciding in order to be heard. At the same time, a case cannot be "moot," no longer fit for judicial resolution because the controversy has passed away.

If there is no real injury alleged in a plaintiff's complaint, or the government is not responsible for it, or there is nothing the court can do about it anyway, the court will say that the plaintiff lacks "standing." To have constitutional standing to sue the government for a constitutional violation, a plaintiff must show three things:

1. a concrete and specific injury that is:
2. caused by the government and
3. redressable in court, meaning that the court has power to award meaningful relief.

Finally, if the court believes that it does not have jurisdiction over a particular issue because the Constitution leaves it entirely up to the executive or legislative branch, the court may decline to decide the case on grounds that it presents a so-called political question.

The Three Branches of the National Government

The Constitution distributes power at the national level of government among three branches. Article I defines the composition and powers of the legislative branch—the U.S.

Congress—which is divided between the House of Representatives and the Senate. In George Washington's famous metaphor, the two chambers act like a cup and saucer of tea, allowing emotions to cool off by having the Senate, the smaller and more deliberate institution, review the legislative handiwork of the House, the more numerous and passionate body.

Article II defines the powers of the executive branch, which consists of the president, the cabinet, and other officials appointed by the president. The Framers wanted the president to be energetic and effective in implementing the laws passed by Congress, but they also knew that with too much power he might turn despotic and tyrannical. The Constitution forbids Congress to award titles of nobility (even to the president) and carefully hems in the president's power to make war, which the Framers considered a constant and awful temptation for executives. Only Congress itself would have power to declare war, not the president; Congress would have the power to raise and support armies; and Congress would have power to regulate commerce both internally and with foreign nations.

Article III sets up the judicial branch, which includes the Supreme Court and other federal courts that Congress may establish. Their job is to interpret the Constitution and the laws passed by Congress and to enforce the rights of the people.

This structure places the lawmaking power in Congress, the bicameral (two-chamber) body that is today supposed to represent the will of the people as they elect their senators and House members. (Before ratification of the Seventeenth Amendment in 1913, state legislatures appointed U.S. senators.) The president is charged with signing or vetoing the laws and policies that Congress adopts and then, when signed into law, enforcing and implementing them.

The powers of the branches are not completely distinct. For example, the Senate must confirm (or reject) the president's nominations to the Supreme Court and other judgeships. The House has power to impeach the president, which it did to President Bill Clinton in 1998, and the Senate has power to convict him and remove him from office, which it refused to do in Clinton's case. In impeachment trials in the Senate, the chief justice presides (as William Rehnquist did in Clinton's case). Each branch has a distinct function, but the Constitution overlaps and blends these functions.

Qualifications to Run for Congress and President

To run for the House of Representatives, you must be at least twenty-five years old, a U.S. citizen for at least seven years, and an inhabitant of the state you are running from.

To run for the U.S. Senate, you must be at least thirty years old, a citizen of the United States for at least nine years, and an inhabitant of the state you are running from.

To run for president, you must be at least thirty years old, a natural-born citizen of the United States, and a resident of the country for at least fourteen years.

WHAT DO YOU Think?

Exercise 1.1. Do you feel committed to our Constitution and Bill of Rights? Why or why not? What do you know about it, and what does it mean to you?

Exercise 1.2. Find the provisions of the Constitution setting forth the age requirements listed above. Why do you think that the Founders established different age requirements for the U.S. House and Senate? Do you think that they are still valid today? Should a very promising twenty-one-year-old be able to run for the House of Representatives or a brilliant twenty-six-year-old for the Senate? Why or why not?

Exercise 1.3. Have you ever thought about running for Congress one day? Why or why not?

Exercise 1.4. What do you think of the requirement that only "natural born" citizens may run for president? In the first decade of the twenty-first century, the governors of two states—California and Michigan—were naturalized U.S. citizens forbidden to run for president. California governor Arnold Schwarzenegger was born in Austria, Michigan governor Jennifer Granholm in Canada. Would you favor a constitutional amendment that removes this restriction? Why or why not? Debate the proposition in class.

Federalism: How the States Share the Power

Article VI of the Constitution makes federal law "the supreme Law of the Land" and thus superior to state law whenever they come into conflict. Still, the Constitution implicitly leaves major areas of responsibility to the states. According to the Tenth Amendment, the powers not delegated to the United States by the Constitution "are reserved to the States respectively, or to the people." Many domains of social life have been left in large part to the states, including family law and zoning, but also public education, where the role of localities and states has always been preeminent. The U.S. Department of Education contributes some funds to local school districts and pushes certain policies along with them, but the vast portion of resources in the public schools comes from the states and their political subdivisions: the counties, cities, and towns.

One of the recurring issues in the Supreme Court's education cases is whether the Court's searching review of local school district decisions is appropriate. Some people argue that the Court should not sit as a "super–school board" to second-guess local educators who know their schools and students best. Others believe that the Court should always aggressively defend basic federal constitutional values, such as the freedoms of speech and due process, against tyranny at the local level. The images of "our federalism" and the profound controversies over it linger close to the surface in the cases examined here.

The Incorporation of the Bill of Rights

Although the provisions of the Bill of Rights originally applied only to congressional actions ("*Congress* shall make no law …"), the Supreme Court has decided that the Bill of Rights binds all of the states and localities as well. Why? In 1868 the Fourteenth Amendment was added to the Constitution; its due process clause provides that "no state shall … deprive any person of life, liberty, or property, without due process of law; nor deny to any person within its jurisdiction the equal protection of the laws." The Court has found that the liberty guaranteed by due process of law includes almost all of the specific rights granted to the people against Congress by the Bill of Rights. Thus state governments may not abridge the rights recognized in the Bill of Rights—such as the right to speak, publish

The Constitution's opening words, "We the People," may be not only the largest but also the most important in the document, infusing the meaning of the entire text.

a newspaper, practice religion, or be free from unreasonable searches and seizures—any more than Congress may. This assimilation of Bill of Rights protections to citizens facing state power is called "incorporation" through the due process clause.

The State Action Requirement

It is important to remember that although the Bill of Rights applies generally against both Congress and the states (and localities), it applies only to *government* actions. Specifically, it applies to what we call "state action"—an action undertaken by a government agency or actor, whether federal, state, or local. This is known as the state action requirement. A private entity is not ordinarily subject to constitutional restraints. (One exception is the Thirteenth Amendment's ban on slavery and involuntary servitude even where the offending actor is a private person or entity.)

Thus, unlike public schools, which are an arm of government, private schools are not bound directly by the Constitution. Private schools may be found to be in violation of a *statute*, a law passed by a federal or state legislature, such as those forbidding job discrimination on the basis of race or gender or requiring "reasonable accommodation" for disabled persons. But private schools may not themselves be found to be in direct violation of the U.S. Constitution or its Bill of Rights.

Judicial Architecture: How Our Court System Works

To understand the cases that appear in the chapters that follow, some background information will be useful, beginning with an overview of the judicial process.

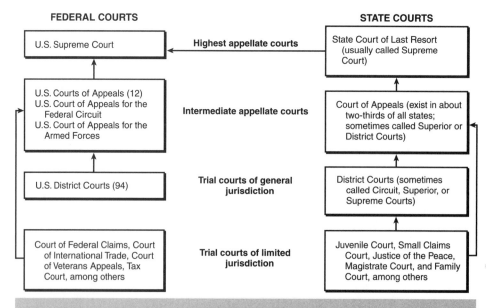

FEDERAL COURTS		STATE COURTS
U.S. Supreme Court	**Highest appellate courts**	State Court of Last Resort (usually called Supreme Court)
U.S. Courts of Appeals (12) U.S. Court of Appeals for the Federal Circuit U.S. Court of Appeals for the Armed Forces	**Intermediate appellate courts**	Court of Appeals (exist in about two-thirds of all states; sometimes called Superior or District Courts)
U.S. District Courts (94)	**Trial courts of general jurisdiction**	District Courts (sometimes called Circuit, Superior, or Supreme Courts)
Court of Federal Claims, Court of International Trade, Court of Veterans Appeals, Tax Court, among others	**Trial courts of limited jurisdiction**	Juvenile Court, Small Claims Court, Justice of the Peace, Magistrate Court, and Family Court, among others

Source: Lee Epstein and Thomas G. Walker, *Constitutional Law for a Changing America: Rights, Liberties, and Justice,* 6th ed. (Washington, D.C.: CQ Press, 2007), 13.

The U.S. Supreme Court is housed in a beautiful building across the street from the Capitol in Washington, D.C. When the Court is in session the plaza in front is filled, both before and after oral arguments, with interested parties, journalists, spectators, lawyers, and, sometimes, protesters.

There are two major branches of the judicial system in the United States: the federal courts and the state courts. Federal courts decide issues of federal law, which means controversies relating to the United States Constitution, federal laws (or statutes) passed by Congress, and regulations issued by federal agencies. The federal system has three levels of courts. The United States District Courts are trial courts that make findings of fact and law in civil cases and render verdicts in federal criminal cases. The United States Circuit Courts of Appeals are those courts where people appeal decisions and verdicts reached in district courts. In the courts of appeals, there are no juries; judges decide all the issues.

The United States Supreme Court is the highest court of appeals. The Supreme Court is the final step in the appeals process; its decisions become the supreme law of the land on constitutional issues. However, the Supreme Court may reject the vast majority of certiorari petitions (seeking the Court's certification for review) that it receives. In fact, the Court agrees to hear less than 1 percent of the cases people try to bring before it.

The handsome Supreme Court building conveys the greatness and majesty of law, but the Court did not have a home of its own for the first 146 years of its existence. After inhabiting relatively undignified quarters in New York City and Philadelphia, the Court came to Washington when the city became the nation's capital, at the start of the nineteenth century. Congress let it use space in the Capitol, where it decided such great cases as *Marbury v. Madison* (1803) and *McCulloch v. Maryland* (1819). In 1929 Chief Justice William Howard Taft, who had been president of the United States from 1909 to 1913, finally convinced Congress to build a permanent home for the Court. Today the Court attracts visitors and protestors alike. Ironically, there has been a good deal of First Amendment litigation about rules restricting First Amendment activity on the plaza in front of the Court, which remains generally unenthusiastic about political free speech on its doorstep.

Like the federal system, the state system usually has three levels of courts, composed of trial, appellate, and supreme courts. The decisions of the state supreme courts may be appealed to the United States Supreme Court if there is a federal question involved. State courts may decide issues relating to both state law and federal law. In most cases, however, the issues that come before state courts deal with state law. Most crimes, such as assault, murder, rape, and burglary, are prosecuted in state court. Each state also has its own constitution, which provides citizens with additional protections beyond those afforded by the U.S. Constitution.

Courts hear two types of cases: criminal and civil. In a criminal prosecution charges are brought by a government prosecutor against a person who has allegedly violated a state or federal criminal statute. For example, if you attack your neighbor, the county or district attorney will prosecute you for violating the state's criminal code; if you are convicted, you might go to jail. Civil suits, in contrast, are brought by one person, company, or government entity against another for a civil wrong, property invasion, or breach of contract. For example, if you don't take care of your tree, and it falls on your neighbor's house, he or she can bring a negligence action against you for damages. This is called a *tort.* You cannot be sent to jail for committing a simple tort, although you can be forced to pay money damages to another party.

Courts will hear the facts and legal claims presented by two parties. The petitioner, or plaintiff, is the party that initiates the lawsuit; the respondent, or defendant, is the party that responds to the lawsuit. (In a case that has been appealed, the appealing party is known as the appellant and the responding party as the appellee.) The courts will then either dismiss the case or grant relief—that is, some monetary benefit or other restitution—based on the evidence and the arguments presented. Depending on the kind of case, courts tap different resources to reach their verdicts and make decisions. Courts analyze the Constitution and other relevant rules of law, such as a statutory law, which is passed by the state legislatures or Congress; an ordinance, which is enacted by a city, suburb, town, municipality, or other local entity; or the common law, which is developed over time from the judgment of courts, as well as case precedent (decisions from earlier cases).

Majority and Dissenting Opinions

You will notice that most of the case excerpts in this book present substantial parts of the majority opinion but also descriptions of, and quotations from, dissenting opinions. A majority opinion typically will first summarize the procedure of the case, which is the path the case took to get to the Supreme Court, and then the facts of the case, that is, what happened that led the parties to a court battle. The procedure and facts are normally followed by the justices' analysis of the issues posed in the case. The majority opinion represents the views of a majority of the justices on the nine-member Court. Occasionally another justice will write a concurring opinion, in which he or she agrees with the majority's result but offers a different analysis or gives the law or facts a different emphasis.

A dissenting opinion expresses a different point of view on major or minor issues in the case and rejects the result reached by the majority of the Court.

It is important to read parts of dissenting opinions along with majority opinions. Many decisions are decided on the slender margin of 5–4, and the simple change of one justice's

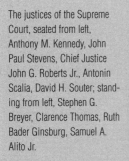

The justices of the Supreme Court, seated from left, Anthony M. Kennedy, John Paul Stevens, Chief Justice John G. Roberts Jr., Antonin Scalia, David H. Souter; standing from left, Stephen G. Breyer, Clarence Thomas, Ruth Bader Ginsburg, Samuel A. Alito Jr.

mind—or the replacement of an outgoing or deceased justice with a newly appointed one—can create a new 5–4 majority in the opposite direction. Well-argued dissenting opinions are often the seeds of a later reversal. An example of a realignment of views took place between 1940 and 1943. In *Minersville School District v. Gobitis* (1940), the Supreme Court upheld compulsory flag salute rituals. But a strong dissenting opinion laid the groundwork for a reversal that followed three years later in *West Virginia State Board of Education v. Barnette* (1943) (see Chapter 2). In the latter case, the Court overruled *Gobitis*, finding that the First Amendment does not allow public schools to force students to pledge allegiance to the flag.

Dissenting opinions focus on the critical questions of the case. They also register the diversity of legal and political thought in our society and remind us that the law is not a "hard science." A court is not a computer that prints out right answers once you enter the facts. The law is a field of contests among competing theories, ideas, analogies, values, interpretations, and beliefs. As Justice Robert H. Jackson once said, "We are not final because we are infallible, but we are infallible only because we are final" (*Brown v. Allen*, 344 U.S. 443, 540 [1953]).

How to Brief a Case

When law students read cases, they often take notes on them and outline them in a way that has come to be known as "briefing a case." You might find it useful to brief cases as you start your own habits of case reading and analysis. To effectively brief a case, you must do the following:

State the procedure—Where did this case come from? A state supreme court after a state appeals court after a state district court? A federal appeals court after a federal district court? What happened in those lower courts? Who won? Who lost? The procedural history of the case is a very quick statement about the path the case has followed in the courts.

Name the parties—Who is the plaintiff? Who is the defendant?

State the facts—Write down the facts of what happened to the parties. What is the story between them? Who did what to whom? What happened of legal significance; that is, what happened that is relevant to deciding the legal issues?

State the issue (or issues)—What are the legal issues that the court must decide to arrive at a decision?

State the holding—What does the court hold or decide? What is the "rule" that it comes up with in answer to the legal issues posed?

State the court's reasoning or rationale—Why does the court decide the way it does? What is the logic or rationale of its holding? What is its analysis?

There is no single right way to brief a case, but these basic features might be useful to you as you dip your toes in the water. If you like the process of case briefing and outlining— and doing it as part of a study group—consider renting the classic 1973 movie about students at Harvard Law School, *The Paper Chase*. It might make you determined to go to law school—or to avoid the experience at all costs! If you don't want to wait for law school to engage your passion for the law, contact the Marshall-Brennan Constitutional Literacy Project at American University's Washington College of Law for information about the annual high school student moot court and essay competitions, which take place in Washington, D.C. or Philadelphia. Check out the Web site at www.wcl.american.edu/ wethestudents.

Further Reading

Cushman, Clare. *The Supreme Court Justices: Illustrated Biographies, 1789–1995.* 2d ed. Washington, D.C.: Congressional Quarterly, 1995.

Greenburg, Jan Crawford. *Supreme Conflict: The Inside Story of the Struggle for Control of the United States Supreme Court.* New York: Penguin Press, 2007.

Hall, Kermit. *The Oxford Companion to the Supreme Court of the United States.* New York: Oxford University Press, 1992.

Stewart, David O. *The Summer of 1787: The Men Who Invented the Constitution.* New York: Simon and Schuster, 2007.

Toobin, Jeffrey. *The Nine: Inside the Secret World of the Supreme Court.* New York: Doubleday, 2007.

Turow, Scott. *One L: The Turbulent True Story of a First Year at Harvard Law School.* Reissued ed. New York: Farrar, Straus, and Giroux, 1988.

VOICES AND CHOICES:
The First Amendment and Student Speech

> "In our system, students may not be regarded as closed-circuit recipients of only that which the State chooses to communicate. They may not be confined to the expression of those sentiments that are officially approved. In the absence of a specific showing of constitutionally valid reasons to regulate their speech, students are entitled to freedom of expression of their views...." JUSTICE ABE FORTAS, *TINKER V. DES MOINES INDEPENDENT COMMUNITY SCHOOL DISTRICT* (1969)

Many people believe that the First Amendment expresses what it means to be an American: a citizen with the right to speak his or her mind. This is ironic because free speech received almost no protection from the Supreme Court until the middle of the twentieth century. Originally, the First Amendment applied only to actions by Congress (not the states), and even then it was thought to be restricted to cases involving "prior restraints" by government against political speech. (Prior restraint refers to official restriction of speech or press publication before it occurs.)

Nonetheless, today the First Amendment guarantees a sweeping and impressive freedom of speech, thought, and conscience against state control. As Justice Robert H. Jackson put it in *West Virginia State Board of Education v. Barnette* (1943), the case you will read first about students and the Pledge of Allegiance, "If there is any fixed star in our constitutional constellation, it is that no official, high or petty, can prescribe what shall be orthodox in politics, nationalism, religion, or other matters of opinion or force citizens to confess by word or act their faith therein. If there are any circumstances which permit an exception, they do not now occur to us."

In *Texas v. Johnson* (1989), Justice William Brennan articulated a corresponding principle: "If there is a bedrock principle underlying the First Amendment, it is that the Government may not prohibit the expression of an idea simply because society finds the idea itself offensive or disagreeable."

Today, the Supreme Court upholds the right to think and speak in ways that are extreme, moderate, profane, sexually offensive, indecent, hostile, radical, reactionary, antiwar, unpopular, and even aggressively antigovernment in content.

At the same time, the Court has permitted government to censor and punish "obscenity" (sexually explicit and grossly offensive pictures or words that lack any serious literary, artistic, political, or scientific value), fighting words (the kind of speech that people would experience as a verbal punch in the nose, such as accusing a stranger in a bar of an inappropriate relationship with his own mother), and incitement of imminent lawless activity (such as encouraging an angry brick-wielding mob in front of city hall to attack the mayor). All in all, the United States of America still protects more freedom of expression than almost any other nation on Earth.

The text of the First Amendment reads:

> Congress shall make no law respecting an establishment of religion, or prohibiting the free exercise thereof; or abridging the freedom of speech, or of the press, or of the right of the people peaceably to assemble, and to petition the Government for a redress of grievances.

Although the First Amendment refers to Congress, the rights contained in the text apply also against states and localities. This is the effect of the "incorporation" doctrine discussed in Chapter 1.

There are six major rights protected by the First Amendment. These can be readily recalled by thinking of the word *GRAPES:*

*G*rievances, Right to petition for a redress of
*R*eligion, Right to no establishment of
*A*ssembly, Right to peaceful
*P*ress, Freedom of the
*E*xercise, Freedom of religious
*S*peech, Freedom of

What images does the First Amendment evoke in your mind? Can you make a collage, painting, or other artistic work that expresses your sense of the First Amendment?

P⬤INTS TO PONDER

The rules of speech differ in different social institutions. How does the basic First Amendment liberty of free expression apply to students in public schools?

- Should students be required to salute and pledge allegiance to the American flag?
- Should students be prevented from wearing clothing with political messages?
- Should students be allowed to wear their hair however they please?
- Should students be able to make speeches and presentations with vulgar or profane language?
- Should students be able to talk and joke about illegal activities such as drug use and underage drinking at school?

Expressive Conduct and the Right Not to Speak

The right to "speak" actually implies a broader right of free expression. The First Amendment protects not only written or spoken words but also what the Court calls *expressive conduct,* which means actions that send a message. Picketing a store, wearing a political button, or painting a picture are all examples.

The decision in *Barnette,* one of many Supreme Court cases dealing with flags and political expression, articulated the idea that the First Amendment protects not just speech and written words but also actions that communicate meaning. It also held that free speech includes a right *not* to speak when a citizen so chooses.

In *Barnette* the Court found that public school students who choose not to join in the Pledge of Allegiance flag salute ritual for reasons of conscience cannot be forced to participate. The case reversed the Supreme Court's earlier decision in *Minersville School District v. Gobitis* (1940), which upheld the expulsion of the child of a Jehovah's Witness who refused to join in the pledge ritual.

The *Barnette* decision was of extraordinary importance because it set a precedent for defending liberty of conscience in the middle of World War II, when the United States and its Allies were struggling to defeat fascism and Nazism. In the three years between *Gobitis* and the Court's change of heart in *Barnette,* the children of Jehovah's Witnesses in public schools across the country faced widespread persecution and harassment for their continuing refusal to salute the flag during the nation's emergency mobilization against Adolf Hitler and the Axis powers. The Jehovah's Witnesses saw flag salutes as violating the prohibitions in the Ten Commandments against idol worship and graven images. They also wanted to show solidarity with 25,000 Jehovah's Witnesses in Germany who had refused to participate in the "Heil Hitler" salute.

The Court's dramatic turnaround on the flag salute was a landmark statement that the values of the Constitution apply during wartime and peacetime alike. The decision illustrates that when it comes to essential controversies, the Court has often changed its mind about what the Constitution provides. Although we might be tempted to think of the Court as operating like a computer—you plug in the data, and the legal answer prints out—in truth the meanings of the Constitution change over time in response to events, changes in social consciousness, and new legal understandings.

JUSTICES: A CLOSER LOOK

The author of the *Barnette* opinion, **JUSTICE ROBERT H. JACKSON** (1892–1954), was raised in farm country outside Jamestown, New York. He graduated from two high schools, Frewsburg High and Jamestown High, where he spent an extra year. He never went to college but finished a two-year course at Albany Law School in a year. He became a lawyer through apprenticeship. After a distinguished career in Franklin Delano Roosevelt's New Deal administration that included stints as solicitor general of the United States and attorney general, Jackson was named to the Supreme Court by FDR in 1941 and served until 1954.

HIGHLIGHTS

- President Roosevelt tried to entice Jackson into electoral politics, encouraging him to run for governor of New York in 1938. His name was even floated as a potential vice presidential running mate for FDR, but Jackson's true passion was law, not electoral politics.
- Speaking of his high school English teacher Mary Willard, who inspired in him a love of language and oratory, Justice Jackson would later say, "Her influence would be hard to overestimate."

The Jehovah's Witnesses argued their case as if it were primarily about the rights of religious free exercise. Justice Jackson quickly shifted the terms of the discussion away from a narrow focus on *religious rights* toward broader principles of *free speech* and *free thought*.

....

WEST VIRGINIA STATE BOARD OF EDUCATION v. BARNETTE

Supreme Court of the United States
Argued March 11, 1943.
Decided June 14, 1943.

Majority OPINION   Justice JACKSON delivered the opinion of the Court.

… The Board of Education on January 9, 1942, … order[ed] that the salute to the flag become "a regular part of the program of activities in the public schools," that all teachers and pupils "shall be required to participate in the salute honoring the Nation represented by the Flag; provided, however, that refusal to salute the Flag be regarded as an Act of insubordination, and shall be dealt with accordingly."

The resolution originally required the "commonly accepted salute to the Flag" which it defined. Objections to the salute as "being too much like Hitler's" were raised by the Parent and Teachers Association, the Boy and Girl Scouts, the Red Cross, and the Federation of Women's Clubs. Some modification appears to have been made in deference to these objections, but no concession was made to Jehovah's Witnesses. What is now required is the "stiff-arm" salute, the saluter to keep the right hand raised with palm turned up while the following is repeated: "I pledge allegiance to the Flag of the United States of America and to the Republic for which it stands; one Nation, indivisible, with liberty and justice for all."

Failure to conform is "insubordination" dealt with by expulsion. Readmission is denied by statute until compliance. Meanwhile the expelled child is "unlawfully absent" and may be proceeded against as a delinquent. His parents or guardians are liable to prosecution, and if convicted are subject to a fine not exceeding $50 and jail term not exceeding thirty days.

… [C]itizens of the United States and of West Virginia, brought suit in the United States District Court for themselves and others similarly situated asking its *injunction* to restrain enforcement of these laws and regulations against Jehovah's Witnesses. The Witnesses are an unincorporated body teaching that the obligation imposed by law of God is superior to that of laws enacted by temporal government. Their religious beliefs include a literal version of Exodus, Chapter 20, verses 4 and 5, which says: "Thou shalt not make unto thee any graven image, or any likeness of anything that is in heaven above, or that is in the earth beneath, or that is in the water under the earth; thou shalt not bow down thyself to them nor serve them." They consider that the flag is an "image" within this command. For this reason they refuse to salute it.

> **Injunction**
> An order from a court commanding or preventing an action.

Children of this faith have been expelled from school and are threatened with exclusion for no other cause. Officials threaten to send them to reformatories maintained for criminally inclined juveniles. Parents of such children have been prosecuted and are threatened with prosecutions for causing delinquency.

... [T]he compulsory flag salute and pledge requires affirmation of a belief and an attitude of mind. It is not clear whether the regulation contemplates that pupils forego any contrary convictions of their own and become unwilling converts to the prescribed ceremony or whether it will be acceptable if they simulate assent by words without belief and by a gesture barren of meaning. It is now a commonplace that censorship or suppression of expression of opinion is tolerated by our Constitution only when the expression presents a clear and present danger of action of a kind the State is empowered to prevent and punish. It would seem that involuntary affirmation could be commanded only on even more immediate and urgent grounds than silence. But here the power of compulsion is invoked without any allegation that remaining passive during a flag salute ritual creates a clear and present danger that would justify an effort even to muffle expression. To sustain the compulsory flag salute we are required to say that a Bill of Rights which guards the individual's right to speak his own mind, left it open to public authorities to compel him to utter what is not in his mind.

... Nor does the issue as we see it turn on one's possession of particular religious views or the sincerity with which they are held. While religion supplies appellees' motive for enduring the discomforts of making the issue in this case, many citizens who do not share these religious views hold such a compulsory rite to infringe constitutional liberty of the individual. It is not necessary to inquire whether non-conformist beliefs will exempt from the duty to salute unless we first find power to make the salute a legal duty.

... The question which underlies the flag salute controversy is whether such a ceremony so touching matters of opinion and political attitude may be imposed upon the individual by official authority under powers committed to any political organization under our Constitution.

Gregory Johnson holds an American flag while another man sets it on fire. In *Texas v. Johnson* (1989), the Supreme Court, on First Amendment grounds, overturned Johnson's conviction for flag burning. In 1990 the Court reaffirmed its decision by ruling the Flag Protection Act unconstitutional.

… The very purpose of a Bill of Rights was to withdraw certain subjects from the vicissitudes of political controversy, to place them beyond the reach of majorities and officials and to establish them as legal principles to be applied by the courts. One's right to life, liberty, and property, to free speech, a free press, freedom of worship and assembly, and other fundamental rights may not be submitted to vote; they depend on the outcome of no elections.

… National unity as an end which officials may foster by persuasion and example is not in question. The problem is whether under our Constitution compulsion as here employed is a permissible means for its achievement.

Struggles to coerce uniformity of sentiment in support of some end thought essential to their time and country have been waged by many good as well as by evil men. Nationalism is a relatively recent phenomenon but at other times and places the ends have been racial or territorial security, support of a dynasty or regime, and particular plans for saving souls. As first and moderate methods to attain unity have failed, those bent on its accomplishment must resort to an ever-increasing severity. As governmental pressure toward unity becomes greater, so strife becomes more bitter as to whose unity it shall be. Probably no deeper division of our people could proceed from any provocation than from finding it necessary to choose what doctrine and whose program public educational officials shall compel youth to unite in embracing. Ultimate futility of such attempts to compel coherence is the lesson of every such effort from the Roman drive to stamp out Christianity as a disturber of its pagan unity, the Inquisition, as a means to religious and dynastic unity, the Siberian exiles as a means to Russian unity, down to the fast failing efforts of our present totalitarian enemies. Those who begin coercive elimination of dissent soon find themselves exterminating dissenters. Compulsory unification of opinion achieves only the unanimity of the graveyard.

It seems trite but necessary to say that the First Amendment to our Constitution was designed to avoid these ends by avoiding these beginnings. There is no mysticism in the American concept of the State or of the nature or origin of its authority. We set up government by consent of the governed, and the Bill of Rights denies those in power any legal opportunity to coerce that consent. Authority here is to be controlled by public opinion, not public opinion by authority.

The case is made difficult not because the principles of its decision are obscure but because the flag involved is our own. Nevertheless, we apply the limitations of the Constitution with no fear that freedom to be intellectually and spiritually diverse or even contrary will disintegrate the social organization. To believe that patriotism will not flourish if patriotic ceremonies are voluntary and spontaneous instead of a compulsory routine is to make an unflattering estimate of the appeal of our institutions to free minds. We can have intellectual individualism and the rich cultural diversities that we owe to exceptional minds only at the price of occasional eccentricity and abnormal attitudes. When they are so harmless to others or to the State as those we deal with here, the price is not too great. But freedom to differ is not limited to things that do not matter much. That would be a mere shadow of freedom. The test of its substance is the right to differ as to things that touch the heart of the existing order.

If there is any fixed star in our constitutional constellation, it is that no official, high or petty, can prescribe what shall be orthodox in politics, nationalism, religion, or other matters of opinion or force citizens to confess by word or act their faith therein. If there are any circumstances which permit an exception, they do not now occur to us.

We think the action of the local authorities in compelling the flag salute and pledge transcends constitutional limitations on their power and invades the sphere of intellect and spirit which it is the purpose of the First Amendment to our Constitution to reserve from all official control....

Affirmed.

Dissenting VOICES

Justice Frankfurter dissented. He began by saying that a person who "belongs to the most vilified and persecuted minority in history" (he was Jewish) is not likely to be insensitive "to the freedoms guaranteed by our Constitution." But he argued that the majority in the case asked the wrong question, because for him the issue was whether the compulsory flag salute was a "reasonable" use of the state's power. He wrote, "[I]t would require more daring than I possess to deny that reasonable legislators could have taken the action which is before us for review." Justice Frankfurter thus thought West Virginia's law was "reasonable."

JUSTICES: A CLOSER LOOK

The dissenter in *Barnette*, **JUSTICE FELIX FRANK-FURTER** (1882–1965), was born in Vienna, Austria. With his family he left Vienna at age twelve for the United States. He attended the City College of New York and Harvard Law School, an institution where he taught for more than two decades. President Franklin Delano Roosevelt nominated him to the Supreme Court in 1939, where he served until 1962.

HIGHLIGHTS

- As a professor at Harvard Law School, Frankfurter was deeply involved in the celebrated Sacco-Vanzetti case, in which two Italian American anarchists, Nicola Sacco and Bartolomeo Vanzetti, were prosecuted on murder charges. Though they proclaimed their innocence, Sacco and Vanzetti were convicted in a politically charged trial and executed by the state of Massachusetts. Frankfurter helped fight, unsuccessfully, to have their convictions overturned. The experience led Frankfurter to join others in establishing the American Civil Liberties Union (ACLU), now America's leading civil liberties organization.

- Frankfurter, who in *Barnette* alluded to being Jewish, was a lifelong Zionist and later a supporter of Israel. During the post–World War I Paris Peace Conference, Frankfurter represented Dr. Chaim Weizmann and the Zionist leaders in negotiations with the Arab states.

Under the First Amendment, should the Court have asked whether the policy was "reasonable" or whether it violated the Barnette kids' freedom of speech?

WHAT DO YOU **Think?**

Exercise 2.1. In *Barnette,* the Court held that the First Amendment prevents school officials from compelling a student to stand and salute the flag during the Pledge of Allegiance. Although public schools may still conduct a Pledge of Allegiance ceremony every morning, students may not be *forced* to participate or punished for not participating. Do you think this decision was right? Why or why not? Write a one-page statement on your assessment of the majority's opinion in *Barnette* and how it relates to your own school's practices. Read your reactions aloud and talk about them.

Exercise 2.2. What does the American flag represent to you? Does the flag have a single meaning or multiple meanings? If someone decides to sit out a flag salute, does it diminish in your eyes either the meaning of the flag or the person? What reasons might a student have for not joining in a flag salute? Do you think that such businesses as Ralph Lauren, Speedo, and Tommy Hilfiger should be able to use the American flag as part of their clothing and advertising and to put it on products such as underarm deodorant? Explore the use of the flag in advertising and popular culture. How many flags can you find as part of commercial advertising and displays?

Exercise 2.3. In *Johnson,* the Supreme Court upheld the right of the people under the First Amendment to use the American flag for expressive purposes, even burning a flag at a political demonstration. Gregory Johnson, a member of the Revolutionary Communist Youth Brigade, set fire to an American flag at the 1984 Republican National Convention in Dallas in order to demonstrate his opposition to the reelection of President Ronald Reagan. The youthful Johnson was convicted of violating a state law making it a crime to "deface, damage or otherwise physically mistreat" the American flag "in a way that the actor knows will seriously offend one or more persons likely to observe or discover his action."

A 5–4 majority on the Supreme Court found that Johnson was engaged in an act of symbolic speech and that the Texas law clearly censored political expression. Writing for the majority, Justice Brennan wrote, "If there is a bedrock principle underlying the First Amendment, it is that the Government may not prohibit the expression of an idea simply because society finds the idea itself offensive or disagreeable." The majority struck down Johnson's conviction as a violation of the First Amendment.

In his dissenting opinion, Justice John Paul Stevens argued, "Even if flag burning could be considered just another species of symbolic speech under the logical application of the rules that the Court has developed in its interpretation of the First Amendment in other contexts, this case has an intangible dimension that makes those rules inapplicable." Justice

Stevens, who is ordinarily a strong champion of free speech, compared the asserted right to burn flags in protest to "a federal right to post bulletin boards and graffiti on the Washington Monument." Is this a perceptive analogy? Why or why not? Make a list of the ways in which this analogy is either accurate or misleading. Hint: Who owns the Washington Monument? Who owns our flags? How many American flags are there across the country?

Since *Johnson,* there have been several attempts to amend the Constitution to give Congress the power to make it a crime to burn or desecrate the flag. Congress has voted several times on versions of the following proposed twenty-eighth amendment:

> "Congress shall have power to prohibit physical desecration of the flag of the United States."

Although the proposed "flag amendment" has repeatedly won two-thirds majorities in the House of Representatives, it has always fallen just short of the two-thirds mark in the Senate. (Article V of the Constitution provides that new amendments must be passed by a two-thirds vote in both the House of Representatives and the Senate and then ratified by three-fourths of the states.) The issue of flag desecration is not going away. But what does "desecration" mean? Look it up. Is it clear that flag burning is a form of desecration?

Federal law today actually recommends burning flags as the proper form of disposal. Indeed, any Boy Scout or Girl Scout knows that this is proper flag protocol. There are undoubtedly students reading this book right now who have burned flags!

Pretend that you and your classmates are senators considering the proposed flag desecration amendment. Research *Texas v. Johnson* and the pros and cons of a constitutional amendment to ban flag desecration. (Check magazine and newspaper articles, as well as Internet commentary.) Prepare a one-minute speech on how you plan to vote and why.

Be sure to consider whether use of the flag by such companies as Ralph Lauren and Speedo for commercial advertising would be permitted under the amendment. The first generation of flag patriots, northern Civil War veterans in the Grand Army of the Republic, considered commercial use of the flag the worst kind of desecration. What about the use of flags in art, in theater, in personal clothing? Also consider more mainstream political uses of the flag, such as writing, "Vote for Jones, not Smith," on a flag design poster or "Boycott oil from Saudi Arabia" on a flag. Earlier flag protectors thought it was desecration to use the flag in any partisan way, since it was the symbol of the whole country. Will such political flag uses be allowed under this amendment?

What *is* a flag exactly? Federal law says that it is the stars-and-stripes design "of any size" and "in any substance." What if you bake a flag-design cake and hot wax drips on it? Is that desecration? What if you use a flag napkin on the Fourth of July to wipe barbecue sauce from your mouth? Is that desecration? How do we know it when we see it?

Exercise 2.4. The combustible mix of public schools, the Pledge of Allegiance, and religion exploded once more in June 2002 when a three-judge panel on the Ninth Circuit ruled, in *Newdow v. U.S. Congress,* that public schools cannot conduct the Pledge of Allegiance with the words "under God" included in the script. We will return to this problem in Chapter 4, but think about this question: What function do the words "under God" now have in the pledge for students who choose to say it? Do these words make it a partially religious statement?

FOR THE CLASS

Channel Fun. Imagine that the Oakland, California, school system has installed televisions in its classrooms. The sets were donated by a for-profit corporation, Channel Fun, in return for Oakland's promise to broadcast in each homeroom at least seven minutes' worth of substantive Channel Fun programming each day—news, features, and sports reports—and three minutes of commercials for fast food, soft drinks, and candy.

Ninth-graders Sandy Rad and Ben Ali walk out of the classroom whenever the commercials appear, saying that they "refuse to be part of this commercial sellout of our education." The school principal tells Sandy and Ben to quit their protest, but they continue to walk out whenever commercials come on. They are suspended. They now appeal their suspensions to federal district court.

Form two teams of students and argue whether the suspensions should be struck down on First Amendment principles found in *Barnette* or whether the school acted reasonably within its powers. What language in *Barnette* do you cite for your position? Select a panel of three federal appeals court judges to determine whether the First Amendment protects the students' right to walk out.

The Right to Speak Freely and Protest (but Not to Disrupt)

Just as students have the right *not* to be forced to profess their belief in officially approved ideas, they also have the right *to* express their own ideas—at least they do if they speak in a way that does not fundamentally interfere with their school's functions. This was the holding of the Court in *Tinker v. Des Moines Independent Community School District* (1969), the dramatic high point of the Supreme Court's commitment to free speech in schools in the last century.

Mary Beth Tinker, here with her brother, John, protested the Vietnam War in 1965 by wearing black armbands to school. After they were suspended by school authorities, the Supreme Court held that public school students have First Amendment rights of political expression that were violated in their case.

The *Tinker* case arose in the heat of national controversy over the Vietnam War, the United States' military action in Indochina in the 1960s and 1970s that caused great political division across the country. Many people supported the war as an intervention on behalf of a besieged ally, South Vietnam, that was resisting Communist aggression. Others considered the long war both unjust and *illegal,* that is, a violation of the Constitution. They maintained that such an aggressive intervention in the affairs of another country, which Congress never declared as a war, took place at huge human and moral cost. Historians and politicians continue to debate the Vietnam War, perhaps our most divisive military experience outside of the Civil War—at least up until the Iraq War.

Many young Americans joined the debate over the justice of the Vietnam War. This case had its origins in November 1965, when a group from Iowa traveled to Washington, D.C., to join a peace march organized by the National Committee for a Sane Nuclear Policy, which featured speeches by Coretta Scott King and Dr. Benjamin Spock. The Iowa marchers included John Tinker and Christopher Eckhardt, aged fifteen and sixteen, respectively, and in the tenth grade at Des Moines public high schools. The boys' families were steeped in progressive causes such as civil rights and the peace movement.

Upon the boys' return to Iowa, Eckhardt and Tinker decided with Tinker's sister Mary Beth, a thirteen-year-old in eighth grade, to express their opposition to the war. Specifically, they wore black armbands to school as a way to mourn the loss of life in Vietnam and to support Sen. Robert F. Kennedy's proposal for an extended truce in the war. When dozens of other students joined in this silent protest, school authorities moved to stop the protests and punish students who wore the armbands. Even in the face of this official hostility (and taunting by students), the Tinkers and Christopher Eckhardt stood their ground and became plaintiffs in this famous case. Mary Beth Tinker, who wrote the preface to this book, recalls how red paint was thrown on her front door, the peace of her home was disturbed by frequent crank calls, and she and her parents came under severe public criticism on the radio and even received death threats. And then the Court handed down its decision, which many students to this day hold close to their hearts.

TINKER v. DES MOINES INDEPENDENT COMMUNITY SCHOOL DISTRICT

Supreme Court of the United States
Argued November 12, 1968.
Decided February 24, 1969.

Majority OPINION Justice FORTAS delivered the opinion of the Court.

Petitioner John F. Tinker, 15 years old, and Christopher Eckhardt, 16 years old, attended high schools in Des Moines, Iowa. Petitioner Mary Beth Tinker, John's sister, was a 13-year-old student in junior high school.

In December 1965, a group of adults and students in Des Moines held a meeting at the Eckhardt home. The group

Petitioner
Party that presents a petition to a court in an effort to seek appeal of a judgment. *See also* **Appellant**, under Chapter 5, *In Re Latasha W.*

JUSTICES: A CLOSER LOOK

JUSTICE ABE FORTAS (1910–1982) wrote the opinion for the majority in *Tinker*. Born in Memphis, Tennessee, Justice Fortas was the youngest of five children. He went to Southwestern College in Memphis and Yale Law School, where he studied under another future justice, William O. Douglas. Fortas's good friend President Lyndon Johnson appointed him to the Supreme Court in 1965. Fortas, a brilliant lawyer and also an accomplished violinist, served on the Court for only four years.

HIGHLIGHTS

- When Fortas was a partner at the prestigious Washington, D.C., firm of Arnold and Porter, he became the court-appointed advocate for Clarence Earl Gideon, the appellant in *Gideon v. Wainwright* (1963). This case established that the government must appoint lawyers for indigent criminal defendants who cannot otherwise afford them.
- Justice Fortas wrote the Court's opinion in *In re Gault* (1967), holding that young people in juvenile proceedings enjoy many of the same constitutional protections as adults, including the right to counsel and the right against self-incrimination.
- Justice Fortas resigned from the Court on May 14, 1969, amid allegations of financial improprieties that led to calls for his impeachment.

determined to publicize their objections to the hostilities in Vietnam and their support for a truce by wearing black armbands during the holiday season and by fasting on December 16 and New Year's Eve. Petitioners and their parents had previously engaged in similar activities, and they decided to participate in the program.

The principals of the Des Moines schools became aware of the plan to wear armbands. On December 14, 1965, they met and adopted a policy that any student wearing an armband to school would be asked to remove it, and if he refused he would be suspended until he returned without the armband. Petitioners were aware of the regulation that the school authorities adopted.

On December 16, Mary Beth and Christopher wore black armbands to their schools. John Tinker wore his armband the next day. They were all sent home and suspended from school until they would come back without their armbands. They did not return to school until after the planned period for wearing armbands had expired—that is, until after New Year's Day....

I

The District Court recognized that the wearing of an armband for the purpose of expressing certain views is the type of symbolic act that is within the Free Speech Clause of the First Amendment. As we shall discuss, the wearing of armbands in the circumstances of this case was entirely divorced from actually or potentially disruptive conduct by those participating in it. It was closely akin to "pure speech" which, we have repeatedly held, is entitled to comprehensive protection under the First Amendment.

First Amendment rights, applied in light of the special characteristics of the school environment, are available to teachers and students. It can hardly be argued that either students or teachers shed their constitutional rights to freedom of speech or expression at the schoolhouse gate. This has been the unmistakable holding of this Court for almost 50 years....

… Our problem lies in the area where students in the exercise of First Amendment rights collide with the rules of the school authorities.

II

The problem posed by the present case does not relate to regulation of the length of skirts or the type of clothing, to hair style, or deportment. It does not concern aggressive, disruptive action or even group demonstrations. Our problem involves direct, primary First Amendment rights akin to "pure speech."

The school officials banned and sought to punish petitioners for a silent, passive expression of opinion, unaccompanied by any disorder or disturbance on the part of petitioners. There is here no evidence whatever of petitioners' interference, actual or nascent, with the schools' work or of collision with the rights of other students to be secure and to be let alone. Accordingly, this case does not concern speech or action that intrudes upon the work of the schools or the rights of other students.

Only a few of the 18,000 students in the school system wore the black armbands. Only five students were suspended for wearing them. There is no indication that the work of the schools or any class was disrupted. Outside the classrooms, a few students made hostile remarks to the children wearing armbands, but there were no threats or acts of violence on school premises.

The District Court concluded that the action of the school authorities was reasonable because it was based upon their fear of a disturbance from the wearing of the armbands. But, in our system, undifferentiated fear or apprehension of disturbance is not enough to overcome the right to freedom of expression. Any departure from absolute regimentation may cause trouble. Any variation from the majority's opinion may inspire fear. Any word spoken, in class, in the lunchroom, or on the campus, that deviates from the views of another person may start an argument or cause a disturbance. But our Constitution says we must take this risk[,] and our history says it is this sort of hazardous freedom—this kind of openness—that is the basis of our national strength and of the independence and vigor of Americans who grow up and live in this relatively permissive … society.

In order for the State in the person of school officials to justify prohibition of a particular expression of opinion, it must be able to show that its action was caused by something more than a mere desire to avoid the discomfort and unpleasantness that always accompany an unpopular viewpoint. Certainly where there is no finding and no showing that engaging in the forbidden conduct would "materially and substantially interfere with the requirements of appropriate discipline in the operation of the school," the prohibition cannot be sustained.

In the present case, the District Court made no such finding, and our independent examination of the record fails to yield evidence that the school authorities had reason to anticipate that the wearing of the armbands would substantially interfere with the work of the school or impinge upon the rights of other students. Even an official memorandum prepared after the suspension that listed the reasons for the ban on wearing the armbands made no reference to the anticipation of such disruption.

On the contrary, the action of the school authorities appears to have been based upon an urgent wish to avoid the controversy which might result from the expression, even by the silent symbol of armbands, of opposition to this Nation's part in the conflagration in Vietnam....

It is also relevant that the school authorities did not purport to prohibit the wearing of all symbols of political or controversial significance. The record shows that students in some of the schools wore buttons relating to national political campaigns, and some even wore the Iron Cross, traditionally a symbol of Nazism. The order prohibiting the wearing of armbands did not extend to these. Instead, a particular symbol—black armbands worn to exhibit opposition to this Nation's involvement in Vietnam—was singled out for prohibition. Clearly, the prohibition of expression of one particular opinion, at least without evidence that it is necessary to avoid material and substantial interference with schoolwork or discipline, is not constitutionally permissible.

In our system, state-operated schools may not be enclaves of totalitarianism. School officials do not possess absolute authority over their students. Students in school as well as out of school are "persons" under our Constitution. They are possessed of fundamental rights which the State must respect, just as they themselves must respect their obligations to the State. In our system, students may not be regarded as closed-circuit recipients of only that which the State chooses to communicate. They may not be confined to the expression of those sentiments that are officially approved. In the absence of a specific showing of constitutionally valid reasons to regulate their speech, students are entitled to freedom of expression of their views....

The principle of these cases is not confined to the supervised and ordained discussion which takes place in the classroom. The principal use to which the schools are dedicated is to accommodate students during prescribed hours for the purpose of certain types of activities. Among those activities is personal intercommunication among the students. This is not only an inevitable part of the process of attending school; it is also an important part of the educational process. A student's rights, therefore, do not embrace merely the classroom hours. When he is in the cafeteria, or on the playing field, or on the campus during the authorized hours, he may express his opinions, even on controversial subjects like the conflict in Vietnam, if he does so without "materially and substantially interfer(ing) with the requirements of appropriate discipline in the operation of the school" and without colliding with the rights of others. But conduct by the student, in class or out of it, which for any reason—whether it stems from time, place, or type of behavior—materially disrupts classwork or involves substantial disorder or invasion of the rights of others is, of course, not immunized by the constitutional guarantee of freedom of speech....

As we have discussed, the record does not demonstrate any facts which might reasonably have led school authorities to forecast substantial disruption of or material interference with school activities, and no disturbances or disorders on the school premises in fact occurred. These petitioners merely went about their ordained rounds in school. Their deviation consisted only in wearing on their sleeve a band of black cloth, not more than two inches wide. They wore it to exhibit their disapproval of the Vietnam hostilities and their advocacy of a truce, to make their views known, and, by their example, to influence others to adopt them. They neither interrupted school activities nor sought to intrude in the school affairs or the lives of others. They caused discussion outside of the classrooms, but no interference with work and no disorder. In the circumstances, our Constitution does not permit officials of the State to deny their form of expression....

Reversed and remanded.

> **Remand**
> To send back to a lower court for further proceedings.

Dissenting VOICES

Justice Hugo Black dissented. Although conceding that the black armbands did not "disrupt" class work, he argued that "the armbands did exactly what the elected school officials and principals foresaw they would, that is, took the students' minds off their classwork and diverted them to thoughts about the highly emotional subject of the Vietnam war."

He warned about the effect that the Court's decision would have on school discipline: "[I]f the time has come when pupils of state-supported schools, kindergartens, grammar schools, or high schools, can defy and flout orders of school officials to keep their minds on their own schoolwork, it is the beginning of a new revolutionary era of permissiveness in this country fostered by the judiciary. The next logical step, it appears to me, would be to hold unconstitutional laws that bar pupils under 21 or 18 from voting, or from being elected members of the boards of education." He observed philosophically: "Change has been said to be truly the law of life but sometimes the old and the tried and true are worth holding."

Justice Black predicted:

> One does not need to be a prophet or the son of a prophet to know that after the Court's holding today some students in Iowa schools and indeed in all schools will be ready, able, and willing to defy their teachers on practically all orders. This is the more unfortunate for the schools since groups of students all over the land are already running loose, conducting break-ins, sit-ins, lie-ins, and smash-ins. Many of these student groups, as is all too familiar to all who read the newspapers and watch the television news programs, have already engaged in rioting, property seizures, and destruction. They have picketed schools to force students not to cross their picket lines and have too often violently attacked earnest but frightened students who wanted an education that the pickets did not want them to get. Students engaged in such activities are apparently confident that they know far more about how to operate public school systems than do their parents, teachers, and elected school officials.

Building on *Barnette*, the Court in *Tinker* established several principles. First, it held that students do not surrender their constitutional rights simply by entering a public school; second, that symbolic dress worn for political reasons is expression protected by the First Amendment; and, third, that student expression can be curtailed or censored only where the school can show it threatens "material and substantial interference" with the school's effective operation or the rights of other students.

These principles were sharply limited in *Hazelwood School District v. Kuhlmeier* (1988), where the Court held that all student expression associated with official academic activities, such as the school newspaper, the school yearbook, assemblies, the student council, and athletic teams, may be regulated or censored in the interests of serving the school's reasonable academic missions and objectives. (We will explore this major exception to the *Tinker* principle in Chapter 3.)

WHAT DO YOU Think?

Exercise 2.5. Do you think that "political" discussion and nonviolent protests have a proper place in public schools? Should high school students be shielded from political controversy, or should they be educated for active participation as citizens in the rough-and-tumble of American society? What about junior high school students? Elementary school students? Will younger children be distracted and lose ground academically if confronted with political discussion? Write a one-page essay answering these questions.

Exercise 2.6. Justice Black thought that *Tinker* would lead to anarchy in the schools. Has it? He also worried that free political discussion at school would lead to students "being elected members of the boards of education." That has actually happened quite successfully in a number of jurisdictions, including Montgomery County, Maryland. Should students under eighteen be allowed to vote to elect fellow students to the school board? Do young people provide necessary and different perspectives on the schools? Are they mature and experienced enough to vote on such issues as a superintendent's contract? Why or why not?

Exercise 2.7. Justice Black worried that a prospeech decision like this could lead to states or localities lowering the voting age. Although the Constitution requires that states permit eighteen-year-olds to vote, some jurisdictions have lowered the voting age further in local elections, which they retain the power to do. Should sixteen-year-olds be allowed to vote in local elections in your city or town? Why or why not?

Exercise 2.8. School teachers in McMinnville, Oregon, went on strike for better pay and working conditions. The school fired them and hired new teachers, which upset many students. Two students, especially angry because their fathers were among the dismissed teachers, wore buttons to school—and gave them to other students—that said, "No scabs," "I'm not listening scab," "Do scabs bleed?," "Scab we will never forget," "Students united for a fair settlement," and "We want our real teachers back." (*Scab* is derogatory slang for someone who takes the job of a striking worker.)

The two students were suspended for refusing to remove the "scab"-related buttons, which the school system claimed to be "disruptive." The students then brought a First Amendment lawsuit, claiming that they had a right to wear political buttons and that they were being punished for leading a protest against the firings.

The district court upheld their suspensions, finding that the anti-"scab" buttons were "offensive" and "inherently disruptive." The students appealed, arguing that their speech was nonviolent political expression that did not disrupt school. The case went to the Ninth Circuit Court of Appeals. It reversed the district court and found that the students were entitled to wear the anti-"scab" buttons because their message was political and nonviolent, like Mary Beth Tinker's, and was not part of a school-sponsored activity. Do you think that political buttons attacking "scabs" disrupt the teaching and learning environment for the newly hired teachers? Are students capable of understanding the dynamics of a workplace conflict? Are you?

Exercise 2.9. Do you agree with the Ninth Circuit that students have a First Amendment right to speak up for striking teachers? Conversely, should teachers have a First Amendment right to speak up for students who have been suspended if they think the suspensions are unfair? Many school districts take the position that teachers are employees who must follow the orders of the principal even if they disagree with the school's actions.

FOR THE **CLASS**

Soft Drinks, Hard Choices. This exercise requires you to integrate your knowledge of the *Barnette* and *Tinker* cases. A hypothetical high school, which has been having money problems, enters a national competition sponsored by Coca-Cola in which it tries to show its "Coca-Cola pride" in order to win educational tools worth tens of thousands of dollars, including televisions, VCRs, computers, and printers. On the appointed day, all hypothetical high school students wear a Coca-Cola T-shirt (donated by the company) to school, that is, all students except senior class clown Randy Rabblerouser, who wears a Pepsi T-shirt. When told by the principal to take it off and put on a Coca-Cola T-shirt, he says, "I'm no robot, man." The principal has invited Coca-Cola executives and local media to drop in at the school throughout the day and has asked an art teacher to videotape students in their Coca-Cola garb. The principal is afraid that Randy's Pepsi T-shirt will be seen by the visiting executives and news reporters or picked up on videotape. He gives Randy one more chance to take off his T-shirt and put on the Coca-Cola shirt, saying, "You are being disruptive of our mission, Randall. There's a lot at stake here." But Randy says, "You can't make me wear the flag of Coke." The principal has a hearing in his office where Randy talks about Mary Beth Tinker and Martin Luther King. The principal says, "If you want to be a civil disobedient, then you pay the price." He suspends Randy for three days for refusing to follow the rules and policies of the school. Randy goes to federal court to ask for an injunction against his suspension.

Divide the classroom into two teams of students and argue before a panel of three (student) federal district judges whether the suspension is constitutional or not. How do you rule and why?

An increasing number of public high schools are signing contracts with large corporations to sell and market their products on campus and at athletic events. For example, the Martin County, Florida, school district in the 1990s approved a $155,000 contract between South Fork High School and Pepsi-Cola in which South Fork contracted to "make its best effort to maximize all sales opportunities for Pepsi-Cola products." Meantime, other groups are pushing for policies to remove sugary drinks from public schools. Many states have passed farm-to-school laws to bring locally grown farm foods into school kitchens and cafeterias.

The Confederate Flag and Other Racially Provocative Symbols

As we saw in *Barnette*, people take flags seriously, and, as we saw in *Tinker*, what students wear to school can be deeply controversial. Put flags and clothes together, and you get an explosive mix.

In *Melton v. Young* (1972), the Sixth Circuit Court of Appeals upheld the suspension of a Brainerd High School student in Chattanooga, Tennessee, for wearing a jacket with the Confederate battle flag emblem sewn on his sleeve. Prior to the incident, there had been racial conflict and fights among students over the school's use of the Confederate flag as an official school symbol. In response, the school dropped the Confederate flag and the song *Dixie* from its school functions (although it kept "the Rebels" for its team name).

Student Rod Melton protested these changes by wearing his jacket with a Confederate patch on the sleeve to school. When he refused to take it off, he was suspended.

The formerly all-white school was integrated in 1966 (twelve years after *Brown v. Board of Education of Topeka, Kansas,* which declared the segregation of public schools unconstitutional). In 1969 the student body consisted of 170 black students and 1,224 white students. The Sixth Circuit majority found that, given the violent reactions to prior displays of the Confederate flag at school, school authorities did not violate the *Tinker* rule by suspending Melton. The judges thought that his expressive conduct threatened a "material and substantial disruption" of the educational process.

A dissenting judge in the case, William E. Miller, took his colleagues to task for failing to distinguish between the school's *official* use of the Confederate emblem, which had indeed caused violent unrest in the past, and a student's *personal* use of the insignia, which he said was never connected to violence at the school. Judge Miller emphasized that the Confederate flag patch "was small; it was worn as a part of an article of clothing; and it had no inherent qualities for causing disruption or disturbance." He argued that, like Mary Beth Tinker's armband, the "emblem was

The Confederate flag remains a lightning rod of controversy. Here, people gather to support the flying of the Confederate flag atop the South Carolina statehouse in Columbia in April 2000. Shortly thereafter, the state legislature voted to remove the flag from atop the capitol but permitted it to be flown on capitol grounds.

worn by the student in a quiet, peaceful and dignified manner with no untoward gestures or remarks." But the majority thought the potential for violence was clear.

The Tenth Circuit Court of Appeals handed down a similar decision in *West v. Derby Unified School District No. 260* (2000). In that case a middle school student who had been involved in racial incidents in the past was suspended for violating a racial harassment and intimidation policy when he drew a Confederate flag design on a piece of paper during class. The court found that the school system acted reasonably in predicting disruption from this incident based on past racial violence and hate group activities at the school. The student's suspension was upheld.

FOR THE CLASS

How Disruptive is the Confederate Flag? Imagine a school in Lancaster, Pennsylvania, where there has been no racial violence in memory and a very small minority student population until recently. After an influx of new students from El Salvador, a high school senior, John Rebell, wears a blue jeans jacket with a Confederate flag patch on the back to school. When several classmates complain, he is told by the principal to remove the patch; he refuses. He is suspended for violating a rule against "disruptive conduct or conduct that will violate the rights of other students." Do you think his suspension is acceptable within the *Tinker* rule? Is it like the *Melton* and *Derby* cases? Should a school have to wait for a disruption to occur before it limits students' rights? Why or why not? Should there be different presumptions about the potential for violence in southern and northern school districts?

Melton was a court of appeals case that the student tried to bring to the Supreme Court through a petition for a *writ of certiorari,* which the Court issues to direct a lower court to deliver a case for review. The Supreme Court has discretion to choose the cases it hears. When the Court declines to hear a case, as it did in *Melton*, it "denies certiorari." The Court denies certiorari in more than 99 percent of the cases in which it is sought. By denying certiorari in *Melton,* the Supreme Court allowed the Sixth Circuit court decision to stand.

WHAT DO YOU Think?

Exercise 2.10. Some people see the Confederate battle flag as a symbol of slavery, secession from the Union, and white supremacy. Others see it as a symbol of regional and historic pride. Who is right? Can we say either side is right? Can the same symbol mean different things to different people? Semioticians—people who study the meaning of signs—often describe flags as "polysemous," meaning that they have multiple meanings. What if someone wore a Confederate flag emblem to your school? What kind of effect do you think it would have? What message might that person be sending?

Exercise 2.11. Do you think that racist and sexist symbols enjoy less First Amendment protection than other speech? Does the Fourteenth Amendment, which guarantees "equal protection of the laws" to all, give government more power to censor racist expression? Why or why not? Does the fact that the United States fought a war against the Confederacy in which hundreds of thousands of Americans died make any difference?

Exercise 2.12. Some nations with different histories and different constitutions ban certain racist symbols that we tolerate. For example, Germany makes it a crime to display a swastika. Should it be a crime to display a swastika in America? What about a Confederate flag? Does our First Amendment protect symbols and words of hate? Does the principle of First Amendment tolerance ask us to tolerate too much?

FOR THE CLASS

Tinker-ing With Uniform Policies. Imagine this taking place in your school district: Parents and school authorities are concerned about student misbehavior. They are also troubled by competition among students to see who can wear the "coolest" clothes, often meaning the most expensive designer clothing and athletic footwear. The school board votes to impose a mandatory school uniform policy in all elementary, junior high, and high schools. The policy requires students to wear solid-color polo-style shirts with collars, oxford-type shirts, or blouses with collars in one of two colors (white or navy blue); khaki pants; and loafers. Boys must wear blue blazers and red ties. Blue jeans, denim, striped materials, checkered materials, and shirts with written messages on them are all prohibited by the new uniform policy.

A group of students goes to federal court to try to stop the policy, arguing that it violates the First Amendment by denying students their expressive freedom as guaranteed in *Tinker*. They also argue that there are better ways to deal with student discipline problems. The school district argues that student dress is not an aspect of First Amendment freedom under *Tinker* and, even if it is, departures from a reasonable dress code threaten material and substantial disruption where there are ongoing problems with student discipline and fashion competition.

Divide the class into two teams of lawyers and a team of justices. Conduct a mock Supreme Court argument where lawyers for the students argue that the policy violates the First Amendment and lawyers for the school district defend it. The justices should ask intelligent questions of both sides.

(For your information, the Fifth Circuit Court of Appeals has upheld similar mandatory uniform policies in Bossier Parish, Louisiana, and Forney, Texas, against student lawsuits.)

A Mystical Ban on Blue Jeans. In a Mystic, Connecticut, local newspaper, a report appears that annual "National Coming Out Day" is coming up on May 5. The story states that gays and lesbians and their supporters will wear blue jeans to show support for gay rights. The Mystic school board learns that many high school students plan to wear blue jeans (which are ordinarily allowed anyway) and that another group of students plans to wear buttons that say, "God Made Adam and Eve, Not Adam and Steve," provided by a local conservative group. The school board announces that "any student who wears blue jeans to school on May 5 or wears a button expressing an opinion about homosexuality will be sent home for the rest of the day." Can the school board do this under Supreme Court case law?

Divide the class into two groups, then take turns making arguments on both sides. Do you think the school board dealt well with the expected expression from students? How would you have handled it if you were on the school board?

Hirsute Lawsuit: Do Boys Have the Right to Wear Long Hair?

According to *Tinker*, students can choose their own dress as long as their choices do not threaten "material" and "substantial" disruption to school activities. In *Karr v. Schmidt* (1972), the Fifth Circuit considered a claim that a student's hairstyle represents a symbolic and expressive choice that deserves First Amendment protection. The plaintiff was Chesley Karr, a sixteen-year-old boy at Coronado High School in El Paso, Texas, who was not allowed to enroll in his junior year of high school because he had grown his hair long and refused to cut it despite his school's repeated demands that he do so.

Karr argued that his hairstyle was deeply personal and related to his sense of style and personal values. He went to federal court and challenged the "boy hair" provisions in the following dress code:

> FOR BOYS
> Hair may be blocked, but is not to hang over the ears or the top of the collar of a standard dress shirt and must not obstruct vision. No artificial means to conceal the length of the hair is to be permitted; i.e., ponytails, buns, wigs, combs, or straps....
> Cleanliness of body and clothing is expected of all students at all times. No child shall be admitted to school or shall be allowed to continue in school who fails to conform to the proper standards of dress.

Karr won a First Amendment and Equal Protection victory in federal district court in Texas, which found that the rule discriminated against boys (since girls could still grow their hair long) and interfered with the boys' personal expression even though their long hair is not "disruptive." The court found that "the presence and enforcement of the hair-cut rule causes far more disruption of the classroom instructional process than the hair it seeks to prohibit."

The district court rejected the argument that the rule was necessary to guarantee cleanliness; long hair can be clean (just as short hair can be dirty!). It also rejected the claim that long hair creates a safety hazard in science laboratories; if true, the court said, this would mean that the rule should apply to girls as well as boys. The court also found that even though fights occurred between long- and short-haired students, the proper course of action for the school board was to "[teach] tolerance" and stop the fighting rather than interfere with personal liberty.

However, the Fifth Circuit Court of Appeals reversed this judgment and found in the school's favor. According to this holding, personal decisions about hair length are *not* protected by the First Amendment; therefore schools may make boys cut their hair. What do you think of the reasoning in the following decision? Would the same decision be made today?

KARR v. SCHMIDT

United States Court of Appeals for the Fifth Circuit
April 28, 1972.

Majority OPINION LEWIS R. MORGAN, Circuit Judge …

III

… Is there a constitutionally protected right to wear one's hair in a public high school in the length and style that suits the wearer? We hold that no such right is to be found within the plain meaning of the Constitution.…

A. The First Amendment.—The most frequently asserted basis for a constitutional right to wear long hair lies in the First Amendment. It is argued that the wearing of long hair is symbolic speech by which the wearer conveys his individuality, his rejection of conventional values, and the like. Accordingly, it is argued that the wearing of long hair is subject to the protection of the First Amendment.…

We find considerable difficulty, however, with the First Amendment approach to this question. First, we think it doubtful that the wearing of long hair has sufficient communicative content to entitle it to the protection of the First Amendment.… For some, no doubt, the wearing of long hair is intended to convey a discrete message to the world. But for many, the wearing of long hair is simply a matter of personal taste or the result of peer group influence. Appellee Karr, for example, has brought this suit not because his hair conveys a message but "because I like my hair long." Surely if we are to have workable rules of constitutional law, the validity of the regulation cannot turn on the plaintiff's subjective motivation in wearing his hair long.

For these reasons, we think it inappropriate that the protection of the First Amendment be extended to the wearing of long hair. Moreover, it is our belief that the Supreme Court's decision in *Tinker* supports this view.…

> The problem posed by the present case does not relate to regulation of the length of skirts or the type of clothing, to hair style, or deportment.… Our problem involves direct, primary First Amendment rights akin to pure speech.

The conclusion is inescapable that this paragraph was intended to delimit the outer reach of the court's holding. We read this language as indicating that the right to style one's hair as one pleases in the public schools does not inherit the protection of the First Amendment.…

In this case, it is evident from the record that the school authorities seek only to accomplish legitimate objectives in promulgating the hair regulation here in question. The record nowhere suggests that their goals are other than the elimination of classroom distraction, the avoidance of violence between long and short haired students, the elimination of potential health hazards, and the elimination of safety hazards resulting from long hair in the science labs.…

Dissenting VOICES

In dissent, Judge John Minor Wisdom, joined by Chief Judge John R. Brown, argued that young people do have a fundamental liberty interest, protected by the Fourteenth Amendment due process clause, in making personal decisions about how to wear their hair.

> **Due Process Clause**
> Clause in the Fifth and Fourteenth Amendments declaring that no person may be deprived of life, liberty, or property without due process of law; interpreted to mean that every individual is entitled to a fair trial with significant protections, such as the right to be heard, to call witnesses, to cross-examine witnesses, and so forth.

He wrote:

> … To me the right to wear one's hair as one pleases, although unspecified in our Bill of Rights, is a 'fundamental' right protected by the Due Process Clause. Hair is a purely personal matter—a matter of personal style which for centuries has been one aspect of the manner in which we hold ourselves out to the rest of the world. Like other elements of costume, hair is a symbol: of elegance, of efficiency, of affinity and association, of non-conformity and rejection of traditional values. A person shorn of the freedom to vary the length and style of his hair is forced against his will to hold himself out symbolically as a person holding ideas contrary, perhaps, to ideas he holds most dear. Forced dress, including forced hair style, humiliates the unwilling complier, forces him to submerge his individuality in the 'undistracting' mass, and in general, smacks of the exaltation of organization over member, unit over component, and state over individual. I always thought this country does not condone such repression.…

Judge Wisdom then asked whether the state had a sufficiently important interest in overruling a student's desire to wear his hair long:

> I ask: What is the important state interest that permits a public school board to deny an education to a boy whose hair is acceptably long to his parents but too long to suit a majority of the School Board of El Paso, Texas?
> I submit that under the First and Fourteenth Amendments, if a student wishes to show his disestablishmentarianism by wearing long hair or has the whim to wear long hair, antidisestablishmentarians on public school boards have no constitutional authority to prevent it.

WHAT DO YOU Think?

Exercise 2.13. What statement are you making (if any) with your hairstyle? Are you making it consciously or unconsciously? What do the style, color, and cut of your hair express about you? The French semiologist Roland Barthes argued that people inevitably make statements with their clothing and hairstyle, and there is no way around it. Do you agree?

Exercise 2.14. If a public high school can ban *long* hair for boys because it may cause fights between long- and short-haired students, can it ban *short* hair for girls by the same rationale? Can a school with a feminist agenda require boys to grow long hair and girls to have short hair to "change outmoded sexist stereotypes"?

Exercise 2.15. Write a one-page essay explaining why hair length and style and color *should* or *should not* be protected by the First Amendment. Should the same rules hold for both boys and girls?

Exercise 2.16. What does *antidisestablishmentarianism* mean? How about *disestablishmentarian*? Do you think that the purpose of freedom of speech is to allow Americans to "dis-establish" religions, authorities, and orthodoxies? Is it a guarantee against the government promoting what we today call "political correctness"?

Double Entendres and Double Standards: Lewd and Suggestive Language in a Student Government Campaign Speech

One of the things that make people most nervous about free speech in school is that teenagers frequently talk about sex and sexuality, sometimes in irreverent and crude ways. In *Bethel School District v. Fraser* (1986), the Supreme Court's anxiety about adolescent sexual innuendo led to a major retreat from its earlier free speech stand in *Tinker*.

The case began when Matthew Fraser, a popular student and quasi–class clown at Bethel High School in Pierce County, Washington, gave a nominating speech for a fellow student running for student government. The theme of the speech was a sophomoric sexual metaphor that included the following sentences:

JUSTICES: A CLOSER LOOK

CHIEF JUSTICE WARREN E. BURGER (1907–1995) was born in St. Paul, Minnesota, where he went to high school, college, and night law school at what is now the William Mitchell College of Law. After a career at the Justice Department and service as a judge on the U.S. Court of Appeals for the District of Columbia circuit, Burger was appointed to the Supreme Court by President Nixon in 1969. Burger remained on the Court until 1986, when he left to devote himself fully to the Commission on the Bicentennial of the Constitution, a post from which he argued for pervasive constitutional education in American schools and colleges.

HIGHLIGHTS

- In high school Burger was president of the student council, a reporter on the student newspaper, and a well-rounded athlete. He was forced to turn down a partial scholarship to Princeton because his family could not afford to pay the difference.
- As chief justice, Burger was the presiding officer of the Supreme Court and voted in every case. When he was part of the majority, he assigned the task of writing opinions to the other justices.
- Burger reduced the time allotted to Supreme Court litigants from two hours per case to one hour per case.

I know a man who is firm—he's firm in his pants, he's firm in his shirt, his character is firm—but most ... of all, his belief in you, the students of Bethel, is firm.... Jeff Kuhlman is a man who takes his point and pounds it in. If necessary, he'll take an issue and nail it to the wall. He doesn't attack things in spurts—he drives hard, pushing and pushing until finally—he succeeds.... Jeff is a man who will go to the very end—even the climax, for each and every one of you.... So vote for Jeff for A.S.B. vice-president— he'll never come between you and the best our high school can be.

The Court found that the school did nothing wrong in disciplining Fraser for this speech. What is the Court's reasoning? How would you have decided this case?

BETHEL SCHOOL DISTRICT NO. 403 v. FRASER

Supreme Court of the United States
Argued March 3, 1986.
Decided July 7, 1986.

Majority OPINION   Chief Justice BURGER delivered the opinion of the Court.

We granted certiorari to decide whether the First Amendment prevents a school district from disciplining a high school student for giving a lewd speech at a school assembly.

> **Writ of Certiorari**
> A writ issued by the U.S. Supreme Court to a lower court directing the lower court to deliver the case for review. *Certiorari* is Latin and means "to be more fully informed."

I

A

On April 26, 1983, respondent Matthew N. Fraser, a student at Bethel High School in Pierce County, Washington, delivered a speech nominating a fellow student for student elective office. Approximately 600 high school students, many of whom were 14-year-olds, attended the assembly. Students were required to attend the assembly or to report to the study hall. The assembly was part of a school-sponsored educational program in self-government.... During the entire speech, Fraser referred to his candidate in terms of an elaborate, graphic, and explicit sexual metaphor.

Two of Fraser's teachers, with whom he discussed the contents of his speech in advance, informed him that the speech was "inappropriate and that he probably should not deliver it," and that his delivery of the speech might have "severe consequences."

During Fraser's delivery of the speech, a school counselor observed the reaction of students to the speech. Some students hooted and yelled; some by gestures graphically simulated the sexual activities pointedly alluded to in respondent's speech. Other students appeared to be bewildered and embarrassed by the speech. One teacher reported that on the day following the speech, she found it necessary to forgo a portion of the scheduled class lesson in order to discuss the speech with the class.

A Bethel High School disciplinary rule prohibiting the use of obscene language in the school provides:

Conduct which materially and substantially interferes with the educational process is prohibited, including the use of obscene, profane language or gestures.

The morning after the assembly, the Assistant Principal called Fraser into her office and notified him that the school considered his speech to have been a violation of this rule. Fraser was presented with copies of five letters submitted by teachers, describing his conduct at the assembly; he was given a chance to explain his conduct, and he admitted to having given the speech described and that he deliberately used sexual innuendo in the speech. Fraser was then informed that he would be suspended for three days, and that his name would be removed from the list of candidates for graduation speaker at the school's commencement exercises.

Fraser sought review of this disciplinary action through the School District's grievance procedures. The hearing officer determined that the speech given by respondent was "indecent, lewd, and offensive to the modesty and decency of many of the students and faculty in attendance at the assembly." The examiner determined that the speech fell within the ordinary meaning of "obscene," as used in the disruptive-conduct rule, and affirmed the discipline in its entirety. Fraser served two days of his suspension, and was allowed to return to school on the third day.

B

... [Fraser] alleged a violation of his First Amendment right to freedom of speech and sought both injunctive relief and monetary damages.... The District Court held that the school's sanctions violated respondent's right to freedom of speech under the First Amendment to the United States Constitution, that the school's disruptive-conduct rule is unconstitutionally vague and overbroad, and that the removal of respondent's name from the graduation speaker's list violated the Due Process Clause of the Fourteenth Amendment because the disciplinary rule makes no mention of such removal as a possible sanction. The District Court awarded [Fraser] $278 in damages, $12,750 in litigation costs and attorney's fees, and enjoined the School District from preventing [him] from speaking at the commencement ceremonies. [Fraser], who had been elected graduation speaker by a write-in vote of his classmates, delivered a speech at the commencement ceremonies on June 8, 1983.

The Court of Appeals for the Ninth Circuit affirmed the judgment of the District Court, holding that [Fraser's] speech was indistinguishable from the protest armband in *Tinker v. Des Moines Independent Community School District*....

We granted certiorari. We reverse.

II

... The Court of Appeals ... appears to have proceeded on the theory that the use of lewd and obscene speech in order to make what the speaker considered to be a point in a nominating speech for a fellow student was essentially the same as the wearing of an armband in *Tinker* as a form of protest or the expression of a political position.

The marked distinction between the political "message" of the armbands in *Tinker* and the sexual content of respondent's speech in this case seems to have been given little weight by the Court of Appeals. In upholding the students' right to engage in a nondisruptive, passive expression of a political viewpoint in *Tinker,* this Court was careful to note that the case did "not concern speech or action that intrudes upon the work of the schools or the rights of other students."

… [W]e turn to consider the level of First Amendment protection accorded to Fraser's utterances and actions before an official high school assembly attended by 600 students.

III

… The undoubted freedom to advocate unpopular and controversial views in schools and classrooms must be balanced against the society's countervailing interest in teaching students the boundaries of socially appropriate behavior. Even the most heated political discourse in a democratic society requires consideration for the personal sensibilities of the other participants and audiences.

In our Nation's legislative halls, where some of the most vigorous political debates in our society are carried on, there are rules prohibiting the use of expressions offensive to other participants in the debate. Senators have been censured for abusive language directed at other Senators. Can it be that what is proscribed in the halls of Congress is beyond the reach of school officials to regulate?

The First Amendment guarantees wide freedom in matters of adult public discourse. A sharply divided Court upheld the right to express an antidraft viewpoint in a public place, albeit in terms highly offensive to most citizens. It does not follow, however, that simply because the use of an offensive form of expression may not be prohibited to adults making what the speaker considers a political point, the same latitude must be permitted to children in a public school.…

Surely it is a highly appropriate function of public school education to prohibit the use of vulgar and offensive terms in public discourse.… The determination of what manner of speech in the classroom or in school assembly is inappropriate properly rests with the school board.…

The pervasive sexual innuendo in Fraser's speech was plainly offensive to both teachers and students—indeed to any mature person. By glorifying male sexuality, and in its verbal content, the speech was acutely insulting to teenage girl students. The speech could well be seriously damaging to its less mature audience, many of whom were only 14 years old and on the threshold of awareness of human sexuality. Some students were reported as bewildered by the speech and the reaction of mimicry it provoked.…

We hold that petitioner School District acted entirely within its permissible authority in imposing sanctions upon Fraser in response to his offensively lewd and indecent speech. Unlike the sanctions imposed on the students wearing armbands in *Tinker*, the penalties imposed in this case were unrelated to any political viewpoint. The First Amendment does not prevent the school officials from determining that to permit a vulgar and lewd speech such as respondent's would undermine the school's basic educational mission. A high school assembly or classroom is no place for a sexually explicit monologue directed towards an unsuspecting audience of teenage students. Accordingly, it was perfectly appropriate for the school to disassociate itself to make the point to the pupils that vulgar speech and lewd conduct is wholly inconsistent with the "fundamental values" of public school education.…

Reversed.

JUSTICES: A CLOSER LOOK

JUSTICE THURGOOD MARSHALL (1908–1993), the first African American Supreme Court justice, was born in Baltimore, Maryland, which he later described as "the most segregated city in the United States." He graduated from a segregated high school and went north to all-black Lincoln University in Pennsylvania. He could not go to law school in Maryland because the state school was for whites only, so he rose before dawn every morning and commuted to Howard Law School in Washington, D.C., where he studied under Dean Charles Hamilton Houston, the architect of the legal strategy to end Jim Crow segregation. Marshall's distinguished career as a civil rights lawyer led to his appointment as solicitor general of the United States, a position from which he argued eighteen cases before the Supreme Court, and later as a federal appeals court judge. President Lyndon Johnson appointed Marshall to the Supreme Court in 1967, and he served until 1991.

HIGHLIGHTS

- As head of the NAACP Legal Defense Fund, Marshall argued along with other civil rights attorneys for the plaintiff black children in *Brown v. Board of Education* (1954), the landmark case that discredited the doctrine of separate but equal and ended legalized segregation in America.

Dissenting VOICES

Justice Marshall dissented, arguing that the school failed to show that the speech was actually "disruptive" of "the educational process."

WHAT DO YOU Think?

Exercise 2.17. The *Fraser* Court found that schools could censor and punish students for "lewd, indecent, or offensive" speech, at least in school-sponsored functions. While reaffirming that high school students have First Amendment rights, it held that such rights are not equal to the rights of adult citizens. After all, grown-ups do have the right to make lewd, indecent, and offensive remarks in public. (Think about *Family Guy, South Park,* Howard Stern, and other raunchy comedies and comedians on TV and radio.)

What was wrong with Fraser's nominating speech? If you were the principal of Bethel High School, how would you have handled it? Do you think that suspension is an effective and appropriate response? What else might have been done?

Exercise 2.18. Chief Justice Burger drew out a gender dimension to the legal conflict and wrote, "By glorifying male sexuality, and in its verbal content, the speech was acutely insulting to teenage girl students." Do you agree with this point? Was it more insulting to girls than to boys? Should girls (must girls) in high school be protected from the hyperactive sexual imaginations of teenage boys?

FOR THE CLASS

Safe Campaigning or Political Abstinence-Only? In 1999 Adam Henery, a sophomore at St. Charles High School in Missouri, was running for junior class president. He signed a contract to follow the school's election rules, including the requirement that all flyers and posters be approved in advance. Adam got approval for his campaign slogan, "Adam Henery: The Safe Choice." On election day, he passed out to fellow students condoms that had his campaign slogan written on the wrapping.

After another student complained, the principal ruled that Adam would be disqualified from holding office, since he failed to clear the distribution of the condoms with the school. Adam argued that the preclearance rule applied only to flyers and posters and maintained that his condom-based message was both preapproved and protected by the First Amendment under *Tinker*. When the votes were counted, Adam had a majority, but the school refused to allow him to take office. He went to court alleging a First Amendment violation and asked to be placed in the office of class president. The court ruled that the school had a reasonable interest in preventing Adam from distributing the condoms and from becoming president. Who's right here? Is this a case of vulgarity and indecency or blatant denial of democracy and free speech? Assume you are the Supreme Court and the case had come to you. How would you rule?

Coed Naked Civil Liberties

Although *Fraser* recognized the authority schools have to censor and punish "lewd, indecent and offensive" student speech, many states have extended to student speakers the broader

After Jeffrey Pyle (left) was sent home for wearing a suggestive T-shirt, he and his brother Jonathan (right) challenged their school's rapidly evolving dress code by designing and wearing a series of sexually provocative and politically pointed T-shirts to class. Today the Pyle brothers are both lawyers.

free speech rights that adults enjoy. State legislatures and state courts can offer the people of a state *more* rights and liberties than they enjoy directly under the U.S. Constitution.

Consider the expansive Student Free Expression law passed by the Massachusetts legislature in 1974:

> The rights of students to freedom of expression in the public schools of the Commonwealth shall not be abridged, provided that such right shall not cause any disruption or disorder within the school. Freedom of expression shall include without limitation the rights and responsibilities of students, collectively and individually, (a) to express their views through speech and symbols, (b) to write, publish, and disseminate their views....

In a very interesting case, *Pyle v. South Hadley School Committee* (1996), the Supreme Judicial Court of Massachusetts used this law to allow students at South Hadley High School in Western Massachusetts to wear T-shirts with funny sexual subtexts that may be offensive to others. While these T-shirts would clearly have gotten them suspended at Bethel High School, where "lewd" speech is forbidden, Massachusetts does not cancel out student speech rights even when someone considers the speech "lewd."

The case started when high school senior Jeffrey Pyle wore a shirt to gym class that his mother had given him bearing this message: "Coed Naked Band. Do It to the Rhythm." The shirt featured an illustration of closely intertwined musical instruments. He was told not to wear it again, but he did and was promptly sent home for violating the school's dress code, which forbids speech that would "harass, threaten, intimidate, or demean an individual or group of individuals because of sex, color, race, religion, handicap, national origin or sexual orientation."

Jeffrey and his brother Jon were outraged and won the support of their mother and father (a professor of constitutional law at Mount Holyoke College) in an irreverent campaign to test the limits of the school's policy. The boys began to wear provocative T-shirts with irreverent political messages, including:

See Dick Drink/See Dick Drive/See Dick Die/Don't Be a Dick
Coed Naked Gerbils [Front]; Some People Will Censor Anything [Back]
Coed Naked Civil Liberties [Front]; Do It to the First Amendment [Back]
Legalize It [with a drawing of a marijuana plant]
A Century of Women on Top/Smith College Centennial/1875–1975
Boring Teacher-Approved Non-Suggestive T-Shirt
Coed Naked Censorship [Front]; They Do It in South Hadley [Back]

The Pyle brothers were disciplined for violating a provision of a new, hastily adopted dress code prohibiting students from wearing clothing that "has comments, pictures, slogans, or designs that are obscene, profane, lewd, or vulgar."

On July 25, 1996, the Massachusetts Supreme Judicial Court upheld the Pyle brothers' claim that their expression was protected by state law because it caused no material disruption of the educational program. "The statute is unambiguous," the court held, "and must be construed as written.... *Our Legislature is free to grant greater rights to the citizens of this Commonwealth than would otherwise be protected under the United States Constitution.*" The court thus read the state law to incorporate the *Tinker* standard and proclaimed broad free speech rights for students in Massachusetts.

WHAT DO YOU **Think?**

Exercise 2.19. Many teachers and students saw Jeffrey Pyle's first T-shirt ("Coed Naked Band. Do It to the Rhythm") as sexist or even sexually harassing. Do you agree? Why or why not? Should students be allowed to wear sexist T-shirts? T-shirts with pictures of nude women (or men)?

Exercise 2.20. Should people have a right to wear "offensive" clothing? How do we know what "offensive" is? Who defines it? What do you find offensive? What do you wear that other people find offensive? (The late comedian Lenny Bruce once said, "My parents came to America to be offensive.")

Exercise 2.21. No student complained to the school administration about any of the Pyle brothers' T-shirts. Is that relevant in trying to decide whether such T-shirts are really "disruptive"? How does *Tinker* approach this problem?

Exercise 2.22. Did the Pyle brothers make a mountain out of a molehill, or did they do the right thing by standing up for their rights? What would you have done?

FOR THE **CLASS**

Draft a Dress Code. Break the class into groups of three. Each group should write a dress code for your school that deals with both general standards of dress and specific standards for "message clothing." Come back together as a class. Read the codes and compare their pros and cons in a class discussion. See if you can come up with a dress code for the school that achieves unanimous support. Is it constitutional?

"BONG HiTS 4 JESUS": Testing the Limits of Free Speech

Although *Tinker* suggested that students might be treated like adult citizens in terms of the right to speak, the *Fraser* decision signaled the Court's second thoughts about relatively unrestrained expression in public schools. In Chapter 3 we will examine cases dealing with the rights of student newspaper reporters and other journalists. We will see how the Supreme Court in the 1980s turned away from broad student rights, substantially limiting the reach of *Tinker*,

When Joe Frederick, an 18-year-old high school student, displayed his now-famous "BONG HiTS 4 JESUS" banner outside of his high school he was suspended. The Supreme Court held that his suspension did not represent a violation of his first amendment rights. Here, Frederick's attorney stands with the banner that started it all.

and upheld broad powers of school authorities to censor and regulate student expression in school-sponsored activities.

In 2007 the Supreme Court carved out another big exception to the rule of free speech in school, holding in a case from Alaska that schools can punish student expression that seems to promote illegal drug use.

···

MORSE v. FREDERICK

Supreme Court of the United States
Argued March 19, 2007.
Decided June 25, 2007.

Majority OPINION Chief Justice ROBERTS delivered the opinion of the Court.

At a school-sanctioned and school-supervised event, a high school principal saw some of her students unfurl a large banner conveying a message she reasonably regarded as promoting illegal drug use. Consistent with established school policy prohibiting such messages at school events, the principal directed the students to take down the banner. One student—among those who had brought the banner to the event—refused to do so. The principal confiscated the banner and later suspended the student.

Our cases make clear that students do not shed their constitutional rights to freedom of speech or expression at the schoolhouse gate. At the same time, we have held that "the constitutional rights of students in public school are not automatically coextensive with the rights of adults in other settings," and that the rights of students "must be 'applied in light of the special characteristics of the school environment.'" Consistent with these principles, we hold that schools may take steps to safeguard those entrusted to their care from speech that can reasonably be regarded as encouraging illegal drug use. We conclude that the school officials in this case did not violate the First Amendment by confiscating the pro-drug banner and suspending the student responsible for it.

I

On January 24, 2002, the Olympic Torch Relay passed through Juneau, Alaska, on its way to the winter games in Salt Lake City, Utah. The torchbearers were to proceed along a street in front of Juneau-Douglas High School (JDHS) while school was in session. Deborah Morse, the school principal, decided to permit staff and students to participate in the Torch Relay as an approved social event or class trip. Students were allowed to leave class to observe the relay from either side of the street. Teachers and administrative officials monitored the students' actions.

… Joseph Frederick, a JDHS senior, was late to school that day. When he arrived, he joined his friends (all but one of whom were JDHS students) across the street from the school to watch the event. Not all the students waited patiently. Some became rambunctious, throwing plastic cola bottles and snowballs and scuffling with their classmates. As the torchbearers and camera crews passed by, Frederick and his friends unfurled a 14-foot banner bearing the phrase: "BONG HiTS 4 JESUS." The large banner was easily readable by the students on the other side of the street.

Principal Morse immediately crossed the street and demanded that the banner be taken down. Everyone but Frederick complied. Morse confiscated the banner and told Frederick to report to her office, where she suspended him for 10 days. Morse later explained that she told Frederick to take the banner down because she thought it encouraged illegal drug use, in violation of established school policy. Juneau School Board Policy No. 5520 states: "The Board specifically prohibits any assembly or public expression that advocates the use of substances that are illegal to minors...." In addition, Juneau School Board Policy No. 5850 subjects "pupils who participate in approved social events and class trips" to the same student conduct rules that apply during the regular school program.

Frederick administratively appealed his suspension, but the Juneau School District Superintendent upheld it, limiting it to time served (8 days). In a memorandum setting forth his reasons, the superintendent determined that Frederick had displayed his banner "in the midst of his fellow students, during school hours, at a school-sanctioned activity." He further explained that Frederick "was not disciplined because the principal of the school 'disagreed' with his message, but because his speech appeared to advocate the use of illegal drugs."

The superintendent continued:

> The common-sense understanding of the phrase 'bong hits' is that it is a reference to a means of smoking marijuana. Given [Frederick's] inability or unwillingness to express any other credible meaning for the phrase, I can only agree with the principal and countless others who saw the banner as advocating the use of illegal drugs. [Frederick's] speech was not political. He was not advocating the legalization of marijuana or promoting a religious belief. He was displaying a fairly silly message promoting illegal drug usage in the midst of a school activity, for the benefit of television cameras covering the Torch Relay. [Frederick's] speech was potentially disruptive to the event and clearly disruptive of and inconsistent with the school's educational mission to educate students about the dangers of illegal drugs and to discourage their use.

Relying on our decision in *Fraser* the superintendent concluded that the principal's actions were permissible because Frederick's banner was "speech or action that intrudes upon the work of the schools."...

Frederick then filed suit alleging that the school board and Morse had violated his First Amendment rights....

We granted certiorari on two questions: whether Frederick had a First Amendment right to wield his banner, and, if so, whether that right was so clearly established that the principal may be held liable for damages. We resolve the first question against Frederick, and therefore have no occasion to reach the second.

II

At the outset, we reject Frederick's argument that this is not a school speech case. The event occurred during normal school hours. It was sanctioned by Principal Morse "as an approved social event or class trip," and the school district's rules expressly provide that pupils in "approved social events and class trips are subject to district rules for student conduct." Teachers and administrators were interspersed among the students and charged with supervising them. The high school band and cheerleaders performed. Frederick, standing among other JDHS students across the street from the school, directed his banner toward the school, making it plainly visible to most students. Under these circumstances, we agree with the superintendent that Frederick cannot "stand in the midst of his fellow students, during school hours, at a school-sanctioned activity and claim he is not at school."

III

The message on Frederick's banner is cryptic. It is no doubt offensive to some, perhaps amusing to others. To still others, it probably means nothing at all. Frederick himself claimed "that the words were just nonsense meant to attract television cameras." But Principal Morse thought the banner would be interpreted by those viewing it as promoting illegal drug use, and that interpretation is plainly a reasonable one.

As Morse later explained, when she saw the sign, she thought that "the reference to a 'bong hit' would be widely understood by high school students and others as referring to smoking marijuana." She further believed that "display of the banner would be construed by students, District personnel, parents and others witnessing the display of the banner, as advocating or promoting illegal drug use"—in violation of school policy.

We agree with Morse. At least two interpretations of the words on the banner demonstrate that the sign advocated the use of illegal drugs. First, the phrase could be interpreted as an imperative: "[Take] bong hits …"—a message equivalent, as Morse explained in her declaration, to "smoke marijuana" or "use an illegal drug." Alternatively, the phrase could be viewed as celebrating drug use—"bong hits [are a good thing]," or "[we take] bong hits"—and we discern no meaningful distinction between celebrating illegal drug use in the midst of fellow students and outright advocacy or promotion.

The pro-drug interpretation of the banner gains further plausibility given the paucity of alternative meanings the banner might bear. The best Frederick can come up with is that the banner is "meaningless and funny." The dissent similarly refers to the sign's message as "curious," "ambiguous," "nonsense," "ridiculous," "obscure," "silly," "quixotic," and "stupid." Gibberish is surely a possible interpretation of the words on the banner, but it is not the only one, and dismissing the banner as meaningless ignores its undeniable reference to illegal drugs.

The dissent mentions Frederick's "credible and uncontradicted explanation for the message—he just wanted to get on television." But that is a description of Frederick's motive for displaying the banner; it is not an interpretation of what the banner says. The *way* Frederick was going to fulfill his ambition of appearing on television was by unfurling a pro-drug banner at a school event, in the presence of teachers and fellow students.

Elsewhere in its opinion, the dissent emphasizes the importance of political speech and the need to foster "national debate about a serious issue," as if to suggest that the banner is political speech. But not even Frederick argues that the banner conveys any sort of political or religious message. Contrary to the dissent's suggestion, this is plainly not a case about political debate over the criminalization of drug use or possession.

IV

The question thus becomes whether a principal may, consistent with the First Amendment, restrict student speech at a school event, when that speech is reasonably viewed as promoting illegal drug use. We hold that she may….

Tinker held that student expression may not be suppressed unless school officials reasonably conclude that it will "materially and substantially disrupt the work and discipline of the school." The essential facts of *Tinker* are quite stark, implicating concerns at the heart of the First Amendment…. Political speech, of course, is "at the core of what the First Amendment is designed to protect." The only interest the Court discerned underlying the school's actions was the "mere desire to avoid the discomfort and unpleasantness that always accompany an unpopular viewpoint," or "an urgent wish to avoid the controversy which might result from the expression." That interest was not enough to justify banning "a silent, passive expression of opinion, unaccompanied by any disorder or disturbance."…

Drawing on the principles applied in our student speech cases, we have held in the Fourth Amendment context that "while children assuredly do not 'shed their constitutional rights … at the schoolhouse gate,' … the nature of those rights is what is appropriate for children in school." In particular, "the school setting requires some easing of the restrictions to which searches by public authorities are ordinarily subject."

Even more to the point, these cases also recognize that deterring drug use by schoolchildren is an "important—indeed, perhaps compelling" interest. Drug abuse can cause severe and permanent damage to the health and well-being of young people:

> School years are the time when the physical, psychological, and addictive effects of drugs are most severe. Maturing nervous systems are more critically impaired by intoxicants than mature ones are; childhood losses in learning are lifelong and profound; children grow chemically dependent more quickly than adults, and their record of recovery is depressingly poor. And of course the effects of a drug-infested school are visited not just upon the users, but upon the entire student body and faculty, as the educational process is disrupted.

Just five years ago, we wrote: "The drug abuse problem among our Nation's youth has hardly abated since *Vernonia* was decided in 1995. In fact, evidence suggests that it has only grown worse."

The problem remains serious today. About half of American 12th graders have used an illicit drug, as have more than a third of 10th graders and about one-fifth of 8th graders. Nearly one in four 12th graders has used an illicit drug in the past month. Some 25% of high schoolers say that they have been offered, sold, or given an illegal drug on school property within the past year….

The "special characteristics of the school environment" and the governmental interest in stopping student drug abuse—reflected in the policies of Congress and myriad school boards, including JDHS—allow schools to restrict student expression that they reasonably regard as promoting illegal drug use. *Tinker* warned that schools may not prohibit student speech because of "undifferentiated fear or apprehension of disturbance" or "a mere desire to avoid the discomfort and unpleasantness that always accompany an unpopular viewpoint." The danger here is far more serious and palpable. The particular concern to prevent student drug abuse at issue here extends well beyond an abstract desire to avoid controversy….

School principals have a difficult job, and a vitally important one. When Frederick suddenly and unexpectedly unfurled his banner, Morse had to decide to act— or not act— on the spot. It was reasonable for her to conclude that the banner promoted illegal drug use— in violation of established school policy—and that failing to act would send a powerful message to the students in her charge, including Frederick, about how serious the school was about the dangers of illegal drug use. The First Amendment does not require schools to tolerate at school events student expression that contributes to those dangers....

It is so ordered.

A Concurring Conclusion

Concurring Opinion

Opinion written by a justice or judge that agrees with the judgment of the majority in a case but that offers a separate explanation or process of reasoning for arriving there.

Justice Thomas concurred and wrote an opinion in which he called for flat-out overruling the *Tinker* decision, something the majority had not called for. He wrote:

In my view, the history of public education suggests that the First Amendment, as originally understood, does not protect student speech in public schools.... Because public schools were initially created as substitutes for private schools, when States developed public education systems in the early 1800's, no one doubted the government's ability to educate and discipline children as private schools did. Like their private counterparts, early public schools were not places for freewheeling debates or exploration of competing ideas. Rather, teachers instilled 'a core of common values' in students and taught them self-control.... Teachers instilled these values not only by presenting ideas but also through strict discipline. Schools punished students for behavior the school considered disrespectful or wrong.... Rules of etiquette were enforced, and courteous behavior was demanded. To meet their educational objectives, schools required absolute obedience.... In short, in the earliest public schools, teachers taught, and students listened. Teachers commanded, and students obeyed. Teachers did not rely solely on the power of ideas to persuade; they relied on discipline to maintain order.

Justice Thomas pointed out that the legal doctrine of *in loco parentis* gave schools the general power "to discipline students, to enforce rules, and to maintain order." He cited with approval an old text stating that "the master" of a school "must govern these pupils, quicken the slothful, spur the indolent, restrain the impetuous, and control the stubborn. He must make rules, give commands, and punish disobedience."

Justice Thomas argued that the school principal's general power to discipline conduct includes the power to regulate and punish speech as well. He pointed approvingly to a Vermont Supreme Court decision upholding the corporal punishment of a student who called his teacher *"Old Jack Seaver"* in front of other students. Justice Thomas quoted this passage from the decision:

Language used to other scholars to stir up disorder and subordination, or to heap odium and disgrace upon the master; writings and pictures placed so as to suggest evil and corrupt language, images and thoughts to the youth who must frequent the school; all such or similar acts tend directly to impair the usefulness of the school, the welfare of the scholars and the authority of the master. By common consent and by the universal custom in our New England schools, the master has always been deemed to have the right to punish such offences. Such power is essential to the preservation of order, decency, decorum and good government in schools.

Justice Thomas assailed the *Tinker* decision, saying that it created a rule not rooted in the First Amendment that is now riddled with exceptions. He wrote:

> Today, the Court creates another exception. In doing so, we continue to distance our-selves from *Tinker*, but we neither overrule it nor offer an explanation of when it op-erates and when it does not. I am afraid that our jurisprudence now says that students have a right to speak in schools except when they don't—a standard continuously de-veloped through litigation against local schools and their administrators. In my view, petitioners could prevail for a much simpler reason: As originally understood, the Constitution does not afford students a right to free speech in public schools.

He concluded:

> I join the Court's opinion because it erodes *Tinker*'s hold in the realm of student speech, even though it does so by adding to the patchwork of exceptions to the *Tinker* standard. I think the better approach is to dispense with *Tinker* altogether, and given the opportunity, I would do so.

Dissenting VOICES

Justice Stevens was joined by Justice Souter and Justice Ginsburg in his dissenting opinion. He wrote:

> In my judgment, the First Amendment protects student speech if the message itself neither violates a permissible rule nor expressly advocates conduct that is illegal and harmful to students. This nonsense banner does neither, and the Court does serious vi-olence to the First Amendment in upholding—indeed, lauding—a school's decision to punish Frederick for expressing a view with which it disagreed.

Justice Stevens said that the Court's test about advocating use of illegal drugs

> invites stark viewpoint discrimination. In this case, for example, the principal has un-abashedly acknowledged that she disciplined Frederick because she disagreed with the pro-drug viewpoint she ascribed to the message on the banner.... [T]he Court's hold-ing in this case strikes at 'the heart of the First Amendment' because it upholds a pun-ishment meted out on the basis of a listener's disagreement with her understanding (or, more likely, misunderstanding) of the speaker's viewpoint.

Even if the school has an interest in restricting speech that advocates the use of illegal substances, Justice Stevens wrote, such an interest would not justify punishment of "an ob-scure message with a drug theme that a third party subjectively—and not very reason-ably—thinks is tantamount to express advocacy."

He continued:

> This is a nonsense message, not advocacy. The Court's feeble effort to divine its hidden meaning is strong evidence of that (positing that the banner might mean, alternatively, "[Take] bong hits," "'bong hits [are a good thing],'" or "[we take] bong hits"). Frederick's credible and uncontradicted explanation for the message—he just wanted to get on television—is also relevant because a speaker who does not intend to per-suade his audience can hardly be said to be advocating anything. But most importantly, it takes real imagination to read a "cryptic" message (the Court's characterization, not mine) with a slanting drug reference as an incitement to drug use. Admittedly, some

high school students (including those who use drugs) are dumb. Most students, however, do not shed their brains at the schoolhouse gate, and most students know dumb advocacy when they see it. The notion that the message on this banner would actually persuade either the average student or even the dumbest one to change his or her behavior is most implausible. That the Court believes such a silly message can be proscribed as advocacy underscores the novelty of its position, and suggests that the principle it articulates has no stopping point.

Even if advocacy could somehow be wedged into Frederick's obtuse reference to marijuana, that advocacy was at best subtle and ambiguous. There is abundant precedent, including another opinion the chief justice announces today, for the proposition that when the "First Amendment is implicated, the tie goes to the speaker".... If this were a close case, the tie would have to go to Frederick's speech, not to the principal's strained reading of his quixotic message.

Justice Stevens saw the majority decision as a frontal assault on the right of students to debate controversial subjects, including the War on Drugs:

Among other things, the Court's ham-handed, categorical approach is deaf to the constitutional imperative to permit unfettered debate, even among high-school students, about the wisdom of the war on drugs or of legalizing marijuana for medicinal use. ("[Students] may not be confined to the expression of those sentiments that are officially approved"). If Frederick's stupid reference to marijuana can in the Court's view justify censorship, then high school students everywhere could be forgiven for zipping their mouths about drugs at school lest some "reasonable" observer censor and then punish them for promoting drugs.

Consider, too, that the school district's rule draws no distinction between alcohol and marijuana, but applies evenhandedly to all "substances that are illegal to minors." Given the tragic consequences of teenage alcohol consumption—drinking causes far more fatal accidents than the misuse of marijuana—the school district's interest in deterring teenage alcohol use is at least comparable to its interest in preventing marijuana use. Under the Court's reasoning, must the First Amendment give way whenever a school seeks to punish a student for any speech mentioning beer, or indeed anything else that might be deemed risky to teenagers? While I find it hard to believe the Court would support punishing Frederick for flying a "WINE SiPS 4 JESUS" banner—which could quite reasonably be construed either as a protected religious message or as a pro-alcohol message—the breathtaking sweep of its opinion suggests it would.

Justice Stevens closed with a series of extraordinary observations about stifling youthful speech critical of government initiatives like the War on Drugs:

Although this case began with a silly, nonsensical banner, it ends with the Court inventing out of whole cloth a special First Amendment rule permitting the censorship of any student speech that mentions drugs, at least so long as someone could perceive that speech to contain a latent pro-drug message.... I mention two personal recollections that have no doubt influenced my conclusion that it would be profoundly unwise to create special rules for speech about drug and alcohol use.

The Vietnam War is remembered today as an unpopular war. During its early stages, however, "the dominant opinion" that Justice Harlan mentioned in his *Tinker* dissent regarded opposition to the war as unpatriotic, if not treason. That dominant opinion strongly supported the prosecution of several of those who demonstrated in Grant

Park during the 1968 Democratic Convention in Chicago, and the vilification of vocal opponents of the war like Julian Bond. In 1965, when the Des Moines students wore their armbands, the school district's fear that they might "start an argument or cause a disturbance" was well founded. Given that context, there is special force to the Court's insistence that "our Constitution says we must take that risk; and our history says that it is this sort of hazardous freedom—this kind of openness—that is the basis of our national strength and of the independence and vigor of Americans who grow up and live in this relatively permissive, often disputatious, society." As we now know, the then-dominant opinion about the Vietnam War was not etched in stone.

Reaching back still further, the current dominant opinion supporting the war on drugs in general, and our antimarijuana laws in particular, is reminiscent of the opinion that supported the nationwide ban on alcohol consumption when I was a student. While alcoholic beverages are now regarded as ordinary articles of commerce, their use was then condemned with the same moral fervor that now supports the war on drugs. The ensuing change in public opinion occurred much more slowly than the relatively rapid shift in Americans' views on the Vietnam War, and progressed on a state-by-state basis over a period of many years. But just as prohibition in the 1920's and early 1930's was secretly questioned by thousands of otherwise law-abiding patrons of bootleggers and speakeasies, today the actions of literally millions of otherwise law-abiding users of marijuana, and of the majority of voters in each of the several States that tolerate medicinal uses of the product, lead me to wonder whether the fear of disapproval by those in the majority is silencing opponents of the war on drugs. Surely our national experience with alcohol should make us wary of dampening speech suggesting—however inarticulately—that it would be better to tax and regulate marijuana than to persevere in a futile effort to ban its use entirely.

Even in high school, a rule that permits only one point of view to be expressed is less likely to produce correct answers than the open discussion of countervailing views. In the national debate about a serious issue, it is the expression of the minority's viewpoint that most demands the protection of the First Amendment. Whatever the better policy may be, a full and frank discussion of the costs and benefits of the attempt to prohibit the use of marijuana is far wiser than suppression of speech because it is unpopular.

WHAT DO YOU Think?

Exercise 2.23. In his dissenting opinion, Justice Stevens says that Joseph's banner "is a nonsense message, not advocacy." What exactly does the banner statement mean? Which of the following meanings seems most likely to you?

"Take bong hits." [Chief Justice Roberts's suggestion]
"Bong hits are a good thing." [Chief Justice Roberts's suggestion]
"We take bong hits." [Chief Justice Roberts's suggestion]
"Marijuana use demonstrates support for Jesus Christ."
"Drug use leads to Christianity."
"Jesus was a psychedelic hippie rebel."
"We use drugs and talk about Jesus."

"Be a religious conscientious objector to the War on Drugs."
"Pay attention to me; I want to get on TV!" [Joseph's own suggestion]
Other?

Exercise 2.24. Given how inscrutable Joseph Frederick's message was, does that suggest that it *should* or *should not* be protected by the First Amendment? Who gets to decide what a young citizen's expression actually means—the student, his classmates, his teacher, his principal, or the Supreme Court?

Exercise 2.25. In his dissenting opinion, Justice Stevens lampoons the whole discipline of Joseph Frederick by saying that most students "do not shed their brains at the school-house gate, and most students know dumb advocacy when they see it. The notion that the message on this banner would actually persuade either the average student or even the dumbest one to change his or her behavior is most implausible." Do you agree or disagree? Would the holding of such a banner actually encourage students to use marijuana? Would you be influenced by it?

Exercise 2.26. Joseph Frederick first asserted that this was not a case about speech at school, since it took place outside of school. Chief Justice Roberts thoroughly rejects this claim, observing that this was an approved class activity with a school band performance and an abundant teacher and administrator presence in the crowd. Do you agree with Joseph's claim that he was not actually at school? Why is this an important first point?

Exercise 2.27. Chief Justice Roberts and Justice Stevens take dramatically different approaches to the War on Drugs, which is the critical backdrop to the case. Chief Justice Roberts records the serious physical and psychological dangers that drugs pose to adolescents and cites pervasive federal and local efforts to prevent drug use by young people.

But Justice Stevens says that the majority opinion "is deaf to the constitutional imperative to permit unfettered debate, even among high school students, about the wisdom of the war on drugs or of legalizing marijuana for medicinal use." He notes that Alaska's Constitution protects the right of adults to possess less than four ounces of marijuana for personal use and that Alaska's voters also passed a ballot measure decriminalizing the use of marijuana for medicinal purposes.

Should high school students be able to freely debate the wisdom of the War on Drugs and drug prohibition in high school, or does that invite advocacy of illegal behavior among young students who may not be able to tell the difference between a policy debate and official academic advice?

Exercise 2.28. Justice Stevens closes his dissenting opinion with a remarkable analysis comparing speech that dissents from the War on Drugs with speech that dissented from the Vietnam War and liquor Prohibition. Is it dangerous for a Supreme Court justice to be inviting a national discussion about the continued wisdom of criminalizing drugs? Is it a thoughtful suggestion to the public?

Exercise 2.29. Which of the following student messages at school, worn on T-shirts, do you think could be censored and punished under the majority opinion? Which not? Discuss and explain.

"Bong hits offend Jesus."
"Song hits 4 Jesus."
"People who are late 4 class 4 Jesus."
"Juneau-Douglas footballers: We hit 4 Jesus."
"Arrest drug users now."
"Jesus forgives bong hits."
"Legalize marijuana."
"Free speech to end the War on Drugs."

Thought Control or Quality Control? The Problem of Library Book Removal

The First Amendment generally protects not only the right to speak but also the right to receive information. Citizens have a right to information even when the government thinks the information in question may be dangerous. In the public school context, the principle of free access to information loses some of its clarity because the Supreme Court has recognized that a school system controls its curriculum, its libraries, and the selection of textbooks. Yet, this general control is not unlimited. For example, school officials cannot ban specific library books for political reasons. Consider the events that led to *Board of Education, Island Trees Union Free School District No. 26 v. Pico*, a 1982 case that established this principle.

After several members of the Island Trees Board of Education went to a conference of the conservative group Parents of New York United (PONYU), they returned home with a list of books that the board members considered "objectionable" and "improper fare." The list of dangerous books included a number that were already in the Island Trees school libraries, among them the following:

Slaughterhouse-Five, by Kurt Vonnegut Jr.
The Naked Ape, by Desmond Morris
Down These Mean Streets, by Piri Thomas
Best Short Stories of Negro Writers, edited by Langston Hughes
Go Ask Alice, by Anonymous
Laughing Boy, by Oliver LaFarge
Black Boy, by Richard Wright
A Hero Ain't Nothin' but a Sandwich, by Alice Childress
Soul on Ice, by Eldridge Cleaver
A Reader for Writers, edited by Jerome Archer
The Fixer, by Bernard Malamud

Because these books had been described at the conference as "anti-American, anti-Christian, anti-Semitic, and just plain filthy," the Board of Education ordered public school

Author Kurt Vonnegut Jr. speaks to reporters about a lawsuit involving a Long Island school board's attempt to ban a number of books, including his best-seller *Slaughterhouse-Five*. High school student Steven Pico and other students challenged the board's decision to remove the books, arguing that it violated their First Amendment rights. Their case went to the Supreme Court, which ruled in the students' favor.

librarians to deliver the books to the board so they could be examined. The board then formed a parent/teacher Book Review Committee to advise it on which books should be taken out of the libraries and which kept in the stacks. The committee recommended the removal of only two books, but the board went ahead and without explanation removed nine of the books from the public school libraries.

When a group of students brought a suit alleging violation of their First Amendment rights, the district court threw it out and held for the Board of Education, finding that it had properly targeted only books that were "vulgar." But a panel of the Second Circuit—and then a closely divided Supreme Court (5–4)—found that the students had a right to go to trial in the case to show that the books were removed as part of an official effort at thought control rather than mere regulation of student access to vulgarity.

There was no majority opinion in *Board of Education v. Pico,* but Justice Brennan announced the judgment of the Supreme Court in an opinion that was joined in full by Justices Marshall and Stevens and in part by Justice Blackmun. Essentially, Justice Brennan found that this case was special because it did not involve textbooks but library books and did not involve selection of books in the first instance but ad hoc *removal* of books that were already selected and purchased. Justice Brennan wrote:

[We] think that the First Amendment rights of students may be directly and sharply implicated by the removal of the books from the shelves of a school library. … [W]e have held that in a variety of contexts "the Constitution protects the right to receive information and ideas." *Stanley v. Georgia.* [W]e do not deny that local school boards have a substantial legitimate role to play in the determination of school library content. [But] that discretion may not be exercised in a narrowly partisan or political manner. If a Democratic school board, motivated by party affiliation, ordered the removal of all books written by or in favor of Republicans, few would doubt that the order violated the constitutional rights of students denied access to those books. The same conclusion would surely apply if an all-white school board, motivated by racial animus, decided to remove all books authored by blacks or advocating racial equality or integration. Our Constitution does not permit the official suppression of ideas.

Justice Rehnquist vigorously dissented from the Court's decision. He wrote:

> I can cheerfully concede [that a Democratic school board could not, for political reasons, remove all books by or in favor of Republicans, and that an all-white school board, motivated by racial animus, could not remove all books authored by blacks or advocating racial equality], but as in so many other cases the extreme examples are seldom the ones that arise in the real world of constitutional litigation. In this case the facts taken most favorably to respondents suggest that nothing of this sort happened. The nine books removed undoubtedly did contain "ideas," but in the light of the excerpts from them ... it is apparent that eight of them contained demonstrable amounts of vulgarity and profanity and the ninth contained nothing that could be considered partisan or political.

WHAT DO YOU Think?

Exercise 2.30. Do you agree with the implication that the Island Trees Board of Education could have refused to purchase these books in the first place? If not, does that mean the board had a *constitutional obligation* to order these books? Does it have a constitutional obligation to order new copies when these become too beat up to use? Or does the decision simply stand for the proposition that books cannot be kept out of libraries for the wrong reasons? What are the right reasons to deny books a place in the library? Should children have access to any books that adults can obtain?

Exercise 2.31. There have been efforts to remove Mark Twain's classic *Huckleberry Finn* from high school curricula and libraries because of its alleged racism and frequent use of the "N-word," perhaps the most toxic word in the English language. Using your school library and the Internet, research the debate over *Huckleberry Finn* and write a two- to three-page paper about various perspectives expressed on this subject.

Do you think that Twain's book should be removed from the schools? If not, how should it be taught with respect to its language, which is undoubtedly experienced as demeaning and painful by many students? Is school the right place to learn how to participate in a civil discourse when one is feeling injured and insulted? Consider Harvard Law professor Randall Kennedy's book *Nigger* (2002), in which he explores the history, legal effect, and social meaning of this still ubiquitous and incendiary epithet. Should we try to suppress books, articles, songs, and cases where the offending word appears, or do you think that campaigns against words cheapen our politics and distract us from what is really important?

FOR THE **CLASS**

Literature and Vulgarity in the High School Library. Do you agree with the premise, apparently shared by justices in both the majority and the dissent in *Pico*, that it is fine to remove books from the library when they are vulgar? Literature, films, and art described as "vulgar" are generally protected under the First Amendment. But, as we know, general rules do not always apply in the school setting. Are there unique dangers to having vulgar literature in a school library? Are there dangers to removing it?

Assume that there is a proposal in your school district to remove from the high school curriculum and school libraries the eleven books at issue in *Pico* on the grounds that they are all vulgar. Transform yourselves into members of the school board and debate whether or not the books should indeed be removed. Can you speak about what the books say? Take a vote in your class.

Viewpoint Neutrality and Religious Speech: Good News for the Free Speech Rights of Religious Americans

When a public school opens its doors in the after-school hours to community groups for educational and civic meetings, it must allow all groups to use the facilities on an equal basis without regard to their politics or philosophical viewpoint. In First Amendment terms, we say that in a "public forum" like this, the government must have a policy of "viewpoint neutrality" toward speech.

Yet, some public schools and universities have thought that they can exclude organizations and speakers with a religious perspective from public speech forums. Indeed, many schools have thought they *must* exclude religious speakers from their facilities on the supposition that letting them in would violate the First Amendment's establishment clause, which prevents government from endorsing or otherwise establishing religion.

Members of the Good News Club stand outside Milford Central School. The club won the right to meet there after the Supreme Court ruled that public schools cannot deny religiously oriented groups an equal right to meet on campus.

But in a string of cases the Supreme Court has made clear that religiously oriented speakers and groups have every equal right to use the facilities and resources of public universities and schools when they are opened up to the public. The Court first defined this principle in *Widmar v. Vincent* (1981), which ruled that religiously oriented student groups must be given equal rights to meet in public schools. This constitutional idea is also written into federal law: The Equal Access Act requires that public high schools receiving federal funds grant equal access to student groups who want to meet on campus without discriminating on the basis of the "religious, political, philosophical or other content of the speech."

In *Lamb's Chapel v. Center Moriches Union Free School District* (1993), the Court considered whether a public school violated the First Amendment when it opened its doors to outside groups for after-school use but refused a group's request to show a religiously oriented film series. The Court ruled that this was speech discrimination on the basis of religious viewpoint and ordered that the group be given access.

Then, in *Rosenberger v. Rector and Visitors of the University of Virginia* (1995), the Court struck down the University of Virginia's practice of funding all student-organized publications on campus except those written from a religious point of view. The plaintiff was a student newspaper, *Wide Awake,* that considered issues such as dating, academic competition, and athletics from a fundamentalist Christian perspective. Justice Kennedy, writing for the majority in *Rosenberger,* found that religion provides a distinct vantage point from which to analyze society, politics, and culture. This viewpoint cannot be suppressed or driven off the field of debate in public settings.

Thus, by the time the Court came to consider *Good News Club v. Milford Central School* in 2001, the die had been cast. The question was whether Milford Central School violated the free speech rights of the Good News Club, a Christian group for children ages six to twelve, by selectively rejecting its application to use the facilities because the group's members were engaged in religious-type activities. Justice Clarence Thomas first considered whether the policy violated the club's free speech rights and then, finding that it did, rejected the argument that the establishment clause somehow required the discrimination.

GOOD NEWS CLUB v. MILFORD CENTRAL SCHOOL

Supreme Court of the United States
Argued February 28, 2001.
Decided June 11, 2001.

Majority OPINION   Justice THOMAS delivered the opinion of the Court.

This case presents two questions. The first question is whether Milford Central School violated the free speech rights of the Good News Club when it excluded the Club from meeting after hours at the school. The second question is whether any such violation is justified by Milford's concern that permitting the Club's activities would violate the Establishment Clause. We conclude that Milford's restriction violates the Club's free speech rights and that no Establishment Clause concern justifies that violation.

Establishment Clause
The religion clause in the First Amendment that prohibits both federal and state governments from formally establishing, coercing, or endorsing a religion or religion in general.

I

... Stephen and Darleen Fournier reside within Milford's district and therefore are eligible to use the school's facilities as long as their proposed use is approved by the school. Together they are sponsors of the local Good News Club, a private Christian organization for children ages 6 to 12. Pursuant to Milford's policy, in September 1996 the Fourniers submitted a request to Dr. Robert McGruder, interim superintendent of the district, in which they sought permission to hold the Club's weekly afterschool meetings in the school cafeteria. The next month, McGruder formally denied the Fourniers' request on the ground that the proposed use—to have "a fun time of singing songs, hearing a Bible lesson and memorizing scripture"—was "the equivalent of religious worship." According to McGruder, the community use policy, which prohibits use "by any individual or organization for religious purposes," foreclosed the Club's activities.

In response to a letter submitted by the Club's counsel, Milford's attorney requested information to clarify the nature of the Club's activities. The Club sent a set of materials used or distributed at the meetings and the following description of its meeting:

"The Club opens its session with Ms. Fournier taking attendance. As she calls a child's name, if the child recites a Bible verse the child receives a treat. After attendance, the Club sings songs. Next Club members engage in games that involve, *inter alia,* learning Bible verses. Ms. Fournier then relates a Bible story and explains how it applies to Club members' lives. The Club closes with prayer. Finally, Ms. Fournier distributes treats and the Bible verses for memorization."

McGruder and Milford's attorney reviewed the materials and concluded that "the kinds of activities proposed to be engaged in by the Good News Club were not a discussion of secular subjects such as child rearing, development of character and development of morals from a religious perspective, but were in fact the equivalent of religious instruction itself." In February 1997, the Milford Board of Education adopted a resolution rejecting the Club's request to use Milford's facilities "for the purpose of conducting religious instruction and Bible study."

... The Club alleged that Milford's denial of its application violated its free speech rights under the First and Fourteenth Amendments....

III

... [W]e first address whether the exclusion constituted viewpoint discrimination. We are guided in our analysis by two of our prior opinions, *Lamb's Chapel* [*v. Center Moriches Union Free School District*] and *Rosenberger* [*v. Rector and Visitors of University of Virginia.*]...

Milford has opened its limited public forum to activities that serve a variety of purposes, including events "pertaining to the welfare of the community." Milford interprets its policy to permit discussions of subjects such as child rearing, and of "the development of character and morals from a religious perspective." For example, this policy would allow someone to use Aesop's Fables to teach children moral values. Additionally, a group could sponsor a debate on whether there should be a constitutional amendment to permit prayer in public schools and the Boy Scouts could meet "to influence a boy's character, development and spiritual growth." In short, any group that "promote[s] the moral and character development of children" is eligible to use the school building.

Just as there is no question that teaching morals and character development to children is a permissible purpose under Milford's policy, it is clear that the Good News Club teaches morals and character development to children. For example, no one disputes that the Club instructs children to overcome feelings of jealousy, to treat others well regardless of how they treat the children, and to be obedient, even if it does so in a nonsecular way. Nonetheless, because Milford found the Club's activities to be religious in nature—"the equivalent of religious instruction itself"—it excluded the Club from use of its facilities.

Applying *Lamb's Chapel* we find it quite clear that Milford engaged in viewpoint discrimination when it excluded the Club from the afterschool forum....

Like the church in *Lamb's Chapel*, the Club seeks to address a subject otherwise permitted under the rule, the teaching of morals and character, from a religious standpoint.... The only apparent difference between the activity of Lamb's Chapel and the activities of the Good News Club is that the Club chooses to teach moral lessons from a Christian perspective through live storytelling and prayer, whereas Lamb's Chapel taught lessons through films. This distinction is inconsequential. Both modes of speech use a religious viewpoint. Thus, the exclusion of the Good News Club's activities, like the exclusion of Lamb's Chapel's films, constitutes unconstitutional viewpoint discrimination....

IV

Milford argues that, even if its restriction constitutes viewpoint discrimination, its interest in not violating the Establishment Clause outweighs the Club's interest in gaining equal access to the school's facilities. In other words, according to Milford, its restriction was required to avoid violating the Establishment Clause. We disagree....

We rejected Establishment Clause defenses similar to Milford's in two previous free speech cases, *Lamb's Chapel* and *Widmar* [*v. Vincent*]....

Milford attempts to distinguish *Lamb's Chapel* and *Widmar* by emphasizing that Milford's policy involves elementary school children. According to Milford, children will perceive that the school is endorsing the Club and will feel coercive pressure to participate, because the Club's activities take place on school grounds, even though they occur during nonschool hours. This argument is unpersuasive.

First, ... [t]he Good News Club seeks nothing more than to be treated neutrally and given access to speak about the same topics as are other groups....

Second, to the extent we consider whether the community would feel coercive pressure to engage in the Club's activities the relevant community would be the parents, not the elementary school children. It is the parents who choose whether their children will attend the Good News Club meetings. Because the children cannot attend without their parents' permission, they cannot be coerced into engaging in the Good News Club's religious activities. Milford does not suggest that the parents of elementary school children would be confused about whether the school was endorsing religion. Nor do we believe that such an argument could be reasonably advanced.

Third, whatever significance we may have assigned in the Establishment Clause context to the suggestion that elementary school children are more impressionable than adults, we have never extended our Establishment Clause jurisprudence to foreclose private religious conduct during nonschool hours merely because it takes place on school premises where elementary school children may be present....

Fourth, even if we were to consider the possible misperceptions by schoolchildren in deciding whether Milford's permitting the Club's activities would violate the Establishment Clause, the facts of this case simply do not support Milford's conclusion. There is no evidence that young children are permitted to loiter outside classrooms after the schoolday has ended. Surely even young children are aware of events for which their parents must sign permission forms. The meetings were held in a combined high school resource room and middle school special education room, not in an elementary school classroom. The instructors are not schoolteachers. And the children in the group are not all the same age as in the normal classroom setting; their ages range from 6 to 12. In sum, these circumstances simply do not support the theory that small children would perceive endorsement here.

Finally, even if we were to inquire into the minds of schoolchildren in this case, we cannot say the danger that children would misperceive the endorsement of religion is any greater than the danger that they would perceive a hostility toward the religious viewpoint if the Club were excluded from the public forum. This concern is particularly acute given the reality that Milford's building is not used only for elementary school children. Students, from kindergarten through the 12th grade, all attend school in the same building. There may be as many, if not more, upperclassmen than elementary school children who occupy the school after hours. For that matter, members of the public writ large are permitted in the school after hours pursuant to the community use policy. Any bystander could conceivably be aware of the school's use policy and its exclusion of the Good News Club, and could suffer as much from viewpoint discrimination as elementary school children could suffer from perceived endorsement....

V

When Milford denied the Good News Club access to the school's limited public forum on the ground that the Club was religious in nature, it discriminated against the Club because of its religious viewpoint in violation of the Free Speech Clause of the First Amendment. Because Milford has not raised a valid Establishment Clause claim, we do not address the question whether such a claim could excuse Milford's viewpoint discrimination....

Dissenting VOICES

Justice Souter, joined by Justice Ginsburg, dissented. They argued that the Good News Club was not engaged in religious speech but religious *worship*. Thus, they maintained that it would indeed violate the establishment clause to have the Club conduct its classes in the school. The justices wrote:

> Good News's classes open and close with prayer. In a sample lesson considered by the District Court, children are instructed that "[t]he Bible tells us how we can have our sins forgiven by receiving the Lord Jesus Christ. It tells us how to live to please Him....

If you have received the Lord Jesus as your Saviour from sin, you belong to God's special group—His family." … The lesson plan instructs the teacher to "lead a child to Christ," and, when reading a Bible verse, to "[e]mphasize that this verse is from the Bible, God's Word" and is "important—and true—because God said it." The lesson further exhorts the teacher to "[b]e sure to give an opportunity for the 'unsaved' children in your class to respond to the Gospel" and cautions against "neglect[ing] this responsibility.'"…

While Good News's program utilizes songs and games, the heart of the meeting is the "challenge" and "invitation," which are repeated at various times throughout the lesson. During the challenge, "saved" children who "already believe in the Lord Jesus as their Savior" are challenged to "stop and ask God for the strength and the 'want' … to obey Him." … They are instructed that "[i]f you know Jesus as your Savior, you need to place God first in your life. And if you don't know Jesus as Savior and if you would like to, then we will—we will pray with you separately, individually.… And the challenge would be, those of you who know Jesus as Savior, you can rely on God's strength to obey Him." …

During the invitation, the teacher "invites" the "unsaved" children "to trust the Lord Jesus to be your Savior from sin," and "receiv[e][him] as your Savior from sin." … The children are then instructed that "[i]f you believe what God's Word says about your sin and how Jesus died and rose again for you, you can have His forever life today. Please bow your heads and close your eyes. If you have never believed on the Lord Jesus as your Savior and would like to do that, please show me by raising your hand. If you raised your hand to show me you want to believe on the Lord Jesus, please meet me so I can show you from God's Word how you can receive His everlasting life." …

It is beyond question that Good News intends to use the public school premises not for the mere discussion of a subject from a particular, Christian point of view, but for an evangelical service of worship calling children to commit themselves in an act of Christian conversion.… The majority avoids this reality only by resorting to the bland and general characterization of Good News's activity as "teaching of morals and character, from a religious standpoint."

WHAT DO YOU Think?

Exercise 2.32. The Good News Club engaged its student members in "education" and "learning" from a religious perspective. But what if it had indeed applied for use of the school's facilities for "religious worship and services"? Many school districts allow their buildings to be used for religious worship on weekends and after hours. Does this violate the establishment clause, as Justices Souter and Ginsburg think? On the other hand, would Milford Central School be violating the free speech (or religious free exercise) rights of the Good News Club by denying it space at school to engage in religious "worship"? These are open questions. Debate them.

Exercise 2.33. Assume that a local atheists' group in your community issues a statement saying, "*Good News Club* is a terrible decision. Our public schools should never allow religious clubs in for any speaking purpose at all because it violates the separation between church and state. Let's make it our policy to keep all religious groups out." A local television news station comes to interview your class about the proposal, and you have to explain whether this proposal is consistent with the First Amendment as explained in the Good News Club case. What do you say? Can a school refuse to let all religious groups in for meetings and forums?

Further Reading

Abraham, Henry J., and Barbara A. Perry. *Freedom and the Court: Civil Rights and Liberties in the United States.* 7th ed. New York: Oxford University Press, 1998.

Bosmajian, Haig. *The Freedom Not to Speak.* New York: New York University Press, 1999.

Fish, Stanley. *There's No Such Thing as Free Speech, and It's a Good Thing, Too.* New York: Oxford University Press, 1994.

Johnson, John W. *The Struggle for Student Rights:* Tinker v. Des Moines *and the 1960s.* Lawrence: University Press of Kansas, 1997.

Kennedy, Randall. *Nigger: The Strange Career of a Troublesome Word.* New York: Pantheon, 2002.

On the Web

Student Press Law Center, www.splc.org.

American Civil Liberties Union, www.aclu.org.

First Amendment Center, www.firstamendmentcenter.org.

FREEDOM OF THE STUDENT PRESS:
All the News the School Sees Fit to Print

"Congress shall make no law … abridging the freedom of speech, or of the press.…" THE FIRST AMENDMENT

"Were it left to me to decide whether we should have a government without newspapers, or newspapers without a government, I should not hesitate a moment to choose the latter." THOMAS JEFFERSON (JANUARY 16, 1787)

From our beginnings, we Americans have prided ourselves on spirited and irreverent journalism. Yet, in the eighteenth century, not long after the Bill of Rights was adopted, newspaper editors were sent to jail under the Alien and Sedition Acts for criticizing President John Adams.

In the twentieth century, the Supreme Court finally declared that the media must be free from government censorship and harsh libel laws. The Court has come to the First Amendment conclusion that a free press is vital to holding government accountable and that debate must be "uninhibited, robust and wide-open" (*New York Times v. Sullivan*, 1964).

However, in public schools, the *student* press does not enjoy the same freedom. Although the 1969 case *Tinker v. Des Moines Independent Community School District* implied that student writers might have a right to publish anything that would not substantially disrupt school, the Court in *Hazelwood School District v. Kuhlmeier* (1988) articulated a much narrower approach to the rights of students working on school-sponsored newspapers, magazines, and yearbooks. The school may act as the "editor" of student speech in these contexts and may therefore censor school-sponsored student expression for any "reasonable" educational purpose.

As you read *Hazelwood* and the cases that follow, consider whether you think student journalists should have the same rights as adult journalists. Has the Supreme Court struck the right balance between the rights of students to express themselves and the interest that schools have in controlling materials that go out under their names?

P**O**INTS TO PONDER

How does the basic First Amendment liberty of freedom of the press apply to school-sponsored student publications?

- Should school officials have the authority to review, regulate, and censor the content of school-sponsored student publications?
- Should school officials have the authority to censor student publications produced outside of school but distributed on school property?
- Should school officials have the authority to punish students for posting critical statements about other students or teachers on the Internet?

Robert Reynolds, principal of Hazelwood East High, stands in front of his school in January 1988 holding a copy of *Spectrum*, the student newspaper that he censored in *Hazelwood*. The Court's decision gave school authorities broad new powers to regulate the content of school-sponsored newspapers and yearbooks for "reasonable" pedagogical purposes.

Freedom of the Student Press in Official School-Sponsored Activities

When a school sponsors an activity in which students express themselves, how much control can it exert over student expression? In the following landmark case, a school principal censored two articles in the student newspaper because he felt that they dealt inappropriately with sensitive themes related to sex and family. The students tried to invoke their *Tinker* rights, asserting that their articles were educationally sound and would not cause "substantial" or "material" disruption of the educational process.

But the Court found that *Tinker* was the wrong standard to use when the school is sponsoring the activity—in this case, the school newspaper. The Court asked only whether the censorship is "reasonably related to legitimate pedagogical concerns." This is a much easier standard for schools to meet.

Read the following decision and think about how *Bethel School District v. Fraser* was a bridge to it. Do you think that the Court went too far in allowing principals and teachers to act as censors, or do you agree that when the school's name is implicated, the school acts as the editor and should get to pick and choose what is published?

HAZELWOOD SCHOOL DISTRICT v. KUHLMEIER

Supreme Court of the United States
Argued October 13, 1987.
Decided January 13, 1988.

Majority OPINION   Justice WHITE delivered the opinion of the Court.

This case concerns the extent to which educators may exercise editorial control over the contents of a high school newspaper produced as part of the school's journalism curriculum.

I

… [T]hree former Hazelwood East students who were staff members of Spectrum, the school newspaper, contend that school officials violated their First Amendment rights by deleting two pages of articles from the May 13, 1983, issue. Spectrum was written and edited by the Journalism II class at Hazelwood East. The newspaper was published every three weeks or so during the 1982–1983 school year. More than 4,500 copies of the newspaper were distributed during that year to students, school personnel, and members of the community.…

The practice at Hazelwood East during the spring 1983 semester was for the journalism teacher to submit page proofs of each Spectrum issue to Principal Reynolds for his review prior to publication. On May 10, Emerson [the journalism instructor] delivered the proofs of the May 13 edition to Reynolds, who objected to two of the articles scheduled to appear in that edition. One of the stories described three Hazelwood East students' experiences with pregnancy; the other discussed the impact of divorce on students at the school.

Reynolds was concerned that, although the pregnancy story used false names "to keep the identity of these girls a secret," the pregnant students still might be identifiable from the text. He also believed that the article's references to sexual activity and birth control were inappropriate for some of the younger students at the school. In addition, Reynolds was concerned that a student identified by name in the divorce story had complained that her father "wasn't spending enough time with my mom, my sister and I" prior to the divorce, "was always out of town on business or out late playing cards with the guys," and "always argued about everything" with her mother. Reynolds believed that the student's parents should have been given an opportunity to respond to these remarks or to consent to their publication. He was unaware that Emerson had deleted the student's name from the final version of the article.

Reynolds believed that there was no time to make the necessary changes in the stories before the scheduled press run and that the newspaper would not appear before the end of the school year if printing were delayed to any significant extent. He concluded that his only options under the circumstances were to publish a four-page newspaper instead of the planned six-page newspaper, eliminating the two pages on which the offending stories appeared, or to publish no newspaper at all. Accordingly, he directed Emerson to withhold from publication the two pages containing the stories on pregnancy and divorce. He informed his superiors of the decision, and they concurred.…

JUSTICES: A CLOSER LOOK

FORBES FIELD 1938 SCHEDULE
SEPT. 11 — NEW YORK GIANTS
OCT. 16 — CLEVELAND RAMS
OCT. 19 — BROOKLYN DODGERS
NOV. 6 — WASHINGTON REDSKINS
NOV. 20 — PHILADELPHIA EAGLES

The author of the *Hazelwood* opinion, **JUSTICE BYRON R. WHITE**, was born in Fort Collins, Colorado, in 1917. At the University of Colorado he earned varsity letters in football, basketball, and baseball and was class valedictorian in 1938. Before earning a Rhodes scholarship to attend Oxford University, "Whizzer" White played football for one year with the Pittsburgh Steelers. At Oxford, White met the playwright George Bernard Shaw and future U.S. president John F. Kennedy. After the outbreak of World War II in Europe, White left Oxford early to study at Yale Law School. He took time off from his studies to play for the Detroit Lions and to serve in the navy, where he again met Kennedy. After the war, White obtained his law degree and served in the Kennedy Justice Department for a year. In 1962 President Kennedy appointed him to the Supreme Court. White sat on the bench until 1993, making him one of the longest-serving justices in history.

HIGHLIGHTS

- In 1938, in his senior year of college, White was selected for Phi Beta Kappa and two days later scored all of Colorado's points in a 17–7 win over the Utah football team, a feat that included a 97-yard touchdown on a punt return. A standout athlete, he made the All-American team that year as a halfback.

II

The question whether the First Amendment requires a school to tolerate particular student speech—the question that we addressed in *Tinker*—is different from the question whether the First Amendment requires a school affirmatively to promote particular student speech. The former question addresses educators' ability to silence a student's personal expression that happens to occur on the school premises. The latter question concerns educators' authority over school-sponsored publications, theatrical productions, and other expressive activities that students, parents, and members of the public might reasonably perceive to bear the imprimatur of the school. These activities may fairly be characterized as part of the school curriculum, whether or not they occur in a traditional classroom setting, so long as they are supervised by faculty members and designed to impart particular knowledge or skills to student participants and audiences.

Educators are entitled to exercise greater control over this second form of student expression to assure that participants learn whatever lessons the activity is designed to teach, that readers or listeners are not exposed to material that may be inappropriate for their level of maturity, and that the views of the individual speaker are not erroneously attributed to the school. Hence, a school may in its capacity as publisher of a school newspaper or producer of a school play "disassociate itself," not only from speech that would "substantially interfere with [its] work … or impinge upon the rights of other students," *Tinker,* but also from speech that is, for example, ungrammatical, poorly written, inadequately researched, biased or prejudiced, vulgar or profane, or unsuitable for immature audiences. A school must be able to set high standards for the student speech that is disseminated under its auspices—standards that may be higher than those demanded by some newspaper publishers or theatrical producers in the "real" world—and may refuse to disseminate student speech that does not meet those standards. In addition, a school must be able to take into account the emotional maturity of the intended audience in determining whether to disseminate student speech on potentially sensitive topics, which might range from the existence of Santa Claus in an elementary school setting to the particulars of teenage sexual activity in a high school setting. A school must also retain the authority to refuse to sponsor student speech that might reasonably be perceived to advocate drug or alcohol use, irresponsible sex, or conduct otherwise inconsistent with "the shared values of a civilized social order," or to associate the school with any position other than neutrality on matters of political controversy....

Accordingly, we conclude that the standard articulated in *Tinker* for determining when a school may punish student expression need not also be the standard for determining when a school may refuse to lend its name and resources to the dissemination of student expression. Instead, we hold that educators do not offend the First Amendment by exercising editorial control over the style and content of student speech in school-sponsored expressive activities so long as their actions are reasonably related to legitimate pedagogical concerns....

We also conclude that Principal Reynolds acted reasonably in requiring the deletion from the May 13 issue of Spectrum of the pregnancy article, the divorce article, and the remaining articles that were to appear on the same pages of the newspaper. The initial paragraph of the pregnancy article declared that "[a]ll names have been changed to keep the identity of these girls a secret." The principal concluded that the students' anonymity was not adequately protected, however, given the other identifying information in the article and the small number of pregnant students at the school.... In addition, he could reasonably have been concerned that the article was not sufficiently sensitive to the privacy interests of the students' boyfriends and parents, who were discussed in the article but who were given no opportunity to consent to its publication or to offer a response. The article did not contain graphic accounts of sexual activity. The girls did comment in the article, however, concerning their sexual histories and their use or nonuse of birth control. It was not unreasonable for the principal to have concluded that such frank talk was inappropriate in a school-sponsored publication distributed to 14-year-old freshmen and presumably taken home to be read by students' even younger brothers and sisters.

The student who was quoted by name in the version of the divorce article seen by Principal Reynolds made comments sharply critical of her father. The principal could reasonably have concluded that an individual publicly identified as an inattentive parent—indeed, as one who chose "playing cards with the guys" over home and family—was entitled to an opportunity to defend himself as a matter of journalistic fairness. These concerns were shared by both of Spectrum's faculty advisers for the 1982–1983 school year, who testified that they would not have allowed the article to be printed without deletion of the student's name....

In sum, we cannot reject as unreasonable Principal Reynolds' conclusion that neither the pregnancy article nor the divorce article was suitable for publication in Spectrum.... Accordingly, no violation of First Amendment rights occurred.

Reversed.

Dissenting VOICES

Justice Brennan, with whom Justice Marshall and Justice Blackmun join, dissented. They took strong exception to the idea that participation on the school newspaper was "just a class exercise in which students learned to prepare papers and hone writing skills." Rather, it was plainly a "forum established to give students an opportunity to express their views while gaining an appreciation of their rights and responsibilities under the First Amendment to the United States Constitution...."

Justice Brennan argued that the school had "violated the First Amendment's prohibitions against censorship of any student expression that neither disrupts classwork nor invades the rights of others, and against any censorship that is not narrowly tailored to serve its purpose."

In *Tinker,* Justice Brennan wrote, "[T]his Court struck the balance. We held that official censorship of student expression—there the suspension of several students until they removed their armbands protesting the Vietnam war—is unconstitutional unless the speech 'materially disrupts classwork or involves substantial disorder or invasion of the rights of others....'"

He then explained what he thought was wrong with the majority's analysis:

> The Court is certainly correct that the First Amendment permits educators "to assure that participants learn whatever lessons the activity is designed to teach...." That is, however, the essence of the *Tinker* test, not an excuse to abandon it. Under *Tinker,* school officials may censor only such student speech as would "materially disrup[t]" a legitimate curricular function. Manifestly, student speech is more likely to disrupt a curricular function when it arises in the context of a curricular activity—one that "is designed to teach" something—than when it arises in the context of a noncurricular activity. Thus, under *Tinker,* the school may constitutionally punish the budding political orator if he disrupts calculus class but not if he holds his tongue for the cafeteria. That is not because some more stringent standard applies in the curricular context. (After all, this Court applied the same standard whether the students in *Tinker* wore their armbands to the "classroom" or the "cafeteria.") It is because student speech in the noncurricular context is less likely to disrupt materially any legitimate pedagogical purpose.
>
> I fully agree with the Court that the First Amendment should afford an educator the prerogative not to sponsor the publication of a newspaper article that is "ungrammatical, poorly written, inadequately researched, biased or prejudiced," or that falls short of the "high standards for ... student speech that is disseminated under [the school's] auspices...." But we need not abandon *Tinker* to reach that conclusion; we need only apply it.

Justice Brennan pointed out that if a school wants to dissociate itself from student speakers, it has easy ways of doing so:

> Dissociative means short of censorship are available to the school. It could, for example, require the student activity to publish a disclaimer, such as the "Statement of Policy" that Spectrum published each school year announcing that "[a]ll ... editorials appearing in this newspaper reflect the opinions of the Spectrum staff, which are not

necessarily shared by the administrators or faculty of Hazelwood East," or it could simply issue its own response clarifying the official position on the matter and explaining why the student position is wrong. Yet, without so much as acknowledging the less oppressive alternatives, the Court approves of brutal censorship....

Justice Brennan closed with unusually strong language assailing the majority's decision:

> The Court opens its analysis in this case by purporting to reaffirm *Tinker's* time-tested proposition that public school students do not "shed their constitutional rights to freedom of speech or expression at the schoolhouse gate." That is an ironic introduction to an opinion that denudes high school students of much of the First Amendment protection that *Tinker* itself prescribed. Instead of "teach[ing] children to respect the diversity of ideas that is fundamental to the American system... [and] ... that our Constitution is a living reality, not parchment preserved under glass," the Court today "teach[es] youth to discount important principles of our government as mere platitudes...." The young men and women of Hazelwood East expected a civics lesson, but not the one the Court teaches them today.
>   I dissent.

WHAT DO YOU Think?

Exercise 3.1. Consider the outcomes in *Tinker, Fraser,* and *Hazelwood.* How have the Supreme Court's holdings changed? Is the Court expanding or constricting the free speech rights of students?

Exercise 3.2. What was wrong with the student-written articles that Hazelwood East censored? Do you think that such articles are appropriate or important for students to write and read? If you were the principal, would you have censored the articles? Why or why not?

Exercise 3.3. Should school only be a place where teachers and administrators transmit knowledge and messages to students or be a place where students also bring knowledge in and circulate their own messages to fellow students and teachers? How does *Tinker v. Des Moines School District* answer this question? How about *Hazelwood*? What image does Justice White have of high school students? What image does Justice Brennan have?

Exercise 3.4. Can school authorities at Hazelwood East censor articles that speak respectfully of the decision of high school students to go through with their pregnancies and have babies, but then publish articles that condemn teen parenthood and urge pregnant students to have abortions? Can school authorities censor one side in a political controversy? Generally, the First Amendment requires government to be *viewpoint neutral,* that is, scrupulously evenhanded among all sides in a political debate. Does *Hazelwood* respect that principle?

FOR THE **CLASS**

Drafting an Editorial Policy for Your School Newspaper. The principal of your school has just appointed your class a school task force to come up with an editorial policy for your school newspaper that respects student speech rights but also prevents embarrassment of the school community and its members. Write a policy explaining what the newspaper will publish and what it will not. Do you leave it wide open? Are there categories of expression that are forbidden, such as obscene, libelous, dangerous, or disruptive speech? What will be the process for defining such categories? Do you attach a disclaimer? Do you forbid only articles that will materially and substantially disrupt school? Do you appoint faculty advisors who have free rein to censor articles for both grammatical and substantive reasons? Does the principal get final say? Bring your policies to class and discuss them as a task force, trying to find consensus for a final recommendation to the principal. Can you agree on the exact wording of a policy?

Squelching Debate: A Different Sort of Blair Witch-Hunt

In October 1996 controversy erupted at Blair High School in Montgomery County, Maryland. Blair has an honors class that permits students to produce television news shows, commentaries, debates, and roundtable talk shows under the supervision of a teacher. They receive academic credit for their work. The TV news shows produced in the high school's studio are broadcast on the Montgomery County Public Schools' local cable channel.

The students had a monthly show called *Shades of Gray.* They planned and produced a debate-format talk show on the subject of whether gays and lesbians should be allowed to marry. Two conservative adult guests appeared to oppose gay marriage, and two liberal adult guests came to speak in favor of it. The show was taped; the teacher who led the class, Christopher Lloyd, praised the students' work, and the show was set to air.

At that point, officials in the school system who run the cable channel decided to preview the tape, which was not their ordinary practice. They notified Mr. Lloyd and the students that their show would not be broadcast because it was "inappropriate" for the station. A series of meetings and phone calls ensued in which the students tried to get the school authorities to explain what was wrong with their debate on gay marriage. On October 23, 1996, Barbara Wood, the program director for the cable channel, sent an e-mail explaining the decision:

> We felt that the gentleman who was a guest on the show [Dr. Frank Kameny] brought
> up the issue of religion and God in a very heated and controversial manner.... We both
> felt it would be inappropriate to air the program for that reason alone.

School authorities apparently reacted negatively when the student host asked a question about the basis of the guests' views on gay marriage. One of the conservative guests, Paula Govers, press secretary for Concerned Women for America, introduced religion into the discussion:

GOVERS: The Concerned Women for America believes that marriage is an institution sanctioned by God, licensed by the state, specifically between one man and one woman, and specifically for the purpose of procreation and should be a covenant between two people that should be a lifetime commitment.

This comment prompted the liberal guests, Dr. Frank Kameny of the Washington, D.C., Gay and Lesbian Activists Alliance and Judith Schaeffer of People for the American Way, to respond:

KAMENY: Paula, you said that the First Amendment guarantees us freedom of religion, and we all have our own views of God. My God gave us homosexuality as a blessing given to us by our creator God to be enjoyed to its fullest—exultantly, exuberantly, joyously. My God sanctifies same-sex marriage even if your God does not, and we are both American citizens and both Gods deserve equal recognition from our—not your—our government.

SCHAEFFER: That's exactly what the First Amendment requires. The government cannot legislate religious beliefs.

KAMENY: If you don't want to enter into a same-sex marriage, don't. But don't tell us just because your God doesn't sanctify it, my God is to be ignored.

GOVERS: Dr. Kameny, you said that your God does sanctify these unions. So your religious beliefs would say it's a good thing and our religious beliefs would say it's not. Why does your view get to trump ours?

KAMENY: It does not. If you believe that, you have an absolute right not to enter into a same-sex marriage.

KRIS ARDIZONNE [the other conservative guest and legal director of the Eagle Forum]: But my taxpayer dollars go to pay for the institution of marriage. And we don't believe in it[same-sex marriage].

KAMENY: And so do the tax dollars of gay people go to pay for marriage as well....

Although the students' teacher and the principal of Blair High School saw this spirited exchange of views as enlightening, the Montgomery County Public Schools officials thought it was inappropriate for the mostly adult audience of the cable channel, an argument the students found ironic.

The Blair students went to the Montgomery County Board of Education to appeal the school superintendent's decision to censor the broadcast of the show. They argued that the decision to censor violated school policy and the First Amendment by discriminating against a speaker because of his religious views. The students quoted the Supreme Court's 1995 decision in *Rosenberger v. University of Virginia,* which struck down the University of Virginia's practice of subsidizing student journals that had secular points of view but declining to subsidize those that had a religious point of view. The Court there stated, "The government must abstain from regulating speech when the specific motivating ideology, or the opinion or perspective of the speaker, is the rationale for the restriction." The students argued that the school system was objecting to "the gentleman who was a guest on the show ... [who] ... brought up the issue of religion and God in a very heated and controversial manner."

When the school system responded that *Hazelwood* gave them the right to edit and censor student speech, the students had an answer. Because the educators in this case—their media teacher and the Blair principal—both favored broadcast of the show, the school system could not claim under *Hazelwood* that their actions were "reasonably related to legitimate pedagogical concerns." The teachers in this case were opposed to censorship.

Meanwhile, the county superintendent argued that the school system's cable channel was government property within the absolute control of school system authorities. He maintained, in any event, that this was reasonable censorship within the meaning of *Hazelwood*, because the topic of gay marriage was sensitive and unsuitable for younger students.

The students never had to go to court, because the school board voted 4–3 to reverse the superintendent and to air the show. The principal, Philip Gainous, subsequently won an award from the Freedom Forum in Virginia for standing up for the First Amendment rights of his students, and many of the students have since gone on to study media and broadcasting in college. Their case has given much force to arguments of students in other schools that they should have the same rights on video and television productions that they have in newspapers and yearbooks. Students in Montgomery County subsequently lobbied their school board to pass a set of guidelines on student speech that incorporates basic First Amendment ideas.

FOR THE CLASS

Too Hot to Handle? Say that you are the student editor of your school-sponsored newspaper. One student writes an article in favor of allowing gays and lesbians to marry. In it she says that marriage offers hundreds of legal, social, and economic benefits that should not be denied to millions of citizens based on whom they love. As the daughter of gay parents, she says that there are many gay people and their families being discriminated against. On the other side of the issue, a fundamentalist Christian student argues that the Bible is clear that marriage must be between a man and a woman. He maintains that allowing homosexuals to marry will destroy the institution. You want to run the two pieces side-by-side, but the principal says he does not want to, arguing that it will upset students on both sides. How would you convince him that it is acceptable? If he does not consent to publish, is he within his rights under *Hazelwood*?

Cyber Censors: Rising Conflicts over Internet Homepages

The *Hazelwood* decision has given school systems greater latitude to censor school newspapers, and many schools have used it to censor student writings deemed offensive, subversive, mischievous, insubordinate, or inappropriate. Still, other schools have stood by policies that codify the old *Tinker* standard, which is much friendlier to student expression.

Censorship of school newspapers, combined with the rise of the Internet and desktop publishing, has led to the return of so-called underground newspapers—unofficial student-written, student-published, and privately circulated newspapers that were common in the 1960s. However, most students today do not bother to publish full-blown newspapers but simply create blogs and engage in the massive and generationally irresistible new speech forums such as Facebook and YouTube. Some simply publish diatribes, screeds, David Letterman–style top ten lists, or wicked satire on their own Internet homepages.

In the 1970s, court decisions about underground newspapers stayed true to the *Tinker* standard: They found that school authorities cannot censor privately distributed student newspapers and magazines unless the educational process is in danger of being disrupted. But today, because of the pervasiveness of the Internet and the immediacy of its power to communicate ideas, many schools are reacting strongly against student speech on the Internet. In a typical case, a student posts stinging criticism of his principal or teachers on an Internet homepage and then school authorities retaliate by suspending him or punishing him academically.

Although no such case has made it to the Supreme Court, several lower courts have ruled on this kind of situation. In *Brandon Beussink v. Woodland R-IV School District* (1998), the United States District Court for the Eastern District of Missouri reversed Woodland High School's disciplinary action against Brandon Beussink, who was at the time a high school junior. Beussink had posted material "highly critical" of the school administration and "used vulgar language to convey his opinion regarding the teachers, the principal, and the school's own homepage."

Although Beussink designed his homepage at home and did not intend for it to be accessed at school, he did show it to a friend, Amanda Brown. Later, after the two friends had a falling out, Brown decided to get back at Beussink by showing his homepage to the school's computer teacher, who promptly reported it to the school principal, Yancy Poorman. Mr. Poorman said that he became "upset" by its contents and immediately suspended Beussink from school for five days. Then, as his anger apparently swelled, he "reconsidered" and suspended Beussink for ten days. Because of the school's absenteeism policy, this suspension would have resulted in Beussink's flunking all of his junior year classes.

Beussink went to court and won an injunction against his discipline on First Amendment grounds. The court found that Beussink's personal Web page caused no disruption in his classes—unlike the suspension itself—and that any fear of disruption was unreasonable. According to district judge Sippel, "Disliking or being upset by the content of a student's speech is not an acceptable justification for limiting student speech under *Tinker*."

In the following case from federal district court in western Pennsylvania, *Killion v. Franklin Regional School District,* another court considered the suspension of a student who had published on the Internet a top ten list of reasons that the school's athletic director was always in a grouchy mood.

10. The School Store doesn't sell [T]winkies.
9. He is constantly tripping over his own chins.
8. The girls at the 900 #'s keep hanging up on him.
7. For him, becoming Franklin's "Athletic Director" was considered "moving up in the world."
6. He has to use a pencil to type and make phone calls because his fingers are unable to hit only one key at a time.

5. As stated in previous list, he's just not getting any.

4. He is no longer allowed in any "All You Can Eat" restaurants.

3. He has constant flashbacks of when he was in high school and the athletes used to pick on him, instead of him picking on the athletes.

2. Because of his extensive gut factor, the "man" hasn't seen his own penis in over a decade.

1. Even it is wasn't for his gut, it would still take a magnifying glass and extensive searching to find it.

The school justified its discipline of this speech on the Web by arguing that it was disruptive, within the meaning of *Tinker*, and lewd and vulgar, within the meaning of *Fraser*. What does the court say? What do you think?

KILLION v. FRANKLIN REGIONAL SCHOOL DISTRICT

United States District Court, Western District of Pennsylvania
March 22, 2001.

OPINION   ZIEGLER, District Judge.

Majority

… Plaintiff, Zachariah Paul ("Paul"), was a student at Franklin Regional High School during the 1998–1999 school year. During March of 1999, Paul, apparently angered by a denial of a student parking permit and the imposition of various rules and regulations for members of the track team (Paul was a member), compiled a "Top Ten" list about the athletic director, Robert Bozzuto. The Bozzuto list contained … statements regarding Bozzuto's appearance, including the size of his genitals. After consulting with friends, Paul composed and assembled the list while at home after school hours. Thereafter, in late March or early April, Paul e-mailed the list to friends from his home computer.… Paul did not print or copy the list to bring it on school premises because, after copying and distributing similar lists in the past, he had been warned that he would be punished if he brought another list to school.

> **Plaintiff**
> Party that brings an original civil suit in a state or federal court.

Several weeks later, several individuals found copies of the Bozzuto Top Ten list in the Franklin Regional High School teachers' lounge and the Franklin Regional Middle School. An undisclosed student had reformatted Paul's original e-mail and distributed the document on school grounds.

On or about May 3, 1999, Paul was called to a meeting with Richard Plutto (principal), Thomas Graham (assistant principal), and Robert Bozzuto (athletic director). Upon questioning, Paul admitted that he had created the contents of the Top Ten list, and that he had e-mailed it to the home computers of several friends from his home computer; however, Paul steadfastly denied bringing the list on school grounds. Plutto or Graham instructed Paul to bring a copy of the original e-mail message the next day.…

The next day, shortly before Paul was scheduled to leave for a track meet, Plutto called Paul to his office. Paul, apparently anticipating that he might be disciplined, called his mother, who arrived shortly thereafter. Paul and Mrs. Killion went to the administrative of-fices where they met with Graham and Bozzuto. Graham and Bozzuto showed Mrs. Killion the Top Ten list, asked if she had seen it, and informed her that Paul was being suspended for ten days because the list contained offensive remarks about a school official, was found on school grounds, and that Paul admitted creating the list. Graham further informed Mrs. Killion that Paul could not participate in any school-related activities, including track and field events during the ten-day suspension.

… [P]laintiffs commenced an action in the Westmoreland County Court of Common Pleas, Pennsylvania, against the School District seeking immediate reinstatement. The parties subsequently entered a settlement agreement wherein plaintiffs agreed to withdraw the complaint in exchange for the School District's agreement to provide Paul with the due process outlined in the Pennsylvania School Code.…

On May 12, plaintiffs Plutto and Graham met for the suspension hearing, which resulted in a ten day suspension. The same day, plaintiffs commenced a civil action in this court seeking a preliminary injunction for First … Amendment violation, and requesting that Paul be allowed to return to school immediately.…

Plaintiffs seek summary judgment contending that defendants violated Paul's First Amendment right of free expression by suspending Paul for speech that was made off school grounds and in the privacy of his home.…

> **Settlement Agreement**
> Resolution of a legal dispute outside of court.
>
> **Civil Action**
> A lawsuit undertaken to protect an individual's private legal rights. Also known as a civil suit.
>
> **Preliminary Injunction**
> A temporary court order for a party to a case to do something or to stop doing something. The injunction lasts until the case has been fully decided on its merits.
>
> **Summary Judgment**
> Resolution of a case by a judge without trial where all of the significant facts of the case are uncontested and one party is entitled to win as a matter of law.

B. First Amendment

1. Freedom of Speech

… Although there is limited case law on the issue, courts considering speech that occurs off school grounds have concluded (relying on Supreme Court decisions) that school officials' authority over off-campus expression is much more limited than expression on school grounds.…

… [W]e find that Paul's suspension violates the First Amendment because defendants failed to satisfy *Tinker's* substantial disruption test. First, defendants failed to adduce any evidence of actual disruption.… There is no evidence that teachers were incapable of teaching or controlling their classes because of the Bozzuto Top Ten list. Indeed, the list was on school grounds for several days before the administration became aware of its existence, and at least one week passed before defendants took any action.…

Further, we note that the speech at issue was not threatening, and, although upsetting to Bozzuto, did not cause any faculty member to take a leave of absence.… Although the intended audience was undoubtedly connected to Franklin Regional High School, the absence of threats or actual disruption leads us to conclude that Paul's suspension was improper.…

Admittedly, Bozzuto, Graham, Plutto and others found the list to be rude, abusive and demeaning.... However, "[d]isliking or being upset by the content of a student's speech is not an acceptable justification for limiting student speech...." Indeed, "the mere desire to avoid 'discomfort' or 'unpleasantness' is not enough to justify restricting student speech.... However, if a school can point to a well-founded expectation of disruption—especially one based on past incidents arising out of similar speech—the restriction may pass constitutional muster." ...

... [D]efendants apparently argue that the Bozzuto list could "impair the administration's ability to appropriately discipline the students." ... We cannot accept, without more, that the childish and boorish antics of a minor could impair the administrators' abilities to discipline students and maintain control....

... Defendants also argue that the suspension was appropriate because Paul's speech was lewd and obscene and therefore punishable.... Plaintiffs rejoin that, "[i]f the Bozzuto list could in fact be considered contraband ... the defendants['] recourse would be to punish those students who actually brought the offending material to school. But to punish the author for work created outside of school is certainly beyond the First Amendment pale."...

Here, defendants argue that Paul's Top Ten list contained several lewd and vulgar statements. Although we agree that several passages from the list are lewd, abusive, and derogatory, we cannot ignore the fact that the relevant speech occurred within the confines of Paul's home, far removed from any school premises or facilities. Further, Paul was not engaged in any school activity or associated in any way with his role as a student when he compiled the Bozzuto Top Ten list.

... Given the out of school creation of the list, absent evidence that Paul was responsible for bringing the list on school grounds, and absent disruption ... we hold ... that defendants could not, without violating the First Amendment, suspend Paul for the mere creation of the Bozzuto Top Ten list.... Plaintiffs' motion for summary judgment must be granted.

WHAT DO YOU Think?

Exercise 3.5. If schools cannot discipline students for posting disparaging comments about teachers on the Internet, can they discipline teachers for posting disparaging comments about students on the Internet? In class make arguments for both sides, assuming that Coach Bozzuto created a similar satirical top ten list about why Paul is always in a bad mood. How can schools create more positive dynamics between students and teachers? Can the Internet become a positive force for communication among students, teachers, and administrators in high schools? Is it possible to foster a culture of "no personal disses" online? How might we do that?

Further Reading

Bollinger, Lee C., and Geoffrey R. Stone, eds. *Eternally Vigilant: Free Speech in the Modern Era.* Chicago: University of Chicago Press, 2002.

Hentoff, Nat. *Free Speech for Me—But Not for Thee: How the American Left and Right Relentlessly Censor Each Other.* New York: HarperCollins, 1992.

On the **Web**

Electronic Frontier Foundation, www.eff.org.
The Freedom Forum and First Amendment Schools Project, www.freedomforum.org.
Society of Professional Journalists, www.spj.org.
Student Press Law Center, www.splc.org.

THE WALL OF SEPARATION BETWEEN CHURCH AND SCHOOL

"Congress shall make no law respecting an establishment of religion, or prohibiting the free exercise thereof...." THE FIRST AMENDMENT

"Believing with you that religion is a matter which lies solely between man & his God, that he owes account to none other for his faith or his worship, that the legitimate powers of government reach actions only, and not opinions, I contemplate with sovereign reverence that act of the whole American people which declared that *their* legislature should make no law respecting an establishment of religion, or prohibiting the free exercise thereof, thus building a wall of separation between church and state." THOMAS JEFFERSON (JANUARY 1, 1802, LETTER TO THE DANBURY BAPTISTS)

The United States of America was founded by people fleeing religious persecution and the merger of state and church in Europe. They wanted to escape the theological warfare, the holy crusades, the inquisitions, and the witchcraft trials that marked centuries of European history.

To ensure that our government would neither impose a religion nor oppress religious minorities, the Framers placed in the First Amendment two related prohibitions: (1) Congress may not "establish" a religion and (2) Congress may not prohibit the "free exercise" of religion. Government thus may neither sponsor nor endorse a religion of its own nor deliberately interfere with citizens' freedom to practice their own faith.

Like Thomas Jefferson, who insisted that there be no theology school at his beloved University of Virginia, most of our Framers were Enlightenment thinkers who wanted to liberate public institutions from religious conflict. They thought that the establishment clause and the free exercise clause reinforced one another and stood best when they stood together to form a "wall of separation" between church and state.

But sometimes the establishment clause and the free exercise clause come into conflict, or at least many people think they do. If we do everything we can to expel religion from the public square, many Americans believe, we will be violating the free exercise of religiously oriented citizens and impoverishing our public life. Others feel equally strongly that if we invite religion into public spaces and activities, we will promote sectarian conflict, hard feelings, and manipulation of religious sentiment by government leaders.

Thus, there has always been religious controversy swirling around public schools, and there is no end in sight. This is because many parents are afraid that powerful religious groups in their community will use the schools as an instrument for fostering specific religious beliefs and marginalizing students who belong to other faiths. Meantime, other parents want their children to remain religiously faithful and fear that the public schools, by teaching secular subjects from a strictly secular perspective, may undermine the hold of religion. Of course, parents who want to place religious faith at the center of their children's education always have the option of sending them to private parochial schools. The Supreme Court recognized this option as a constitutional right in *Pierce v. Society of Sisters* (1925), which struck down an Oregon law that tried to compel all students to go to public school. Justice McReynolds wrote that children are not "the mere creature of the state" and parents retain the liberty to define their upbringing.

The original constitutional problem in public schools was raised by the issue of organized school prayer, where teachers and administrators lead or encourage prayer to God among students. It has been clear since 1962 that this practice violates the establishment clause. On the other hand, public school students are always free to say prayers on their own at school so long as they are not disruptive of the educational process. As the Marshall-Brennan fellows like to say, "As long as there are pop math quizzes, there *will* be prayer in the public schools." This freedom to pray on one's own in a nondisruptive way is guaranteed by freedom of speech and religion.

A trickier problem is how to reconcile the free speech rights of students who want to meet and pray at school with the establishment clause principle that government may not endorse religion. Yet another controversy focuses on the development by states and cities of school voucher plans that make public dollars available to families to send their children to private schools, including religious schools.

In this chapter we will learn where the Supreme Court has drawn different lines in this rocky field and ask how teachers and students can reconcile competing constitutional values in the classroom.

P⬤INTS TO PONDER

How do the First Amendment's religion clauses affect students and teachers in public schools?

- Should school officials be able to establish morning prayer for all students?
- Should nondenominational prayers be allowed during official school functions?
- Should public high school students be allowed to elect fellow students to make "solemnizing" invocations at football games?
- Should public school officials be allowed to post the Ten Commandments in classrooms?
- Should government be allowed to ask students to pledge allegiance to the American flag "under God"?
- Should state and local governments be allowed to spend public dollars on school vouchers that families can use for tuition at private religious schools?
- Can a state design a college scholarship program for gifted students to go to college to study any subject except for devotional theology?
- Do student religious clubs and organizations have a right to meet in public schools?
- Do people with religious points of view have equal speech rights in public schools?
- Should religious beliefs ever excuse students from completing their state-required schooling?

Freedom from Establishment of Religion at School

The Supreme Court has long struggled to find a clean test for deciding whether a government practice survives a challenge under the establishment clause. The traditional test is found in *Lemon v. Kurtzman* (1971), which provided that a challenged government practice must (1) have a primarily secular (not religious) purpose; (2) have a primarily secular effect; and (3) avoid "excessive entanglement" with religion. If a practice failed to meet any one of these requirements, it violated the establishment clause.

Most justices have expressed dissatisfaction with the *Lemon* test, but it is still in use; Justice Scalia even likened it to a Frankenstein monster that occasionally sits up in the coffin and scares the justices. But the Court has not been able to develop a consensus alternative.

Justice O'Connor proposed her "endorsement" test, which suggests that any governmental endorsement of a specific religion or of religion in general violates the establishment clause, in essence by violating the "effects" prong of the Lemon test.

Justice Kennedy's "coercion" test would invalidate on establishment clause grounds only those practices that actually coerce people into participating in religious exercises.

Meantime, the most conservative justices have been promoting the acceptability of what they call "ceremonial deism," historically rooted public practices that invoke theistic belief, such as "under God" in the Pledge of Allegiance or "In God We Trust" on the dollar bill, but do not directly try to establish a church. As you go through the cases in this chapter, think about which of these standards works best to effectuate underlying establishment clause values; or perhaps you could develop a new standard.

Beginning with *Engel v. Vitale* in 1962, the Supreme Court has read the establishment clause to prevent governmental promotion of religion or departure from strict neutrality in matters of religion at school. In *Engel* the Court found it unconstitutional for school authorities to lead students in organized school prayer. Many politicians vehemently disagree

In *Santa Fe v. Doe*, the Court struck down school-organized and student-led prayer exercises at public high school football games. Private schools are not affected by the decision. Here, private school football players pray before a game in Rolling Fork, Mississippi, in August 2000.

with this holding and blame it for the nation's perceived moral demise. Some even link it to disasters such as the 1999 Columbine High School killings in Littleton, Colorado. Others think the ban on organized school prayer is critical to maintaining Thomas Jefferson's "wall of separation" between church and state. Do you agree with the Court's decision that school-led prayers violate the establishment clause?

ENGEL v. VITALE

Supreme Court of the United States
Argued April 3, 1962.
Decided June 25, 1962.

Majority OPINION   Justice BLACK delivered the opinion of the Court.

The respondent Board of Education of Union Free School District No. 9, New Hyde Park, New York, acting in its official capacity under state law, directed the School District's principal to cause the following prayer to be said aloud by each class in the presence of a teacher at the beginning of each school day:

> **Respondent**
> Party that answers to a petition for review in court. *See also* **Appellee**, under Chapter 5, *Cass.*

> Almighty God, we acknowledge our dependence upon Thee, and we beg Thy blessings upon us, our parents, our teachers and our Country.

JUSTICES: A CLOSER LOOK

JUSTICE HUGO L. BLACK (1886–1971) wrote the majority opinion for this decision. He was the last of eight children born to a storekeeper and farmer in Clay County, Alabama. Skipping college, he went to the University of Alabama Law School, where he graduated with honors. After a distinguished career as a progressive reformer in public life, including stints as a judge, prosecutor, and U.S. senator, Black was appointed to the Supreme Court by President Franklin Delano Roosevelt in 1937. He served thirty-one years.

HIGHLIGHTS

- Justice Black attended medical school for one year at age seventeen.
- As a county prosecuting attorney in Alabama, he ran a successful grand jury investigation of the Bessamer, Alabama, police department, which was known for its barbaric torture chamber. Despite his brief membership in the Ku Klux Klan, Black demonstrated a passionate concern for human rights that later became a hallmark of his jurisprudence.
- Justice Black was an absolutist about the freedoms of speech and religion. He was fond of saying that "no law means *no law* abridging these rights." He was buried with a ten-cent copy of the Constitution in his pocket.

... [T]he parents of ten pupils brought this action in a New York State Court insisting that use of this official prayer in the public schools was contrary to the beliefs, religions, or religious practices of both themselves and their children. Among other things, these parents challenged the constitutionality of the School District's regulation ordering the recitation of this particular prayer on the ground that these actions of official governmental agencies violate that part of the First Amendment of the Federal Constitution which commands that "Congress shall make no law respecting an establishment of religion." ... The New York Court of Appeals ... sustained an order of the lower state courts which had upheld the power of New York to use the Regents' prayer as a part of the daily procedures of its public schools so long as the schools did not compel any pupil to join in the prayer over his or his parents' objection. We think that by using its public school system to encourage recitation of the Regents' prayer, the State of New York has adopted a practice wholly inconsistent with the Establishment Clause. There can, of course, be no doubt that New York's program of daily classroom invocation of God's blessings as prescribed in the Regents' prayer is a religious activity. It is a solemn avowal of divine faith and supplication for the blessings of the Almighty....

The petitioners contend among other things that the state laws requiring or permitting use of the Regents' prayer must be struck down as a violation of the Establishment Clause because that prayer was composed by governmental officials as a part of a governmental program to further religious beliefs. For this reason, petitioners argue, the State's use of the Regents' prayer in its public school system breaches the constitutional wall of separation between Church and State. We agree with that contention since we think that the constitutional prohibition against laws respecting an establishment of religion must at least mean that in this country it is no part of the business of government to compose official prayers for any group of the American people to recite as a part of a religious program carried on by government....

There can be no doubt that New York's state prayer program officially establishes the religious beliefs embodied in the Regents' prayer. The respondents' argument to the contrary, which is largely based upon the contention that the Regents' prayer is "non-denominational" and the fact that the program, as modified and approved by state courts, does not require all pupils to recite the prayer but permits those who wish to do so to remain silent or be excused from the room, ignores the essential nature of the program's constitutional defects. Neither the fact that the prayer may be denominationally neutral nor the fact that its observance on the part of the students is voluntary can serve to free it from the limitations of the Establishment Clause as it might from the Free Exercise Clause....

Free Exercise Clause
The religion clause in the First Amendment guaranteeing people the right to worship and believe as they please (or not at all) against deliberate interference by government.

Although these two clauses may in certain instances overlap, they forbid two quite different kinds of governmental encroachment upon religious freedom. The Establishment Clause does not depend upon any showing of direct governmental compulsion and is violated by the enactment of laws which establish an official religion whether those laws operate directly to coerce nonobserving individuals or not. When the power, prestige and financial support of government is placed behind a particular religious belief, the indirect coercive pressure upon religious minorities to conform to the prevailing officially approved religion is plain. But the purposes underlying the Establishment Clause go much further than that. Its first and most immediate purpose rested on the belief that a union of government and religion tends to destroy government and to degrade religion.... The Establishment Clause thus stands as an expression of principle on the part of the Founders of our Constitution that religion is too personal, too sacred, too holy, to permit its "unhallowed perversion" by a civil magistrate. Another purpose of the Establishment Clause rested upon an awareness of the historical fact that governmentally established religions and religious persecutions go hand in hand. The Founders knew that only a few years after the Book of Common Prayer became the only accepted form of religious services in the established Church of England, an Act of Uniformity was passed to compel all Englishmen to attend those services and to make it a criminal offense to conduct or attend religious gatherings of any other kind....

It has been argued that to apply the Constitution in such a way as to prohibit state laws respecting an establishment of religious services in public schools is to indicate a hostility toward religion or toward prayer. Nothing, of course, could be more wrong. It is neither sacrilegious nor antireligious to say that each separate government in this country should stay out of the business of writing or sanctioning official prayers and leave that purely religious function to the people themselves and to those the people choose to look to for religious guidance.

The judgment of the Court of Appeals of New York is reversed and the cause remanded for further proceedings not inconsistent with this opinion.

Dissenting VOICES

Justice Stewart, dissenting, wrote,

> [T]his decision is wrong.... With all respect, I think the Court has misapplied a great constitutional principle. I cannot see how an 'official religion' is established by letting those who want to say a prayer say it. On the contrary, I think that to

JUSTICES: A CLOSER LOOK

JUSTICE POTTER STEWART (1915–1985) was born in Jackson, Michigan, on January 23, 1915. He went to prep school at Hotchkiss. Upon graduating from Yale University, he went to Cambridge, England, on a Henry Fellowship and one year later entered Yale Law School. Stewart served on active duty in the navy, practiced privately, and was a judge on the United States Court of Appeals for the Sixth Circuit before President Dwight Eisenhower appointed him to the Supreme Court in 1958. He served until 1981.

HIGHLIGHTS

- During World War II, Stewart served as a deck officer on oil tankers.
- On the Court, Justice Stewart was well known for his pithy and witty statements in opinions. About obscenity, he said: "I shall not today further attempt to define the kinds of material I understand to be embraced within that shorthand description; and perhaps I could never succeed in intelligibly doing so. But I know it when I see it." In a capital punishment case, he wrote that arbitrary imposition of the death penalty is "cruel and unusual in the way that being struck by lightning is cruel and unusual."

deny the wish of these school children to join in reciting this prayer is to deny them the opportunity of sharing in the spiritual heritage of our Nation....

WHAT DO YOU Think?

Exercise 4.1. Imagine that your class had to recite these words in unison every morning: "Almighty God, we acknowledge our dependence upon Thee, and we beg Thy blessings upon us, our parents, our teachers and our Country." How would you feel about it? Would it make anyone uncomfortable? Are there atheist students who might be offended by having to recite the prayer? Are there religious students who would have cause to object?

Exercise 4.2. The Supreme Court ruled in *Engel v. Vitale* that schools could not organize moments of prayer. In *Wallace v. Jaffree* (1985), the Court upheld the practice of calling for "moments of silence" for meditation and reflection (which can include voluntary prayer). Because the students could think, meditate, pray, or perhaps review their multiplication tables or perform French conjugations during this moment, the Court found that it did not violate the establishment clause. (Silence may be rare in a public school, but it is not unconstitutional.)

In Virginia, today, all students now begin the day with "the daily observance of one minute of silence in each classroom." State law provides that "each pupil may, in the exercise of his or her individual choice, meditate, pray or engage in any other silent activity which does not interfere with, distract or impede other pupils in the like exercise of individual choice."

Is it constitutional to mention religion in this way? Some students objected that Virginia's policy is a dressed-up form of school-endorsed prayer. Others clearly liked the chance to begin the day by focusing their minds and did not view the moment of silence as a religious imposition. What do you think of Virginia's policy? The Fourth Circuit Court of Appeals upheld the law against a challenge by some students and the American Civil Liberties Union in *Brown v. Gilmore* (2001).

Exercise 4.3. In September 2006 Kearny High School junior Matthew LaClair, age seventeen, secretly made two recordings of his eleventh-grade history class in Kearny, New Jersey. He was concerned about what he saw as his teacher's attempts to promote religion and proselytize in class. After Matthew's parents brought a lawsuit alleging that their son's First Amendment rights were being violated, the school reprimanded the teacher, David Paszkiewicz, and transferred Matthew to a different class. The school later agreed to educate teachers about the establishment clause and the proper teaching of evolution. Here is part of the classroom discussion that LaClair recorded and then used to challenge his teacher's methods:

DAVID PASZKIEWICZ: I'm going to keep this short—every day we'll devote five minutes or so to you guys trying to make an atheist out of me.

FEMALE STUDENT: Let's say I show up at the Gates of Heaven or the Gates of Hell and I see Jesus, and then I realize, Okay, this is real now, I believe, I won't denounce Christ. Is that too late?

PASZKIEWICZ: It's like a soccer game. Once you get that red card, you're out of the game. You get a warning. How many yellow cards do you get? Two. After the second one, you're done. This life is the playing field.

FEMALE STUDENT: For a Muslim who's never seen the Bible, how is He trying to get him to follow Him if he's never heard of it?

PASZKIEWICZ: He's in the Koran, you know—they've heard of Him. Man has a conscience. Everybody on this planet has this concept of right or wrong. My dog doesn't bite me because he's suffering from PMS—it's instinct. If he feels threatened, he bites me. I'm using that figuratively, because my dog wouldn't bite anybody. But you guys know what I'm saying about dogs, right? There is no such thing as a bad dog—they operate on instinct. Humans are different. We're moral beings. You take any culture on this planet; it has a basic concept of right and wrong. What they worship may be different, but there's something inside of them that tells them there's something greater than them. Find me a culture that doesn't have a god, I'll give you an A+ for the class. Don't use the Soviet Union, because their god lives with Satan.

FEMALE STUDENT: Isn't there, like, a culture that doesn't believe in anything? Atheists?

PASZKIEWICZ: Does an atheist have a concept of justice? Where does that come from?

FEMALE STUDENT: I don't know—their human, um, brain?

PASZKIEWICZ: The highest value in public education is tolerance, but tolerance of what? There are a lot of things I don't want my kids tolerating. Ethnic diversity? Yes. Deviant sexual behavior? No. I still believe in the concept of sin. All that stuff is considered old-fashioned nowadays. Let's suppose you have a religious family. You surrender your kid to the state from preschool on through the twelfth grade. Mom and Dad are trying to tell you that the Bible is God's word, and their lives are deeply rooted in faith, yet the "smart" people—I say that in quotations, because they're not really all that smart—the teachers you're exposed to, never once will you see them crack open a Bible, never once will you hear them quote it, and never once will you hear a prayer from their lips. Over the course of twelve years, what's the transfer? Smart people don't have faith, don't believe.

MALE STUDENT: But then there's people like me—my mom and my dad never go to church.

PASZKIEWICZ: Well, that's their prerogative, but should they impose that on the rest of the world?

MALE STUDENT: What would you do if one of your kids after a while said, "Thanks for teaching me all this, but I don't agree, I don't have faith"?

PASZKIEWICZ: Until you're eighteen, you have to do it. If my kid is age twelve and he's telling me, "Dad, I appreciate your time and effort, but I've decided in my twelve years of wisdom I'm going to stop going to church"—after I break his backside, we're going to have a little attitude adjustment. He's gonna get in the car with the rest of the family and go to church.

MALE STUDENT: Isn't the whole point of public school so that you can separate personal beliefs from nonreligious teachings?

PASZKIEWICZ: Mm, no. The purpose of public school is to provide free education for people that can't afford education. What it's become is social engineering.

MALE STUDENT: What if some students don't believe in the Bible?

PASZKIEWICZ: That's their prerogative. What if the student doesn't believe in evolution?

MALE STUDENT: Well, evolution is scientific.

PASZKIEWICZ: Is it?

MALE STUDENT: Yes. I could get you a whole bunch of information on it.

PASZKIEWICZ: Yeah, I'm thirty-eight years old; I've seen the information on it. Take the big bang theory. The theory is that there was nothing out there, there was no matter. But yet nothing exploded and created something. Let me give you a clue, guys: If there's nothing, it can't explode! Okay? And that is supposed to have created order, all of the order you see in the universe. How many of you have ever witnessed an explosion? Did you ever see a firecracker blow up? Did you ever see a fireworks show? Did you ever see a gun fire? Did you see the twin towers collapse on TV? Did any of these ever create order? You know what, no explosion has ever created order in all of recorded human history. That's observation. Nobody ever recorded an explosion creating order, yet we make this assumption about an event that occurred a billion years ago? That's not scientific. There's nothing scientific about it. It sounds cool on paper, but it defies human reason.

MALE STUDENT: If I have faith, if I truly, truly believe that a man, let's say, 2,766 years old, with a blue face and a pink shirt—and he always wears the same thing—if I have true faith that that man created the universe, does that mean that it really happened?

PASZKIEWICZ: No. It's a good argument, though. You guys were following what he's saying, right? Some of you probably disagree with what I've put on the board. That's okay—you're not going to be tested on it, you understand. You're going to be tested on populism.

Do you think that Paszkiewicz abused his official position by trying to endorse a religious program in class? Alternatively, does it violate his free speech rights as a citizen to reprimand him for expressing his opinion in class if he is clear that students won't be "tested" on it? Must teachers leave their religious beliefs at home and stick to the formal curriculum? How well did Paszkiewicz answer the students' questions? Do you think he would have ended up converting students to his views over time had his classroom discussion not been recorded?

Graduating from Invocation and Benediction

After *Engel v. Vitale,* many school systems tried to get around the Court's decision by having teachers and students read excerpts from the Bible rather than from a prayer composed by the school system. In Pennsylvania, state law provided that "at least ten verses from the Holy Bible shall be read, without comment, at the opening of each public school on each school day." The Schempp family, who were Unitarians, challenged the practice of having students read passages from the New Testament and then together recite the Lord's Prayer.

In *Abington School District v. Schempp* (1963), the Supreme Court found that this practice also violates the establishment clause by putting the government in the position of leading a religious exercise. Indeed, because the schools were having students read from the New Testament, the policy automatically excluded and offended Jewish students as well as atheists and students from other faiths. The Court emphasized that there is nothing wrong with a public school teaching about religion as a fact in the world, such as "the history of religion" or even the Bible as literature. But these inquiries into religion, "when presented objectively as part of a secular program of education," are a world apart from inviting (or requiring) students to participate in a sectarian religious ritual. Thus, whether the school system composes a prayer or selects Bible passages for reading, it is unconstitutional if its purpose is a kind of devotional worship rather than academic study and critique.

But even after *Schempp*, many local school system officials and teachers continued to lead students in group prayer at ceremonial events, such as graduations and homecoming games. Then in 1992 the Supreme Court decided *Lee v. Weisman*, which held that public school officials could not invite clergy members to open graduation with an invocation prayer or close it with a benediction. Do you think that the Court pushed things too far with this decision, as Justice Scalia suggests, or is this ruling necessary to allow all students, regardless of religious belief, to enjoy "one of life's most significant occasions," as Justice Kennedy argues?

LEE v. WEISMAN

Supreme Court of the United States
Argued November 6, 1991.
Decided June 24, 1992.

Majority OPINION   Justice KENNEDY delivered the opinion of the Court.

School principals in the public school system of the city of Providence, Rhode Island, are permitted to invite members of the clergy to offer invocation and benediction prayers as part of the formal graduation ceremonies for middle schools and for high schools. The question before us is whether including clerical members who offer prayers as part of the official school graduation ceremony is consistent with the Religion Clauses of the First Amendment, provisions the Fourteenth Amendment makes applicable with full force to the States and their school districts.

I

Deborah Weisman graduated from Nathan Bishop Middle School, a public school in Providence, at a formal ceremony in June 1989.... For many years it has been the policy of the Providence School Committee and the Superintendent of Schools to permit principals to invite members of the clergy to give invocations and benedictions at middle school and high school graduations. Many, but not all, of the principals elected to include prayers as part of the graduation ceremonies. Acting for himself and his daughter, Deborah's father,

Deborah Weisman, right, and her sister Merith stand outside the Supreme Court. Deborah's middle school principal had invited a rabbi to deliver a nonsectarian invocation and benediction at her graduation ceremony in Rhode Island. Her father, Daniel, challenged the practice. In *Lee v. Weisman* (1992), the Supreme Court ruled in his favor, stating that the practice violated the First Amendment's establishment clause.

Daniel Weisman, objected to any prayers at Deborah's middle school graduation, but to no avail. The school principal, petitioner Robert E. Lee, invited a rabbi to deliver prayers at the graduation exercises for Deborah's class. Rabbi Leslie Gutterman, of the Temple Beth El in Providence, accepted.

It has been the custom of Providence school officials to provide invited clergy with a pamphlet entitled "Guidelines for Civic Occasions," prepared by the National Conference of Christians and Jews. The Guidelines recommend that public prayers at nonsectarian civic ceremonies be composed with "inclusiveness and sensitivity," though they acknowledge that "[p]rayer of any kind may be inappropriate on some civic occasions." The principal gave Rabbi Gutterman the pamphlet before the graduation and advised him the invocation and benediction should be nonsectarian. Rabbi Gutterman's [invocation was] as follows:

> God of the Free, Hope of the Brave:
>
> For the legacy of America where diversity is celebrated and the rights of minorities are protected, we thank You. May these young men and women grow up to enrich it.
>
> For the liberty of America, we thank You. May these new graduates grow up to guard it.
>
> For the political process of America in which all its citizens may participate, for its court system where all may seek justice we thank You. May those we honor this morning always turn to it in trust.
>
> For the destiny of America we thank You. May the graduates of Nathan Bishop Middle School so live that they might help to share it.
>
> May our aspirations for our country and for these young people, who are our hope for the future, be richly fulfilled.
>
> AMEN...

B

... The District Court held that petitioners' practice of including invocations and benedictions in public school graduations violated the Establishment Clause of the First Amendment, and it enjoined petitioners from continuing the practice....

On appeal, the United States Court of Appeals for the First Circuit affirmed.... We granted certiorari and now affirm.

> **Establishment Clause**
> The religion clause in the First Amendment that prohibits both federal and state governments from formally establishing, coercing, or endorsing a religion or religion in general.

II

These dominant facts mark and control the confines of our decision: State officials direct the performance of a formal religious exercise at promotional and graduation ceremonies for secondary schools. Even for those students who object to the religious exercise, their attendance and participation in the state-sponsored religious activity are in a fair and real sense obligatory, though the school district does not require attendance as a condition for receipt of the diploma.

... The government involvement with religious activity in this case is pervasive, to the point of creating a state-sponsored and state-directed religious exercise in a public school. Conducting this formal religious observance conflicts with settled rules pertaining to prayer exercises for students, and that suffices to determine the question before us.

The principle that government may accommodate the free exercise of religion does not supersede the fundamental limitations imposed by the Establishment Clause. It is beyond dispute that, at a minimum, the Constitution guarantees that government may not coerce anyone to support or participate in religion or its exercise.... The State's involvement in the school prayers challenged today violates these central principles.

The State's role did not end with the decision to include a prayer and with the choice of a clergyman. Principal Lee provided Rabbi Gutterman with a copy of the "Guidelines for Civic Occasions," and advised him that his prayers should be nonsectarian. Through these means the principal directed and controlled the content of the prayers....

Petitioners argue, and we find nothing in the case to refute it, that the directions for the content of the prayers were a good-faith attempt by the school to ensure that the sectarianism which is so often the flashpoint for religious animosity be removed from the graduation ceremony. The concern is understandable, as a prayer which uses ideas or images identified with a particular religion may foster a different sort of sectarian rivalry than an invocation or benediction in terms more neutral. The school's explanation, however, does not resolve the dilemma caused by its participation. The question is not the good faith of the school in attempting to make the prayer acceptable to most persons, but the legitimacy of its undertaking that enterprise at all when the object is to produce a prayer to be used in a formal religious exercise which students, for all practical purposes, are obliged to attend....

The degree of school involvement here made it clear that the graduation prayers bore the imprint of the State and thus put school-age children who objected in an untenable position. We turn our attention now to consider the position of the students, both those who desired the prayer and those who did not.

To endure the speech of false ideas or offensive content and then to counter it is part of learning how to live in a pluralistic society, a society which insists upon open discourse towards the end of a tolerant citizenry. And tolerance presupposes some mutuality of obligation. It is argued that our constitutional vision of a free society requires confidence in our own ability to accept or reject ideas of which we do not approve, and that prayer at a high school graduation does nothing more than offer a choice. By the time they are seniors, high school students no doubt have been required to attend classes and assemblies and to complete assignments exposing them to ideas they find distasteful or immoral or absurd or all of these. Against this background, students may consider it an odd measure of justice to be subjected during the course of their educations to ideas deemed offensive and irreligious, but to be denied a brief, formal prayer ceremony that the school offers in return. This argument cannot prevail, however. It overlooks a fundamental dynamic of the Constitution. The First Amendment protects speech and religion by quite different mechanisms. Speech is protected by ensuring its full expression even when the government participates, for the very object of some of our most important speech is to persuade the government to adopt an idea as its own. The method for protecting freedom of worship and freedom of conscience in religious matters is quite the reverse. In religious debate or expression the government is not a prime participant, for the Framers deemed religious establishment antithetical to the freedom of all. The Free Exercise Clause embraces a freedom of conscience and worship that has close parallels in the speech provisions of the First Amendment, but the Establishment Clause is a specific prohibition on forms of state intervention in religious affairs with no precise counterpart in the speech provisions. The explanation lies in the lesson of history that was and is the inspiration for the Establishment Clause, the lesson that in the hands of government what might begin as a tolerant expression of religious views may end in a policy to indoctrinate and coerce. A state-created orthodoxy puts at grave risk that freedom of belief and conscience which are the sole assurance that religious faith is real, not imposed.

The lessons of the First Amendment are as urgent in the modern world as in the 18th century when it was written. One timeless lesson is that if citizens are subjected to state-sponsored religious exercises, the State disavows its own duty to guard and respect that sphere of inviolable conscience and belief which is the mark of a free people. To compromise that principle today would be to deny our own tradition and forfeit our standing to urge others to secure the protections of that tradition for themselves.

As we have observed before, there are heightened concerns with protecting freedom of conscience from subtle coercive pressure in the elementary and secondary public schools. … What to most believers may seem nothing more than a reasonable request that the nonbeliever respect their religious practices, in a school context may appear to the nonbeliever or dissenter to be an attempt to employ the machinery of the State to enforce a religious orthodoxy.

We need not look beyond the circumstances of this case to see the phenomenon at work. The undeniable fact is that the school district's supervision and control of a high school graduation ceremony places public pressure, as well as peer pressure, on attending students to stand as a group or, at least, maintain respectful silence during the invocation and benediction.... There can be no doubt that for many, if not most, of the students at the graduation, the act of standing or remaining silent was an expression of participation in the rabbi's prayer. That was the very point of the religious exercise. It is of little comfort to a dissenter, then, to be told that for her the act of standing or remaining in silence signifies mere respect, rather than participation. What matters is that, given our social conventions, a reasonable dissenter in this milieu could believe that the group exercise signified her own participation or approval of it.

Finding no violation under these circumstances would place objectors in the dilemma of participating, with all that implies, or protesting. We do not address whether that choice is acceptable if the affected citizens are mature adults, but we think the State may not, consistent with the Establishment Clause, place primary and secondary school children in this position.... To recognize that the choice imposed by the State constitutes an unacceptable constraint only acknowledges that the government may no more use social pressure to enforce orthodoxy than it may use more direct means....

There was a stipulation in the District Court that attendance at graduation and promotional ceremonies is voluntary. The argument lacks all persuasion. Everyone knows that in our society and in our culture high school graduation is one of life's most significant occasions....

The importance of the event is the point the school district and the United States rely upon to argue that a formal prayer ought to be permitted, but it becomes one of the principal reasons why their argument must fail. Their contention ... is that the prayers are an essential part of these ceremonies because for many persons an occasion of this significance lacks meaning if there is no recognition, however brief, that human achievements cannot be understood apart from their spiritual essence. We think the Government's position that this interest suffices to force students to choose between compliance or forfeiture demonstrates fundamental inconsistency in its argumentation. It fails to acknowledge that what for many of Deborah's classmates and their parents was a spiritual imperative was for Daniel and Deborah Weisman religious conformance compelled by the State.... The Constitution forbids the State to exact religious conformity from a student as the price of attending her own high school graduation. This is the calculus the Constitution commands....

We do not hold that every state action implicating religion is invalid if one or a few citizens find it offensive. People may take offense at all manner of religious as well as nonreligious messages, but offense alone does not in every case show a violation. We know too that sometimes to endure social isolation or even anger may be the price of conscience or nonconformity. But, by any reading of our cases, the conformity required of the student in this case was too high an exaction to withstand the test of the Establishment Clause. The prayer exercises in this case are especially improper because the State has in every practical sense compelled attendance and participation in an explicit religious exercise at an event of singular importance to every student, one the objecting student had no real alternative to avoid....

... We recognize that, at graduation time and throughout the course of the educational process, there will be instances when religious values, religious practices, and religious persons will have some interaction with the public schools and their students. But these matters, often questions of accommodation of religion, are not before us. The sole question presented is whether a religious exercise may be conducted at a graduation ceremony in circumstances where, as we have found, young graduates who object are induced to conform. No holding by this Court suggests that a school can persuade or compel a student to participate in a religious exercise. That is being done here, and it is forbidden by the Establishment Clause of the First Amendment.

For the reasons we have stated, the judgment of the Court of Appeals is *Affirmed.*

Dissenting VOICES

Justice Scalia, joined by Chief Justice Rehnquist, Justice White, and Justice Thomas, dissented in an opinion insisting that religious prayers have featured prominently in official public ceremonies throughout our history. The majority's opinion, Justice Scalia wrote, therefore —

> lays waste a tradition that is as old as public school graduation ceremonies themselves, and that is a component of an even more longstanding American tradition of nonsectarian prayer to God at public celebrations generally....
>
> From our Nation's origin, prayer has been a prominent part of governmental ceremonies and proclamations. The Declaration of Independence, the document marking our birth as a separate people, "appealed to the Supreme Judge of the world for the rectitude of our intentions" and avowed "a firm reliance on the protection of divine Providence." In his first inaugural address, after swearing his oath of office on a Bible, George Washington deliberately made a prayer a part of his first official act as President.... Such supplications have been a characteristic feature of inaugural addresses ever since.

Justice Scalia argued that the majority's claim that students were subtly "coerced" into participating in invocation and benediction was "incoherent."

He explained:

> The Court's notion that a student who simply sits in "respectful silence" during the invocation and benediction (when all others are standing) has somehow joined or would somehow be perceived as having joined in the prayers is nothing short of ludicrous. We indeed live in a vulgar age. But surely "our social conventions" have not coarsened to the point that anyone who does not stand on his chair and shout obscenities can reasonably be deemed to have assented to everything said in his presence. Since the Court does not dispute that students exposed to prayer at graduation ceremonies retain (despite "subtle coercive pressures") the free will to sit, there is absolutely no basis for the Court's decision. It is fanciful enough to say that "a reasonable dissenter," standing head erect in a class of bowed heads, "could believe that the group exercise signified her own participation or approval of it." It is beyond the absurd to say that she could entertain such a belief while pointedly declining to rise.

Even if we "assume the very worst, that the nonparticipating graduate is 'subtly coerced' ...to stand," Justice Scalia continued, this does not establish participation "in a religious exercise." Standing might simply imply an expression of respect for other people's religious beliefs and prayers, which is a "fundamental civic virtue that government (including the public schools) can and should cultivate."

But Justice Scalia did not run away from endorsing use of the ceremonial religious prayers that the majority banned at graduation:

> The narrow context of the present case involves a community's celebration of one of the milestones in its young citizens' lives, and it is a bold step for this Court to seek to banish from that occasion, and from thousands of similar celebrations throughout this land, the expression of gratitude to God that a majority of the community wishes to make. The issue before us today is not the abstract philosophical question whether the alternative of frustrating this desire of a religious majority is to be preferred over the alternative of imposing "psychological coercion," or a feeling of exclusion, upon non-believers. Rather, the question is *whether a mandatory choice in favor of the former has been imposed by the United States Constitution.* As the age-old practices of our people show, the answer to that question is not at all in doubt.

He concluded with an argument that organized prayer at public ceremonies promotes tolerance rather than intolerance:

> The Founders of our Republic knew the fearsome potential of sectarian religious belief to generate civil dissension and civil strife. And they also knew that nothing, absolutely nothing, is so inclined to foster among religious believers of various faiths a toleration —no, an affection—for one another than voluntarily joining in prayer together, to the God whom they all worship and seek. Needless to say, no one should be compelled to do that, but it is a shame to deprive our public culture of the opportunity, and indeed the encouragement, for people to do it voluntarily. The Baptist or Catholic who heard and joined in the simple and inspiring prayers of Rabbi Gutterman on this official and patriotic occasion was inoculated from religious bigotry and prejudice in a manner that cannot be replicated. To deprive our society of that important unifying mecha-nism, in order to spare the nonbeliever what seems to me the minimal inconvenience of standing or even sitting in respectful nonparticipation, is as senseless in policy as it is unsupported in law.

Even after *Lee v. Weisman,* many schools remained defiant about maintaining religious practices. School-organized prayers continued to be a common feature of athletic games throughout the 1990s. Nowhere was this practice more ingrained than in varsity high school football games in the South, especially Texas, where high school football itself is a kind of religion.

In 2000 the Supreme Court took a case involving a challenge to organized football game prayers in the Santa Fe Independent School District in Texas. For many years, this over-whelmingly Southern Baptist community had students elect a "student council chaplain" who prayed over the loud speaker before football games. After litigation forced the school to drop the student chaplain position, the school adopted a two-part policy. It first allowed students to have a pregame speaker to "solemnize" football games if they wanted. Second, if they decided to have such a solemnizing speaker, the policy allowed them to elect the stu-dent who would give the statement or prayer.

A Mormon family and a Catholic family brought suit against this policy, alleging that it was yet another assault on the establishment clause in a district where the rights of religious minorities were routinely violated. They claimed that the football field was part of the school and the school system should not be involved with religious prayer at all. Electing the student to give a prayerful invocation made matters worse by turning the different religious groups in the school into political parties. The school district answered that students did not have to choose to have a solemnizing statement and the statement did not have to be a religious one. It said the case was premature and the plaintiffs were making a mountain out of a molehill. The Supreme Court majority disagreed. Do you?

SANTA FE INDEPENDENT SCHOOL DISTRICT v. DOE

Supreme Court of the United States
Argued March 29, 2000.
Decided June 19, 2000.

Majority OPINION   Justice STEVENS delivered the opinion of the Court.

Prior to 1995, the Santa Fe High School student who occupied the school's elective office of student council chaplain delivered a prayer over the public address system before each varsity football game for the entire season. This practice, along with others, was challenged in District Court as a violation of the Establishment Clause of the First Amendment.... [T]he school district [then] adopted a different policy that permits, but does not require, prayer initiated and led by a student at all home games....

I

> **Litigate**
> To sue or seek a resolution to a conflict in the courts.

Respondents are two sets of current or former students and their respective mothers. One family is Mormon and the other is Catholic. The District Court permitted respondents (Does) to litigate anonymously to protect them from intimidation or harassment.

... [Respondents] alleged that the District had engaged in several proselytizing practices, such as promoting attendance at a Baptist revival meeting, encouraging membership in religious clubs, chastising children who held minority religious beliefs, and distributing Gideon Bibles on school premises. They also alleged that the District allowed students to read Christian invocations and benedictions from the stage at graduation ceremonies, and to deliver overtly Christian prayers over the public address system at home football games.

On May 10, 1995, the District Court entered an interim order [providing] that "nondenominational prayer" consisting of "an invocation and/or benediction" could be presented by a senior student or students selected by members of the graduating class. The text of the prayer was to be determined by the students, without scrutiny or preapproval by school officials. References to particular religious figures "such as Mohammed, Jesus, Buddha, or the like" would be permitted "as long as the general thrust of the prayer is non-proselytizing."

In response the District adopted a series of policies over several months dealing with prayer at school functions....

The August policy, which was titled "Prayer at Football Games,"... authorized two student elections, the first to determine whether "invocations" should be delivered, and the second to select the spokesperson to deliver them.... [I]t contained two parts, an initial statement that omitted any requirement that the content of the invocation be "nonsectarian and nonproselytising," and a fallback provision that automatically added that limitation if the preferred policy should be enjoined. On August 31, 1995 ... "[t]he district's high school students voted to determine whether a student would deliver prayer at varsity football games.... The students chose to allow a student to say a prayer at football games." A week later, in a separate election, they selected a student "to deliver the prayer at varsity football games."

The [October policy] is essentially the same as the August policy, though it omits the word "prayer" from its title, and refers to "messages" and "statements" as well as "invocations."...

... We conclude, as did the Court of Appeals, that ... ["the District's policy permitting student-led, student-initiated prayer at football games violates the Establishment Clause."]

II

... The fact that the District's policy provides for the election of the speaker only after the majority has voted on her message identifies an obvious distinction between this case and the typical election of a "student body president, or even a newly elected prom king or queen." [This footnote text has been inserted here for clarity.] ...

... While Santa Fe's majoritarian election might ensure that *most* of the students are represented, it does nothing to protect the minority; indeed, it likely serves to intensify their offense.

Moreover, the District has failed to divorce itself from the religious content in the invocations. It has not succeeded in doing so, either by claiming that its policy is "one of neutrality rather than endorsement" or by characterizing the individual student as the "circuit-breaker" in the process. Contrary to the District's repeated assertions that it has adopted a "hands-off" approach to the pregame invocation, its policy involves both perceived and actual endorsement of religion.... [T]he "degree of school involvement" makes it clear that the pregame prayers bear "the imprint of the State and thus put school-age children who objected in an untenable position."

The District has attempted to disentangle itself from the religious messages by developing the two-step student election process. The text of the October policy, however, exposes the extent of the school's entanglement. The elections take place at all only because the school "board *has chosen to permit* students to deliver a brief invocation and/or message." The elections thus "shall" be conducted "by the high school student council" and "[u]pon advice and direction of the high school principal." The decision whether to deliver a message is first made by majority vote of the entire student body, followed by a choice of the speaker in a separate, similar majority election. Even though the particular words used by the speaker are not determined by those votes, the policy mandates that the "statement or invocation" be "consistent with the goals and purposes of this policy," which are "to solemnize the event, to promote good sportsmanship and student safety, and to establish the appropriate environment for the competition."

In addition to involving the school in the selection of the speaker, the policy, by its terms, invites and encourages religious messages. The policy itself states that the purpose of the message is "to solemnize the event." A religious message is the most obvious method of solemnizing an event. Moreover, the requirements that the message "promote good sportsmanship" and "establish the appropriate environment for competition" further narrow the types of message deemed appropriate, suggesting that a solemn, yet nonreligious, message, such as commentary on United States foreign policy, would be prohibited. Indeed, the only type of message that is expressly endorsed in the text is an "invocation"—a term that primarily describes an appeal for divine assistance. In fact, as used in the past at Santa Fe High School, an "invocation" has always entailed a focused religious message. Thus, the expressed purposes of the policy encourage the selection of a religious message, and that is precisely how the students understand the policy. The results of the elections ... make it clear that the students understood that the central question before them was whether prayer should be a part of the pregame ceremony....

The actual or perceived endorsement of the message, moreover, is established by factors beyond just the text of the policy. Once the student speaker is selected and the message composed, the invocation is then delivered to a large audience assembled as part of a regularly scheduled, school-sponsored function conducted on school property. The message is broadcast over the school's public address system, which remains subject to the control of school officials. It is fair to assume that the pregame ceremony is clothed in the traditional indicia of school sporting events, which generally include not just the team, but also cheerleaders and band members dressed in uniforms sporting the school name and mascot. The school's name is likely written in large print across the field and on banners and flags. The crowd will certainly include many who display the school colors and insignia on their school T-shirts, jackets, or hats and who may also be waving signs displaying the school name. It is in a setting such as this that "[t]he board has chosen to permit" the elected student to rise and give the "statement or invocation."

In this context the members of the listening audience must perceive the pregame message as a public expression of the views of the majority of the student body delivered with the approval of the school administration. In cases involving state participation in a religious activity, one of the relevant questions is "whether an objective observer, acquainted with the text, legislative history, and implementation of the statute, would perceive it as a state endorsement of prayer in public schools." Regardless of the listener's support for, or objection to, the message, an objective Santa Fe High School student will unquestionably perceive the inevitable pregame prayer as stamped with her school's seal of approval....

According to the District, the secular purposes of the policy are to "foste[r] free expression of private persons ... as well [as to] solemniz[e] sporting events, promot[e] good sportsmanship and student safety, and establis[h] an appropriate environment for competition." ... [H]owever, the District's approval of only one specific kind of message, an "invocation," is not necessary to further any of these purposes. Additionally, the fact that only one student is permitted to give a content-limited message suggests that this policy does little to "foste[r] free expression." Furthermore, regardless of whether one considers a sporting event an appropriate occasion for solemnity, the use of an invocation to foster such solemnity is impermissible when, in actuality, it constitutes prayer sponsored by the school.

School sponsorship of a religious message is impermissible because it sends the ancillary message to members of the audience who are nonadherents "that they are outsiders, not full members of the political community, and an accompanying message to adherents that they are insiders, favored members of the political community." ... The delivery of such a message —over the school's public address system, by a speaker representing the student body, under the supervision of school faculty, and pursuant to a school policy that explicitly and implicitly encourages public prayer—is not properly characterized as "private" speech.

III

The District next argues that its football policy does not coerce students to participate in religious observances. Its argument has two parts: first, that there is no impermissible government coercion because the pregame messages are the product of student choices; and second, that there is really no coercion at all because attendance at an extracurricular event, unlike a graduation ceremony, is voluntary.

[T]he issue resolved in the first election was "whether a student would deliver prayer at varsity football games" and the controversy in this case demonstrates that the views of the students are not unanimous on that issue.

One of the purposes served by the Establishment Clause is to remove debate over this kind of issue from governmental supervision or control. [T]he "preservation and transmission of religious beliefs and worship is a responsibility and a choice committed to the private sphere." The two student elections authorized by the policy, coupled with the debates that presumably must precede each, impermissibly invade that private sphere. The election mechanism reflects a device the District put in place that determines whether religious messages will be delivered at home football games. The mechanism encourages divisiveness along religious lines in a public school setting, a result at odds with the Establishment Clause. Although it is true that the ultimate choice of student speaker is "attributable to the students" the District's decision to hold the constitutionally problematic election is clearly "a choice attributable to the State."

... Attendance at a high school football game, unlike showing up for class, is certainly not required in order to receive a diploma. Moreover, we may assume that the District is correct in arguing that the informal pressure to attend an athletic event is not as strong as a senior's desire to attend her own graduation ceremony.

There are some students, however, such as cheerleaders, members of the band, and, of course, the team members themselves, for whom seasonal commitments mandate their attendance, sometimes for class credit. The District also minimizes the importance to many students of attending and participating in extracurricular activities as part of a complete educational experience. To assert that high school students do not feel immense social pressure, or have a truly genuine desire, to be involved in the extracurricular event that is American high school football is "formalistic in the extreme."

... [T]he delivery of a pregame prayer has the improper effect of coercing those present to participate in an act of religious worship.... "[W]hat to most believers may seem nothing more than a reasonable request that the nonbeliever respect their religious practices, in a school context may appear to the nonbeliever or dissenter to be an attempt to employ the machinery of the State to enforce a religious orthodoxy." The constitutional command will not permit the District "to exact religious conformity from a student as the price" of joining her classmates at a varsity football game....

The judgment of the Court of Appeals is, accordingly, affirmed.

Dissenting VOICES

Chief Justice Rehnquist, joined by Justice Scalia and Justice Thomas, dissented, and declared that the Court's opinion "bristles with hostility to all things religious in public life. Neither the holding nor the tone of the opinion is faithful to the meaning of the Establishment Clause."

Chief Justice Rehnquist defended the neutrality of the election process at the high school, arguing that any attempt to judge its constitutionality under the establishment clause was premature. He wrote that

> the election permitted by the policy is a two-fold process whereby students vote first on whether to have a student speaker before football games at all, and second, if the students vote to have such a speaker, on who that speaker will be.... It is conceivable that the election could become one in which student candidates campaign on platforms that focus on whether or not they will pray if elected. It is also conceivable that the election could lead to a Christian prayer before 90 percent of the football games. If, upon implementation, the policy operated in this fashion, we would have a record before us to review whether the policy, as applied, violated the Establishment Clause or unduly suppressed minority viewpoints. But it is possible that the students might vote not to have a pregame speaker, in which case there would be no threat of a constitutional violation. It is also possible that the election would not focus on prayer, but on public speaking ability or social popularity. And if student campaigning did begin to focus on prayer, the school might decide to implement reasonable campaign restrictions.
>
> But the Court ignores these possibilities by holding that merely granting the student body the power to elect a speaker that may choose to pray, "regardless of the students' ultimate use of it, is not acceptable." ... The Court so holds despite that any speech that may occur as a result of the election process here would be *private,* not *government,* speech. The elected student, not the government, would choose what to say. Support for the Court's holding cannot be found in any of our cases. And it essentially invalidates all student elections. A newly elected student body president, or even a newly elected prom king or queen, could use opportunities for public speaking to say prayers. Under the Court's view, the mere grant of power to the students to vote for such offices, in light of the fear that those elected might publicly pray, violates the Establishment Clause.

Chief Justice Rehnquist thought that the case should turn on the fact that any speech given by a student would be "private" in nature:

> Here ... the potential speech at issue, if the policy had been allowed to proceed, would be a message or invocation selected or created by a student. That is, if there were speech

at issue here, it would be *private* speech. The "crucial difference between *government* speech endorsing religion, which the Establishment Clause forbids, and *private* speech endorsing religion, which the Free Speech and Free Exercise Clauses protect," applies with particular force to the question of endorsement....

WHAT DO YOU **Think?**

Exercise 4.4. Suzie Smith was named valedictorian of your high school graduating class by virtue of her grade point average. She is a devout Muslim who has written her valedictorian address about the importance of Muhammad in her life and why she thinks students who abuse drugs and alcohol or belong to gangs need to discover Muhammad in their personal lives. She wants to finish by inviting her fellow graduates to come with her to her mosque before they leave for college or work. The principal is nervous about letting her give such a speech, but students in the past have always been allowed to speak about the topic of their choice, and their remarks are traditionally edited for length, clarity, and style only. The principal does not want to be sued by non-Muslim parents, but she also does not want to be sued by Suzie and her family.

Knowing that you are taking this class, the principal asks your advice on how to handle the situation without violating the establishment clause or Suzie's free speech and free exercise of religion rights. How will you advise the principal to act in this majority Christian community? (What if Suzie were a Methodist? A Jehovah's Witness? A Hare Krishna? Would that change your views?) Discuss the problem with your classmates and come up with what you think is sound legal and policy advice for the principal.

Exercise 4.5. With the score tied and five minutes to go in John Jay High School's big football game against John Marshall High, the charismatic quarterback of the Jay team, Jed Belmon, asks all of the players on offense to join hands in the huddle and follow him in a prayer to God for victory. "Dear God," he says, "thank you for your support all season. Please let us score just one more touchdown on the play-action 76 post pattern. Amen." When the team scores and wins the championship, Jed tells the newspapers the story of the prayer in the huddle. His wide receiver, Tom Sherberg, says that the prayer violated the establishment clause; Jed says that this is ridiculous. Who is right? Meantime, the coach for Marshall High School wants to have the victory handed to his team because he says that the prayer was also "unconstitutional and unfair." Does he have a solid argument? What if the prayer had been sent into the huddle by another player?

FOR THE **CLASS**

Interviewing the Justices. Select two students to play the anchors of an evening television news talk show. The anchors have an unusual assignment: They will be interviewing the nine Supreme Court justices about their opinions in *Santa Fe v. Doe*. Select

one set of students to play Justice Stevens (who wrote the Court's majority opinion) and the five justices who agreed with him. Select a second set of students to play Chief Justice Rehnquist (who wrote the dissenting opinion) and the two justices who dissented alongside him. Try to get to the bottom of the views of each justice. Why did those who sided with the majority think that the football invocation violated the establishment clause? How did they think that such statements affected students, team players, cheerleaders, and fans? And why did the dissenters object to the majority's decision? The news anchors should invite additional student guests to play teachers and students to discuss their own thoughts about the case. (This exercise is for fun; in reality, Supreme Court justices rarely discuss their opinions in public, and almost never in a format like this.)

Government Aid to Private Religious Schools: When Does It Cross the Line?

Government may not give tax dollars directly to religious schools for the purpose of teaching religion. After all, the establishment clause prevents the government from establishing religions or taxing the public to support them.

Yet many public services and dollars are spent on churches in a way that poses no constitutional problem. For example, if a church is on fire, the fire department can put the fire out without violating the First Amendment. Police officers can help churches, mosques, and synagogues if they have been vandalized or burglarized. Cities can provide sewerage and garbage collection. These forms of public aid are part of universal government services that do not bolster the specifically religious mission of the churches.

In the following case the Supreme Court considered the constitutionality of a New Jersey township's policy of reimbursing parents for the cost of sending their children to private school, including private religious school, on public buses. The plaintiffs attacking the policy argued that it was designed to make parochial school cheaper and to indirectly subsidize religious schools. The township argued that it was part of a universal policy to pay for all kids, whether in public or private school, to get to school safely and on time. What do you think? What does the Court decide?

EVERSON v. BOARD OF EDUCATION OF THE TOWNSHIP OF EWING

Supreme Court of the United States
Argued November 20, 1946.
Decided February 10, 1947.

OPINION   Justice BLACK delivered the opinion of the Court.

Majority

A New Jersey statute authorizes its local school districts to make rules and contracts for the transportation of children to and from schools. The appellee, a township board of education, acting pursuant to this statute, authorized reimbursement to parents of money expended by them for the bus transportation of their children on regular buses operated by the public transportation system. Part of this money was for the payment of transportation of some children in the community to Catholic parochial schools. These church schools give their students, in addition to secular education, regular religious instruction conforming to the religious tenets and modes of worship of the Catholic Faith.

> **Statute**
> A law passed by Congress or a state legislature.

The New Jersey statute is challenged as a "law respecting an establishment of religion." The First Amendment, as made applicable to the states by the Fourteenth, commands that a state "shall make no law respecting an establishment of religion, or prohibiting the free exercise thereof...." These words of the First Amendment reflected in the minds of early Americans a vivid mental picture of conditions and practices which they fervently wished to stamp out in order to preserve liberty for themselves and for their posterity. Doubtless their goal has not been entirely reached; but so far has the Nation moved toward it that the expression "law respecting an establishment of religion," probably does not so vividly remind present-day Americans of the evils, fears, and political problems that caused that expression to be written into our Bill of Rights....

The "establishment of religion" clause of the First Amendment means at least this: Neither a state nor the Federal Government can set up a church. Neither can pass laws which aid one religion, aid all religions, or prefer one religion over another. Neither can force nor influence a person to go to or to remain away from church against his will or force him to profess a belief or disbelief in any religion. No person can be punished for entertaining or professing religious beliefs or disbeliefs, for church attendance or non-attendance. No tax in any amount, large or small, can be levied to support any religious activities or institutions, whatever they may be called, or whatever form they may adopt to teach or practice religion....

We must consider the New Jersey statute in accordance with the foregoing limitations. New Jersey cannot consistently with the "establishment of religion" clause of the First Amendment contribute tax-raised funds to the support of an institution which teaches the tenets and faith of any church. On the other hand, other language of the amendment commands that New Jersey cannot hamper its citizens in the free exercise of their own religion. While we do not mean to intimate that a state could not provide transportation only to children attending public schools, we must be careful, in protecting the citizens of New Jersey against state-established churches, to be sure that we do not inadvertently prohibit New Jersey from extending its general state law benefits to all its citizens without regard to their religious belief. Measured by these standards, we cannot say that the First Amendment prohibits New Jersey from spending tax-raised funds to pay the bus fares of parochial school pupils as a part of a general program under which it pays the fares of pupils attending public and other schools.... That Amendment requires the state to be neutral in its relations with groups of religious believers and non-believers; it does not require the state to be their adversary. State power is no more to be used so as to handicap religions than it is to favor them....

The First Amendment has erected a wall between church and state. That wall must be kept high and impregnable. We could not approve the slightest breach. New Jersey has not breached it here.

Affirmed.

Dissenting VOICES

Justice Rutledge, joined by Justice Frankfurter, Justice Jackson, and Justice Burton, dissented. They argued that New Jersey's payment of transportation costs for parochial school students is unavoidably a transfer of public money to support religious institutions, a kind of transfer disallowed under the establishment clause:

> Not simply an established church, but any law respecting an establishment of religion is forbidden. The Amendment was broadly but not loosely phrased.... Here parents pay money to send their children to parochial schools and funds raised by taxation are used to reimburse them. This not only helps the children to get to school and the parents to send them. It aids them in a substantial way to get the very thing which they are sent to the particular school to secure, namely, religious training and teaching....

This is precisely what the Framers wanted to avoid, Justice Rutledge argued: New Jersey's policy "exactly fits the type of exaction and the kind of evil at which Madison and Jefferson struck. Under the test they framed it cannot be said that the cost of transportation is no part of the cost of education or of the religious instruction given...."

According to Justice Rutledge, paying for transportation to religious school should be no more allowable than paying for religious books:

> Payment of transportation is no more, nor is it any the less essential to education, whether religious or secular, than payment for tuitions, for teachers' salaries, for buildings, equipment and necessary materials. Nor is it any the less directly related, in a school giving religious instruction, to the primary religious objective all those essential items of cost are intended to achieve.

WHAT DO YOU Think?

Exercise 4.6. *Everson* may have been an easy case because the city buses simply got the children to the schoolhouse door; government action did not follow students inside the religious schools. What would you think about a local policy of reimbursing all parents of children in public or private school for the cost of any schoolbooks they buy, including both secular and religious books? What would you think about a city policy, designed to make teaching a more attractive option for talented college graduates, that gave teachers a 10 percent bonus for working in the city at public or private schools, including religious schools?

School Vouchers: Making Education Redeemable in Secular or Religious Schools

In the 1990s several school districts developed school voucher policies that gave parents tuition vouchers redeemable at public, private, or religious schools. Critics attacked these programs as a violation of the establishment clause. Defenders said they passed constitutional muster on the grounds that the parents, not the government, decided whether to allocate the voucher money to religious schools or nonreligious ones.

As the Supreme Court heard oral arguments on February 20, 2002, about the constitutionality of school voucher plans, both supporters and opponents rallied outside.

The table was set for victory for voucher proponents in a series of cases upholding the constitutionality of universal and formally neutral programs whose benefits went heavily to religious institutions. In *Mueller v. Allen* (1983), the Supreme Court rejected an establishment clause attack on a Minnesota program authorizing tax deductions for various educational expenses, including private school tuition costs, even though 96 percent of the program's beneficiaries were parents of children in religious schools. The Court found it compelling that the class of beneficiaries was "all parents," including those who sent their children to nonreligious private schools. The program thus respected the principle of private choice, since public funds were made available to religious schools "only as a result of numerous, private choices of individual parents of school-age children."

The Court used the same logic in *Witters v. Washington Department of Services for the Blind* (1986). It rejected an establishment clause challenge to a vocational scholarship program that provided tuition aid to a student at a religious institution who was studying to become a pastor. The Court observed that the state's scholarship program was open to all private and public schools and that any aid that went to religious institutions did so "only as a result of the genuinely independent and private choices of aid recipients."

Finally, in *Zobrest v. Catalina Foothills School District* (1993), the Court refused a challenge to a federal program that permitted sign-language interpreters to assist deaf children enrolled in religious schools. The Court stated that "government programs that neutrally provide benefits to a broad class of citizens defined without reference to religion are not readily subject to an establishment clause challenge." The program, the Court found, distributes sign-language or other interpretive benefits "neutrally to any child qualifying as 'disabled.' … Its primary beneficiaries were 'disabled' children, not sectarian schools."

By the time the Court took up the school voucher question in 2002, it was easy for the majority to analyze the issue and settle the constitutional controversy (though certainly not the political one). In *Zelman v. Simmons-Harris* (2002), the Court upheld the state of

Ohio's educational voucher program for poor students in the failing Cleveland City School District, which had been placed under state control. The state made the tuition vouchers available to less affluent families, who could then use them either to attend private school or to go to public schools but get extra tutoring help. The plaintiffs argued that the plan violated the establishment clause because fully 96 percent of those who transferred out of public schools enrolled their children in parochial religious schools.

Yet the Court found that there was no constitutional problem because the Ohio plan relied on the "private choice" of eligible families to choose among public schools (with bolstered tutoring services), secular private schools, and religious private schools. The fact that most school vouchers were redeemed at religious schools was deemed incidental and therefore not fatal to the program.

Do you agree with the majority, which saw the policy as neutral, or the dissenters, who saw school vouchers as a clever and unlawful way to channel public money directly into the coffers of religious institutions?

ZELMAN v. SIMMONS-HARRIS

Supreme Court of the United States
Argued February 20, 2002.
Decided June 27, 2002.

OPINION   Chief Justice REHNQUIST delivered the opinion of the Court.

Majority

The State of Ohio has established a pilot program designed to provide educational choices to families with children who reside in the Cleveland City School District. The question presented is whether this program offends the Establishment Clause of the United States Constitution. We hold that it does not.

There are more than 75,000 children enrolled in the Cleveland City School District. The majority of these children are from low-income and minority families. Few of these families enjoy the means to send their children to any school other than an inner-city public school. For more than a generation, however, Cleveland's public schools have been among the worst performing public schools in the Nation....

... [T]he Pilot Project Scholarship Program ... provides two basic kinds of assistance to parents of children in a covered district. First, the program provides tuition aid for students in kindergarten through third grade, expanding each year through eighth grade, to attend a participating public or private school of their parent's choosing. Second, the program provides tutorial aid for students who choose to remain enrolled in public school....

Any private school, whether religious or nonreligious, may participate in the program and accept program students so long as the school is located within the boundaries of a covered district and meets statewide educational standards. Participating private schools must agree not to discriminate on the basis of race, religion, or ethnic background, or to "advocate or foster unlawful behavior or teach hatred of any person or group on the basis of race, ethnicity, national origin, or religion." Any public school located in a school district adjacent to the covered district may also participate in the program....

The program has been in operation within the Cleveland City School District since the 1996–1997 school year. In the 1999–2000 school year, 56 private schools participated in the program, 46 (or 82%) of which had a religious affiliation. None of the public schools in districts adjacent to Cleveland have elected to participate. More than 3,700 students participated in the scholarship program, most of whom (96%) enrolled in religiously affiliated schools. Sixty percent of these students were from families at or below the poverty line. In the 1998–1999 school year, approximately 1,400 Cleveland public school students received tutorial aid. This number was expected to double during the 1999–2000 school year....

... [O]ur jurisprudence with respect to true private choice programs has remained consistent and unbroken. Three times we have confronted Establishment Clause challenges to neutral government programs that provide aid directly to a broad class of individuals, who, in turn, direct the aid to religious schools or institutions of their own choosing. Three times we have rejected such challenges....

> **Jurisprudence**
> The fundamental and linked principles of a body of law or legal system.

We believe that the program challenged here is a program of true private choice, consistent with *Mueller, Witters,* and *Zobrest,* and thus constitutional. As was true in those cases, the Ohio program is neutral in all respects toward religion. It is part of a general and multifaceted undertaking by the State of Ohio to provide educational opportunities to the children of a failed school district. It confers educational assistance directly to a broad class of individuals defined without reference to religion, *i.e.,* any parent of a school-age child who resides in the Cleveland City School District. The program permits the participation of *all* schools within the district, religious or nonreligious. Adjacent public schools also may participate and have a financial incentive to do so. Program benefits are available to participating families on neutral terms, with no reference to religion. The only preference stated anywhere in the program is a preference for low-income families, who receive greater assistance and are given priority for admission at participating schools.

There are no "financial incentive[s]" that "ske[w]" the program toward religious schools. ... The program here in fact creates financial *dis*incentives for religious schools, with private schools receiving only half the government assistance given to community schools and one-third the assistance given to magnet schools. Adjacent public schools, should any choose to accept program students, are also eligible to receive two to three times the state funding of a private religious school. Families too have a financial disincentive to choose a private religious school over other schools. Parents that choose to participate in the scholarship program and then to enroll their children in a private school (religious or nonreligious) must copay a portion of the school's tuition. Families that choose a community school, magnet school, or traditional public school pay nothing. Although such features of the program are not necessary to its constitutionality, they clearly dispel the claim that the program "creates ... financial incentive[s] for parents to choose a sectarian school."

Respondents suggest that even without a financial incentive for parents to choose a religious school, the program creates a "public perception that the State is endorsing religious practices and beliefs." But we have repeatedly recognized that no reasonable observer would think a neutral program of private choice, where state aid reaches religious schools solely as a result of the numerous independent decisions of private individuals, carries with it the *imprimatur* of government endorsement....

... It is true that 82% of Cleveland's participating private schools are religious schools, but it is also true that 81% of private schools in Ohio are religious schools. To attribute constitutional significance to this figure would lead to the absurd result that a neutral school-choice program might be permissible in some parts of Ohio, such as Columbus, where a lower percentage of private schools are religious schools but not in inner-city Cleveland, where Ohio has deemed such programs most sorely needed, but where the preponderance of religious schools happens to be greater....

The constitutionality of a neutral educational aid program simply does not turn on whether and why, in a particular area, at a particular time, most private schools are run by religious organizations, or most recipients choose to use the aid at a religious school....

In sum, the Ohio program is entirely neutral with respect to religion. It provides benefits directly to a wide spectrum of individuals, defined only by financial need and residence in a particular school district. It permits such individuals to exercise genuine choice among options public and private, secular and religious. The program is therefore a program of true private choice. In keeping with an unbroken line of decisions rejecting challenges to similar programs, we hold that the program does not offend the Establishment Clause.

The judgment of the Court of Appeals is reversed.

Dissenting VOICES

Justice Souter filed a dissent and was joined by Justices Stevens, Ginsburg, and Breyer. They thought that the Cleveland plan violates the establishment clause because

> the overwhelming proportion of large appropriations for voucher money must be spent on religious schools if it is to be spent at all, and will be spent in amounts that cover almost all of tuition. The money will thus pay for eligible students' instruction not only in secular subjects but in religion as well, in schools that can fairly be characterized as founded to teach religious doctrine and to imbue teaching in all subjects with a religious dimension.

The dissenters argued that the program was not really "neutral," since less state money was offered for parents to employ tutors to help their children in public schools than for them to pay for their children to go to private school.

The dissenters further rejected the idea that the poor families exercised a truly meaningful "choice" in where to send their children to school. There is, they wrote,

> no way to interpret the 96.6% of current voucher money going to religious schools as reflecting a free and genuine choice by the families that apply for vouchers. The 96.6% reflects, instead, the fact that too few nonreligious school desks are available and few but religious schools can afford to accept more than a handful of voucher students. And contrary to the majority's assertion ... public schools in adjacent districts hardly have a financial incentive to participate in the Ohio voucher program, and none has.... For the overwhelming number of children in the voucher scheme, the only alternative

to the public schools is religious. And it is entirely irrelevant that the State did not deliberately design the network of private schools for the sake of channeling money into religious institutions."

WHAT DO YOU Think?

Exercise 4.7. The majority in *Zelman* found that Ohio's plan did not violate the establishment clause because the choice of where to send the children to school was made by parents, not the state. Thus, when 96 percent of the 3,700 participating students chose religious schools, this was a merely contingent and accidental, not necessary, feature of the program. Indeed, only forty-six of fifty-six participating private schools were religiously affiliated. But would the Court reach the same result if 100 percent of participating students went to religious schools and all fifty-six private schools had been religious? Would such a program still be constitutional? Conversely, would the dissenters still think the Ohio plan was unlawful even if only 5 percent of participating students were in religious schools?

The First Amendment and the Ten Commandments

Law and religion have much in common, especially this: They both organize themselves around revered founding texts. In the case of American law, our controlling text is the Constitution and its Bill of Rights; in the case of Christianity, for example, it is the Bible How far can a school system go in inserting biblical text in a classroom before it bumps into the First Amendment? Can a state require public school teachers to hang on the walls of their classrooms a display of the Ten Commandments? Consider the following landmark case, in which the Court said no.

The debate over public display of the Ten Commandments in government buildings reached a fever pitch in Montgomery, Alabama, in 2003. Despite a court order for the removal of a Ten Commandments monument, Alabama chief justice Roy Moore refused to comply and was subsequently suspended. Here, workers remove the Commandments from public view in the Alabama Judicial Building.

STONE v. GRAHAM

Supreme Court of the United States
Decided November 17, 1980.
Per Curiam.

OPINION PER CURIAM.

Majority

A Kentucky statute requires the posting of a copy of the Ten Commandments, purchased with private contributions, on the wall of each public classroom in the State.

... We conclude that Kentucky's statute requiring the posting of the Ten Commandments in public schoolrooms had no secular legislative purpose, and is therefore unconstitutional.

The Commonwealth [of Kentucky] insists that the statute in question serves a secular legislative purpose, observing that the legislature required the following notation in small print at the bottom of each display of the Ten Commandments: "The secular application of the Ten Commandments is clearly seen in its adoption as the fundamental legal code of Western Civilization and the Common Law of the United States."

Per Curiam
By the court as a whole, rather than by a single author. It generally indicates the majority or plurality opinion (if not the unanimous opinion of the court), but there can still be concurring or dissenting opinions.

The trial court found the "avowed" purpose of the statute to be secular, even as it labeled the statutory declaration "self-serving." Under this Court's rulings, however, such an "avowed" secular purpose is not sufficient to avoid conflict with the First Amendment. In *Abington School District v. Schempp* this Court held unconstitutional the daily reading of Bible verses and the Lord's Prayer in the public schools, despite the school district's assertion of such secular purposes as "the promotion of moral values, the contradiction to the materialistic trends of our times, the perpetuation of our institutions and the teaching of literature."

The pre-eminent purpose for posting the Ten Commandments on schoolroom walls is plainly religious in nature. The Ten Commandments are undeniably a sacred text in the Jewish and Christian faiths, and no legislative recitation of a supposed secular purpose can blind us to that fact. The Commandments do not confine themselves to arguably secular matters, such as honoring one's parents, killing or murder, adultery, stealing, false witness, and covetousness. Rather, the first part of the Commandments concerns the religious duties of believers: worshipping the Lord God alone, avoiding idolatry, not using the Lord's name in vain, and observing the Sabbath Day.

This is not a case in which the Ten Commandments are integrated into the school curriculum, where the Bible may constitutionally be used in an appropriate study of history, civilization, ethics, comparative religion, or the like. Posting of religious texts on the wall serves no such educational function. If the posted copies of the Ten Commandments are to have any effect at all, it will be to induce the schoolchildren to read, meditate upon, perhaps to venerate and obey, the Commandments. However desirable this might be as a matter of private devotion, it is not a permissible state objective under the Establishment Clause.

It does not matter that the posted copies of the Ten Commandments are financed by voluntary private contributions, for the mere posting of the copies under the auspices of the legislature provides the "official support of the State … Government" that the Establishment Clause prohibits. Nor is it significant that the Bible verses involved in this case are merely posted on the wall, rather than read aloud … for "it is no defense to urge that the religious practices here may be relatively minor encroachments on the First Amendment."

[T]he judgment below is reversed.

Dissenting VOICES

Justice Rehnquist dissented, taking the majority to task for not accepting Kentucky's effort to integrate the Ten Commandments into the life of students at school.

> The Establishment Clause does not require that the public sector be insulated from all things which may have a religious significance or origin. This Court has recognized that "religion has been closely identified with our history and government," and that "[t]he history of man is inseparable from the history of religion.…" Kentucky has decided to make students aware of this fact by demonstrating the secular impact of the Ten Commandments.

WHAT DO YOU Think?

Exercise 4.8. If a teacher cannot post the Ten Commandments in the classroom, can he or she integrate a recitation of the Ten Commandments into a teaching unit on the tale of Exodus during a Western literature class? Can a public high school offer a course on the Bible and teach about various books and chapters so long as the material is presented from a literary perspective? Why or why not? What is the difference between posting the Ten Commandments in the front of the room and teaching about the Bible in literature class? Is there a danger of offending religious students by teaching the Bible as literature rather than the revealed word of God? Would such offense reflect an unconstitutional establishment of religion?

Exercise 4.9. Even for those who think that posting the Ten Commandments is a good idea and should be allowed under the First Amendment, a major problem remains: Which version should be displayed? There are multiple versions of the Ten Commandments, with different wordings and orderings used by different churches and religions. For example, here are the Ten Commandments according to the Community Baptist Church of Harvest, in Alabama (www.communitybaptistharvestal.com/ten_full.html), which drew them from the book of Exodus 20:3–17. The numbers offered are the line numbers from Exodus, not the Commandment numbers; however, note that the Ten Commandments in this version are not ten at all.

3. Thou shalt have no other gods before me.
4. Thou shalt not make unto thee any graven image, or any likeness *of any thing* that *is* in heaven above, or that *is* in the earth beneath, or that *is* in the water under the earth:
5. Thou shalt not bow down thyself to them, nor serve them: for I the LORD thy God *am* a jealous God, visiting the iniquity of the fathers upon the children unto the third and fourth *generation* of them that hate me;
6. And shewing mercy unto thousands of them that love me, and keep my commandments.
7. Thou shalt not take the name of the LORD thy God in vain; for the LORD will not hold him guiltless that taketh his name in vain.
8. Remember the sabbath day, to keep it holy.
9. Six days shalt thou labour, and do all thy work:
10. But the seventh day *is* the sabbath of the LORD thy God: *in it* thou shalt not do any work, thou, nor thy son, nor thy daughter, thy manservant, nor thy maidservant, nor thy cattle, nor thy stranger that *is* within thy gates:
11. For *in* six days the LORD made heaven and earth, the sea, and all that in them *is*, and rested the seventh day: wherefore the LORD blessed the sabbath day, and hallowed it.
12. Honour thy father and thy mother: that thy days may be long upon the land which the LORD thy God giveth thee.
13. Thou shalt not kill.
14. Thou shalt not commit adultery.
15. Thou shalt not steal.
16. Thou shalt not bear false witness against thy neighbour.
17. Thou shalt not covet thy neighbour's house, thou shalt not covet thy neighbour's wife, nor his manservant, nor his maidservant, nor his ox, nor his ass, nor any thing that *is* thy neighbour's.

Contrast this version with the translation of the Ten Commandments that hung on the wall of Alabama state court judge Roy Moore's courtroom in the 1990s. (A federal district court forced Judge Moore to take down the display, but the controversy propelled him to run for chief justice of the Alabama State Supreme Court in 2000. He won. As chief justice he proceeded to erect another Ten Commandments display in the state supreme court building, only to have another federal court order him to take it down. In the end, the court's business proceeded without the Ten Commandments display hanging and Moore was removed as chief justice by the Alabama Court of the Judiciary in November 2003 for refusing to comply with the court order.)

1. You shall have no other gods before me.
2. You shall not take the name of the Lord your God in vain.
3. You shall not make unto yourself any graven image.
4. Remember the sabbath day, to keep it holy.
5. Honor your father and your mother: that your days may be long.
6. You shall not kill.

7. You shall not commit adultery.
8. You shall not steal.
9. You shall not bear false witness against your neighbour.
10. You shall not covet.

Dozens of variations of the Ten Commandments can be found online; the Roman Catholic, Anglican, Jewish, and Lutheran religions and churches use different translations of the Decalogue, as it is called. The questions of proper order, arrangement, and phraseology, as well as correct meaning and interpretation, themselves raise profound issues of theological doctrine and belief. Does the sheer variety in Ten Commandments presentations reinforce the argument that government should not be meddling in religion and endorsing religious texts, or does all this variety suggest that the Ten Commandments are truly a common denominator for most people?

Exercise 4.10. The Kentucky law included a note that read: "The secular application of the Ten Commandments is clearly seen in its adoption as the fundamental legal code of Western Civilization and the Common Law of the United States." It is not entirely clear what this statement means, but as far as you can interpret it, is it correct? Pick one of the versions of the Ten Commandments above. Make a list of which Commandments are indeed part of our legal code and common law. Which ones are not? Which Commandments could *not* be made law because of the First Amendment ban on religious establishment? Conversely, are there important legal principles and criminal prohibitions that are not contained in the Ten Commandments (the freedom of speech, the free exercise of religion, the ban on rape, the law against genocide, and so forth)?

FOR THE CLASS

Talk Show Debate. On June 17, 1999, in the wake of continuing public concern about the April 20 massacre at Columbine High School in Littleton, Colorado—in which two students roamed the school with guns and shot fellow students and teachers—the U.S. House of Representatives passed a law purporting to give states the power to post the Ten Commandments in public buildings, including public schools. One representative, criticizing the Court's decision in *Stone v. Graham,* said that had the Ten Commandments been posted on the wall at Columbine High, the massacre never would have happened. Do you agree? Set up a TV-style talk show in which a moderator has several guests on either side of the issue. Discuss whether having the Ten Commandments in the classroom will stop school violence.

Season's Greetings! The Court's Agonizing Ambivalence over Christmas Nativity Displays

In 1984 the Supreme Court rendered a decision in *Lynch v. Donnelly,* a case testing the constitutionality of a Christmas display erected by the city of Pawtucket, Rhode Island, in a park in the heart of the city's shopping district.

A nativity scene on the lawn of a Tipton, Iowa, courthouse includes a disclaimer after a complaint filed by the Iowa Civil Liberties Union.

The Pawtucket display included many of the traditional figures and decorations associated with Christmas, including Santa Claus, reindeer, candy-striped poles, a Christmas tree, carolers, cutout figures of a clown, a dancing elephant, a robot, a teddy bear, hundreds of colored lights, a "season's greetings" banner, and at its very center a Christmas crèche (nativity scene). This crèche, which had been part of the annual display for four decades, featured the infant Jesus, Mary and Joseph, angels, shepherds, kings, and barn animals. The Rhode Island American Civil Liberties Union (ACLU) challenged the city's practice of spending public money to prepare and stage the display.

Chief Justice Burger, for the majority, rejected the ACLU's establishment clause attack. He observed that our official history is "replete with official references to the value and invocation of Divine guidance," noting the observance of Thanksgiving and Christmas as religious holidays and the employment of congressional chaplains to conduct daily prayers in the House and Senate. Elaborating the theme of "ceremonial deism," he invoked the motto "In God We Trust" on our dollars and the language "One nation under God" as part of the Pledge of Allegiance to the American flag. Declining to "take a rigid, absolutist view of the establishment clause," Chief Justice Burger found that the crèche scene in Pawtucket was no more religious than these ceremonial invocations upheld in the past and that the crèche had a legitimate secular purpose in celebrating the Christmas holiday and depicting its origins.

In Justice O'Connor's concurrence, she voted to uphold the display but reached the conclusion based on reasoning different from "ceremonial deism." For her, the critical question under the establishment clause was whether the practice constituted a governmental "endorsement" of religion. Such an endorsement violates the establishment clause because it sends "a message to nonadherents that they are outsiders, not full members of the political community, and an accompanying message to adherents that they are insiders, favored members of the political community." Justice O'Connor found that the "evident purpose of including the crèche in the larger display was not promotion of the religious content of the crèche but celebration of the public holiday through its traditional symbols." This "is a legitimate secular purpose." Moreover, the effect of having the crèche as part of the holiday display is not religious, since "the overall holiday setting changes what viewers may fairly understand to be the purpose of the display." In other words, the reindeer, the robot, the elves, Santa Claus, and the elephant counteracted the religiosity of the manger scene.

The four dissenters in *Lynch*—Justices Brennan, Marshall, Blackmun, and Stevens—considered the majority's opinion an outrageous betrayal of establishment clause principles. They saw the religious endorsement as clear. Justice Brennan could find no secular purpose in having the crèche at all and quoted testimony by town officials that its actual purpose was to "keep Christ in Christmas." The effect of the nativity scene, he argued, was "to place the government's imprimatur of approval on the particular religious beliefs exemplified by the crèche." He rejected the claim that the overall holiday context somehow removed the religious character of the central manger scene, for "the crèche retains a specifically Christian religious meaning," which is "the characteristically Christian belief that a divine savior was brought into the world and that the purpose of this miraculous birth was to illuminate a path toward salvation and redemption."

Justice O'Connor later became the "swing vote," and her "endorsement" analysis became decisive, in *County of Allegheny v. American Civil Liberties Union, Greater Pittsburgh Chapter* (1989), which considered two more holiday displays. The first one was a crèche nativity scene, decorated only with an angel and a banner proclaiming, "Gloria in Excelsis Deo," placed on the grand staircase of the Allegheny County Courthouse. The second was a Hanukkah menorah placed next to a Christmas tree and a sign saluting "liberty" outside the City-County Building.

A five-person majority on the Court, including Justice O'Connor, voted to strike down the crèche because it was placed centrally inside the county courthouse and in such a way that its bare religious message was unadorned by such secular holiday imagery as reindeer or dancing elephants.

However, the majority upheld the outdoor display of the menorah and Christmas tree as a mere secular recognition "that both Christmas and Hanukkah are part of the same winter-holiday season." Justice Kennedy, writing for himself and Chief Justice Rehnquist and Justices White and Scalia, would have allowed both displays as less religious in nature than other cases of "ceremonial deism" accepted by the Court. Justices Brennan, Marshall, and Stevens would have struck down both displays as impermissible placement of "indisputably" religious symbols on public property for purely religious reasons.

Where would you come down on this tough problem? Pretend your class is your city or county council and a group has proposed that you set up a holiday display in a major public park near a shopping center and a high school. Some people don't want it. Most people do. Some want a nativity scene, and others do not. What creative responses can you come up with? What will you do? How will you make sure that any holiday display is constitutional? If you have a nativity scene, do you need to add some reindeer, some elves, and some dancing elephants to offset the religious message?

FOR THE CLASS

Draft a School Board Policy on Holiday Programs. During the Christmas/Hanukkah/Kwanzaa period, public and secular private schools explore how to properly observe a holiday season saturated with religious feeling. No school wants to be the grinch that steals the joy of the holiday season, but how do you put on holiday programs that do not cross the line? After all, many religions—Judaism, Islam, Hinduism, for example—do not celebrate Christmas at all, and some that do, such as Greek Orthodox or Serbian Orthodox, celebrate Christmas at a different time of year.

Many public schools have students sing songs and perform skits in holiday shows that celebrate Christmas because Christianity is the majority religion in the local area. Should schools be required to offer a sampling of religious traditions so that every child's tradition is represented? What about atheist families that object to any religious overtones in official school programs? Should there be no mention at all of Christmas, Hanukkah, or Kwanzaa? Turn your class into a school board to discuss this big problem. Vote on a systemwide policy for appropriate holiday programs and decorations.

One Nation, under Canada, with Constitutional Controversy for All: New Conflict over the Pledge of Allegiance

Michael Newdow, a doctor and lawyer who argued his own case that resulted in the Pledge of Allegiance being called unconstitutional in the Ninth Circuit Court of Appeals, talks to the press about the pledge at his home on June 27, 2002, in Sacramento, California. After the ruling against the "under God" language he received death threats on his answering machine. The U.S. Supreme Court reversed.

The Supreme Court's landmark decision in *West Virginia v. Barnette* (1943) did not put an end to public controversy over the Pledge of Allegiance in public schools. Today we face lively debate over whether the words "under God" violate the establishment clause.

The Pledge of Allegiance was written in 1892 (on the 400th anniversary of Christopher Columbus's arrival in America) and has been modified over the years. The original pledge was written by Francis Bellamy, a Baptist minister, socialist, and antiracist agitator who sought to unify the country around the American flag. He wanted to replace the continuing salutes and nostalgic rituals developing around the Confederate battle flag in the South with a culture of national allegiance to the flag of freedom. Bellamy was emphatic that his pledge avoid mention of God, because he thought it would be socially divisive. The pledge proved hugely popular and spread across the country.

But in 1954, at the height of the cold war and just several weeks after the Supreme Court's decision in *Brown v. Board of Education,* Congress added the words "under God" to the codified Pledge of Allegiance in federal law. President Dwight D. Eisenhower said, "In this way we are reaffirming the transcendence of religious faith in America's heritage and future; in this way we shall constantly strengthen those spiritual weapons which forever will be our country's most powerful resource in peace and war."

In the following remarkable case brought in the Ninth Circuit Court of Appeals in 2002, Dr. Michael Newdow—a father, a doctor, a lawyer, and an atheist—argued that the addition of the words "under God" to the Pledge of Allegiance violated the establishment clause. After hearing him argue his case and the government response, a three-judge panel struck down government-run Pledge of Allegiance rituals that include the words "under God." The U.S. Senate voted 99–0 in June 2002 to denounce the decision, and a firestorm of criticism swept the country. The decision was then "stayed" (put on hold); however, the full Ninth Circuit Court of Appeals affirmed the ruling of the three-judge panel. Here is the panel decision.

NEWDOW v. U.S. CONGRESS

United States Court of Appeals for the Ninth Circuit
Argued March 14, 2002.
Decided June 26, 2002.

Majority OPINION   GOODWIN, Circuit Judge.

Michael Newdow appeals a judgment dismissing his challenge to the constitutionality of the words "under God" in the Pledge of Allegiance to the Flag. Newdow argues that the addition of these words by a 1954 federal statute to the previous version of the Pledge of Allegiance (which made no reference to God) and the daily recitation in the classroom of the Pledge of Allegiance, with the added words included, by his daughter's public school teacher are violations of the Establishment Clause of the First Amendment to the United States Constitution.

FACTUAL AND PROCEDURAL BACKGROUND

Newdow is an atheist whose daughter attends public elementary school in the Elk Grove Unified School District ("EGUSD") in California. In accordance with state law and a school district rule, EGUSD teachers begin each school day by leading their students in a recitation of the Pledge of Allegiance ("the Pledge"). The California Education Code requires that public schools begin each school day with "appropriate patriotic exercises" and that "[t]he giving of the Pledge of Allegiance to the Flag of the United States of America shall satisfy" this requirement....

DISCUSSION

... D. Establishment Clause

... Over the last three decades, the Supreme Court has used three interrelated tests to analyze alleged violations of the Establishment Clause in the realm of public education: the three-prong test set forth in *Lemon v. Kurtzman;* the "endorsement" test, first articulated by Justice O'Connor in her concurring opinion in *Lynch v. Donnelly,* and later adopted by a majority of the Court in *County of Allegheny v. ACLU;* and the "coercion" test first used by the Court in *Lee v. Weisman.*

We are free to apply any or all of the three tests, and to invalidate any measure that fails any one of them. Although this court has typically applied the *Lemon* test to alleged Establishment Clause violations, we are not required to apply it if a practice fails one of the other tests. Nevertheless, for purposes of completeness, we will analyze the school district policy and the 1954 Act under all three tests.

We first consider whether the 1954 Act and the EGUSD's policy of teacher-led Pledge recitation survive the endorsement test.

In the context of the Pledge, the statement that the United States is a nation "under God" is an endorsement of religion. It is a profession of a religious belief, namely, a belief in monotheism. The recitation that ours is a nation "under God" is not a mere acknowledgment that many Americans believe in a deity. Nor is it merely descriptive of the undeniable historical significance of religion in the founding of the Republic. Rather, the phrase "one nation under God" in the context of the Pledge is normative. To recite the Pledge is not to describe the United States; instead, it is to swear allegiance to the values for which the flag stands: unity, indivisibility, liberty, justice, and—since 1954—monotheism. The text of the official Pledge, codified in federal law, impermissibly takes a position with respect to the purely religious question of the existence and identity of God. A profession that we are a nation "under God" is identical, for Establishment Clause purposes, to a profession that we are a nation "under Jesus," a nation "under Vishnu," a nation "under Zeus," or a nation "under no god," because none of these professions can be neutral with respect to religion. "[T]he government must pursue a course of complete neutrality toward religion." Furthermore, the school district's practice of teacher-led recitation of the Pledge aims to inculcate in students a respect for the ideals set forth in the Pledge, and thus amounts to state endorsement of these ideals. Although students cannot be forced to participate in recitation of the Pledge, the school district is nonetheless conveying a message of state endorsement of a religious belief when it requires public school teachers to recite, and lead the recitation of, the current form of the Pledge.

The Pledge, as currently codified, is an impermissible government endorsement of religion because it sends a message to unbelievers "that they are outsiders, not full members of the political community, and an accompanying message to adherents that they are insiders, favored members of the political community." ... To be sure, no one is obligated to recite this phrase ... but it borders on sophistry to suggest that the reasonable atheist would not feel less than a full member of the political community every time his fellow Americans recited, as part of their expression of patriotism and love for country, a phrase he believed to be false.

Similarly, the policy and the Act fail the coercion test. The policy and the Act place students in the untenable position of choosing between participating in an exercise with religious content or protesting. "What to most believers may seem nothing more than a reasonable request that the nonbeliever respect their religious practices, in a school context may appear to the nonbeliever or dissenter to be an attempt to employ the machinery of the State to enforce a religious orthodoxy." Although the defendants argue that the religious content of "one nation under God" is minimal, to an atheist or a believer in certain non-Judeo-Christian religions or philosophies, it may reasonably appear to be an attempt to enforce a "religious orthodoxy" of monotheism, and is therefore impermissible. The coercive effect of this policy is particularly pronounced in the school setting given the age and impressionability of schoolchildren, and their understanding that they are required to adhere to the norms set by their school, their teacher and their fellow students. The mere fact that a pupil is required to listen every day to the statement "one nation under God" has a coercive effect. The coercive effect of the Act is apparent from its context and legislative history, which indicate that the Act was designed to result in the daily recitation of the words "under God" in school classrooms.... Therefore, the policy and the Act fail the coercion test.

Finally we turn to the *Lemon* test, the first prong of which asks if the challenged policy has a secular purpose. Historically, the primary purpose of the 1954 Act was to advance religion, in conflict with the first prong of the *Lemon* test. The federal defendants "do not dispute that the words 'under God' were intended to recognize a Supreme Being," at a time when the government was publicly inveighing against atheistic communism. Nonetheless, the federal defendants argue that the Pledge must be considered as a whole when assessing whether it has a secular purpose. They claim that the Pledge has the secular purpose of "solemnizing public occasions, expressing confidence in the future, and encouraging the recognition of what is worthy of appreciation in society."

The flaw in defendants' argument is that it looks at the text of the Pledge "as a whole," and glosses over the 1954 Act.

We apply the purpose prong of the *Lemon* test to the amendment that added the words "under God" to the Pledge, not to the Pledge in its final version. The legislative history of the 1954 Act reveals that the Act's *sole* purpose was to advance religion, in order to differentiate the United States from nations under communist rule. "[T]he First Amendment requires that a statute must be invalidated if it is entirely motivated by a purpose to advance religion." The purpose of the 1954 Act was to take a position on the question of theism, namely, to support the existence and moral authority of God, while "deny[ing] ... atheistic and materialistic concepts." Such a purpose runs counter to the Establishment Clause, which prohibits the government's endorsement or advancement not only of one particular religion at the expense of other religions, but also of religion at the expense of atheism.

[T]he Court has unambiguously concluded that the individual freedom of conscience protected by the First Amendment embraces the right to select any religious faith or none at all. This conclusion derives support not only from the interest in respecting the individual's freedom of conscience, but also from the conviction that religious beliefs worthy of respect are the product of a free and voluntary choice by the faithful, and from recognition of the fact that the political interest in forestalling intolerance extends beyond intolerance among Christian sects—or even intolerance among "religions"—to encompass intolerance of the disbeliever and the uncertain.

Similarly, the school district policy also fails the *Lemon* test. Although it survives the first prong of *Lemon* because, as even Newdow concedes, the school district had the secular purpose of fostering patriotism in enacting the policy, the policy fails the second prong. The second *Lemon* prong asks "whether the challenged government action is sufficiently likely to be perceived by adherents of the controlling denominations as an endorsement, and by the nonadherents as a disapproval, of their individual religious choices." Given the age and impressionability of schoolchildren, as discussed above, particularly within the confined environment of the classroom, the policy is highly likely to convey an impermissible message of endorsement to some and disapproval to others of their beliefs regarding the existence of a monotheistic God. Therefore the policy fails the effects prong of *Lemon*, and fails the *Lemon* test. In sum, both the policy and the Act fail the *Lemon* test as well as the endorsement and coercion tests....

The Supreme Court's Curious Response to *Newdow v. U.S. Congress*

When this ruling on behalf of Michael Newdow was appealed to the U.S. Supreme Court in *Elk Grove Unified School District v. Newdow* (2004), the Court reversed the decision on most curious grounds. It found that Michael Newdow, as the father in the case, had no "standing" to challenge the wording of the Pledge of Allegiance because he was not the legal custodian of his daughter, who lived with her mother. The Court felt that he did not have a sufficient legal stake in the outcome of the case to justify handing down a decision. Thus, the constitutional issue was postponed for another day and remains a live question.

Although the Court majority did not address the merits of the underlying constitutional issue, three justices—Chief Justice Rehnquist, Justice O'Connor, and Justice Thomas—wanted to. They would have decided that it does not violate the establishment clause to include the words "under God" in the Pledge.

Chief Justice Rehnquist wrote that

> [G]overnment can, in a discrete category of cases, acknowledge or refer to the divine without offending the Constitution. This category of 'ceremonial deism' most clearly encompasses such things as the national motto ('In God We Trust'), religious references in traditional patriotic songs such as the 'Star-Spangled Banner,' and the words with which the Marshal of this Court opens each of its sessions ('God save the United States and this honorable Court'). These references are not minor trespasses upon the Establishment Clause to which I turn a blind eye. Instead, their history, character, and context prevent them from being constitutional violations at all.

Chief Justice Rehnquist treated "under God" in the Pledge of Allegiance as another harmless instance of "ceremonial deism." He invoked several key factors for that finding, including the fact that the country has used the phrase for fifty years:

> In that time, the Pledge has become, alongside the singing of the 'Star-Spangled Banner,' our most routine ceremonial act of patriotism; countless schoolchildren recite it daily, and their religious heterogeneity reflects that of the Nation as a whole. As a result, the Pledge and the context in which it is employed are familiar and nearly inseparable in the public mind.

He was also persuaded by the fact that the "under God" language did not pick and choose among many competing religions but spoke in broad terms. "It does not refer to a nation 'under Jesus' or 'under Vishnu,' but instead acknowledges religion in a general way: a simple reference to a generic 'God.'"

Chief Justice Rehnquist also cited the Pledge's "minimal religious content."

> [Michael Newdow's] challenge focuses on only two of the Pledge's 31 words. Moreover, the presence of those words is not absolutely essential to the Pledge, as demonstrated by the fact that it existed without them for over 50 years. As a result, students who wish to avoid saying the words 'under God' still can consider themselves

meaningful participants in the exercise if they join in reciting the remainder of the Pledge.

WHAT DO YOU **Think?**

Exercise 4.11. Would it make sense to compel the government to drop "under God" in the Pledge of Allegiance and then simply to allow students who want to add it in their verbal recitation of the Pledge to do so? Or should "under God" be left in the Pledge and then those who want to omit it while speaking be allowed to do so? Which solution makes more sense under the First Amendment?

Exercise 4.12. Do you agree with the Supreme Court's ruling on Michael Newdow's standing? Imagine that a child is being punished for praying at her locker. Would the Supreme Court reject a lawsuit by the student's father on "standing" grounds if the child lived primarily with her mother? Also, would the Supreme Court find there is no standing if the child lived primarily with the father and the mother sued?

Exercise 4.13. Some people are insisting that if "under God" is dropped from the Pledge, something needs to replace it. What are the pros and cons of the following candidates? Which ones are constitutional?

- "one nation, under Jesus Christ"
- "one nation, under Vishnu"
- "one nation, under Canada"
- "one nation, under the Constitution"
- "one nation, under the threat of global warming"
- "one nation, under the Supreme Court"
- "one nation, under the will of the people"

Exercise 4.14. Between its decisions in *Gobitis* in 1940 and *Barnette* in 1943, the Supreme Court changed its mind about the constitutionality of requiring students to pledge allegiance or face suspension or expulsion. (See Chapter 2.) One of the reasons the Court changed course is that Jehovah's Witness children were facing serious harassment by classmates and punishment at school for refusing to participate. Are students who object to saying "under God" facing similar problems today? If not, does this make it less likely that the Supreme Court will act on their behalf? Should this issue even be relevant?

The Free Exercise Rights of Religious Americans

As we have seen, one issue courts face is how schools may, or may not, make religion a part of the educational experience. Another is the extent to which parents can use religion to keep their kids *out* of school or particular school activities.

In this famous decision about the free exercise of religion, the Supreme Court upheld the right of Amish families to stop sending their children to school after eighth grade. Does the holding apply broadly to people and children of *all* faiths, or are there unique, compelling facts about the Amish community that justify this exception?

··

WISCONSIN v. YODER

Supreme Court of the United States
Argued Dec. 8, 1971.
Decided May 15, 1972.

Majority OPINION　Chief Justice BURGER delivered the opinion of the Court....

Respondents Jonas Yoder and Wallace Miller are members of the Old Order Amish religion, and respondent Adin Yutzy is a member of the Conservative Amish Mennonite Church. They and their families are residents of Green County, Wisconsin. Wisconsin's compulsory school-attendance law required them to cause their children to attend public or private school until reaching age 16 but the respondents declined to send their children, ages 14 and 15, to public school after they complete the eighth grade. The children were not enrolled in any private school, or within any recognized exception to the compulsory attendance law, and they are conceded to be subject to the Wisconsin statute.

... [R]espondents were charged, tried, and convicted of violating the compulsory attendance law in Green County Court and were fined the sum of $5 each. Respondents defended on the ground that the application of the compulsory-attendance law violated their rights under the First and Fourteenth Amendments. The trial testimony showed that respondents believed, in accordance with the tenets of Old Order Amish communities generally, that their children's attendance at high school, public or private, was contrary to the Amish religion and way of life. They believed that by sending their children to high school, they would not only expose themselves to the danger of the censure of the church community, but also endanger their own salvation and that of their children. The State stipulated that respondents' religious beliefs were sincere....

A related feature of Old Order Amish communities is their devotion to a life in harmony with nature and the soil, as exemplified by the simple life of the early Christian era that continued in America during much of our early national life. Amish beliefs require members of the community to make their living by farming or closely related activities....

Amish objection to formal education beyond the eighth grade is firmly grounded in these central religious concepts. They object to the high school, and higher education generally, because the values they teach are in marked variance with Amish values and the Amish way of life.... The high school tends to emphasize intellectual and scientific accomplishments, self-distinction, competitiveness, worldly success, and social life with other students. Amish society emphasizes informal learning through doing; a life of "goodness," rather than a life of intellect; wisdom, rather than technical knowledge; community welfare, rather than competition; and separation from, rather than integration with, contemporary worldly society.

Formal high school education beyond the eighth grade is contrary to Amish beliefs, not only because it places Amish children in an environment hostile to Amish beliefs ... but also because it takes them away from their community, physically and emotionally, during the crucial and formative adolescent period of life. During this period, the children must acquire Amish attitudes favoring manual work and self-reliance and the specific skills needed to perform the adult role of an Amish farmer or housewife. They must learn to enjoy physical labor. Once a child has learned basic reading, writing, and elementary mathematics, these traits, skills, and attitudes admittedly fall within the category of those best learned through example and "doing" rather than in a classroom. And, at this time in life, the Amish child must also grow in his faith and his relationship to the Amish community if he is to be prepared to accept the heavy obligations imposed by adult baptism. In short, high school attendance with teachers who are not of the Amish faith and may even be hostile to it interposes a serious barrier to the integration of the Amish child into the Amish religious community....

... The testimony of Dr. Donald A. Erickson, an expert witness on education, showed that the Amish succeed in preparing their high school age children to be productive members of the Amish community. He described their system of learning through doing the skills directly relevant to their adult roles in the Amish community as "ideal" and perhaps superior to ordinary high school education. The evidence also showed that the Amish have an excellent record as law-abiding and generally self-sufficient members of society....

I

There is no doubt as to the power of a State, having a high responsibility for education of its citizens, to impose reasonable regulations for the control and duration of basic education.... [A] State's interest in universal education, however highly we rank it, is not totally free from a balancing process when it impinges on fundamental rights and interests, such as those specifically protected by the Free Exercise Clause of the First Amendment, and the traditional interest of parents with respect to the religious upbringing of their children....

It follows that in order for Wisconsin to compel school attendance beyond the eighth grade against a claim that such attendance interferes with the practice of a legitimate religious belief, it must appear either that the State does not deny the free exercise of religious belief by its requirement, or that there is a state interest of sufficient magnitude to override the interest claiming protection under the Free Exercise Clause....

The essence of all that has been said and written on the subject is that only those interests of the highest order and those not otherwise served can overbalance legitimate claims to the free exercise of religion....

II

We come then to the quality of the claims of the respondents concerning the alleged encroachment of Wisconsin's compulsory school-attendance statute on their rights and the rights of their children to the free exercise of the religious beliefs they and their forbears have adhered to for almost three centuries. In evaluating those claims we must be careful to determine whether the Amish religious faith and their mode of life are, as they claim, inseparable and interdependent. A way of life, however virtuous and admirable, may not be interposed as a barrier to reasonable state regulation of education if it is based on purely secular considerations; to have the protection of the Religion Clauses, the claims must be rooted in religious belief.... Thus, if the Amish asserted their claims because of their subjective evaluation and rejection of the contemporary secular values accepted by the majority, much as Thoreau rejected the social values of his time and isolated himself at Walden Pond, their claims would not rest on a religious basis....

... [T]he record in this case abundantly supports the claim that the traditional way of life of the Amish is not merely a matter of personal preference, but one of deep religious conviction, shared by an organized group, and intimately related to daily living. That the Old Order Amish daily life and religious practice stem from their faith is shown by the fact that it is in response to their literal interpretation of the Biblical injunction from the Epistle of Paul to the Romans, "be not conformed to this world...." This command is fundamental to the Amish faith. Moreover, for the Old Order Amish, religion is not simply a matter of theocratic belief. As the expert witnesses explained, the Old Order Amish religion pervades and determines virtually their entire way of life, regulating it with the detail of the Talmudic diet through the strictly enforced rules of the church community....

The impact of the compulsory-attendance law on respondents' practice of the Amish religion is not only severe, but inescapable, for the Wisconsin law affirmatively compels them, under threat of criminal sanction, to perform acts undeniably at odds with fundamental tenets of their religious beliefs. Nor is the impact of the compulsory-attendance law confined to grave interference with important Amish religious tenets from a subjective point of view. It carries with it precisely the kind of objective danger to the free exercise of religion that the First Amendment was designed to prevent. As the record shows, compulsory school attendance to age 16 for Amish children carries with it a very real threat of undermining the Amish community and religious practice as they exist today; they must either abandon belief and be assimilated into society at large, or be forced to migrate to some other and more tolerant region.

In sum, the unchallenged testimony of acknowledged experts in education and religious history, almost 300 years of consistent practice, and strong evidence of a sustained faith pervading and regulating respondents' entire mode of life support the claim that enforcement of the State's requirement of compulsory formal education after the eighth grade would gravely endanger if not destroy the free exercise of respondents' religious beliefs.

III

... We turn, then, to the State's broader contention that its interest in its system of compulsory education is so compelling that even the established religious practices of the Amish must give way. Where fundamental claims of religious freedom are at stake, however, we cannot accept such a sweeping claim; despite its admitted validity in the generality of cases, we must searchingly examine the interests that the State seeks to promote by its requirement for compulsory education to age 16, and the impediment to those objectives that would flow from recognizing the claimed Amish exemption.

The State advances two primary arguments in support of its system of compulsory education. It notes ... that some degree of education is necessary to prepare citizens to participate effectively and intelligently in our open political system if we are to preserve freedom and independence. Further, education prepares individuals to be self-reliant and self-sufficient participants in society. We accept these propositions.

However, the evidence adduced by the Amish in this case is persuasively to the effect that an additional one or two years of formal high school for Amish children in place of their long-established program of informal vocational education would do little to serve those interests.... It is one thing to say that compulsory education for a year or two beyond the eighth grade may be necessary when its goal is the preparation of the child for life in modern society as the majority live, but it is quite another if the goal of education be viewed as the preparation of the child for life in the separated agrarian community that is the keystone of the Amish faith.

... No one can question the State's duty to protect children from ignorance but this argument does not square with the facts disclosed in the record. Whatever their idiosyncrasies as seen by the majority, this record strongly shows that the Amish community has been a highly successful social unit within our society, even if apart from the conventional "mainstream." Its members are productive and very law-abiding members of society; they reject public welfare in any of its usual modern forms....

The State, however, supports its interest in providing an additional one or two years of compulsory high school education to Amish children because of the possibility that some such children will choose to leave the Amish community, and that if this occurs they will be ill-equipped for life.... However, on this record, that argument is highly speculative. There is no specific evidence of the loss of Amish adherents by attrition, nor is there any showing that upon leaving the Amish community Amish children, with their practical agricultural training and habits of industry and self-reliance, would become burdens on society because of educational shortcomings. Indeed, this argument of the State appears to rest primarily on the State's mistaken assumption, already noted, that the Amish do not provide any education for their children beyond the eighth grade, but allow them to grow in "ignorance." To the contrary, not only do the Amish accept the necessity for formal schooling through the eighth grade level, but continue to provide what has been characterized by the undisputed testimony of expert educators as an "ideal" vocational education for their children in the adolescent years....

Insofar as the State's claim rests on the view that a brief additional period of formal education is imperative to enable the Amish to participate effectively and intelligently in our democratic process, it must fall. The Amish alternative to formal secondary school education has enabled them to function effectively in their day-to-day life under self-imposed limitations on relations with the world, and to survive and prosper in contemporary society as a separate, sharply identifiable and highly self-sufficient community for more than 200 years in this country. In itself this is strong evidence that they are capable of fulfilling the social and political responsibilities of citizenship without compelled attendance beyond the eighth grade at the price of jeopardizing their free exercise of religious belief....

V

... [W]e hold ... that the First and Fourteenth amendments prevent the State from compelling respondents to cause their children to attend formal high school to age 16....

Affirmed.

Dissenting VOICES

Justice Douglas dissented in part, because he thought that the majority decision ignored the rights of young people. He rejected "the Court's conclusion that the matter is within the dispensation of parents alone. The Court's analysis assumes that the only interests at stake in the case are those of the Amish parents on the one hand, and those of the State on the other."

He argued that the case could not be resolved without hearing from the Amish children themselves:

> Religion is an individual experience. It is not necessary, nor even appropriate, for every Amish child to express his views on the subject in a prosecution of a single adult. Crucial, however, are the views of the child whose parent is the subject of the suit. Frieda Yoder has in fact testified that her own religious views are opposed to high-school education. I therefore join the judgment of the Court as to respondent Jonas Yoder. But Frieda Yoder's views may not be those of Vernon Yutzy or Barbara Miller. I must dissent, therefore, as to respondents Adin Yutzy and Wallace Miller as their motion to dismiss also raised the question of their children's religious liberty.

Invoking *Barnette* and *Tinker*, Justice Douglas reminded the Court that "children are 'persons' within the meaning of the Bill of Rights. We have so held over and over again." Thus, their rights both to religious liberty and to education count:

JUSTICES: A CLOSER LOOK

JUSTICE WILLIAM O. DOUGLAS (1898–1980) was born poor and sickly in the town of Maine, Minnesota. Because he had polio, he was small and faced ridicule from other children. He turned to sports and outdoor activities to build up his body and self-esteem and thus began a lifelong passion for nature and the environment. He went to Whitman College in Walla Walla, Washington, and in the fall of 1922 hitch-hiked his way across the country, sleeping and eating with hobos, to enter Columbia Law School, where he graduated second in his class. Douglas spent many years at the Securities and Exchange Commission and was a key component of the New Deal brain trust in Washington, D.C. President Franklin Delano Roosevelt appointed him to the Supreme Court in 1939. He served as a justice for thirty-six years, longer than any other justice of his time.

HIGHLIGHTS

- Douglas was married four times. When he was sixty-eight years old, he married a twenty-three-year-old college student.
- Douglas was the foremost naturalist, explorer, and hiker ever to serve on the Court, and he frequently hiked the C&O Canal in Washington, D.C.
- A prolific writer, Justice Douglas was especially fond of writing about his adventuresome travels abroad.

On this important and vital matter of education, I think the children should be entitled to be heard. While the parents, absent dissent, normally speak for the entire family, the education of the child is a matter on which the child will often have decided views. He may want to be a pianist or an astronaut or an oceanographer. To do so he will have to break from the Amish tradition.

It is the future of the student, not the future of the parents, that is imperiled by today's decision. If a parent keeps his child out of school beyond the grade school, then the child will be forever barred from entry into the new and amazing world of diversity that we have today. The child may decide that is the preferred course, or he may rebel. It is the student's judgment, not his parents', that is essential if we are to give full meaning to what we have said about the Bill of Rights and of the right of students to be masters of their own destiny.... The child, therefore, should be given an opportunity to be heard before the State gives the exemption which we honor today.

Justice Douglas also rejected "the emphasis of the Court on the 'law and order' record of this Amish group of people" as a distraction from the real constitutional issue of whether invoking the free exercise of religion exempts people from truancy laws. "A religion is a religion," Justice Douglas wrote, "irrespective of what the misdemeanor or felony records of its members might be. I am not at all sure how the Catholics, Episcopalians, the Baptists, Jehovah's Witnesses, the Unitarians, and my own Presbyterians would make out if subjected to such a test...."

WHAT DO YOU **Think?**

Exercise 4.15. Do you think that the Yoder right to opt out of school after eighth grade should attach to other religious communities too? Must other faith communities first show that their "way of life" is threatened by high school education? On what basis does the Court find that Amish children are getting a sufficient education and sufficient exposure to democratic principles? Since the Amish do not vote, in what sense are they being prepared in a meaningful way for democratic citizenship in their community?

Exercise 4.16. The Amish, who number more than 100,000, mostly in Pennsylvania, Ohio, and Indiana, have a religious practice called *Rumspringa,* which is translated from Pennsylvania Dutch as a period of "running around." During this period, sixteen-year–old boys and girls are permitted to live outside the otherwise strictly conservative rules of the Amish community. They are allowed to see movies, watch television, socialize with "English" (non-Amish) youngsters, and engage in many other activities forbidden at any other time. Thus, given that some small number of Amish teenagers will subsequently leave their community, why shouldn't they indeed be forced to go to high school? Will they be prepared for adulthood if they don't go?

Exercise 4.17. The 2002 documentary film *The Devil's Playground* follows several Amish youth through Rumspringa and shows dramatic footage of them smoking, drinking alcohol, using such drugs as crystal meth and crack cocaine, having premarital sexual relations, getting into car accidents, and generally spinning out of control. In 1997 two young Amish men—Abner King Stoltzfus, twenty-three, and Abner Stoltzfus, twenty-four —were arrested in Lancaster County, Pennsylvania, by state police on charges of dealing cocaine in conjunction with a vicious motorcycle gang called the Pagans. After a sensational trial (one headline read, "Horse and Druggies"), the two defendants were convicted and sentenced to a year in a halfway house. Does the holding in Yoder take into account the Rumspringa rite of passage? Does the Court's decision reflect more of an idealized image of the Amish than the reality of the community's somewhat more familiar problems?

FOR THE CLASS

Religious Freedom or Child Neglect? As Justice Douglas suggests, this decision values the religious wishes of Amish parents but undervalues the rights of Amish children to a high school education that might prepare them to make their own decisions about their future. Who was right in this case, the Yoders or the state of Wisconsin?

It is not clear how *Yoder* would be decided today. In *Employment Division v. Smith* (1990), the Supreme Court rejected a free exercise challenge by members of the Native American Church to state policies banning the use of peyote, which the Indians see as an important part of their sacrament. The Court found that *incidental* burdens on religious exercise do not trigger scrutiny. Neutral and universally applicable laws not undertaken for purposes of religious harassment are presumed to be legitimate. Thus, a truancy law such as Wisconsin's would also be so presumed.

The Theory of Evolution and the Story of Creation: An Ongoing Duel in the Classroom

What happens in high school classrooms when science makes discoveries about the natural world that contradict the religious beliefs of a large number of citizens? Should such scientific theories be taught? Should they be censored? Should they be balanced with "equal time" for religiously based theories? Or is there no place at all for religious indoctrination in the classroom?

Nowhere has this problem been posed more dramatically than in the science classroom when it comes to teaching about human evolution and the doctrine that is sometimes called Darwinism. The classroom war between evolutionary science and religious creationism has gone on for more than seventy-five years.

One of the most famous trials in our nation's history was the so-called Scopes Monkey Trial, which took place in the sweltering summer of 1925 in Tennessee. The case, which arose in the midst of rising religious fundamentalism, involved the criminal prosecution of John T. Scopes, a twenty-four-year-old science teacher and football coach, for teaching evolution in violation of a recently passed state law banning the theory of evolution from the classroom. Scopes had the support of the American Civil Liberties Union and was represented by the legendary Clarence Darrow, who wanted to show that the antievolution statute was an attempt to establish a religious law and substitute nonsense for knowledge.

Don Aguillard, a teacher at Acadiana High School in Scott, Louisiana, filed suit against the state's equal time for creation science law in 1981. Six years later, in *Edwards v. Aguillard*, the Supreme Court found that law to be in violation of the establishment clause.

The lawyer for the state of Tennessee was the eloquent populist orator William Jennings Bryan. A former secretary of state in the Woodrow Wilson administration, Bryan saw the trial as a showdown between evolution and Christianity.

The key moment in the trial arrived when Darrow called Bryan himself to the stand and examined him on whether or not he believed that everything recorded in the Bible was literally true. After interrogating him about biblical stories such as the Tower of Babel and Jonah being swallowed by the whale, Darrow zeroed in on the origins of Earth:

CLARENCE DARROW: "Do you think the earth was made in six days?"

WILLIAM JENNINGS BRYAN: "Not six days of 24 hours.... My impression is they were periods...."

DARROW: "Now, if you call those periods, they may have been a very long time?"

BRYAN: "They might have been."

DARROW: "The creation might have been going on for a very long time?"

BRYAN: "It might have continued for millions of years...."

Thus Darrow exploded Bryan's determination not to depart from the biblical text and radically shifted public sentiment in favor of Scopes and evolution. Still, the jury returned with a guilty verdict and the judge ordered Scopes to pay a fine of $100, the lowest allowed under the law. In his parting words to the court, Scopes said: "Your Honor, I feel that I have been convicted of violating an unjust statute. I will continue in the future ... to oppose this law in any way I can. Any other action would be in violation of my idea of academic freedom." Scopes's conviction was later reversed in the Tennessee Supreme Court on technical grounds.

The Scopes trial did not put the controversy over teaching evolution to rest. In 1968 the issue finally reached the Supreme Court in the landmark case *Epperson v. Arkansas*. There the Court struck down a similar "antievolution" law in Arkansas that made it illegal for public school teachers "to teach the theory or doctrine that mankind ascended or descended from a lower order of animals." The Court found that this law violated the establishment clause of the First Amendment because it "selects from the body of knowledge a particular segment which it proscribes for the sole reason that it is deemed to conflict with a particular religious doctrine." The Court said that it was "clear that fundamentalist sectarian conviction was … the law's reason for existence."

Epperson was a relatively easy case. But what about *Edward v. Aguillard,* a case that reached the Court almost twenty years later in 1987? In that decision, the Supreme Court struck down a Louisiana statute that prevented public school teachers from "teaching the theory of evolution in public schools unless accompanied by instruction in 'creation science,'" the controversial scientific claims developed to support the belief in the biblical version of creation. Despite the fact that the stated purpose of this law was to enhance academic freedom, the Court considered this a "sham," since the law did "not grant teachers a flexibility that they did not already possess to supplement the present science curriculum with the presentation of theories, besides evolution, about the origin of life." Rather, it was clear that the "primary purpose of the Creationism Act … [was] … to endorse a particular religious doctrine."

WHAT DO YOU Think?

Exercise 4.18. Does the holding in *Epperson* make sense, because the clear purpose of the law struck down was to undermine the teaching of evolution with a wholly religious doctrine? Or has the Court unfairly taken sides in a legitimate scientific controversy by declaring one viewpoint religious and in effect banning it? Does the decision actually ban the teaching of creation science even when teachers undertake it voluntarily, or does it just forbid a mandatory "equal time" arrangement? Research "creation science" and "intelligent design theory," both of which are efforts to mobilize scientific evidence and principles in defense of biblical accounts of creation. Are they science or dressed-up religion?

Exercise 4.19. Does the separation of church and state imply that schools can teach scientific truths but not religious truths? What is the difference between science and religion? How do we define each of them? We have a "scientific method." Do we have a "religious method"? Is it fair to religious followers to be in public schools that declare scientific findings "the truth"?

FOR THE CLASS

Evolution Controversy. Imagine a fundamentalist Christian student, Heather Bouler, whose parents do not want her to participate in biology class when evolution is being taught. The teacher is assigning a three-page research paper on the life and work of Charles Darwin and a final exam on modern evolutionary scientific findings. Heather's parents refuse to send her to the class, and the school is threatening to fail her for the whole semester if she does not do her evolution-related work. The family sues in federal court for an injunction against any moves to punish Heather and for her right to study creationism when the rest of the class is studying evolution. Does Heather have a free exercise right to opt out of the evolution section of the biology course? Form two teams and argue Heather's side and the school district's side. Heather's team can start with the *Yoder* decision, and the school's team with the *Smith* decision.

School Board Exercise. Pretend that your class is a school board trying to define a policy governing the teaching of evolution and creation in high school classes. Consider the following options:

1. Teach only the theory of evolution.
2. Teach only the theory of evolution, but include scientific criticisms of it. Explain that many Christians believe in creation for religious reasons.
3. Teach both the theory of evolution and creation science as two equally plausible alternatives.
4. Allow each individual teacher to teach whatever he or she wants according to individual conscience and belief.
5. Allow each individual school to select its preferred curriculum.
6. Teach only creation science, explaining that while this practice is unconstitutional, the school will engage in it as a form of civil disobedience.
7. Teach only the theory of evolution, but allow individual teachers to state their personal beliefs about the origins of humanity.

After discussing the options (including any others you think of), try to form a majority consensus around a solution and take a vote. Do you think your plan is constitutional?

On the Web

First Amendment Center. "A Teacher's Guide to Religion in the Public Schools." www.firstamendmentcenter.org.

"Religion in the Public Schools: A Joint Statement of Current Law." Pamphlet created jointly by a number of religious and public policy organizations. Available at: www.ed.gov/Speeches/04-1995/prayer.html.

U.S. Department of Education. "Religious Expression in Public Schools." www.ed.gov/Speeches/08-1995/religion.html.

THE FOURTH AMENDMENT: SEARCHING THE STUDENT BODY

"The right of the people to be secure in their persons, houses, papers, and effects, against unreasonable searches and seizures, shall not be violated...." THE FOURTH AMENDMENT

"A people who mean to be their own governors, must arm themselves with the power knowledge gives." JAMES MADISON (1822)

Americans generally want to be free from surveillance. But we also want to live in safe environments, free from crime, and this means we often willingly grant large powers to the police and other government agents to protect us. Americans' desire for intensified security measures rose in the wake of the attacks of September 11, 2001, and the explicit threats of Osama Bin Laden and other al-Qaida figures; the anthrax attacks that mysteriously followed; random acts of violence such as the sniper killings in the fall of 2002 that terrified millions in Maryland, Virginia, and Washington, D.C.; and the shooting sprees at schools and universities, such as the horror visited on Virginia Tech University by a mentally ill student in April 2007.

At the same time, many Americans have come to fear that the anxiety-ridden environment and "preemptive" law enforcement tactics of the new century will enable government to trample our freedoms. This kind of fear motivated the authors of our Constitution to add the Bill of Rights shortly after the document was adopted. While the Constitution organized the government to protect us against chaos and violence, the Bill of Rights set forth the inviolable freedoms of the people. Read through the Bill of Rights and pick out the numerous ways that the Framers tried to protect us against unbridled police power.

The tension between our competing desires for security and freedom affects the governance of public schools. While schools work to stop violence, students struggle to maintain not only their safety but also their liberty and privacy. This chapter examines when government authorities may invade students' expectations of privacy and liberty—and when they may not.

The Fourth Amendment does not forbid all government searches and seizures, only *unreasonable* ones. In the world outside of school, the police and government agents cannot conduct a search of your home or person without a search warrant issued by a magistrate and based on probable cause that a crime has been (or is being) committed. In practice, the Supreme Court has relaxed this warrant requirement. In *Terry v. Ohio* (1968), the Supreme Court authorized police officers to "stop and frisk" people on the street through a "pat-down" of the outer garments of their clothing if the police have "reasonable suspicion" to believe that the individuals may be armed and dangerous. This holding has empowered the police in encounters with people on the street and has led to vigorous debate in recent years about whether law enforcement officers unfairly target citizens based on race, ethnicity, and age. What has been your experience?

In the context of public schools, the Supreme Court has granted school authorities broad discretion to search students and their belongings. While many students feel that public officials should not be able to search their clothing, lockers, or persons without a search warrant and probable cause, many school officials believe that there should be no limits on their authority to search students. But the Supreme Court has developed an approach that comes down between these two polar positions.

In *New Jersey v. T. L. O.* (1985), the Court did away with the need for schools to show probable cause and to get search warrants when they want to search, but it did require them to have "reasonable suspicion" of individual students' wrongdoing before searching their persons or belongings. Many students believe the decision went too far in sacrificing their rights.

Yet the Court went further in *Vernonia School District 47J v. Acton* (1995) and *Pottawatomie County v. Earls* (2002) by upholding *random* drug testing of students on athletic teams and in other extracurricular activities, dispensing with even the "reasonable suspicion" requirement.

In Chapter 6, we will examine a case, *Chicago v. Morales* (1999), in which the Supreme Court struck down a city ordinance that prohibited "loitering" (hanging around with no apparent purpose) by "street gang members" because the language of the ordinance was impermissibly vague and thus violated due process.

P⬤INTS TO PONDER

How does the right to be free from unreasonable searches and seizures apply to public school students?

- Should school officials have the authority to search students' belongings without a search warrant or probable cause that a crime has been committed?
- Can school authorities require student athletes to participate in random drug testing even if there is no reason to think that they are using drugs?
- Can school authorities require anyone who participates in any extracurricular activity to undergo random drug testing?
- Can school authorities subject students to strip searches?
- Should government have the power to arrest and prosecute street gang members and their associates for loitering in public places?
- What kinds of expectations of privacy do you have in your locker?
- Do you think metal detectors violate your right to privacy?

Reduced Privacy Rights at School

"Smokin' in the Boys' Room," a rock song from the 1970s, reminded America's youth that "smoking ain't allowed in school." In the following Supreme Court case, a high school freshman in New Jersey was caught smoking in the girls' room. This infraction triggered a series of escalating searches of the girl's belongings, and the high school's vice principal found marijuana in her purse. This discovery led to a trial court's finding that the girl—identified only as T. L. O.—was criminally delinquent.

The Supreme Court took the case to determine whether the searches of T. L. O.'s purse were lawful. If not, the evidence would be excluded—this is the effect of the "exclusionary rule"—and the conviction reversed. Despite the fact that the school had no search warrant and no probable cause to search, the Court upheld the delinquency finding. Why?

NEW JERSEY v. T. L. O.

Supreme Court of the United States
Argued March 28, 1984.
Reargued October 2, 1984.
Decided January 15, 1985.

Majority OPINION   Justice WHITE delivered the opinion of the Court....

I

On March 7, 1980, a teacher at Piscataway High School in Middlesex County, N.J., discovered two girls smoking in a lavatory. One of the two girls was ... T. L. O., who at that time was a 14-year-old high school freshman. Because smoking in the lavatory was a violation of a school rule, the teacher took the two girls to the Principal's office, where they met with Assistant Vice Principal Theodore Choplick. In response to questioning by Mr. Choplick, T. L. O.'s companion admitted that she had violated the rule. T. L. O., however, denied that she had been smoking in the lavatory and claimed that she did not smoke at all.

Mr. Choplick asked T. L. O. to come into his private office and demanded to see her purse. Opening the purse, he found a pack of cigarettes, which he removed from the purse and held before T. L. O. as he accused her of having lied to him. As he reached into the purse for the cigarettes, Mr. Choplick also noticed a package of cigarette rolling papers. In his experience, possession of rolling papers by high school students was closely associated with the use of marihuana. Suspecting that a closer examination of the purse might yield further evidence of drug use, Mr. Choplick proceeded to search the purse thoroughly. The search revealed a small amount of marihuana, a pipe, a number of empty plastic bags, a substantial quantity of money in one-dollar bills, an index card that appeared to be a list of students who owed T. L. O. money, and two letters that implicated T. L. O. in marihuana dealing.

Mr. Choplick notified T. L. O.'s mother and the police, and turned the evidence of drug dealing over to the police. At the request of the police, T. L. O.'s mother took her daughter to police headquarters, where T. L. O. confessed that she had been selling marihuana at the high school. On the basis of the confession and the evidence seized by Mr. Choplick, the State brought delinquency charges against T. L. O. in the Juvenile and Domestic Relations Court of Middlesex County. Contending that Mr. Choplick's search of her purse violated the Fourth Amendment, T. L. O. moved to suppress the evidence found in her purse as well as her confession, which, she argued, was tainted by the allegedly unlawful search. The Juvenile Court denied the motion to suppress. Although the court concluded that the Fourth Amendment did apply to searches carried out by school officials, it held that

> a school official may properly conduct a search of a student's person if the official has a reasonable suspicion that a crime has been or is in the process of being committed, or reasonable cause to believe that the search is necessary to maintain school discipline or enforce school policies.

> **Reasonable Suspicion**
> The level of suspicion required for school officials to search a student's belongings or person; this is a weaker standard than probable cause.

Applying this standard, the court concluded that the search conducted by Mr. Choplick was a reasonable one. The initial decision to open the purse was justified by Mr. Choplick's well-founded suspicion that T. L. O. had violated the rule forbidding smoking in the lavatory. Once the purse was open, evidence of marihuana violations was in plain view, and Mr. Choplick was entitled to conduct a thorough search to determine the nature and extent of T. L. O.'s drug-related activities. Having denied the motion to suppress, the court on March 23, 1981, found T. L. O. to be a delinquent and on January 8, 1982, sentenced her to a year's probation....

... [W]e are satisfied that the search did not violate the Fourth Amendment.

II

In determining whether the search at issue in this case violated the Fourth Amendment, we are faced initially with the question whether that Amendment's prohibition on unreasonable searches and seizures applies to searches conducted by public school officials. We hold that it does....

... In carrying out searches and other disciplinary functions pursuant to such policies, school officials act as representatives of the State, not merely as surrogates for the parents, and they cannot claim the parents' immunity from the strictures of the Fourth Amendment.

III

... To receive the protection of the Fourth Amendment, an expectation of privacy must be one that society is "prepared to recognize as legitimate." The State of New Jersey has argued that because of the pervasive supervision to which children in the schools are necessarily subject, a child has virtually no legitimate expectation of privacy in articles of personal property "unnecessarily" carried into a school. This argument has two factual premises: (1) the fundamental incompatibility of expectations of privacy with the maintenance of a sound educational environment; and (2) the minimal interest of the child in bringing any items of personal property into the school. Both premises are severely flawed.

Although this Court may take notice of the difficulty of maintaining discipline in the public schools today, the situation is not so dire that students in the schools may claim no legitimate expectations of privacy. We have recently recognized that the need to maintain order in a prison is such that prisoners retain no legitimate expectations of privacy in their cells, but it goes almost without saying that "[t]he prisoner and the schoolchild stand in wholly different circumstances, separated by the harsh facts of criminal conviction and incarceration." We are not yet ready to hold that the schools and the prisons need be equated for purposes of the Fourth Amendment.

Nor does the State's suggestion that children have no legitimate need to bring personal property into the schools seem well anchored in reality. Students at a minimum must bring to school not only the supplies needed for their studies, but also keys, money, and the necessaries of personal hygiene and grooming. In addition, students may carry on their persons or in purses or wallets such nondisruptive yet highly personal items as photographs, letters, and diaries. Finally, students may have perfectly legitimate reasons to carry with them articles of property needed in connection with extracurricular or recreational activities. In short, schoolchildren may find it necessary to carry with them a variety of legitimate, noncontraband items, and there is no reason to conclude that they have necessarily waived all rights to privacy in such items merely by bringing them onto school grounds.

Against the child's interest in privacy must be set the substantial interest of teachers and administrators in maintaining discipline in the classroom and on school grounds. Maintaining order in the classroom has never been easy, but in recent years, school disorder has often taken particularly ugly forms: drug use and violent crime in the schools have become major social problems. Even in schools that have been spared the most severe disciplinary problems, the preservation of order and a proper educational environment requires close supervision of schoolchildren, as well as the enforcement of rules against conduct that would be perfectly permissible if undertaken by an adult....

How, then, should we strike the balance between the schoolchild's legitimate expectations of privacy and the school's equally legitimate need to maintain an environment in which learning can take place? It is evident that the school setting requires some easing of the restrictions to which searches by public authorities are ordinarily subject. The warrant requirement, in particular, is unsuited to the school environment: requiring a teacher to obtain a warrant before searching a child suspected of an infraction of school rules (or of the criminal law) would unduly interfere with the maintenance of the swift and informal disciplinary procedures needed in the schools....

The school setting also requires some modification of the level of suspicion of illicit activity needed to justify a search. Ordinarily, a search—even one that may permissibly be carried out without a warrant—must be based upon "probable cause" to believe that a violation of the law has occurred. However, "probable cause" is not an irreducible requirement of a valid search....

... Rather, the legality of a search of a student should depend simply on the reasonableness, under all the circumstances, of the search. Determining the reasonableness of any search involves a twofold inquiry: first, one must consider "whether the ... action was justified at its inception"[;] second, one must determine whether the search as actually conducted "was reasonably related in scope to the circumstances which justified the interference in the first place." Under ordinary circumstances, a search of a student by a teacher or other school official will be "justified at its inception" when there are reasonable grounds for suspecting that the search will turn up evidence that the student has violated or is violating either the law or the rules of the school. Such a search will be permissible in its scope when the measures adopted are reasonably related to the objectives of the search and not excessively intrusive in light of the age and sex of the student and the nature of the infraction....

IV

... The incident that gave rise to this case actually involved two separate searches, with the first—the search for cigarettes—providing the suspicion that gave rise to the second—the search for marihuana. Although it is the fruits of the second search that are at issue here, the validity of the search for marihuana must depend on the reasonableness of the initial search for cigarettes, as there would have been no reason to suspect that T. L. O. possessed marihuana had the first search not taken place. Accordingly, it is to the search for cigarettes that we first turn our attention.

The New Jersey Supreme Court pointed to two grounds for its holding that the search for cigarettes was unreasonable. First, the court observed that possession of cigarettes was not in itself illegal or a violation of school rules. Because the contents of T. L. O.'s purse would therefore have "no direct bearing on the infraction" of which she was accused (smoking in a lavatory where smoking was prohibited), there was no reason to search her purse. Second, even assuming that a search of T. L. O.'s purse might under some circumstances be reasonable in light of the accusation made against T. L. O., the New Jersey court concluded that Mr. Choplick in this particular case had no reasonable grounds to suspect that T. L. O. had cigarettes in her purse. At best, according to the court, Mr. Choplick had "a good hunch."

Both these conclusions are implausible. T. L. O. had been accused of smoking, and had denied the accusation in the strongest possible terms when she stated that she did not smoke at all. Surely it cannot be said that under these circumstances, T. L. O.'s possession of cigarettes would be irrelevant to the charges against her or to her response to those charges. T. L. O.'s possession of cigarettes, once it was discovered, would both corroborate the report that she had been smoking and undermine the credibility of her defense to the charge of smoking. To be sure, the discovery of the cigarettes would not prove that T. L. O. had been smoking in the lavatory; nor would it, strictly speaking, necessarily be inconsistent with her claim that she did not smoke at all. But it is universally recognized that evidence, to be relevant to an inquiry, need not conclusively prove the ultimate fact in issue, but only have "any tendency to make the existence of any fact that is of consequence to the determination of the action more probable or less probable than it would be without the evidence." ...

Of course, the New Jersey Supreme Court also held that Mr. Choplick had no reasonable suspicion that the purse would contain cigarettes. This conclusion is puzzling. A teacher had reported that T. L. O. was smoking in the lavatory. Certainly this report gave Mr. Choplick reason to suspect that T. L. O. was carrying cigarettes with her; and if she did have cigarettes, her purse was the obvious place in which to find them. Mr. Choplick's suspicion that there were cigarettes in the purse … was the sort of "common-sense conclusio[n] about human behavior" upon which "practical people"—including government officials—are entitled to rely…. It cannot be said that Mr. Choplick acted unreasonably when he examined T. L. O.'s purse to see if it contained cigarettes.

Our conclusion that Mr. Choplick's decision to open T. L. O.'s purse was reasonable brings us to the question of the further search for marihuana once the pack of cigarettes was located. The suspicion upon which the search for marihuana was founded was provided when Mr. Choplick observed a package of rolling papers in the purse as he removed the pack of cigarettes. Although T. L. O. does not dispute the reasonableness of Mr. Choplick's belief that the rolling papers indicated the presence of marihuana, she does contend that the scope of the search Mr. Choplick conducted exceeded permissible bounds when he seized and read certain letters that implicated T. L. O. in drug dealing. This argument, too, is unpersuasive. The discovery of the rolling papers concededly gave rise to a reasonable suspicion that T. L. O. was carrying marihuana as well as cigarettes in her purse. This suspicion justified further exploration of T. L. O.'s purse, which turned up more evidence of drug-related activities: a pipe, a number of plastic bags of the type commonly used to store marihuana, a small quantity of marihuana, and a fairly substantial amount of money. Under these circumstances, it was not unreasonable to extend the search to a separate zippered compartment of the purse; and when a search of that compartment revealed an index card containing a list of "people who owe me money" as well as two letters, the inference that T. L. O. was involved in marihuana trafficking was substantial enough to justify Mr. Choplick in examining the letters to determine whether they contained any further evidence. In short, we cannot conclude that the search for marihuana was unreasonable in any respect….

Reversed.

Dissenting VOICES

Justice Brennan, joined by Justice Marshall, concurred in part and dissented in part. His opinion criticized the majority's abandonment of "probable cause" of a crime or rule-breaking as the right standard for initiating searches at school. He wrote:

> Today's decision sanctions school officials to conduct full-scale searches on a "reasonableness" standard whose only definite content is that it *is not* the same test as the "probable cause" standard found in the text of the Fourth Amendment. In adopting this unclear, unprecedented, and unnecessary departure from generally applicable Fourth Amendment standards, the Court carves out a broad exception to standards that this Court has developed over years of considering Fourth Amendment problems.

Justice Stevens, joined by Justices Marshall and Brennan, filed his own decision, partly concurring and partly dissenting. He argued that Mr. Choplick

> overreacted to what appeared to be nothing more than a minor infraction—a rule prohibiting smoking in the bathroom of the freshmen's and sophomores' building. It is, of course, true that he actually found evidence of serious wrongdoing by T. L. O., but no one claims that the prior search may be justified by his unexpected discovery. As far as

the smoking infraction is concerned, the search for cigarettes merely tended to corroborate a teacher's eyewitness account of T. L. O.'s violation of a minor regulation designed to channel student smoking behavior into designated locations. Because this
conduct was neither unlawful nor significantly disruptive of school order or the educational process, the invasion of privacy associated with the forcible opening of T. L.
O.'s purse was entirely unjustified at its inception.

Justice Stevens believed that the majority decision shifted the balance of power far too
dramatically toward school officials: "Although I agree that school administrators must
have broad latitude to maintain order and discipline in our classrooms, that authority is
not unlimited." He emphasized that the

schoolroom is the first opportunity most citizens have to experience the power of government. Through it passes every citizen and public official, from schoolteachers to po-
licemen and prison guards. The values they learn there, they take with them in life. One
of our most cherished ideals is the one contained in the Fourth Amendment: that the
government may not intrude on the personal privacy of its citizens without a warrant
or compelling circumstance. The Court's decision today is a curious moral for the
Nation's youth.

WHAT DO YOU **Think?**

Exercise 5.1. The *T. L. O.* decision allows searches of students' property whenever
school officials have "reasonable suspicion" that a particular individual is engaging in
something criminal or impermissible under school rules. This degree of suspicion is lower
than the "probable cause" showing required of police officers seeking a warrant to search
property belonging to adults. *Probable cause* implies that there are facts that would lead a
reasonable person to believe that some criminal activity is likely taking place. *Reasonable
suspicion* implies that a search would turn up some evidence that a crime is taking place.
How do these two standards differ?

Exercise 5.2. Should school officials and teachers be authorized to search students
when they are on school property but not in the school building? The Supreme Court has
not treated this issue, but most lower courts do permit such searches so long as reasonable
suspicion exists that laws or school rules are being violated. What about searches of students' cars parked on school property? The general rule for cars on the street, as the
Supreme Court elucidated in *California v. Acevedo* (1991), is that if police have probable
cause to think there is criminal contraband inside a car, they may search the car without a
search warrant. This is because the mobility of cars creates a kind of traveling urgency.
Does this probable cause standard apply to a student's car in the school parking lot, or is
reasonable suspicion enough? The Court has not decided this issue. What do you think?
Does it make a real difference?

Exercise 5.3. In deciding whether a search is "reasonable" under *New Jersey v. T. L. O.,* the Court conducts a two-part analysis. First, it sees whether the search was "justified at its inception"—that is, whether there were reasonable grounds for suspecting the search would turn up evidence that the student was violating either the law or school rules. Second, it asks whether the search was reasonably related in scope to the purpose of the search and not overly intrusive in light of the student's age and sex and the nature of the infraction. To analyze this second issue, the Court must balance the importance of the government's interest against the level of violation of legitimate privacy rights.

For this exercise, draw a line down the middle of a piece of paper and make two columns. At the top of the left-hand column, write "Level of Privacy Intrusion"; at the top of the right-hand column, write "Nature of Government Interest." To do a balancing test, you must compare the severity of the privacy intrusion against the weight of the government interest. (For example, in *Vernonia School District v. Acton,* which deals with drug testing of student athletes, there is a dignity invasion against the normal solitude and privacy people enjoy in going to the bathroom, as well as an invasion of the privacy usually experienced in medical information contained in one's own body fluids. These privacy intrusions must be balanced against the government's interest in protecting students from harm in playing sports under the influence of drugs and its interest in establishing student athletes as school role models.)

Read through the following list of procedures established at various public high schools facing the problems of drug and alcohol use among students. In the "Intrusion" column of your chart, list what you think the intrusion on personal privacy is for each procedure and rank how intrusive you think the procedure is on a scale of one to ten (ten being the highest) and why. In the "Government Interest" column, write down what you think the government interest is in the drug testing policy and how high that interest ranks on a scale of one to ten. If you think an example is not a "search" at all, write it on your chart and explain why.

(a) Students entering the building at Madison High must walk through a metal detector.

(b) Students at Hamilton High must walk through a metal detector and put their book bags through an X-ray machine before entering the building.

(c) Jefferson High reserves the right to "tap" all the pay phones in the hallways of the school and listen in on conversations. Students are informed of this practice at the beginning of each school year.

(d) Martin Luther King High has a counselor available to talk to students about their problems. Any teacher can "sign out" from the counselor's office student files that contain notes kept on each student's sessions.

(e) Big City High has video cameras in the hallways filming the rows of student lockers. If students act suspiciously around their lockers, the principal searches their lockers for drugs or weapons. Videotapes are routinely turned over to the police.

(f) Small City High conducts random locker searches of all boys' lockers and has removed all doors from the toilet stalls in the girls' bathroom.

(g) At Kaynine High, trained police dogs sniff outside student lockers, and school officials open and search lockers when the dogs bark and alert teachers to the presence of narcotics.

(h) Southeast High has trained police dogs at school doorways sniffing each student's backpack or bookbag as students enter the building.

(i) Detection High places young-looking undercover police officers into the senior class to befriend students and uncover information about drug dealing and about students obtaining abortions without the parental consent required under state law. They turn in several of their "friends."

(j) As a requirement for advancing to the next grade at J. Edgar Hoover High, all students must take a polygraph ("lie-detector") test and answer one question: "Did you cheat on any of your final exams this year?"

(k) At Thomas Paine High's homecoming dance, all of the chaperones carry an alcohol tester. Throughout the dance, the chaperones may approach any student and have him or her blow into the machine. If alcohol is detected, a red light goes on and the student's parents are called to take the student home.

(l) At John Marshall High's homecoming dance, students who test positive using the same device are expelled.

(m) At Lyndon B. Johnson Middle School in Kansas City, when students make phone calls from the school office, the calls are taped (unbeknownst to the callers) and the assistant principal listens to them after school.

(n) Any student who seeks to run for student council at Richard Nixon High School in Irvine, California, must make all medical, educational, and psychiatric records available to the principal of the school in order to pass a "character" screening for eligibility to run.

A Fluid Analysis of the Fourth Amendment: Drug Tests and Extracurricular Activities

Although *New Jersey v. T. L. O.* gave schools much latitude to search the *belongings* of students, it did not directly deal with the question of when school officials can search the *bodies* of students. A case came before the Court that dealt with just this issue: *Vernonia School District v. Acton* (1995).

James Acton, a seventh grader, went out for the football team at a public school in Oregon. He made the team but was denied the right to join it when he refused to sign forms giving his consent to urinalysis drug testing before the season began and periodically on a random basis throughout the season. The school cited two interests in the drug testing: protecting students from harm caused by mental impairment during athletic activity and maintaining athletes as proper "role models" for other students. In *Acton* (1995), the Court found these interests important enough, and the privacy invasion slight enough, to permit the school district to maintain its drug-testing policy.

The *Acton* decision was written narrowly, seemingly as if to allow drug testing only against interscholastic student athletes. But high school administrators across the country took the football and ran with it, so to speak; many imposed drug testing on students in *all* extracurricular activities, students on overnight field trips and camping trips, and students who run for student council. Compulsory drug testing was destined to return to the Court. In the following case, the Court considered the constitutionality of a high school testing all students who participate in competitive extracurricular activities, including the Academic

Tenth grader James Acton, center, along with friends and family members, leaves the Supreme Court on March 28, 1995, after the Court considered his challenge to Vernonia school district's compulsory urinalysis drug testing of student athletes, a policy to which he was subjected in junior high school. Although plaintiffs in a case like this may attend the Court's oral argument to see their lawyers argue on their behalf, the Court's rules forbid lawyers to introduce their clients to the Court.

Team, Future Farmers of America, band, choir, and cheerleading. The Court upheld the drug-testing program. In hindsight, the *Acton* case looks less like a narrow exception for random compulsory drug testing of athletes and more like a foot in the door to randomly testing everyone. Is that going to be the next step after this case?

BOARD OF EDUCATION OF INDEPENDENT SCHOOL DISTRICT NO. 92 OF POTTAWATOMIE COUNTY v. EARLS

Supreme Court of the United States
Argued March 19, 2002.
Decided June 27, 2002.

Majority OPINION

Justice THOMAS delivered the opinion of the Court.

The Student Activities Drug Testing Policy implemented by the Board of Education of Independent School District No. 92 of Pottawatomie County (School District) requires all students who participate in competitive extracurricular activities to submit to drug testing. Because this Policy reasonably serves the School District's important interest in detecting and preventing drug use among its students, we hold that it is constitutional.

I

The city of Tecumseh, Oklahoma, is a rural community located approximately 40 miles southeast of Oklahoma City. The School District administers all Tecumseh public schools. In the fall of 1998, the School District adopted the Student Activities Drug Testing Policy

(Policy), which requires all middle and high school students to consent to drug testing in order to participate in any extracurricular activity. In practice, the Policy has been applied only to competitive extracurricular activities sanctioned by the Oklahoma Secondary Schools Activities Association, such as the Academic Team, Future Farmers of America, Future Homemakers of America, band, choir, pom pon, cheerleading, and athletics. Under the Policy, students are required to take a drug test before participating in an extracurricular activity, must submit to random drug testing while participating in that activity, and must agree to be tested at any time upon reasonable suspicion. The urinalysis tests are designed to detect only the use of illegal drugs, including amphetamines, marijuana, cocaine, opiates, and barbiturates, not medical conditions or the presence of authorized prescription medications.

… Lindsay Earls was a member of the show choir, the marching band, the Academic Team, and the National Honor Society. Daniel James sought to participate in the Academic Team. Together with their parents, Earls and James … challeng[ed] the Policy both on its face and as applied to their participation in extracurricular activities. They alleged that the Policy violates the Fourth Amendment as incorporated by the Fourteenth Amendment and requested injunctive and declarative relief. They also argued that the School District failed to identify a special need for testing students who participate in extracurricular activities, and that the "Drug Testing Policy neither addresses a proven problem nor promises to bring any benefit to students or the school." …

Injunctive Relief
A court order meant to force an organization or person either to do something or to stop doing it.

Declarative Relief
A binding declaration by a court defining the rights and duties of parties in a case. Also known as declaratory relief.

Lindsay Earls, second right; Graham Boyd, center, an attorney for the American Civil Liberties Union representing Tecumseh School District students challenging the district's random drug testing policy; and others listen to a reporter's question in front of the Supreme Court on March 19, 2002. Sharon Smith, holding sign, who supports the random testing, lost her daughter Angela, shown on sign, to drugs.

How Many LIVES Can Be SAVED With Just A Little Cup?

If student drug testing was done in school, perhaps she would be alive today!
Angie 1979–1998

www.momstell.com

II

… In *Vernonia* [*School Dist. 47J v. Acton*], this Court held that the suspicionless drug testing of athletes was constitutional. The Court, however, did not simply authorize all school drug testing, but rather conducted a fact-specific balancing of the intrusion on the children's Fourth Amendment rights against the promotion of legitimate governmental interests. Applying the principles of *Vernonia* to the somewhat different facts of this case, we conclude that Tecumseh's Policy is also constitutional.

A

We first consider the nature of the privacy interest allegedly compromised by the drug testing.…

A student's privacy interest is limited in a public school environment where the State is responsible for maintaining discipline, health, and safety. Schoolchildren are routinely required to submit to physical examinations and vaccinations against disease. Securing order in the school environment sometimes requires that students be subjected to greater controls than those appropriate for adults.

JUSTICES: A CLOSER LOOK

to Washington to work for Sen. John Danforth and later worked for several federal agencies in the Reagan administration. In 1990 Thomas was appointed to the U.S. Court of Appeals for the District of Columbia, and in 1991 President George H.W. Bush nominated him to fill the seat of Associate Justice Thurgood Marshall.

HIGHLIGHTS

- Thomas's nomination to the Court was controversial and divisive, not only because of his conservative legal and political views but also because of the release of sensational allegations that he had sexually harassed a former lawyer with the Equal Employment Opportunity Commission (EEOC), Anita Hill. The Senate voted to confirm Thomas 52–48, the closest margin in a Supreme Court confirmation battle in the twentieth century.
- Thomas votes reliably with the conservatives on the Court but is silent during the Court's oral arguments as the other justices pepper the advocates with questions. At one point, he had not asked a question of oral advocates appearing before the Supreme Court for more than two years.

JUSTICE CLARENCE THOMAS (1948–) was born in the impoverished hamlet of Pin Point, Georgia. At a Catholic boarding school in the South, Thomas faced racial hostility. In the 1960s he marched against the Vietnam War and identified with the Black Panthers while at Holy Cross College. At Yale Law School, Thomas experienced misgivings about affirmative action, a policy that he thought stigmatized him. He moved

Respondents argue that because children participating in nonathletic extracurricular activities are not subject to regular physicals and communal undress, they have a stronger expectation of privacy than the athletes tested in *Vernonia.* This distinction, however, was not essential to our decision in *Vernonia,* which depended primarily upon the school's custodial responsibility and authority.

In any event, students who participate in competitive extracurricular activities voluntarily subject themselves to many of the same intrusions on their privacy as do athletes. Some of these clubs and activities require occasional off-campus travel and communal undress. All of them have their own rules and requirements for participating students that do not apply to the student body as a whole. For example, each of the competitive extracurricular activities governed by the Policy must abide by the rules of the Oklahoma Secondary Schools Activities Association, and a faculty sponsor monitors the students for compliance with the various rules dictated by the clubs and activities. This regulation of extracurricular activities further diminishes the expectation of privacy among schoolchildren. We therefore conclude that the students affected by this Policy have a limited expectation of privacy.

B

Next, we consider the character of the intrusion imposed by the Policy. Urination is "an excretory function traditionally shielded by great privacy." But the "degree of intrusion" on one's privacy caused by collecting a urine sample "depends upon the manner in which production of the urine sample is monitored."

Under the Policy, a faculty monitor waits outside the closed restroom stall for the student to produce a sample and must "listen for the normal sounds of urination in order to guard against tampered specimens and to insure an accurate chain of custody." The monitor then pours the sample into two bottles that are sealed and placed into a mailing pouch along with a consent form signed by the student. This procedure is virtually identical to that reviewed in *Vernonia,* except that it additionally protects privacy by allowing male students to produce their samples behind a closed stall. Given that we considered the method of collection in *Vernonia* a "negligible" intrusion, the method here is even less problematic.

In addition, the Policy clearly requires that the test results be kept in confidential files separate from a student's other educational records and released to school personnel only on a "need to know" basis. Respondents nonetheless contend that the intrusion on students' privacy is significant because the Policy fails to protect effectively against the disclosure of confidential information and, specifically, that the school "has been careless in protecting that information: for example, the Choir looked at students' prescription drug lists and left them where other students could see them." But the choir teacher is someone with a "need to know," because during off-campus trips she needs to know what medications are taken by her students. Even before the Policy was enacted the choir teacher had access to this information. In any event, there is no allegation that any other student did see such information. This one example of alleged carelessness hardly increases the character of the intrusion.

Moreover, the test results are not turned over to any law enforcement authority. Nor do the test results here lead to the imposition of discipline or have any academic consequences. Rather, the only consequence of a failed drug test is to limit the student's privilege of participating in extracurricular activities. Indeed, a student may test positive for drugs twice and still be allowed to participate in extracurricular activities. After the first positive test, the school contacts the student's parent or guardian for a meeting. The student may continue to participate in the activity if within five days of the meeting the student shows proof of receiving drug counseling and submits to a second drug test in two weeks. For the second positive test, the student is suspended from participation in all extracurricular activities for 14 days, must complete four hours of substance abuse counseling, and must submit to monthly drug tests. Only after a third positive test will the student be suspended from participating in any extracurricular activity for the remainder of the school year, or 88 school days, whichever is longer.

Given the minimally intrusive nature of the sample collection and the limited uses to which the test results are put, we conclude that the invasion of students' privacy is not significant.

C

Finally, this Court must consider the nature and immediacy of the government's concerns and the efficacy of the Policy in meeting them. This Court has already articulated in detail the importance of the governmental concern in preventing drug use by schoolchildren. The drug abuse problem among our Nation's youth has hardly abated since *Vernonia* was decided in 1995. In fact, evidence suggests that it has only grown worse. As in *Vernonia*, "the necessity for the State to act is magnified by the fact that this evil is being visited not just upon individuals at large, but upon children for whom it has undertaken a special responsibility of care and direction." The health and safety risks identified in *Vernonia* apply with equal force to Tecumseh's children. Indeed, the nationwide drug epidemic makes the war against drugs a pressing concern in every school.

Additionally, the School District in this case has presented specific evidence of drug use at Tecumseh schools. Teachers testified that they had seen students who appeared to be under the influence of drugs and that they had heard students speaking openly about using drugs. A drug dog found marijuana cigarettes near the school parking lot. Police officers once found drugs or drug paraphernalia in a car driven by a Future Farmers of America member. And the school board president reported that people in the community were calling the board to discuss the "drug situation." We decline to second-guess the finding of the District Court that "[v]iewing the evidence as a whole, it cannot be reasonably disputed that the [School District] was faced with a 'drug problem' when it adopted the Policy." ...

Furthermore, this Court has not required a particularized or pervasive drug problem before allowing the government to conduct suspicionless drug testing.... [T]he need to prevent and deter the substantial harm of childhood drug use provides the necessary immediacy for a school testing policy. Indeed, it would make little sense to require a school district to wait for a substantial portion of its students to begin using drugs before it was allowed to institute a drug testing program designed to deter drug use.

Given the nationwide epidemic of drug use, and the evidence of increased drug use in Tecumseh schools, it was entirely reasonable for the School District to enact this particular drug testing policy....

Respondents also argue that the testing of nonathletes does not implicate any safety concerns, and that safety is a "crucial factor" in applying the special needs framework. They contend that there must be "surpassing safety interests" or "extraordinary safety and national security hazards," in order to override the usual protections of the Fourth Amendment. Respondents are correct that safety factors into the special needs analysis, but the safety interest furthered by drug testing is undoubtedly substantial for all children, athletes and nonathletes alike. We know all too well that drug use carries a variety of health risks for children, including death from overdose.

We also reject respondents' argument that drug testing must presumptively be based upon an individualized reasonable suspicion of wrongdoing because such a testing regime would be less intrusive. In this context, the Fourth Amendment does not require a finding of individualized suspicion, and we decline to impose such a requirement on schools attempting to prevent and detect drug use by students. Moreover, we question whether testing based on individualized suspicion in fact would be less intrusive. Such a regime would place an additional burden on public school teachers who are already tasked with the difficult job of maintaining order and discipline. A program of individualized suspicion might unfairly target members of unpopular groups. The fear of lawsuits resulting from such targeted searches may chill enforcement of the program, rendering it ineffective in combating drug use. In any case, this Court has repeatedly stated that reasonableness under the Fourth Amendment does not require employing the least intrusive means, because "[t]he logic of such elaborate less-restrictive-alternative arguments could raise insuperable barriers to the exercise of virtually all search-and-seizure powers."

Finally, we find that testing students who participate in extracurricular activities is a reasonably effective means of addressing the School District's legitimate concerns in preventing, deterring, and detecting drug use. While in *Vernonia* there might have been a closer fit between the testing of athletes and the trial court's finding that the drug problem was "fueled by the 'role model' effect of athletes' drug use," such a finding was not essential to the holding. *Vernonia* did not require the school to test the group of students most likely to use drugs, but rather considered the constitutionality of the program in the context of the public school's custodial responsibilities. Evaluating the Policy in this context, we conclude that the drug testing of Tecumseh students who participate in extracurricular activities effectively serves the School District's interest in protecting the safety and health of its students.

III

Within the limits of the Fourth Amendment, local school boards must assess the desirability of drug testing schoolchildren. In upholding the constitutionality of the Policy, we express no opinion as to its wisdom. Rather, we hold only that Tecumseh's Policy is a reasonable means of furthering the School District's important interest in preventing and deterring drug use among its schoolchildren. Accordingly, we reverse the judgment of the Court of Appeals....

Dissenting VOICES

Justice Ginsburg, joined by Justices Stevens, O'Connor, and Souter, dissented. She took the majority to task for extending to schools permission to randomly drug test not only student athletes but any student involved in extracurricular activities. The Pottawatomie County policy "is not reasonable, it is capricious, even perverse [because it] targets for testing a student population least likely to be at risk from illicit drugs and their damaging effects."

Justice Ginsburg rejected the majority's effort to compare the students in chorus, orchestra, academic competitions, and Future Farmers of America to the students participating in varsity athletics. "Schools regulate student athletes discretely because competitive school sports by their nature require communal undress," she wrote, "and, more important, expose students to physical risks that schools have a duty to mitigate." Thus, interscholastic athletics "require close safety and health regulation; a school's choir, band, and academic team do not."

Justice Ginsburg elaborated this point, emphasizing that,

> school sports are not for the bashful. They require 'suiting up' before each practice or event, and showering and changing afterwards. Public school locker rooms, the usual sites for these activities, are not notable for the privacy they afford. The locker rooms in Vernonia are typical: No individual dressing rooms are provided; shower heads are lined up along a wall, unseparated by any sort of partition or curtain; not even all the toilet stalls have doors.

She further stated that these conditions do not exist for students on the math team or Future Homemakers of America. Rather,

> extracurricular activities other than athletics ... serve students of all manners: the modest and shy along with the bold and uninhibited. Activities of the kind plaintiff-respondent Lindsay Earls pursued—choir, show choir, marching band, and academic team—afford opportunities to gain self-assurance, to "come to know faculty members in a less formal setting than the typical classroom," and to acquire "positive social supports and networks [that] play a critical role in periods of heightened stress."

Justice Ginsburg lampooned the majority's attempt to equate the safety risks facing cheerleaders and band members to those faced by football and soccer players:

> The School District cites the dangers faced by members of the band, who must "perform extremely precise routines with heavy equipment and instruments in close proximity to other students," and by Future Farmers of America, who "are required to individually control and restrain animals as large as 1500 pounds." For its part, the United States acknowledges that "the linebacker faces a greater risk of serious injury if he takes the field under the influence of drugs than the drummer in the halftime band," but parries that "the risk of injury to a student who is under the influence of drugs while playing golf, cross country, or volleyball (sports covered by the policy in *Vernonia*) is scarcely any greater than the risk of injury to a student ... handling a 1500-pound steer (as [Future Farmers of America] members do) or working with cutlery or other sharp

instruments (as [Future Homemakers of America] members do)." One can demur to the Government's view of the risks drug use poses to golfers ... for golfers were surely as marginal among the linebackers, sprinters, and basketball players targeted for testing in Vernonia as steer-handlers are among the choristers, musicians, and academic-team members subject to urinalysis in Tecumseh. Notwithstanding nightmarish images of out-of-control flatware, livestock run amok, and colliding tubas disturbing the peace and quiet of Tecumseh, the great majority of students the School District seeks to test in truth are engaged in activities that are not safety sensitive to an unusual degree.

Finally, Justice Ginsburg pressed the essential irrationality of the program, which singles out students who are involved in extracurricular activities and thus less likely to be using drugs. She wrote:

Nationwide, students who participate in extracurricular activities are significantly less likely to develop substance abuse problems than are their less-involved peers. Even if students might be deterred from drug use in order to preserve their extracurricular eligibility, it is at least as likely that other students might forgo their extracurricular involvement in order to avoid detection of their drug use. Tecumseh's policy thus falls short doubly if deterrence is its aim: It invades the privacy of students who need deterrence least, and risks steering students at greatest risk for substance abuse away from extracurricular involvement that potentially may palliate drug problems.

WHAT DO YOU **Think?**

Exercise 5.4. The four dissenters in *Earls* describe the majority decision as "perverse," because studies show that students in competitive extracurricular activities are *less* prone to use drugs than students who are not involved at school in this way. Does this point resonate with you? Would it make more sense to drug test students *not* involved in extracurriculars? Would this be constitutional? Is it less defensible because everyone must go to school (according to the truancy laws) but no one must participate in an extracurricular program?

Exercise 5.5. How effective is random drug testing in preventing, deterring, and detecting drug use among students? Divide the class into three groups—parents, students, and teachers—and act out a community discussion about how best to counteract drug use. Consider drug testing along with other options, such as education by physicians and health trainers, free drug treatment, peer counseling, and so on. What is your plan? Is it constitutional?

Exercise 5.6. Is the dissenters' solution fair in that it would allow drug testing for student athletes but not other students involved in after-school activities? Do student athletes really have less expectation of privacy? Are they really in more danger than other students? Is it fair to treat them as role models in a way that the school does not treat members of the chess team or Future Homemakers of America?

Exercise 5.7. Imagine a community with a big gang and drug problem such as Los Angeles. Could the school board impose random drug testing on all high school students? Argue pro and con based on the majority decision in *Earls*.

BROWNSBURG COMMUNITY SCHOOL CORPORATION
STUDENT DRUG TESTING PROGRAM
CONSENT FORM

BROWNSBURG EAST MIDDLE SCHOOL
RANDOM DRUG TESTING

Please check **ONLY ONE** of the appropriate spaces indicating that your son/daughter **will, or will not** participate in the random drug testing as outlined in the Student Handbook.

Student drug testing is mandatory for all students who wish to participate in extracurricular activities and/or those who wish to drive to school.

1. ____ My son/daughter **will participate** in the random drug testing.

        Reasons for participation: CHECK ALL THAT APPLY
        ___Voluntary   ___Extracurricular involvement

        ___Extracurricular Activities: CHECK ALL THAT APPLY

___Baseball	___Band	___Art Club
___Basketball	___Choir	___Computer Club
___Track	___Musical	___Pride
___Cross Country	___VOICE Club	___Gateway to Technology
___Football	___Honor Society	___Club Cook
___Golf	___Speech	___Fellowship Christian Athletes
___Soccer	___Newspaper	___Science Club
___Softball	___Class Officer	___Academic Super Bowls
___Volleyball	___Student Council	___Destination Imagination
___Wrestling	___Yearbook	___Quiz Bowl
___Intramurals	___DECA	
___Swimming	___Science Olympiad	
___Tennis	___Project XL	
___Cheerleading		

OR

2. _____ My son/daughter **will not participate** in the random drug testing. I understand this choice prohibits my son/daughter from participating in extracurricular activities for the 2007-2008 school year.

_____   _____
    Print Student Name   Grade for 2007-2008

_____   _____   _____
    Parent Signature   Student Signature   Date

I understand that if I change my mind about student drug testing, this form must be completed again and turned in to the Director of Student Assistance. Changes will not take effect until written notice is received. This form is valid for the entire 2007-2008 school year.

This sample student drug testing consent form comes from a school district outside Indianapolis, Indiana. The Supreme Court has upheld the constitutionality of random drug testing in schools for students who participate in any extracurricular activity.

Strip Searches

Whether a search is reasonable depends on the context within which it takes place. A school's need to search must be balanced against the invasion of student privacy that the search requires.

The Fourth Amendment does not protect expectations of privacy that are unreasonable. An expectation of privacy must be one that society is prepared to recognize as legitimate. Although no Supreme Court cases deal with the issue of strip searches in schools, at least one federal court of appeals has considered the issue, along with several state courts of appeals. Consider the following case from Indiana.

....

Doe v. Renfrow

United States Court of Appeals, Seventh Circuit
Argued April 3, 1980.
Decided July 18, 1980.

Majority

OPINION PER CURIAM

Petitioner Diane Doe is a thirteen-year-old student at Highland Junior High School in Highland, Indiana, a community of approximately thirty thousand residents. Highland has one junior high school and one senior high school, located in adjacent buildings. There are 2,780 students total enrolled in the two schools.

On the morning of March 23, 1979, [Doe] went to her first-period class as usual. Shortly before 9:15, when the class was scheduled to adjourn, Doe's teacher ordered everyone to remain seated until further notice. An assistant principal, accompanied by a police-trained German shepherd, a dog handler, and a uniformed police officer, then entered the classroom as one of six teams conducting simultaneous raids at the Highland schools. For the next 2-1/2 hours, Doe and her classmates were required to sit quietly in their seats with their belongings in view and their hands upon their desks. They were forbidden to use the washroom unless accompanied by an escort. Uniformed police officers and school administrators were stationed in the halls. Guards were posted at the schoolhouse doors. While no student was allowed to leave the schoolhouse, representatives of the press and other news media, on invitation of the school authorities, were permitted to enter the classrooms to observe the proceedings.

The dogs were led up and down each aisle of the classroom, from desk to desk, and from student to student. Each student was probed, sniffed, and inspected by at least 1 of the 14 German shepherds detailed to the school. When the search teams assigned to Doe's classroom reached Doe, the police dog pressed forward, sniffed at her body and repeatedly pushed its nose and muzzle into her legs. The uniformed officer then ordered Doe to stand and empty her pockets, apparently because the dog "alerted" to the presence of drugs. However, no drugs were found. After Doe emptied her pockets, the dogs again sniffed her body and again it apparently "alerted." Doe was then escorted to the nurses' office for a more thorough physical inspection.

Doe was met at the nurse's office by two adult women, one a uniformed police officer. After denying that she had ever used marihuana, Doe was ordered to strip. She did so, removing her clothing in the presence of the two women. The women then looked over Doe's body, inspected her clothing, and touched and examined the hair on her head. Again, no drugs were found. Doe was subsequently allowed to dress and was escorted back to her classroom.

Each of the 2,780 students present at Highland Junior and Senior High Schools that day was subjected to the mass detention and general exploratory search. Eleven students, including Doe, were subjected to body searches. Although the police dogs "alerted" 50 times, no junior high school students, and only 17 senior high school students, were found to be in possession of contraband. This contraband included marihuana, drug "paraphernalia," and three cans of beer.

It does not require a constitutional scholar to conclude that a nude search of a thirteen-year-old child is an invasion of constitutional rights of some magnitude. More than that: it is a violation of any known principle of human decency. Apart from any constitutional readings and rulings, simple common sense would indicate that the conduct of the school officials in permitting such a nude search was not only unlawful but outrageous under "settled indisputable principles of law."

[The court] accords immunity to school officials who act in good faith and within the bounds of reason. We suggest as strongly as possible that the conduct herein described exceeded the "bounds of reason" by two and a half country miles. It is not enough for us to declare that the little girl involved was indeed deprived of her constitutional and basic human rights. We must also permit her to seek damages from those who caused this humiliation and did indeed act as though students "shed at the schoolhouse door rights guaranteed by any constitutional provision."

Dissenting VOICES

Judge Swygert dissented, arguing that the use of police dogs to sniff the students on a mass basis itself constituted a search without probable cause or reasonable suspicion.

> I am deeply troubled by this court's holding that the dragnet inspection of the entire student body of the Highland Senior and Junior High Schools by trained police dogs and their dog-handlers did not [itself] constitute a search under the Fourth Amendment. No doctrine of in loco parentis or diminished constitutional rights for children in a public school setting excuses this alarming invasion by police and school authorities of the constitutional rights of thousands of innocent children.

WHAT DO YOU Think?

Exercise 5.8. Judge Swygert considered not only the individual strip search but also the dragnet dog-sniff search to be unlawful. What do you think about a police offensive in which dogs are brought to do a thorough search of everyone and everything at school? Is that lawful? Keep Judge Swygert's views in mind as we discuss locker searches later in the chapter.

Exercise 5.9. Why does the appeals court say that a strip search of a student violates the basic principles of human decency? What are those principles and how do we discover them? What is so upsetting about a strip search?

Exercise 5.10. Respond to this statement: Given the presence not only of drugs but of guns and other weapons in many schools, strip searches may be necessary under certain circumstances to maintain the health and safety of the student population in certain schools.

Exercise 5.11. You are the principal of a large urban high school that shows signs of gang activity, including graffiti on the walls of the school and rival gang fights in the school parking lot. Lately, gang activity has increased and parents have called you asking what your plans are to step up security. A respected teacher informs you that he overheard several students in his remedial math class talking about how easy it is to bring stun guns, which are legal in your state, to school. You are worried about this and decide that something needs to be done. Would it be acceptable to gather all the students you suspect are gang members in the gym, based on their clothing and dress, and strip-search them? If not, what can you do to stop this problem before someone gets hurt?

In the Georgia Court of Appeals case *Thomas ex rel. Thomas v. Roberts*, a group of schoolchildren sued their teacher, a county police officer, their school's assistant principal and principal, the school district, and the county, alleging that they had been subject to unconstitutional strip searches. In this case, a class of fifth-grade students was strip-searched in October 1996 after an envelope containing $26 disappeared from the teacher's desk. The boys were taken into the boys' bathroom in groups of four or five and asked to drop their pants. Some of the boys dropped both their pants and their underwear. Officer Billingslea, a male, searched the boys. As each boy dropped his pants, Billingslea visually inspected the boys' underwear to ensure that the money was not inside. The girls were taken into the girls' bathroom in groups of four or five at a time. Their female teacher, Ms. Morgan, then asked the girls to lower their pants and lift their dresses or shirts. Most of the girls were asked to lift their bras and expose their breasts to ensure that the money was not hidden under their bras.

The United States District Court for the Northern District of Georgia decided in favor of the school, and the students appealed. The Eleventh Circuit Court of Appeals held that the strip searches of schoolchildren, which were conducted without individualized suspicion, were unreasonable. Although the limited search of students from another classroom for the stolen funds was reasonable, the county could be held liable for its officer's unconstitutional conduct.

In *Holmes v. Montgomery*, the Kentucky Court of Appeals in 2003 decided in favor of two young women who sued their school for violating their Fourth Amendment rights by strip-searching them. On November 17, 1998, during a middle school physical education class, a student reported missing a pair of shorts. The classroom teachers told the students they would be given five minutes to return the missing shorts, but no one turned them in. After the students were given an additional five minutes, the teacher brought in a security guard and an assistant principal, who informed the students they would be searched to find the shorts. The students were taken in pairs to a locker room and searched. They were forced to expose their underwear by raising their shirts above their bras and by lowering their pants below their knees.

Applying the logic from *T. L. O.* and *Doe v. Renfrow,* the district court agreed that the strip search violated the Fourth Amendment rights of the young women, especially in light of the fact that the school board policy stated, "In no instance shall the school official strip search any student."

Locker Searches and Drug-Sniffing Dogs

The Supreme Court has not definitively ruled on locker searches, but lower courts have applied the principles of other Supreme Court rulings to disputes involving locker searches. Generally, the courts are finding that schools do not require reasonable suspicion to search lockers that they allow students to use on their property. Courts are divided, however, about whether schools need reasonable suspicion to search closed personal items, such as backpacks or purses, that are found inside the lockers.

In the following Pennsylvania decision, the principal of a school facing a serious drug problem escorted two police officers and a trained drug-sniffing dog around the school to each of the twelve hundred student lockers in the school. When the dog barked at a locker, an officer opened it and searched everything inside—backpacks, purses, clothes, gym bags—and the lockers next to it.

Most students consider the contents of their lockers private, but as in *Commonwealth of Pennsylvania v. Cass,* lower courts have upheld school policies that treat lockers as school property, searchable at any time. Here, a police officer and drug dog inspect lockers in a Decatur, Alabama, high school.

The police found marijuana, a pipe, a roach clip, and rolling papers in a student's gym bag and proceeded to arrest him and bring charges against him. Did the mass suspicionless search of lockers by a drug-sniffing dog violate the student's Fourth Amendment rights? Even if the school could open his locker without suspicion, could it then open his zipped gym bag? The Supreme Court of Pennsylvania found nothing wrong with the search.

Commonwealth of Pennsylvania v. Cass

Supreme Court of Pennsylvania
Argued Septemer 18, 1996.
Decided January 7, 1998.

Majority OPINION　Justice CAPPY.

This case presents the question of what level of protection public school students are entitled to during a school wide search under the Fourth Amendment to the United States Constitution and Article I, Section 8 of the Pennsylvania Constitution. For the reasons that follow we find that public school students have a limited expectation of privacy while in the school environment. In balancing this limited privacy interest against the need to maintain a safe and secure environment for all public school students, we find that public school students are subject to a search by school officials when the decision to search is reasonable given all the circumstances present at the inception of the search and the search itself is reasonably limited in its scope to the objective which initially prompted the search. Applying this principle, we reverse the decision of the Superior Court.

The actions which prompted this appeal occurred on April 12, 1994 at the Harborcreek High School in Harborcreek Township, Erie County, Pennsylvania. The school principal announced to the students that morning that a safety inspection would be conducted. The students were to remain in their classes until the inspection was completed. The inspection was in actuality a search of all the student lockers, 2,000 in number, for the presence of drugs and/or drug paraphernalia. In order to expedite the search process, the principal enlisted the aid of two police officers and a trained drug dog. The methodology for the search was that the Erie police officer who was designated as the dog handler would take the dog to each locker in the school accompanied by school officials. When the dog "alerted" to a particular locker, the other officer, along with school officials, would open that locker, and any lockers adjacent thereto, and search the contents. Based upon the alerts by the dog, a total of 18 lockers were searched during the inspection. Appellee's locker was the only one of the 18 lockers searched which was found to contain contraband. The search of appellee's locker resulted in the seizure of a small amount of marijuana, a pipe, a roach clip and rolling papers. Appellee was subject to a ten-day out of school suspension and required to attend counseling. In addition, appellee was charged criminally with possession of a small amount of marijuana and possession

Appellee
The party that responds to an appeal. This party is generally seeking affirmance of a lower court's decision. *See also* **Respondent**, under Chapter 4, *Engel*.

of drug paraphernalia. In connection with the criminal charges, appellee filed a motion to suppress the items seized from his locker during the safety inspection.

At the suppression hearing the school principal testified that the search was undertaken due to concerns which had arisen over the preceding months indicating that drugs were being sold within the school. The principal offered several reasons for his heightened concern as to drug activity within the school: information received from unnamed students; observations from teachers of suspicious activity by the students, such as passing small packages between themselves in the hallways; increased use of the student assistance program for counseling students with drug problems; calls from concerned parents; observation of a growing number of students carrying beepers; students in possession of large amounts of money; and increased use of pay phones by students. The principal also testified that he had observed students exhibiting physical signs of drug use such as dilated pupils while in the school nurse's office. Armed with this information the principal decided upon the course of conduct described above as the most efficient method of searching the 2,000 lockers in the school. The principal testified that he had not received any specific information implicating appellee as being involved in drug activity. The parties all agree that the search, as undertaken, was a general search as opposed to a particularized search which would have focused on a certain student or, in this case, a certain locker. The principal also offered in support of his decision to undertake this generalized search the Harborcreek school code which provides as follows:

> School authorities may search a student's locker and seize any illegal materials. Prior to a locker search a student shall be notified and given an opportunity to be present. However, where school authorities have a reasonable suspicion that the locker contains materials which pose a threat to the health, welfare, and safety of students in the school, students' lockers may be searched without prior warning.

Upon considering all the evidence presented by the Commonwealth, the trial court granted the motion to suppress. The trial court held that probable cause was not required before school officials could conduct a search of a students' locker and that a search of a student locker would be valid upon a showing of reasonable suspicion. Applying the reasonable suspicion standard to the facts in this case, the trial court concluded that the search at issue did not meet the necessary legal standard. Although the trial court recognized the good intentions of the principal ... the court concluded that "good intentions" alone could not justify the sweeping search which was undertaken here in the absence of some level of articulable suspicion. The court found the principal's generalized suspicions to fall short of an objective reasonable belief that would justify the search. The Superior Court affirmed the decision of the trial court. This court granted the Commonwealth's Petition for Allowance of Appeal, and for the reasons that follow, now reverse....

Suppression Hearing

A court hearing to determine whether a particular piece of evidence can be admitted and used at trial or will be "suppressed" because it was obtained unlawfully.

Probable Cause

Sufficient reason to believe that a person has committed, or is committing, a crime or that a place contains evidence connected with a crime.

Based on the holding of *Acton*, we conclude that the search at Harborcreek High School, as conducted, was a practical means to effectuate the principal's compelling concerns over possible drug use, that it was minimally intrusive as it affected a limited privacy interest of the students, and thus, it was compatible with the Fourth Amendment. Accordingly, we hold that the trial court erred in granting the motion to suppress under the Fourth Amendment....

Dissenting VOICES

Justice Zappala dissented and, in his opinion, objected to the court's permission for the use of drug-detection dogs in school lockers without initial probable cause to believe there was criminal evidence there. For Justice Zappala, the key point was that the contraband was found in a locker "by police officers," not teachers, "and the contraband seized" was used to make "a criminal prosecution." Thus, normal Fourth Amendment rules should apply, meaning that the police should have had to obtain a search warrant from a judge based on probable cause.

Metal Detectors and the Constitution

In the wake of continuing incidents of school violence across America, many public schools have introduced metal detectors as a way to keep guns, knives, and other weapons out. Does your school district use metal detectors? Are they an effective deterrent? Do they violate your freedom from unreasonable searches and seizures?

The U.S. Supreme Court has not considered the issue of metal detectors in schools, but a number of lower courts have decided that metal detectors do not violate students' Fourth Amendment rights. Consider the following.

In Re Latasha W.

California Court of Appeal, Second District
Decided January 27, 1998.

Majority OPINION   NEAL, Associate Justice

Summary

Random metal detector weapon searches of high school students do not violate the Fourth Amendment constitutional ban on unreasonable searches and seizures.

Facts and Proceedings Below

Appellant is a high school student. Before appellant enrolled, her high school had instituted a written policy for daily weapons searches, in order to protect students and staff. The

Appellant
The party that appeals a lower court's decision. This party is usually seeking reversal of the lower court's decision. *See also* **Petitioner**, under Chapter 2, *Tinker*.

searches were to be made at random, and persons to be searched selected on neutral criteria. Parents and students were given notice before institution of this practice, and again at frequent intervals. Searches were conducted using a hand-held metal detector, waved next to the student's person. Students were asked to open jackets or pockets to reveal items which triggered the detector. The day appellant was searched the assistant principal determined that those students who entered the attendance office without hall passes, and those who were late, within a half-hour after 8:09 a.m., would be searched. Appellant was one of eight to ten students who met these criteria and were searched. After the metal detector beeped, she was asked to open her pocket, revealing a knife.

Appellant was charged in a juvenile court petition with the crime of bringing on school grounds a knife with a blade longer than 2.5 inches. The trial court denied appellant's motion to suppress the knife as unlawfully seized, sustained the petition, and ordered appellant home on probation.

This appeal followed. Appellant challenges only the ruling denying her motion to suppress.

Discussion

We find no California case addressing the propriety of a search such as occurred here, but courts in other states have upheld against Fourth Amendment challenge similar searches of students without individualized suspicion.... The school cases just cited are part of a larger body of law holding that "special needs" administrative searches, conducted without individualized suspicion, do not violate the Fourth Amendment where the government need is great, the intrusion on the individual is limited, and a more rigorous standard of suspicion is unworkable.

The searches involved here met the standard for constitutionality.

The need of schools to keep weapons off campuses is substantial. Guns and knives pose a threat of death or serious injury to students and staff. The California Constitution, article I, section 28, subdivision (c), provides that students and staff of public schools have "the inalienable right to attend campuses which are safe, secure and peaceful."

The searches in the present case were minimally intrusive. Only a random sample of students was tested. Students were not touched during the search, and were required to open pockets or jackets only if they triggered the metal detector.

Finally, no system of more suspicion-intense searches would be workable. Schools have no practical way to monitor students as they dress and prepare for school in the morning, and hence no feasible way to learn that individual students have concealed guns or knives on their persons, save for those students who brandish or display the weapons. And, by the time weapons are displayed, it may well be too late to prevent their use.

The search here did not violate the Fourth Amendment.

Disposition

The judgment is affirmed.

WHAT DO YOU **Think?**

Exercise 5.12. Your parents are involved in the Parent-Teacher Association at your school, where there is considerable concern that students' fears for their personal safety are interfering with their education. At the next monthly meeting, the hot topics on the agenda are whether metal detectors and guards should be posted at all entrances to the school, whether a new identification (ID) system should be imposed whereby students are required to wear their photo ID badges around their necks at all times, and how to raise money for these potential new security measures. Using facts about your own school district, prepare a memorandum outlining arguments in favor of and against installation of metal detectors and guards in your school and adoption of the new ID system. If you do not like this plan, what do you suggest instead?

Exercise 5.13. Although schools have a duty to protect children in their care, some argue that young people in crime-ridden neighborhoods carry weapons only for self-protection and the protection of younger siblings and relatives. Is carrying a weapon a good way to keep safe? Does gun control reduce violence or increase it?

FOR THE **Class**

Searching for an Answer. Many schools have stationed police officers in the hallways or at the front door, or they patrol on campus. Oftentimes these officers are involved in searches of student lockers, belongings, and bodies. Should the school still get to search students without a warrant and on the lesser reasonable suspicion standard if police officers are present and involved? The Supreme Court has not ruled on this question, but other courts have been allowing schools to conduct their searches even with the involvement of police officers. Resulting evidence can be used in criminal prosecutions. Is this fair, or is it an end run around the Fourth Amendment?

Divide your class into two groups and debate whether you think drugs should be suppressed as evidence in a criminal prosecution of an eighteen-year-old high school senior for narcotics possession if the drugs were found as part of a warrantless search by a school-based police officer of the student's closed backpack in his closed locker at school. (Assume that he was suspended from school for ten days but is not challenging the suspension.)

Further **Reading**

Arbetman, Lee, and Edward O'Brien. *Street Law: A Course in Practical Law.* 5th ed. St. Paul, Minn.: West Educational Publishing, 1994.

Cole, David. *No Equal Justice: Race and Class in the American Criminal Justice System.* New York: New Press, 1999.

LaFave, Wayne R. *Search and Seizure: a Treatise on the Fourth Amendment.* 4th ed. St. Paul, Minn.: Thomson/West, 2004.

THE CONSTITUTION AND STURENT DISCIPLINE: "Due Process" and "Cruel and Unusual Punishment" at School

"In America the law is king."   THOMAS PAINE, *COMMON SENSE*

"[N]or shall any State deprive any person of life, liberty, or property, without due process of law."   THE FOURTEENTH AMENDMENT

"Excessive bail shall not be required, nor excessive fines imposed, nor cruel and unusual punishment inflicted."   THE EIGHTH AMENDMENT

When students misbehave, school authorities do not have to bring them to court to suspend or even expel them. Disciplinary punishment is deemed civil, not criminal, in nature. Therefore, a school system can set up its own disciplinary process to investigate, judge, and punish students for misconduct.

But what kind of process *is* due a student in trouble at school? Can a school suspend or expel students without telling them why or giving them a chance to explain their side of the story? Are there any kinds of physical discipline at school so severe that they violate the Eighth Amendment's ban on cruel and unusual punishment?

P■INTS TO PONDER

Should procedural due process rights and Eighth Amendment protections against cruel and unusual punishment be extended to public school students?

- What procedural rights to be heard do students have when facing suspension and other forms of discipline?
- When young people are not at school, does the government have the power to arrest and prosecute them for associating with street gang members in public places and loitering "with no apparent purpose"?
- Should schoolteachers be allowed to use physical force to discipline students? If so, how much?

Due Process

When school officials want to suspend students from school for several days or weeks, should the students first get a fair hearing in which they have an opportunity to tell their side of the story?

The opportunity to be heard is the foundation of procedural due process. Due process generally requires some kind of official proceeding and hearing before the government can take action against someone. The hearings and trial required before a person can be convicted of a crime are the most important examples, but motorists also get a hearing before their driver's licenses are removed and teachers get a hearing before they are fired.

The events in the following case, *Goss v. Lopez,* occurred in Columbus, Ohio, in 1971, during a period of unrest in American high schools over school policies that many African Americans and members of other racial minority groups saw as discriminatory. The student civil disobedience that gave rise to the *Goss* decision came after a series of polarizing events in the city of Columbus, which was beset by racial conflict. A few weeks before the protests began, authorities at Central High School cancelled a student-organized Black History Week assembly because they objected to its themes and to certain speakers invited by the students. The anger of African American students grew after two black students were shot by white perpetrators off-campus on the evening of February 25, 1971. The next day big protests at high schools and junior high schools led to summary discipline—that is, suspensions without any real due process. Principals believed that they had this authority, since they had exercised it for decades.

Yet in the famous *In re Gault* (1967) case, the Supreme Court had found that minors charged with criminal conduct could not be declared juvenile delinquents by states unless they had been given basic due process in court. Although the Court found that minors do not enjoy all of the protections that apply to adult criminal defendants, it found that they do have a right to be represented by counsel, to be notified of the charges against them, to have an adversarial hearing, and, perhaps most controversially, to remain silent and not testify against themselves in accordance with the Fifth Amendment's ban on compulsory self-incrimination. Change was in the air, and many civil rights and civil liberties groups believed that if due process applied to young people being criminally prosecuted, it should also apply to young people facing academic discipline.

In most of the incidents discussed in *Goss v. Lopez,* school officials suspended students without filing formal charges, without giving them an opportunity to be heard or to challenge the administrators' conclusions, and without submitting the cases to any consideration by neutral third parties.

The Court struck down the discipline in these cases, which mostly involved ten-day suspensions; it found that there must be a fair hearing before a student is suspended or otherwise disciplined. Note that a hearing before a principal is not a trial: There is no right to be represented by an actual lawyer, to cross-examine witnesses, or to produce evidence. But the idea of some due process—any due process—for high school students was revolutionary nonetheless, as evidenced by the vigorous dissent in this 5–4 case. Dissenting, Justice

Powell, a former president of the School Board of Richmond, Virginia, complained about the Court's tampering with the realm of local education and its dangerous permissiveness toward juvenile insubordination.

....

GOSS v. LOPEZ

Supreme Court of the United States
Argued October 16, 1974.
Decided January 22, 1975.

Majority OPINION   Justice WHITE delivered the opinion of the Court....

The nine [students] each ... alleged that he or she had been suspended from public high school in Columbus for up to 10 days without a hearing.... The complaint sought a declaration that [the Ohio law] was unconstitutional in that it permitted public school administrators to deprive plaintiffs of their rights to an education without a hearing of any kind, in violation of the procedural due process component of the Fourteenth Amendment. It also sought to enjoin the public school officials from issuing future suspensions and to require them to remove references to the past suspensions from the records of the students in question.

... [T]he suspensions arose out of a period of widespread student unrest ... during February and March 1971. Six of the named plaintiffs, Rudolph Sutton, Tyrone Washington, Susan Cooper, Deborah Fox, Clarence Byars, and Bruce Harris, were students at the Marion-Franklin High School and were each suspended for 10 days on account of disruptive or disobedient conduct committed in the presence of the school administrator who ordered the suspension. One of these, Tyrone Washington, was among a group of students demonstrating in the school auditorium while a class was being conducted there. He was ordered by the school principal to leave, refused to do so, and was suspended. Rudolph Sutton, in the presence of the principal, physically attacked a police officer who was attempting to remove Tyrone Washington from the auditorium. He was immediately suspended. The other four Marion-Franklin students were suspended for similar conduct. None was given a hearing to determine the operative facts underlying the suspension, but each, together with his or her parents, was offered the opportunity to attend a conference, subsequent to the effective date of the suspension, to discuss the student's future.

Two named plaintiffs, Dwight Lopez and Betty Crome, were students at the Central High School and McGuffey Junior High School, respectively. The former was suspended in connection with a disturbance in the lunchroom which involved some physical damage to school property. Lopez testified that at least 75 other students were suspended from his school on the same day. He also testified below that he was not a party to the destructive conduct but was instead an innocent bystander. Because no one from the school testified with regard to this incident, there is no evidence in the record indicating the official basis for concluding otherwise. Lopez never had a hearing.

Betty Crome was present at a demonstration at a high school other than the one she was attending. There she was arrested together with others, taken to the police station, and released without being formally charged. Before she went to school on the following day, she was notified that she had been suspended for a 10-day period. Because no one from the school testified with respect to this incident, the record does not disclose how the McGuffey Junior High School principal went about making the decision to suspend Crome, nor does it disclose on what information the decision was based. It is clear from the record that no hearing was ever held....

II

At the outset, [the school administrators] contend that because there is no constitutional right to an education at public expense, the Due Process Clause does not protect against expulsions from the public school system. This position misconceives the nature of the issue and is refuted by prior decisions. The Fourteenth Amendment forbids the State to deprive any person of life, liberty, or property without due process of law....

Here, on the basis of state law, [the students] plainly had legitimate claims of entitlement to a public education.... It is true that the Code permits school principals to suspend students for up to 10 days; but suspensions may not be imposed without any grounds whatsoever. All of the schools had their own rules specifying the grounds for expulsion or suspension. Having chosen to extend the right to an education, Ohio may not withdraw that right on grounds of misconduct, absent fundamentally fair procedures to determine whether the misconduct has occurred.

... "The Fourteenth Amendment, as now applied to the States, protects the citizen against the State itself and all of its creatures—Boards of Education not excepted." ... [T]he State is constrained to recognize a student's legitimate entitlement to a public education as a property interest which is protected by the Due Process Clause and which may not be taken away for misconduct without adherence to the minimum procedures required by that Clause.

The Due Process Clause also forbids arbitrary deprivations of liberty. "Where a person's good name, reputation, honor, or integrity is at stake because of what the government is doing to him," the minimal requirements of the Clause must be satisfied. School authorities here suspended appellees from school for periods of up to 10 days based on charges of misconduct. If sustained and recorded, those charges could seriously damage the students' standing with their fellow pupils and their teachers as well as interfere with later opportunities for higher education and employment. It is apparent that the claimed right of the State to determine unilaterally and without process whether that misconduct has occurred immediately collides with the requirements of the Constitution....

A short suspension is, of course, a far milder deprivation than expulsion. But, "education is perhaps the most important function of state and local governments," and the total

> **Due Process Clause**
> Clause in the Fifth and Fourteenth Amendments declaring that no person may be deprived of life, liberty, or property without due process of law; interpreted to mean that every individual is entitled to a fair trial with significant protections, such as the right to be heard, to call witnesses, to cross-examine witnesses, and so forth.

exclusion from the educational process for more than a trivial period, and certainly if the suspension is for 10 days, is a serious event in the life of the suspended child. Neither the property interest in educational benefits temporarily denied nor the liberty interest in reputation, which is also implicated, is so insubstantial that suspensions may constitutionally be imposed by any procedure the school chooses, no matter how arbitrary.

III

"Once it is determined that due process applies, the question remains what process is due." ...

... "The fundamental requisite of due process is the opportunity to be heard," a right that "has little reality or worth unless one is informed that the matter is ending and can choose for himself whether to ... contest." At the very minimum, therefore, students facing suspension and the consequent interference with a protected property interest must be given some kind of notice and afforded *some* kind of hearing. "Parties whose rights are to be affected are entitled to be heard; and in order that they may enjoy that right they must first be notified."

... The student's interest is to avoid unfair or mistaken exclusion from the educational process, with all of its unfortunate consequences. The Due Process Clause will not shield him from suspensions properly imposed, but it disserves both his interest and the interest of the State if his suspension is in fact unwarranted. The concern would be mostly academic if the disciplinary process were a totally accurate, unerring process, never mistaken and never unfair. Unfortunately, that is not the case, and no one suggests that it is. Disciplinarians, although proceeding in utmost good faith, frequently act on the reports and advice of others; and the controlling facts and the nature of the conduct under challenge are often disputed....

The difficulty is that our schools are vast and complex. Some modicum of discipline and order is essential if the educational function is to be performed. Events calling for discipline are frequent occurrences and sometimes require immediate, effective action. Suspension is considered not only to be a necessary tool to maintain order but a valuable educational device. The prospect of imposing elaborate hearing requirements in every suspension case is viewed with great concern, and many school authorities may well prefer the untrammeled power to act unilaterally, unhampered by rules about notice and hearing. But it would be a strange disciplinary system in an educational institution if no communication was sought by the disciplinarian with the student in an effort to inform him of his dereliction and to let him tell his side of the story in order to make sure that an injustice is not done. "[F]airness can rarely be obtained by secret, one-sided determination of facts decisive of rights...."

"Secrecy is not congenial to truth-seeking and self-righteousness gives too slender an assurance of rightness. No better instrument has been devised for arriving at truth than to give a person in jeopardy of serious loss notice of the case against him and opportunity to meet it."

... Students facing temporary suspension have interests qualifying for protection of the Due Process Clause, and due process requires, in connection with a suspension of 10 days or less, that the student be given oral or written notice of the charges against him and, if he denies them, an explanation of the evidence the authorities have and an opportunity to present his side of the story....

... We hold only that, in being given an opportunity to explain his version of the facts at this discussion, the student first be told what he is accused of doing and what the basis of the accusation is....

Dissenting VOICES

Justice Powell, joined by Chief Justice Burger and Justices Blackmun and Rehnquist, dissented, criticizing the majority for discarding the "informal method of resolving differences" that most schools used in favor of the new "constitutionalized procedure." They thought this would be a very cumbersome change and doubted whether requiring the principal to listen to the student's "version of the events" prior to suspension (or soon after) would actually "assure in any meaningful sense greater protection than that already afforded under Ohio law."

The dissenters predicted that furnishing even minimal due process to students before suspension would lead courts to take up a host of in-school controversies. Justice Powell wrote:

> Teachers and other school authorities are required to make many decisions that may have serious consequences for the pupil. They must decide, for example, how to grade the student's work, whether a student passes or fails a course, whether he is to be promoted, whether he is required to take certain subjects, whether he may be excluded from interscholastic athletics or other extracurricular activities, whether he may be removed from one school and sent to another, whether he may be bused long distances when available schools are nearby, and whether he should be placed in a "general," "vocational," or "college-preparatory" track.

In all of these cases, Justice Powell pointed out, students could argue that they were being denied an educational benefit and injured by adverse action of their teachers. As he put it, "It hardly need be said that if a student, as a result of a day's suspension, suffers 'a blow' to his 'self esteem,' 'feels powerless,' views 'teachers with resentment,' or feels 'stigmatized by his teachers,' identical psychological harms will flow from many other routine and necessary school decisions."

By making school judgments subject to constitutional rules, Justice Powell thought the majority was suddenly substituting the "discretion and judgment of federal courts across the land" for the on-the-ground wisdom of "the 50 state legislatures, the 14,000 school boards, and the 2,000,000 teachers who heretofore have been responsible for the administration of the American public school system."

WHAT DO YOU Think?

Exercise 6.1. In Justice Powell's dissenting opinion, he suggests that a disciplinary suspension from school is no big deal. It "leaves no scars" and "affects no reputations." He even suggests that "it often may be viewed by the young as a badge of some distinction and a welcome holiday." Do you agree? Is suspension so commonplace and even desirable that a school's decision to suspend should trigger no constitutional protections for students? Debate Justice Powell's position.

Exercise 6.2. What are the stages of the disciplinary process at your school? Are there published rules available from the school or the school board? Do you think that these rules comply with the (rather minimal) requirements of *Goss v. Lopez*? (Note that schools can give more protection, but not less, than what is suggested by *Goss*.) Draft your own set of ideal rules for disciplinary proceedings in school. Would you give students more rights or fewer rights than they have now? Would you allow the testimony of witnesses? Opening and closing statements? The opportunity to open the hearing to the public and the media? Should students be involved in the process as judges, prosecutors, or defenders? Should the principal decide on the final action, or should a panel made up of teachers or administrators (or both) and students make that decision? Compare your rules with those of your classmates.

Exercise 6.3. If you were suspended for ten days, how would you react? How would your parents and friends react? What would you do with your days during that time? Make a one-page schedule of how you would spend your time. Could you make productive use of your time away from school?

The Crime of Hanging Out with Gang Members: "Loitering with No Apparent Purpose" in Chicago and the Due Process Clause

In many American cities, teenage gangs are a way of life, a tradition going back decades if not centuries. Gangs become especially important to young people when family structures break down. Many gangs get involved in criminal activity, such as trafficking in guns and drugs, and not a few gang members die in the shocking spirals of violence the United States witnesses when turf fights take place. To outsiders who live and work near gangs, their habits and practices can be utterly terrifying. Oftentimes gangs congregate around public high schools, causing problems in the school environment.

Fear of violent gangs led the Chicago City Council to pass an ordinance in 1992 against "loitering" by "criminal street gang members." The council defined loitering as "remaining in any one place with no apparent purpose." This strange and mysterious wording provoked a lawsuit after more than 42,000 people were arrested in Chicago for violating the terms of the ordinance.

In *City of Chicago v. Morales*, Morales claimed that the language of the antiloitering ordinance was unconstitutionally "vague" in that it did not define specifically what conduct was forbidden, leaving citizens in the dark as to how to remain law abiding. Criminal laws that suffer from vagueness invite arbitrary and discriminatory enforcement by the police and thus violate due process under the Fourteenth Amendment. The Supreme Court agreed and struck it down. Was this a boon for liberty and the Bill of Rights or, as Justice Thomas insists in dissent, a victory for criminal gangs and disorder on the streets?

....

CITY OF CHICAGO v. MORALES

Supreme Court of the United States
Argued December 9, 1998.
Decided June 10, 1999.

OPINION   Justice STEVENS announced the judgment of the Court and delivered the opinion of the Court with respect to Parts I, II, and V, and an opinion with respect to Parts III, IV, and VI, in which Justice SOUTER and Justice GINSBURG join.

In 1992, the Chicago City Council enacted the Gang Congregation Ordinance, which prohibits "criminal street gang members" from "loitering" with one another or with other persons in any public place. The question presented is whether the Supreme Court of Illinois correctly held that the ordinance violates the Due Process Clause of the Fourteenth Amendment to the Federal Constitution.

I

... The [city] council found that a continuing increase in criminal street gang activity was largely responsible for the city's rising murder rate, as well as an escalation of violent and drug related crimes. It noted that in many neighborhoods throughout the city, "the burgeoning presence of street gang members in public places has intimidated many law abiding citizens." Furthermore, the council stated that gang members "establish control over identifiable areas ... by loitering in those areas and intimidating others from entering those areas; and ... [m]embers of criminal street gangs avoid arrest by committing no offense punishable under existing laws when they know the police are present...." It further found that "loitering in public places by criminal street gang members creates a justifiable fear for the safety of persons and property in the area" and that "[a]ggressive action is necessary to preserve the city's streets and other public places so that the public may use such places without fear." Moreover, the council concluded that the city "has an interest in discouraging all persons from loitering in public places with criminal gang members."

The ordinance creates a criminal offense punishable by a fine of up to $500, imprisonment for not more than six months, and a requirement to perform up to 120 hours of community service. Commission of the offense involves four predicates. First, the police officer must reasonably believe that at least one of the two or more persons present in a "public place" is a "criminal street gang membe[r]." Second, the persons must be "loitering," which the ordinance defines as "remain[ing] in any one place with no apparent purpose." Third, the officer must then order "all" of the persons to disperse and remove themselves "from the area." Fourth, a person must disobey the officer's order. If any person, whether a gang member or not, disobeys the officer's order, that person is guilty of violating the ordinance.

Two months after the ordinance was adopted, the Chicago Police Department promulgated General Order 92-4 to provide guidelines to govern its enforcement. That order purported to establish limitations on the enforcement discretion of police officers "to ensure that the anti-gang loitering ordinance is not enforced in an arbitrary or discriminatory way." The limitations confine the authority to arrest gang members who violate the ordinance to sworn "members of the Gang Crime Section" and certain other designated officers, and establish detailed criteria for defining street gangs and membership in such gangs. In addition, the order directs district commanders to "designate areas in which the presence of gang members has a demonstrable effect on the activities of law abiding persons in the surrounding community," and provides that the ordinance "will be enforced only within the designated areas." ...

II

During the three years of its enforcement, the police issued over 89,000 dispersal orders and arrested over 42,000 people for violating the ordinance....

V

... [T]his ordinance, for reasons that are not explained in the findings of the city council, requires no harmful purpose and applies to nongang members as well as suspected gang members. It applies to everyone in the city who may remain in one place with one suspected gang member as long as their purpose is not apparent to an officer observing them. Friends, relatives, teachers, counselors, or even total strangers might unwittingly engage in forbidden loitering if they happen to engage in idle conversation with a gang member.

Ironically, the definition of loitering in the Chicago ordinance not only extends its scope to encompass harmless conduct, but also has the perverse consequence of excluding from its coverage much of the intimidating conduct that motivated its enactment. As the city council's findings demonstrate, the most harmful gang loitering is motivated either by an apparent purpose to publicize the gang's dominance of certain territory, thereby intimidating nonmembers, or by an equally apparent purpose to conceal ongoing commerce in illegal drugs.... [W]e assume that the ordinance means what it says and that it has no application to loiterers whose purpose is apparent. The relative importance of its application to harmless loitering is magnified by its inapplicability to loitering that has an obviously threatening or illicit purpose....

VI

... [T]he ordinance does not provide sufficiently specific limits on the enforcement discretion of the police "to meet constitutional standards for definiteness and clarity." We recognize the serious and difficult problems testified to by the citizens of Chicago that led to the enactment of this ordinance. We are mindful that the preservation of liberty depends in part on the maintenance of social order. However, in this instance the city has enacted an ordinance that affords too much discretion to the police and too little notice to citizens who wish to use the public streets.

Accordingly, the judgment of the Supreme Court of Illinois is Affirmed.

Dissenting VOICES

Justice Thomas, joined by Chief Justice Rehnquist and Justice Scalia, dissented, arguing that "the Court has unnecessarily sentenced law-abiding citizens to lives of terror and misery. The ordinance is not vague.... Nor does it violate the Due Process Clause. The asserted 'freedom to loiter for innocent purposes,' is in no way 'deeply rooted in this Nation's history and tradition.'"

Justice Thomas refuted the idea that the police had been granted too much power under the ordinance:

> A majority of the Court believes that this scheme vests too much discretion in police officers. Nothing could be further from the truth. Far from according officers too much discretion, the ordinance merely enables police officers to fulfill one of their traditional functions. Police officers are not, and have never been, simply enforcers of the criminal law. They wear other hats—importantly, they have long been vested with the responsibility for preserving the public peace. Nor is the idea that the police are also *peace officers* simply a quaint anachronism. In most American jurisdictions, police officers continue to be obligated, by law, to maintain the public peace....

Justice Thomas argued that "the police inevitably must exercise discretion" and the law "cannot rigidly constrain their every action." Although he did not want to "suggest that a police officer enforcing the Gang Congregation Ordinance will never make a mistake" or act in bad faith to "enforce the ordinance in an arbitrary or discriminatory way," he maintained that "our decisions should not turn on the proposition that such an event will be anything but rare." In other words, the police should be given the benefit of the doubt.

Justice Thomas scolded the Court for focusing on the rights of "gang members and their companions," which it could do only because

> the people who will have to live with the consequences of today's opinion do not live in our neighborhoods. Rather, the people who will suffer from our lofty pronouncements are people like Ms. Susan Mary Jackson; people who have seen their neighborhoods literally destroyed by gangs and violence and drugs. They are good, decent people who must struggle to overcome their desperate situation, against all odds, in order to raise their families, earn a living, and remain good citizens. As one resident described: "There is only about maybe one or two percent of the people in the city causing these problems maybe, but it's keeping 98 percent of us in our houses and off the streets and afraid to shop." By focusing exclusively on the imagined "rights" of the two percent, the Court today has denied our most vulnerable citizens the very thing that Justice Steves elevates above all else—the "freedom of movement." And that is a shame.

WHAT DO YOU Think?

Exercise 6.4. The majority in *Morales* is eager to curb the discretion of the police to order people to move from place to place in public. The dissenters are just as eager to empower the police to keep "public order" by clearing the streets. Do you think the police should have the power to tell people where to stand or congregate in public if no crime is being committed?

Exercise 6.5. Do you think most young people have positive or negative attitudes about how they are treated by the police? Why? What has your experience been?

Exercise 6.6. Do citizens have a constitutional right to "hang out" in public places? If not, what are pubic places for? Must you have an "apparent purpose" to be in a public place? (What if the "apparent purpose" is a criminal one, as the majority suggests? Does that make the whole ordinance ridiculous?)

Exercise 6.7. Laws that are found to be "void for vagueness" are the ones written in too obscure and confusing a way to give people actual notice of what is criminal activity and what is innocent activity. We say that vague laws violate due process because they 1) fail to give people proper notice of what they cannot do and 2) invite arbitrary and discriminatory enforcement by the police. Which of the following prohibitions seem to you to be overly vague—and therefore unconstitutional? Why?

1. "Students shall not loiter near school premises after hours in such a way as to disturb the neighbors."
2. "Only a reasonable number of students shall enter a convenience store at any one time."
3. "No more than one other person under the age of 18 may ride in a car driven by a person under the age of 18."
4. "No loud talking on the bus."
5. "It is a violation of the school's conduct code to do another student's homework for him or her, although it is not an offense to help another student understand the concepts."
6. "It is an offense punishable by suspension to act in a manner that brings unwelcome attention to our school."
7. "Students may not leave campus without permission between 8:00 AM and 3:30 PM."
8. "Students may not leave campus without good reason between 8:00 AM and 3:30 PM."
9. "It is a violation of school rules to loiter in the halls during class periods."
10. "It is a violation of school rules to loiter in the halls at any point with no apparent purpose."

Exercise 6.8. Justice Thomas contends that the Court is wrong to focus on the "rights" of people facing arrest under the ordinance. He wants to defend the "freedom" of people intimidated by gang members who want the police to arrest the people hanging around. Whose rights should the Court focus on under the due process clause in this case? Are the rights of these two groups comparable or is this a comparison of apples and oranges?

Corporal Punishment

The Eighth Amendment protects citizens against cruel and unusual punishment. This right comes into play when someone convicted of a crime claims that his or her punishment is exceptionally painful, disproportionate, or outrageous.

In the following case, students who were paddled on the buttocks multiple times by their teachers asserted that they had been subjected to cruel and unusual punishment. The Supreme Court disagreed. It found that the Eighth Amendment ban on cruel and unusual punishment simply does not apply to the application of corporal punishment in schools. Why not?

•••

INGRAHAM v. WRIGHT

Supreme Court of the United States
Argued November 2–3, 1976.
Decided April 19, 1977.

Willie Wright, shown here in April 1977, administered paddling to the rear ends of students in a Florida public school. The Court ruled that such corporal punishment was not "cruel and unusual" within the meaning of the Eighth Amendment.

Majority OPINION   Justice POWELL delivered the opinion of the Court.

This case presents [a question] concerning the use of corporal punishment in public schools: … whether the paddling of students as a means of maintaining school discipline constitutes cruel and unusual punishment in violation of the Eighth Amendment.…

> **Corporal Punishment**
> The use of hitting, spanking, or other forms of physical correction to discipline children.

I

… In the 1970-1971 school year many of the 237 schools in Dade County used corporal punishment as a means of maintaining discipline pursuant to Florida legislation and a local School Board regulation. The statute then in effect authorized limited corporal punishment … proscribing [only] punishment which was "degrading or unduly severe" or which was inflicted without prior consultation with the principal or the teacher in charge of the school. The regulation contained explicit directions and limitations. The authorized punishment consisted of paddling the recalcitrant student on the buttocks with a flat wooden paddle measuring less than two feet long, three to four inches wide, and about one-half inch thick. The normal punishment was limited to one to five "licks" or blows with the paddle and resulted in no apparent physical injury to the student.

School authorities viewed corporal punishment as a less drastic means of discipline than suspension or expulsion. Contrary to the procedural requirements of the statute and regulation, teachers often paddled students on their own authority without first consulting the principal.

... The evidence, consisting mainly of the testimony of 16 students, suggests that the regime at Drew [High School] was exceptionally harsh. The testimony of Ingraham and Andrews, in support of their individual claims for damages, is illustrative. Because he was slow to respond to his teacher's instructions, Ingraham was subjected to more than 20 licks with a paddle while being held over a table in the principal's office. The paddling was so severe that he suffered a hematoma requiring medical attention and keeping him out of school for several days. Andrews was paddled several times for minor infractions. On two occasions he was struck on his arms, once depriving him of the full use of his arm for a week....

II

... We ... begin by examining the way in which our traditions and our laws have responded to the use of corporal punishment in public schools.

The use of corporal punishment in this country as a means of disciplining school children dates back to the colonial period.... Despite the general abandonment of corporal punishment as a means of punishing criminal offenders, the practice continues to play a

JUSTICES: A CLOSER LOOK

an air force intelligence officer, Powell launched a career in corporate law in Virginia and became increasingly active in local affairs in Richmond. As chairman of the Richmond School Board between 1952 and 1961, he defended racial segregation in the schools during a time when much of the South had declared a policy of "massive resistance" to *Brown v. Board of Education* (1954). President Richard Nixon appointed Powell to the Supreme Court in 1971. He retired in 1987.

HIGHLIGHTS

- Powell served in North Africa during World War II and was decorated with the Legion of Merit, the Bronze Star, and the French Croix de Guerre. He was instrumental in cracking the Nazis' secret Ultra code.

- As a lawyer, Powell was a member of the board of directors of eleven large corporations, including Philip Morris.

JUSTICE LEWIS F. POWELL JR. (1907-1998) was born in a suburb of Norfolk, Virginia. He went to Washington and Lee University for both undergraduate and law school study and also took a year at Harvard Law School. After service in World War II as role in the public education of school children in most parts of the country....

At common law a single principle has governed the use of corporal punishment since before the American Revolution: Teachers may impose reasonable but not excessive force to discipline a child.... The basic doctrine has not changed. The prevalent rule in this country today privileges such force as a teacher or administrator "reasonably believes to be necessary for [the child's] proper control, training, or education." To the extent that the force is excessive or unreasonable, the educator in virtually all States is subject to possible civil and criminal liability.

> **Common Law**
> Body of law that develops over time from the judgments of courts; contrasted with statutory law, which is written by legislatures.

... All of the circumstances are to be taken into account in determining whether the punishment is reasonable in a particular case. Among the most important considerations are the seriousness of the offense, the attitude and past behavior of the child, the nature and severity of the punishment, the age and strength of the child, and the availability of less severe but equally effective means of discipline.

Of the 23 States that have addressed the problem through legislation, 21 have authorized the moderate use of corporal punishment in public schools.... Only two States, Massachusetts and New Jersey, have prohibited all corporal punishment in their public schools....

Against this background of historical and contemporary approval of reasonable corporal punishment, we turn to the constitutional questions before us.

III

The Eighth Amendment provides: "Excessive bail shall not be required, nor excessive fines imposed, nor cruel and unusual punishments inflicted." An examination of the history of the Amendment and the decisions of this Court construing the proscription against cruel and unusual punishment confirms that it was designed to protect those convicted of crimes. We adhere to this longstanding limitation and hold that the Eighth Amendment does not apply to the paddling of children as a means of maintaining discipline in public schools....

C

Petitioners ... urge nonetheless that the prohibition should be extended to ban the paddling of schoolchildren. Observing that the Framers of the Eighth Amendment could not have envisioned our present system of public and compulsory education, with its opportunities for noncriminal punishments, petitioners contend that extension of the prohibition against cruel punishments is necessary lest we afford greater protection to criminals than to schoolchildren. It would be anomalous, they say, if schoolchildren could be beaten without constitutional redress, while hardened criminals suffering the same beatings at the hands of their jailers might have a valid claim under the Eighth Amendment. Whatever force this logic may have in other settings, we find it an inadequate basis for wrenching the Eighth Amendment from its historical context and extending it to traditional disciplinary practices in the public schools.

The prisoner and the schoolchild stand in wholly different circumstances, separated by the harsh facts of criminal conviction and incarceration. The prisoner's conviction entitles the State to classify him as a "criminal," and his incarceration deprives him of the freedom "to be with family and friends and to form the other enduring attachments of normal life." Prison brutality is "part of the total punishment to which the individual is being subjected for his crime and, as such, is a proper subject for Eighth Amendment scrutiny." Even so, the protection afforded by the Eighth Amendment is limited. After incarceration, only the "unnecessary and wanton infliction of pain," constitutes cruel and unusual punishment forbidden by the Eighth Amendment.

The schoolchild has little need for the protection of the Eighth Amendment. Though attendance may not always be voluntary, the public school remains an open institution. Except perhaps when very young, the child is not physically restrained from leaving school during school hours; and at the end of the school day, the child is invariably free to return home. Even while at school, the child brings with him the support of family and friends and is rarely apart from teachers and other pupils who may witness and protest any instances of mistreatment.

The openness of the public school and its supervision by the community afford significant safeguards against the kinds of abuses from which the Eighth Amendment protects the prisoner. In virtually every community where corporal punishment is permitted in the schools, these safeguards are reinforced by the legal constraints of the common law. Public school teachers and administrators are privileged at common law to inflict only such corporal punishment as is reasonably necessary for the proper education and discipline of the child; any punishment going beyond the privilege may result in both civil and criminal liability....

We conclude that when public school teachers or administrators impose disciplinary corporal punishment, the Eighth Amendment is inapplicable....

Affirmed.

Dissenting VOICES

Justice White dissented forcefully and was joined by Justices Marshall, Brennan, and Stevens. He rejected the Court's conclusion that corporal punishment in public schools, no matter how severe, could never qualify as "cruel and unusual punishment" within the meaning of the Eighth Amendment. He wondered why certain punishments, such as beatings in the face, "are so barbaric and inhumane" that they could never lawfully be imposed on prisoners but could now theoretically be imposed on students without violating the Eighth Amendment.

Justice White argued that if a punishment (such as tar and feathering) violates the cruel and unusual punishment clause for prisoners, then also it "may not be imposed on persons for less culpable acts, such as breaches of school discipline." He wrote:

> [I]f it is constitutionally impermissible to cut off someone's ear for the commission of murder, it must be unconstitutional to cut off a child's ear for being late to class. Although there were no ears cut off in this case, the record reveals beatings so severe

that if they were inflicted on a hardened criminal for the commission of a serious crime, they might not pass constitutional muster.

Justice White rejected the majority's argument, based on "vague and inconclusive" history, that the Eighth Amendment was designed to protect criminals but not students. "Certainly the fact that the Framers did not choose to insert the word 'criminal' into the language of the Eighth Amendment is strong evidence that the Amendment was designed to prohibit all inhumane or barbaric punishments, no matter what the nature of the offense for which the punishment is imposed."

Justice White was not satisfied that students suffering excessively harsh corporal punishment at school might have other legal claims to press in state or federal court:

> Nor is it an adequate answer that schoolchildren may have other state and constitutional remedies available to them. Even assuming that the remedies available to public school students are adequate under Florida law, the availability of state remedies has never been determinative of the coverage or of the protections afforded by the Eighth Amendment. The reason is obvious. The fact that a person may have a state-law cause of action against a public official who tortures him with a thumbscrew for the commission of an antisocial act has nothing to do with the fact that such official conduct is cruel and unusual punishment prohibited by the Eighth Amendment.

Justice White concluded with this analysis:

> The issue presented in this phase of the case is limited to whether corporal punishment in public schools can *ever* be prohibited by the Eighth Amendment. I am therefore not suggesting that spanking in the public schools is in every instance prohibited by the Eighth Amendment. My own view is that it is not. I only take issue with the extreme view of the majority that corporal punishment in public schools, no matter how barbaric, inhumane, or severe, is never limited by the Eighth Amendment. Where corporal punishment becomes so severe as to be unacceptable in a civilized society, I can see no reason that it should become any more acceptable just because it is inflicted on children in the public schools.

WHAT DO YOU **Think?**

Exercise 6.9. Justice Powell, who had strong views about education, thought that students could not be compared to prisoners and schools could not be likened to prisons. Thus he found that the Eighth Amendment, which forbids "cruel and unusual punishment," should not apply to what happens to students in the school environment. But if we cannot define "corporal punishment" as a form of "punishment" for Eighth Amendment purposes, then what is it exactly? Is it a form of education? Justice Powell clearly thought that some kinds of corporal punishment could be fairly deemed "reasonably necessary for the proper education and discipline of the child." Does Justice White agree that punitive hitting can constitute part of a student's education? Do you?

Exercise 6.10. The Supreme Court has often said that the Eighth Amendment prohibits two kinds of government practices: those that were cruel and unusual when the Constitution was written and those that offend the "evolving standards" of decency of the society. Do you think that the standards of American society have changed sufficiently in the last two decades such that corporal punishment today might violate the Eighth Amendment? Why or why not? When you become adults and have children of your own, how would you feel about public school teachers and administrators imposing corporal punishment on your children?

FOR THE **CLASS**

Punishment Policy. Even though a specific action may not be unconstitutional, people can still say that it makes for *bad policy* and legislate against it. Does corporal punishment make for bad policy or good policy? Assume that the school board for your community asks you to draft a policy for teachers on the use of physical punishment in the classroom. Draft a policy on when—if ever—physical force or corporal punishment may be used against students in the classroom. (Remember that teachers and administrators sometimes act in self-defense and intervene to stop fights.) Present your policy to your classmates as if they were members of the school board and give them the opportunity to ask questions. You should be prepared to defend your policy.

In Loco Parentis. In states that still allow corporal punishment, the practice is often justified by virtue of the fact that the school is acting *in loco parentis,* in the place of the parents. Do you think that schools should therefore have to receive the written or oral authorization of the parents before hitting their children? Divide the class in half and debate such a proposal.

Corporal Punishment in the Aftermath of *Ingraham v. Wright*

Ingraham v. Wright was a major disappointment to the opponents of corporal punishment in school, but they redoubled their efforts in the states over the next two decades. At the time of the decision, in 1977, only two states banned corporal punishment, but by 1998 twenty-five states banned corporal punishment outright, and even in those states that had not discontinued it, many counties and cities had adopted policies against the practice.

Furthermore, although *Ingraham* established that corporal punishment in schools does not violate the Eighth Amendment, a number of federal circuit courts have found that *excessive* physical force against students does violate their due process rights. In the 1980 case of *Hall v. Tawney,* the Fourth Circuit Court of Appeals allowed money damages to a seventh-grade West Virginia student who had been beaten so severely with a thick rubber paddle that she had to receive emergency medical treatment and was hospitalized for ten days.

Similarly, the Tenth Circuit allowed for monetary damages in a civil rights lawsuit based on extreme corporal punishment in the 1987 New Mexico case of *Garcia v. Miera.* The plaintiff in *Garcia,* a nine-year-old student, was held upside down by her ankles while the school principal beat her on the front of her legs with a paddle that was "split right down the middle, so it was two pieces, and when it hit it clapped and grabbed." After the paddling, the student's classroom teacher noticed blood coming through her clothes. The student's injuries left a permanent scar. Responding to complaints from the student's parents, the principal agreed not to spank the child again without first contacting her parents. But she was again seriously injured a month later.

The Third Circuit, in the 1988 Pennsylvania case of *Metzger v. Osbeck,* also allowed students to sue schools for injuries suffered in severe attacks by teachers. In *Metzger,* a teacher punished a student for using abusive language by choking the student while lifting him from the ground. The student lost consciousness and fell facedown on a concrete floor, suffering lip lacerations, a broken nose, broken teeth, and other injuries.

The courts have generally allowed students to recover money damages against schools where there is a severe injury and the force applied was wholly disproportionate to the underlying problem or misbehavior.

WHAT DO YOU **Think?**

Exercise 6.11. Research how much violence there is in the schools in your community —among students and teachers or other employees—and then find out what sorts of things are being done to stop it. Based on your research and interviews, what strategies and policies can you suggest to reduce violence and "increase the peace" in your community?

Exercise 6.12. Do you think that violence is natural and instinctive behavior or a learned response that can be unlearned as well? Do schools have a responsibility to educate students about the practice of nonviolence?

Further **Reading**

Devine, John. *Maximum Security: The Culture of Violence in Inner-City Schools.* Chicago: University of Chicago Press, 1996.

Hyman, Irwin A., and James H. Wise, eds. *Corporal Punishment in American Education: Readings in History, Practice, and Alternatives.* Philadelphia: Temple University Press, 1979.

Lantieri, Linda, and Janet Patti. *Waging Peace in Our Schools.* Boston: Beacon Press, 1998.

On the **Web**

Keep Schools Safe Project, www.keepschoolssafe.org.

Parents and Teachers against Violence in Education (PTAVE), www.nospank.net.

EQUAL PROTECTION AGAINST RACE DISCRIMINATION: From Segregation to Multicultural Democracy

"[N]or shall any State deprive any person of life, liberty, or property, without due process of law; nor deny to any person within its jurisdiction the equal protection of the laws." THE FOURTEENTH AMENDMENT

"All we say to America is be true to what you said on paper. If I lived in China or even Russia, or any totalitarian country, maybe I could understand some of these illegal injunctions. Maybe I could understand the denial of certain basic First Amendment privileges, because they haven't committed themselves to that over there. But somewhere I read of the freedom of assembly. Somewhere I read of the freedom of speech. Somewhere I read of the freedom of press. Somewhere I read that the greatness of America is the right to protest for right." DR. MARTIN LUTHER KING (APRIL 3, 1968, MEMPHIS, TENNESSEE; "I'VE BEEN TO THE MOUNTAINTOP," SPEECH GIVEN THE NIGHT BEFORE HIS ASSASSINATION)

All laws draw lines. For example, we allow sixteen-year-olds to drive cars, but we make it illegal for anyone who is just fifteen to do so. The courts accept this classification even though some fifteen-and-a-half-year-olds might make excellent drivers and some seventeen-year-olds are clearly bad drivers. The line drawn at age sixteen is thought to be reasonable, and the courts do not view classifications based on age as inherently suspicious or discriminatory.

Similarly, most localities will allow people to enroll their children in their public schools only if they live within the borders of the jurisdiction. The Supreme Court views *residency* as a reasonable qualification for school attendance and does not approach residency requirements as demanding any special government justification beyond a simple "rational basis."

But the Supreme Court's deference to government classifications falls away when the lines drawn are based on race or ethnicity. The Fourteenth Amendment was added to the Constitution in 1868 precisely as part of the post–Civil War effort to purge the land of white supremacy and racism. It took nearly a century for the traditionally conservative Supreme Court to act on this high promise, but the Court made it clear starting in the 1950s that the amendment's equal protection clause forbids the use of racial or ethnic categories to separate, demean, stigmatize, or disadvantage people. Racial line drawing by government is presumptively unconstitutional. Any official classification by race or ethnicity draws "strict scrutiny" by the courts.

Under strict scrutiny, a racially discriminatory law or policy can survive only if (a) the government demonstrates that it has a "compelling interest" in having it and (b) the government shows that it has chosen "narrowly tailored" means of achieving its compelling interest. Essentially, there must be no other way to advance the state's interest that is less constitutionally offensive. This tough test means that few race-based laws will ever survive.

The turning point for the Court and for civil rights in America arrived in 1954 with *Brown v. Board of Education of Topeka,* which struck down government segregation of public schools. The decision was negatively received by many whites; however, a wave of movement building, civil disobedience, federal and state legislative changes, and more judicial decisions proclaiming the unconstitutionality and unfairness of racial and ethnic discrimination ensued. The period of the twentieth-century civil rights movement stands as a remarkable moment of social transformation—and young people were critical to it. In 1964 waves of college and high school students recruited from all over America went to Mississippi to join the Freedom Summer campaign of the Student Nonviolent Coordinating Committee (SNCC) with the idea of opening up a deeply racist society through voter registration, education of young children, and political mobilization to challenge the state's racist Democratic Party. This kind of organizing changed the consciousness of the country, but it was very costly too: Three young civil rights activists— Michael Schwerner, James Chaney, and Andrew Goodman—were killed by racists in Mississippi that summer, and numerous churches were bombed and many other activists murdered.

By the late 1970s and 1980s, a deep weariness about making interracial progress had set in on the Supreme Court and in the rest of government. The use of race for purposes of affirmative action in employment and education provoked furious controversy and ended up eliciting numerous Supreme Court decisions striking down affirmative action plans for the sin of having overly rigid goals. (*Affirmative action* is a term used to describe deliberate efforts by colleges and universities as well as employers to recruit and attract women and members of racial and ethnic minority groups as students or employees.)

In the twenty-first century, the Court has forbidden local jurisdictions to use race-based assignments of students to elementary or high schools as a way to promote integration, although it permitted a generalized kind of race-based affirmative action to take place at the college level.

P**INTS** TO PONDER

Do students have a right to attend integrated schools or only the right to attend schools that are not segregated by law?

- Why did it take so long after passage of the Fourteenth Amendment for schools to desegregate?
- Why does *equal protection* mean that schools cannot separate students by race?
- Can public school districts take the race of students into account for the purpose of creating integrated school communities?
- What other techniques are available to foster integration?
- Can colleges and universities make conscious efforts and take "affirmative action" to recruit and admit students from traditionally underrepresented minority groups?

The Persistent Legacy of Slavery and Racism

Slavery was America's original sin. It was given the force of law for centuries until the Civil War and the Thirteenth Amendment abolished it. Today, even though most Americans take pride in the diversity of our society, we still grapple with the complicated legacies of racism and discrimination.

Children in African American and other minority communities have often been the victims of racial exclusion and violence. Yet the country has placed a large burden of hope on them to liberate America from the injustices of the past. *Brown v. Board of Education,* one of the most famous of the Supreme Court's twentieth-century rulings, deals with the rights of black schoolchildren not to be forced into segregated schools. The decision led to a

Under the Jim Crow system of "separate but equal" racial segregation, African American children were segregated from whites and forced to go to underfunded schools with underpaid teachers and poor resources.

JUSTICES:
A CLOSER LOOK

JUSTICE HENRY BILLINGS BROWN (1836–1913) authored the *Plessy v. Ferguson* opinion, which up-held the doctrine of "separate but equal." Brown was born into an affluent New England family and received his education at a prep school, Yale University, and Harvard Law School. After a career as a marshal, United States attorney, lawyer, and judge, Brown was appointed by President Benjamin Harrison to the Supreme Court in 1890. He served until 1906.

HIGHLIGHTS

- Justice Brown employed a substitute to avoid the draft during the Civil War.
- Late in his life, Justice Brown acknowledged that he had been naive to think that the Louisiana statute in *Plessy v. Ferguson* was not meant principally to keep African Americans out of white train cars.

period of intense conflict—and violence—in which children, especially African American children, were put on the front lines of the struggle to create an integrated America.

Brown has become the central symbol of the nation's commitment to an interracial, integrated, and "color-blind" society. It marked a turning point for the Supreme Court, which historically has been a force for racial conservatism. For example, in 1857 the Court upheld the expansion of slavery in the infamous *Dred Scott* case and found that African Americans were not "citizens" eligible to sue in federal court within the meaning of the Constitution. In 1896 the Court ruled in support of the Jim Crow doctrine of "separate but equal" in *Plessy v. Ferguson* by upholding racial segregation in public places and services. More than fifty years later, however, the Court, in *Brown*, found unanimously that "in the field of public education the doctrine of 'separate but equal' has no place." The Court in 1954 ruled that "[s]eparate educational facilities are inherently unequal." Between 1896, when the Court found that the equal protection clause *allows* racially segregated public facilities, and 1954, when it found that the equal protection clause *forbids* racially segregated public facilities, the language of the Constitution did not change. So what changed the mind of the Court? Cultural attitudes? The war against fascism and Nazism? The emergence of the cold war? The stirrings of a civil rights movement? Why did the Supreme Court (with an entirely new membership) make a reversal in its reading of the Constitution? What does the reversal teach us about the nature of Supreme Court interpretation? Is it controlled by science, logic, morality, rhetoric, emotion, politics, or some combination thereof?

BROWN v. BOARD OF EDUCATION OF TOPEKA

Supreme Court of the United States
Argued December 9, 1952.
Reargued December 7–9, 1953.
Decided May 17, 1954.

Majority

OPINION   Chief Justice WARREN delivered the opinion of the Court.

These cases come to us from the States of Kansas, South Carolina, Virginia, and Delaware....

In each of the cases, minors of the Negro race, through their legal representatives, seek the aid of the courts in obtaining admission to the public schools of their community on a nonsegregated basis. In each instance, they have been denied admission to schools attended by white children under laws requiring or permitting segregation according to race. This segregation was alleged to deprive the plaintiffs of the equal protection of the laws under the Fourteenth Amendment. [Segregation has been legally justified by] the so-called "separate but equal" doctrine announced by this Court in *Plessy v. Ferguson*. Under that doctrine, equality of treatment is accorded when the races are provided substantially equal facilities, even though these facilities be separate....

The plaintiffs contend that segregated public schools are not "equal" and cannot be made "equal," and that hence they are deprived of the equal protection of the laws....

In the instant cases ... there are findings that the Negro and white schools involved have been equalized, or are being equalized, with respect to buildings, curricula, qualifications and salaries of teachers, and other "tangible" factors. Our decision, therefore, cannot turn on merely a comparison of these tangible factors in the Negro and white schools involved in each of the cases. We must look instead to the effect of segregation itself on public education.

In approaching this problem, we cannot turn the clock back to 1868 when the Amendment was adopted, or even to 1896 when *Plessy v. Ferguson* was written. We must consider public education in the light of its full development and its present place in American life throughout the Nation. Only in this way can it be determined if segregation in public schools deprives these plaintiffs of the equal protection of the laws.

Today, education is perhaps the most important function of state and local governments. Compulsory school attendance laws and the great expenditures for education both demonstrate our recognition of the importance of education to our democratic society. It is required in the performance of our most basic public responsibilities, even service in the armed forces. It is the very foundation of good citizenship. Today it is a principal instrument in awakening the child to cultural values, in preparing him for later professional training, and in helping him to adjust normally to his environment. In these days, it is doubtful that any child may reasonably be expected to succeed in life if he is denied the opportunity of an education. Such an opportunity, where the state has undertaken to provide it, is a right which must be made available to all on equal terms.

We come then to the question presented: Does segregation of children in public schools solely on the basis of race, even though the physical facilities and other "tangible" factors may be equal, deprive the children of the minority group of equal educational opportunities? We believe that it does.

In *Sweatt v. Painter,* in finding that a segregated law school for Negroes could not provide them equal educational opportunities, this Court relied in large part on "those qualities which are incapable of objective measurement but which make for greatness in a law school." In *McLaurin v. Oklahoma State Regents,* the Court, in requiring that a Negro admitted to a white graduate school be treated like all other students, again resorted to intangible considerations: "... his ability to study, to engage in discussions and exchange views with other students, and, in general, to learn his profession." Such considerations apply with added force to children in grade and high schools. To separate them from others of similar age and qualifications solely because of their race generates a feeling of inferiority as to their status in the community that may affect their hearts and minds in a way unlikely ever to be undone. The effect of this separation on their educational opportunities was well stated by a finding in the Kansas case by a court which nevertheless felt compelled to rule against the Negro plaintiffs:

> Segregation of white and colored children in public schools has a detrimental effect upon the colored children. The impact is greater when it has the sanction of the law; for the policy of separating the races is usually interpreted as denoting the inferiority of the Negro group. A sense of inferiority affects the motivation of a child to learn. Segregation with the sanction of law, therefore, has a tendency to [retard] the educational and mental development of Negro children and to deprive them of some of the benefits they would receive in a racial[ly] integrated school system.

Whatever may have been the extent of psychological knowledge at the time of *Plessy v. Ferguson,* this finding is amply supported by modern authority. Any language in *Plessy v. Ferguson* contrary to this finding is rejected.

JUSTICES: A CLOSER LOOK

JUSTICE JOHN MARSHALL HARLAN (1833–1911) disagreed with the Court majority in *Plessy v. Ferguson;* he wrote that the statute at issue "interfered with the personal freedom of citizens."

Justice Harlan was born in Boyle County, Kentucky. He studied nearby at Centre College and acquired his legal education from professors at Transylvania University. President Rutherford B. Hayes appointed him to the Supreme Court in 1877, where he remained until his death.

HIGHLIGHTS

- Harlan was named for the influential John Marshall, the fourth chief justice of the United States.
- Harlan opposed the secessionists during the Civil War, although he firmly believed in a slave owner's right to slaves as property.
- He also opposed the Emancipation Proclamation and Thirteenth Amendment, abolishing slavery.
- Harlan formed and fought with the 10th Kentucky Volunteers on the side of the Union during the Civil War.
- He was raised to defend slavery but came to abhor racists. He developed the metaphor of "color-blindness" to analyze the meaning of the equal protection guarantee.

We conclude that in the field of public education the doctrine of "separate but equal" has no place. Separate educational facilities are inherently unequal. Therefore, we hold that the plaintiffs and others similarly situated for whom the actions have been brought are, by reason of the segregation complained of, deprived of the equal protection of the laws guaranteed by the Fourteenth Amendment....

... We have now announced that ... segregation is a denial of the equal protection of the laws....

Many people think that by allowing busing and limited affirmative action in education, the Court has followed through on the promise of *Brown*. Others, noting the Court's growing hostility to affirmative action and opposition to inter–school district remedies, think that the Court has taken up its former, passive role in the face of pervasive racism in society. Still others think that the Court should have no special commitment to racial integration and justice but should simply make sure that government is always "color-blind" in its policies. What do you think? Does the Court have a special responsibility to promote racial integration?

WHAT DO YOU **Think?**

Exercise 7.1. The *Brown* Court found segregation unconstitutional because it had such a negative effect on black children: "To separate them from others of similar age and qualifications solely because of their race generates a feeling of inferiority as to their status in the community that may affect their hearts and minds in a way unlikely ever to be undone." What do you think of this as the rationale for the Court's holding? Contrast it with the following hypothetical rationales that the Court might have used:

1. "To segregate white and black children solely because of their race generates a feeling of false inferiority in the black children *and a feeling of false superiority in the white children* that may affect their hearts and minds in a way unlikely ever to be undone."
2. "Segregation is a creation of white supremacy, which was invalidated by the Thirteenth Amendment's ban on slavery and the Fourteenth Amendment's guarantee of equal protection."
3. "The Constitution is color-blind, and so government may never take race into account for any purpose whatsoever."
4. "The premise of American democracy is liberty for all persons, but there is no liberty where the state segregates people on the basis of race."

Exercise 7.2. The Court in *Brown* seems to assume that all students are either black or white. Where do you suppose children who are neither "black" nor "white" fit into the picture? Do you think that the presence of millions of Hispanic, Asian American, and Native American children in the United States improves the prospects for good race relations? What about students who cannot be readily categorized or who refuse to be defined or classified by race? Hold a class debate on this proposition: "Students should never be forced by a school to identify with a specific racial or ethnic background."

Two Steps Forward, One Step Back: "Massive Resistance" and the Reaction to *Brown*

Although the *Brown* decision was met with jubilation in the African American community and among its civil rights allies in other racial groups, the decision set off a furious reaction among whites in the Deep South. Almost every elected official there—from governors to school board members—denounced the *Brown* decision and the Supreme Court. In Virginia, politicians and the white establishment declared a policy of "massive resistance" to federally sanctioned desegregation. Ku Klux Klan membership swelled across the South, and racist violence spread. Many cars featured bumper stickers that read: "Impeach Earl Warren."

In Arkansas white politicians swore they would never integrate. On September 2, 1957, Gov. Orval Faubus declared that blood would "run in the streets" if black children tried to attend Central High School. He ordered the Arkansas National Guard to surround Central High to stop any attempt at integrating the student body. Elizabeth Eckford, an African American high school student at the time, was taunted and threatened when she tried to enter the school. Black students did not successfully integrate Central High School until the Supreme Court made it clear that the state had no power to stand in the way and President Dwight Eisenhower federalized the National Guard and ordered the troops to guarantee the safe passage of the students through the screaming mobs.

The following famous Supreme Court decision, *Cooper v. Aaron*, determined that the defiance of government officials in Arkansas was unconstitutional, and that no state could exempt itself from the commands of equal protection and the supremacy clause, which makes the Constitution and federal laws supreme to state laws and power.

Paratroopers escort members of the so-called "Little Rock Nine" from Central High School on September 27, 1957. These nine African American students led the process of integrating Arkansas's public schools.

COOPER v. AARON

Supreme Court of the United States
Argued September 11, 1958.
Decided September 12, 1958.

[The school board of Little Rock, Arkansas, filed a petition to postpone desegregation plans of public schools due to "extreme public hostility." The district court granted the relief sought and the court of appeals reversed.]

Majority OPINION   Opinion of the Court by Chief Justice WARREN, Justice BLACK, Justice FRANKFURTER, Justice DOUGLAS, Justice BURTON, Justice CLARK, Justice HARLAN, Justice BRENNAN, and Justice WHITTAKER.

... We are urged to uphold a suspension of the Little Rock School Board's plan to do away with segregated public schools in Little Rock until state laws and efforts to upset and nullify our holding in *Brown v. Board of Education* have been further challenged and tested in the courts. We reject these contentions....

The constitutional rights of [the children] are not to be sacrificed or yielded to the violence and disorder which have followed upon the actions of the Governor and Legislature.

JUSTICES: A CLOSER LOOK

CHIEF JUSTICE EARL WARREN (1891–1974) wrote the majority opinion in *Brown*. He was born to a working-class family in Los Angeles and labored on the railroads as a boy. He worked his way through college and law school at the University of California. After serving as a district attorney, state attorney general, and three-term governor, Warren was appointed to the Supreme Court in 1953 by President Dwight Eisenhower. He retired in 1969.

HIGHLIGHTS

- Warren was the first governor of California to be elected three times. In one primary election, he won both the Republican and Democratic nominations.

- Justice Warren was chair of the commission that investigated the assassination of President John F. Kennedy, a commission whose work continues to be controversial today.

- As attorney general of California and a candidate for governor, Warren favored the internment and relocation of persons of Japanese ancestry on the West Coast during World War II. Yet he became a key force on the Court against racial discrimination and segregation. Justice Warren later called his decision to back the internment of Japanese Americans the major regret of his life.

As this Court said some 41 years ago in an unanimous opinion in a case involving another aspect of racial segregation: "It is urged that this proposed segregation will promote the public peace.... [T]his aim cannot be accomplished by laws or ordinances which deny rights created or protected by the Federal Constitution." Thus law and order are not here to be preserved by depriving the Negro children of their constitutional rights....

... The command of the Fourteenth Amendment is that no "State" shall deny to any person within its jurisdiction the equal protection of the laws. "... Whoever, by virtue of public position under a State government, ... denies or takes away the equal protection of the laws, violates the constitutional inhibition; and as he acts in the name and for the State, and is clothed with the State's power, his act is that of the State. This must be so, or the constitutional prohibition has no meaning." ...

It is, of course, quite true that the responsibility for public education is primarily the concern of the States, but it is equally true that such responsibilities, like all other state activity, must be exercised consistently with federal constitutional requirements as they apply to state action. The Constitution created a government dedicated to equal justice under law. The Fourteenth Amendment embodied and emphasized that ideal. State support of segregated schools through any arrangement ... cannot be squared with the Amendment's command that no State shall deny to any person within its jurisdiction the equal protection of the laws. The right of a student not to be segregated on racial grounds in schools so maintained is indeed so fundamental and pervasive that it is embraced in the concept of due process of law. The basic decision in *Brown* was unanimously reached by this Court and that decision is now unanimously reaffirmed. The principles announced in that decision and the obedience of the States to them, according to the command of the Constitution, are indispensable for the protection of the freedoms guaranteed by our fundamental charter for all of us. Our constitutional ideal of equal justice under law is thus made a living truth.

[*Reversed.*]

Just as white politicians in Arkansas used any legal or illegal means they could scare up to block the schoolhouse doors, white politicians in Virginia experimented with even more creative ways to stop desegregation. The school board in Prince Edward County, Virginia, simply closed down the public schools and reopened them as state-supported private schools. In *Griffin v. County School Board of Prince Edward County,* the Supreme Court also rejected that tactic. What was its reasoning?

GRIFFIN v. COUNTY SCHOOL BOARD OF PRINCE EDWARD COUNTY

Supreme Court of the United States
Argued March 30, 1964.
Decided May 25, 1964.

[In 1959, following the order of the Supreme Court to desegregate public schools, Prince Edward County, Virginia, simply closed its public schools. In their place, private, for-white-students-only schools opened with the support of state and local authorities.]

OPINION

Majority

Justice BLACK delivered the opinion of the Court.

... Having as early as 1956 resolved that they would not operate public schools "wherein white and colored children are taught together," the Supervisors of Prince Edward County refused to levy any school taxes for the 1959–1960 school year.... As a result, the county's public schools did not reopen in the fall of 1959 and have remained closed ever since, although the public schools of every other county in Virginia have continued to operate.... An offer to set up private schools for colored children in the county was rejected, the Negroes of Prince Edward preferring to continue the legal battle for desegregated public schools, and colored children were without formal education from 1959 to 1963, when federal, state, and county authorities cooperated to have classes conducted for Negroes and whites in school buildings owned by the county....

For reasons to be stated, we agree with the District Court that, under the circumstances here, closing the Prince Edward County school while public schools in all the other counties of Virginia were being maintained denied the petitioners and the class of Negro students they represent the equal protection of the laws guaranteed by the Fourteenth Amendment....

II

... Virginia law, as here applied, unquestionably treats the school children of Prince Edward differently from the way it treats the school children of all other Virginia counties. Prince Edward children must go to a private school or none at all; all other Virginia children can go to public schools. Closing Prince Edward's schools bears more heavily on Negro children in Prince Edward County since white children there have accredited private schools which they can attend, while colored children until very recently have had no available private schools, and even the school they now attend is a temporary expedient. Apart from this expedient, the result is that Prince Edward County school children, if they go to school in their own county, must go to racially segregated schools which, although designated as private, are beneficiaries of county and state support.

A State, of course, has a wide discretion in deciding whether laws shall operate statewide or shall operate only in certain counties.... But the record in the present case could not be clearer that Prince Edward's public schools were closed and private schools operated in their place with state and county assistance, for one reason, and one reason only: to ensure, through measures taken by the county and the State, that white and colored children in Prince Edward County would not, under any circumstances, go to the same school. Whatever nonracial grounds might support a State's allowing a county to abandon public schools, the object must be a constitutional one, and grounds of race and opposition to desegregation do not qualify as constitutional.

... Accordingly, we agree with the District Court that closing the Prince Edward schools and meanwhile contributing to the support of the private segregated white schools that took their place denied petitioners the equal protection of the laws....

The judgment of the Court of Appeals is reversed, the judgment of the District Court is affirmed, and the cause is remanded to the District Court with directions to enter a decree which will guarantee that these petitioners will get the kind of education that is given in the State's public schools....

It is so ordered.

In cases such as *Cooper* and *Griffin*, the Court was able to knock down the most overt brands of resistance to desegregating public schools. It also disallowed schemes that maintained separate black and white schools but gave individual students the freedom to "switch" from one to another. In *Swann v. Charlotte-Mecklenburg Board of Education* (1971), the Court also gave district courts enforcing *Brown* the green light to order the busing of students from one neighborhood to another—a controversial practice that led to brutal racist violence in many places, including Boston.

However difficult, courts tried to make integration work, but in many places official attempts to evade *Brown*'s mandate were ingenious and successful. Yet even where desegregation did take hold, the underlying social dynamics often would not cooperate. In a sociological sense, the heart of the problem was "white flight," as countless white families decided to move rather than face the possibility of integration. With whites relocating across city and county lines in order to escape the implications of *Brown*, the question became whether courts could follow them by ordering desegregation and busing across school district lines.

In *Milliken v. Bradley* (1974), the Supreme Court found that federal courts may not normally order desegregation plans that cut across the lines of different school districts. A lower court had tried to order a desegregation plan that included not only Detroit but also fifty-three neighboring suburbs. The Court rejected this approach, finding that municipal boundary lines were not automatically part of the problem of racial segregation and must be respected by the judiciary. Justice Marshall called the majority decision "a giant step backwards" that threatened to create black and white school districts. Many people believe that this decision encouraged white flight to the suburbs, halting the progress that had been made since 1954.

WHAT DO YOU **Think?**

Exercise 7.3. As the Supreme Court grew more conservative in the last three decades of the twentieth century, it lost much of its fervor and energy for ending segregation in schools. In *Missouri v. Jenkins* (1995), the Court overturned an effort by a district court to encourage integration in Kansas City, Missouri, by ordering the creation of an urban magnet school with well-paid teachers that would attract students from the mostly white suburban and private schools. The majority in this decision found that such relief goes too far—that the district court exceeded its authority in ordering the creation of the school and higher pay for the teachers. Do you agree?

Exercise 7.4. Write a one- to two-page letter back in time to Chief Justice Warren and the Reverend Martin Luther King, whose 1963 "I have a dream" speech at the Lincoln

Memorial brought the civil rights movement's struggle alive for America. Tell them what your own city, county, or private school system is like today—whether or not it is segregated or integrated or some mixture thereof. Include a description of the situation at your own school and indicate whether you think the teachers and students are living up to the ideals of integration championed by Chief Justice Warren and Dr. King. Give your school system a grade, somewhere between F and A+, on its efforts to break down racial and ethnic barriers. Hang the letters on your class bulletin board to share with your fellow students. What do people think of your observations?

FOR THE **CLASS**

Can Race and Gender Segregation Ever Help? The Frederick Douglass School Thought Experiment.

In response to growing signs that African American teenage boys are at disproportionate risk of academic failure, delinquency, depression, drug and alcohol abuse, and illiteracy, several cities have begun to experiment with special schools set up just for them. The theory is that this at-risk population needs African American male role models, closer supervision and discipline, and a curriculum geared to meet special needs. Private schools set up on this theory have had some impressive academic success.

Critics argue that not all young African American males are at risk, while many girls and young people from other backgrounds are at risk and could benefit from the same investment of resources. Further, critics maintain that setting up race- and sex-segregated schools violates the whole spirit and meaning of *Brown,* which insists that children learn best when they are not artificially segregated. Supporters of such schools note that schools are de facto segregated anyway, and that this formalized and positive group experience is the only possible solution to deal with a serious crisis within the most disadvantaged portion of the American population.

Assume that a group of citizens in your city or town wants to charter a public school called the Frederick Douglass School that would admit only African American boys. Have two teams of students research and debate this issue as a matter of both policy and constitutional law in front of the school board. Would a city-funded, all-black, male school be a good idea where you live? Would it violate equal protection as described in *Brown?* Why or why not? Would such a school stigmatize its students? Would it stigmatize those students who are excluded? Are the answers the same when it comes to race and gender? Make sure that you distinguish between *policy* arguments ("It's a bad idea") and *constitutional* arguments ("It would violate equal protection"). Both kinds of arguments are acceptable in discussion before a legislative body, such as a school board, but make sure you know which is which.

After the debate, each member of the class should write a one- or two-page essay stating (1) whether such a school is a good idea and (2) whether it would be constitutional. (It is fine to say that it is a bad idea but constitutional or a good idea but unconstitutional.)

The Right to Love

Laws segregating schools were not the only racially discriminatory statutes that the Supreme Court tackled in the second half of the last century. In 1967 the Court struck down as a violation of equal protection state laws forbidding interracial marriage between whites and nonwhites. These "antimiscegenation" statutes, which were common throughout the United States, were used in the South to maintain the cultural system of white supremacy and to keep racial groups socially separate. Because they were based on racist notions of rigid biological differences among racial groups, these laws stigmatized and shamed children who were born to parents of different racial and ethnic ancestries.

In *Loving v. Virginia* (1967), the Court invalidated Virginia's law against interracial marriage. Virginia argued that its policy did not violate equal protection, because it applied equally against whites and African Americans; that is, it was just as illegal for a white person to marry an African American as for an African American to marry a white. But the Court rejected this line of reasoning because it said that the whole purpose of the law was to continue "white supremacy." This seems obvious today; why was it so controversial back then?

WHAT DO YOU Think?

Exercise 7.5. There have been reports of public high school principals who have tried to ban interracial couples from attending their senior proms together. Do such bans violate equal protection? Does *Loving v. Virginia* imply that young people should be able to date whomever they want? Why or why not? (In 1983 the Supreme Court upheld the decision of the Internal Revenue Service [IRS] to revoke Bob Jones University's charitable tax exemption because the private university in South Carolina had a rule expelling all students who dated or married "outside their own race" or who advocated interracial dating. The Court found that the IRS acted properly in ruling that this policy brought Bob Jones University outside the class of "charitable" institutions.)

Exercise 7.6. More and more children of "mixed" parentage have grown up to achieve fame in their profession and in the broader society—people such as Sen. Barack Obama, D-Ill. and golf pro Tiger Woods. Have such figures reduced the sense of racial distance and hostility in American life? What does the presidential campaign of Senator Obama in 2008 suggest about the distance America has traveled since the Loving decision was handed down?

Can Public Schools Deliberately Integrate Students Today?

Many school systems remain racially divided today. More than two-thirds of African American and Hispanic children still go to schools having an African American and Hispanic majority; many white children still go to schools with all or mostly white student bodies.

More than a half-century after the decision in *Brown*, persistent patterns of racial isolation and separation cannot easily be traced in direct fashion to the old segregation laws. Thus, the courts have overwhelmingly declared school districts to be "unitary," that is, no longer operating under the direct or indirect effects of legalized segregation. They have pulled the plug on most judicial desegregation orders.

But what about communities that are dissatisfied with the progress they have made and seek to create integrated schools? Are they empowered under the equal protection clause to use race as the basis for assigning children to particular schools? Or does the equal protection clause actually forbid them to do so?

What about state universities unhappy about the low numbers of African American and Hispanic students on campus? Can they take race and ethnicity into account in their very competitive admissions processes to bring more diversity to campus?

In *Parents Involved in Community Schools v. Seattle School District No. 1* (2007), the Supreme Court *rejected* the use of race as a factor for assigning students to public high schools and elementary schools. In *Barbara Grutter v. Lee Bollinger* (2003) and *Jennifer Gratz v. Lee Bollinger* (2003), the Supreme Court *upheld* the use of race in college and graduate school admissions for the purpose of promoting educational "diversity."

In the case from Seattle, Washington, the community had struggled with racially separate schools for decades despite the fact there had never been official segregation by law in the city. In 1998 the Seattle School District developed a plan for assigning students to the ten city high schools in which incoming ninth graders would rank their top choices. If there were too many students applying to a particular school, the district used a series of "tiebreakers" to decide who would be admitted. The first tiebreaker favored students who already had a sibling currently enrolled at the chosen school. The second tiebreaker considered the racial makeup of the school and the race of the applicant with the goal of achieving an integrated student body that matched the school district's overall balance of 41 percent white and 59 percent nonwhite students.

The companion case, *Crystal D. Meredith v. Jefferson County Board of Education*, came from Louisville, Kentucky, where the Jefferson County Public Schools had been officially segregated for many decades and then placed under a court desegregation order from 1975 to 2000. At that point the schools were declared to be "unitary" and thus rid of the "vestiges" of their old segregation policy.

In 2001 Jefferson County voluntarily adopted a student assignment plan for the city's 97,000 students, two-thirds of whom are white and one-third of whom are black. That plan was intended to integrate the city's schools and required all public schools to have a minimum black enrollment of 15% and a maximum black enrollment of 50%. Thus, a student's race was taken into account in the process of making school assignments and transfers.

Why does the Court strike down the Seattle and Louisville plans in the following decision? Do you agree that equal protection requires government to be "color-blind" even when it seeks to integrate? (Note that different justices agreed with different parts of Chief Justice Roberts's opinion. When the Supreme Court first began, its decisions were always unanimous; today, many important decisions are divided and justices pick and choose which parts of the Court's reasoning they adhere to.)

PARENTS INVOLVED IN COMMUNITY SCHOOLS v. SEATTLE SCHOOL DIST. NO. 1

Supreme Court of the United States
Argued December 4, 2006.
Decided* June 28, 2007.

*Together with *Meredith, Custodial Parent and Next Friend of McDonald v. Jefferson County Bd. of Ed et al.*, on certiorari to the United States Court of Appeals for the Sixth Circuit.

Majority OPINION   Chief Justice ROBERTS announced the judgment of the Court and delivered the opinion of the Court with respect to Parts I, II, III-A, and III-C, and an opinion with respect to Parts III-B and IV, in which Justices SCALIA, THOMAS, and ALITO join.

The school districts in these cases voluntarily adopted student assignment plans that rely upon race to determine which public schools certain children may attend.... Parents of students denied assignment to particular schools under these plans solely because of their race brought suit, contending that allocating children to different public schools on the basis of race violated the Fourteenth Amendment guarantee of equal protection. The Courts of Appeals below upheld the plans. We granted certiorari, and now reverse.

I

Both cases present the same underlying legal question—whether a public school that had not operated legally segregated schools or has been found to be unitary may choose to classify students by race and rely upon that classification in making school assignments....

III

A

It is well established that when the government distributes burdens or benefits on the basis of individual racial classifications, that action is reviewed under strict scrutiny.... In order to satisfy this searching standard of review, the school districts must demonstrate that the use of individual racial classifications in the assignment plans here under review is "narrowly tailored" to achieve a "compelling" government interest.

... [O]ur prior cases, in evaluating the use of racial classifications in the school context, have recognized two interests that qualify as compelling. The first is the compelling interest of remedying the effects of past intentional discrimination. Yet the Seattle public schools have not shown that they were ever segregated by law, and were not subject to court-ordered

> **Strict Scrutiny**
> The legal standard of review applied to suspect classifications, such as race, under equal protection and to burdens on fundamental rights, such as reproductive freedom or free speech, under due process or the First Amendment in which the government must show the court that it has used the least restrictive means to advance a compelling state interest.

In *Parents Involved in Community Schools v. Seattle School Dist. No. 1*, parents successfully challenged a school assignment plan that required schools to enroll minimum and maximum numbers of African American students. In 2000 Deborah Stallworth, here in November 2006 with her son, Austin Johnson, had successfully fought a plan that would have required Johnson to be bused to a school across town rather than attend his neighborhood school.

desegregation decrees. The Jefferson County public schools [were found to have] "eliminated the vestiges associated with the former policy of segregation and its pernicious effects," and thus had achieved "unitary" status. Jefferson County accordingly does not rely upon an interest in remedying the effects of past intentional discrimination in defending its present use of race in assigning students.

Nor could it. We have emphasized that the harm being remedied by mandatory desegregation plans is the harm that is traceable to segregation, and that "the Constitution is not violated by racial imbalance in the schools, without more." …

The second government interest we have recognized as compelling for purposes of strict scrutiny is the interest in diversity in higher education upheld in *Grutter*. …

The entire gist of the analysis in *Grutter* was that the admissions program at issue there focused on each applicant as an individual, and not simply as a member of a particular racial group. The classification of applicants by race upheld in *Grutter* was only as part of a "highly individualized, holistic review." As the Court explained, "the importance of this individualized consideration in the context of a race-conscious admissions program is paramount." The point of the narrow tailoring analysis in which the *Grutter* Court engaged was to ensure that the use of racial classifications was indeed part of a broader assessment of diversity, and not simply an effort to achieve racial balance, which the Court explained would be "patently unconstitutional."

In the present cases, by contrast, race is not considered as part of a broader effort to achieve "exposure to widely diverse people, cultures, ideas, and viewpoints"; race, for some students, is determinative standing alone. The districts argue that other factors, such as student preferences, affect assignment decisions under their plans, but under each plan when race comes into play, it is decisive by itself. It is not simply one factor weighed with others in reaching a decision, as in *Grutter;* it is *the* factor. Like the University of Michigan undergraduate plan struck down in *Gratz* ... the plans here "do not provide for a meaningful individualized review of applicants" but instead rely on racial classifications in a "nonindividualized, mechanical" way.

Even when it comes to race, the plans here employ only a limited notion of diversity, viewing race exclusively in white/nonwhite terms in Seattle and black/"other" terms in Jefferson County. The Seattle "Board Statement Reaffirming Diversity Rationale" speaks of the "inherent educational value" in "providing students the opportunity to attend schools with diverse student enrollment." But under the Seattle plan, a school with 50 percent Asian-American students and 50 percent white students but no African-American, Native-American, or Latino students would qualify as balanced, while a school with 30 percent Asian-American, 25 percent African-American, 25 percent Latino, and 20 percent white students would not. It is hard to understand how a plan that could allow these results can be viewed as being concerned with achieving enrollment that is "broadly diverse." ...

B

Perhaps recognizing that reliance on *Grutter* cannot sustain their plans, both school districts assert additional interests, distinct from the interest upheld in *Grutter,* to justify their race-based assignments. In briefing and argument before this Court, Seattle contends that its use of race helps to reduce racial concentration in schools and to ensure that racially concentrated housing patterns do not prevent nonwhite students from having access to the most desirable schools. Jefferson County has articulated a similar goal, phrasing its interest in terms of educating its students "in a racially integrated environment." Each school district argues that educational and broader socialization benefits flow from a racially diverse learning environment, and each contends that because the diversity they seek is racial diversity—not the broader diversity at issue in *Grutter*—it makes sense to promote that interest directly by relying on race alone.

The parties and their *amici* dispute whether racial diversity in schools in fact has a marked impact on test scores and other objective yardsticks or achieves intangible socialization benefits. The debate is not one we need to resolve, however, because it is clear that the racial classifications employed by the districts are not narrowly tailored to the goal of achieving the educational and social benefits asserted to flow from racial diversity. In design and operation, the plans are directed only to racial balance, pure and simple, an objective this Court has repeatedly condemned as illegitimate.

> ### Amicus Curiae
> A "friend of the court" who is not a direct party to a case but files a brief to offer advice and useful information to the court. The plural is *Amici Curiae,* for "friends of the court."

The plans are tied to each district's specific racial demographics, rather than to any pedagogic concept of the level of diversity needed to obtain the asserted educational benefits. ...

This working backward to achieve a particular type of racial balance, rather than working forward from some demonstration of the level of diversity that provides the purported benefits, is a fatal flaw under our existing precedent. We have many times over reaffirmed that "[r]acial balance is not to be achieved for its own sake."

Accepting racial balancing as a compelling state interest would justify the imposition of racial proportionality throughout American society, contrary to our repeated recognition that "at the heart of the Constitution's guarantee of equal protection lies the simple command that the Government must treat citizens as individuals, not as simply components of a racial, religious, sexual or national class." ...

C

... The districts have also failed to show that they considered methods other than explicit racial classifications to achieve their stated goals. Narrow tailoring requires "serious, good faith consideration of workable race-neutral alternatives." ...

IV

... Before *Brown*, schoolchildren were told where they could and could not go to school based on the color of their skin. The school districts in these cases have not carried the heavy burden of demonstrating that we should allow this once again—even for very different reasons. For schools that never segregated on the basis of race, such as Seattle, or that have removed the vestiges of past segregation, such as Jefferson County, the way "to achieve a system of determining admission to the public schools on a nonracial basis" is to stop assigning students on a racial basis. The way to stop discrimination on the basis of race is to stop discriminating on the basis of race....

It is so ordered.

Dissenting VOICES

Justice Breyer, joined by Justices Stevens, Souter, and Ginsburg, filed a dissenting opinion characterized by what he admitted to be "exceptional length" but also by extraordinary passion, indeed anger at what he saw as the Court's sweeping betrayal of the promise of *Brown*.

Justice Breyer pointed out that the Court had before "consistently and unequivocally approved" of local governments developing "race-conscious" plans to undo the structural effects of school segregation, both in its legalized and de facto forms. This permission to school districts to deliberately bring about integration "represents a constitutional principle firmly rooted in federal and state law." While the equal protection clause might not *require* active desegregation efforts by cities and counties long after official segregation is over, it certainly allows such efforts. The equal protection clause, he wrote, "has always distinguished in practice between state action that excludes and thereby subordinates racial minorities and state action that seeks to bring together people of all races."

According to Justice Breyer, the histories of Louisville and Seattle disclose "complex circumstances and a long tradition of conscientious efforts by local school boards to resist racial segregation in public schools." The Court thus made its decision in a way harshly indifferent to the long-term struggle in these cities to overcome racism, promote interracial education, and create a unified civic life.

Justice Breyer was convinced that the cities' plans were "supported by compelling state interests and are narrowly tailored to accomplish those goals." Just as student body diversity was deemed to be a compelling interest at the university level, it was the same, or even more so, in public primary and secondary schools, where younger students actually stand to gain even more from learning in a multiracial environment where they can be exposed to children from many different backgrounds and life experiences.

Justice Breyer denounced the plurality's approach for risking "serious harm to the law and for the Nation." He stressed that there is a major difference between government using race to exclude and degrade people and government using race to include and uplift people. He argued that the Court's decision "slows down and sets back the work of local school boards to bring about racially diverse schools." He thought that the decision undermines the capacity of local school districts to integrate. "Yesterday, school boards had available to them a full range of means to combat segregated schools. Today, they do not."

Justice Breyer thought that the Court had trampled the power of local schools to deal with the vexing issues caused by racism:

> And what of respect for democratic local decisionmaking by States and school boards? For several decades this Court has rested its public school decisions upon *Swann*'s basic view that the Constitution grants local school districts a significant degree of leeway where the inclusive use of race-conscious criteria is at issue. Now localities will have to cope with the difficult problems they face (including resegregation) deprived of one means they may find necessary.

He thought that the Court had inverted the meaning of Equal Protection:

> And what of the long history and moral vision that the Fourteenth Amendment itself embodies? The plurality cites in support those who argued in *Brown* against segregation, and Justice Thomas likens the approach that I have taken to that of segregation's defenders. But segregation policies did not simply tell schoolchildren "where they could and could not go to school based on the color of their skin," ... they perpetuated a caste system rooted in the institutions of slavery and 80 years of legalized subordination.

Finally, looking to the future, Justice Breyer demanded to know,

> [W]hat of the hope and promise of *Brown?* For much of this Nation's history, the races remained divided. It was not long ago that people of different races drank from separate fountains, rode on separate buses, and studied in separate schools. In this Court's finest hour, *Brown v. Board of Education* challenged this history and helped to change it. For *Brown* held out a promise. It was a promise embodied in three Amendments designed to make citizens of slaves. It was the promise of true racial equality—not as a matter of fine words on paper, but as a matter of everyday life in the Nation's cities and schools. It was about the nature of a democracy that must work for all Americans. It sought one law, one Nation, one people, not simply as a matter of legal principle but in terms of how we actually live.
>
> Not everyone welcomed this Court's decision in *Brown*. Three years after that decision was handed down, the Governor of Arkansas ordered state militia to block the doors of a white schoolhouse so that black children could not enter. The President of the United States dispatched the 101st Airborne Division to Little Rock, Arkansas, and federal troops were needed to enforce a desegregation decree. Today, almost 50 years

later, attitudes toward race in this Nation have changed dramatically. Many parents, white and black alike, want their children to attend schools with children of different races. Indeed, the very school districts that once spurned integration now strive for it. The long history of their efforts reveals the complexities and difficulties they have faced. And in light of those challenges, they have asked us not to take from their hands the instruments they have used to rid their schools of racial segregation, instruments that they believe are needed to overcome the problems of cities divided by race and poverty. The plurality would decline their modest request.

The plurality is wrong to do so. The last half-century has witnessed great strides toward racial equality, but we have not yet realized the promise of *Brown*. To invalidate the plans under review is to threaten the promise of *Brown*. The plurality's position, I fear, would break that promise. This is a decision that the Court and the Nation will come to regret.

WHAT DO YOU **Think?**

Exercise 7.7. Justice Kennedy, who signed on to the plurality decision striking down Seattle's plan, nonetheless emphasized that Seattle and Louisville are "free to devise race-conscious measures to address the problem in a general way and without treating each student in different fashion solely on the basis of a systematic, individual typing by race." Specifically, he suggested,

> strategic site selection of new schools; drawing attendance zones with general recognition of the demographics of neighborhoods; allocating resources for special programs; recruiting students and faculty in a targeted fashion; and tracking enrollments, performance, and other statistics by race. These mechanisms are race conscious but do not lead to different treatment based on a classification that tells each student he or she is to be defined by race, so it is unlikely any of them would demand strict scrutiny to be found permissible.

If you were on the Seattle School Board, would you feel that it is still important in the aftermath of this decision to find ways to promote racial integration? Why or why not? What steps would you take to integrate the city's ten high schools now that the Supreme Court has ordered you not to take account of race or ethnicity in school assignments? Evaluate Justice Kennedy's suggestions and see if you can come up with useful ideas that would not be struck down by the Court.

Exercise 7.8. Some scholars, such as law professor Darren Hutchinson, argue that like many politicians the Supreme Court in the twenty-first century is suffering from "racial exhaustion." Is your generation also exhausted with trying to integrate people and break down racial and ethnic fear? Is it a waste of time for the local governments of Seattle and Louisville to try?

Exercise 7.9. Why does the Census Bureau in the Commerce Department ask all persons in the United States about their race and ethnicity on the census every ten years? What purposes does it serve? Should we give up that practice and follow France and other countries in keeping no records of "race" and refusing to recognize it as a legal category? Is this approach logically required by the Court's ideas about "color-blindness"?

Exercise 7.10. What is "color-blindness"? Are you color-blind in forming friendships and in your social life? When you make friends with people from a different group or background, do you try to ignore and never mention their race, their religion, their ethnicity, their gender, their sexual orientation? Do you ignore your own? Or do you incorporate these things into your understanding of your friends and yourself and try to talk about them sometimes? Have a discussion in which you explore the ways in which these identity characteristics are either irrelevant or relevant. Should the government be "color-blind" even if the society is not?

Race and Ethnicity in College and Graduate School Admissions: Affirmative Action or "Reverse Discrimination"?

The formal dismantling of college admission barriers for African Americans in the 1950s and 1960s did not mean automatic integration of the traditionally all-white state colleges and universities. Many state schools had developed campus cultures—-complete with blackface minstrel shows at fraternity rush parties and Confederate flags flapping in the wind—that were, at best, cold and hostile to African Americans. Many universities were openly racist and resisted integration, going so far in some cases as to alter admissions standards to make it more difficult for black students to enter. The University of Maryland at College Park refused to allow Dr. Martin Luther King to come to its campus in 1964 but the same year hosted a political rally for segregationist Alabama governor George Wallace, who "attracted the largest crowd in the history of the University" and stirred an "emotional intensity" among the thousands assembled that "exceeded that of a football game," according to a federal district court reviewing the university's history.

Although the Supreme Court began to order the desegregation of universities in 1950 in *Sweatt v. Painter,* the federal government in 1969—nineteen years later—was still calling on nine southern and border states, including Maryland, to integrate their state university systems.

Yet, even where doors were opened up a bit, after centuries of racial oppression and exclusion, there were precious few minority students prepared to compete against their affluent white counterparts in the increasingly competitive college and graduate school admissions process. Thus, to counter their own histories of segregation and discrimination, many state (and private) universities voluntarily undertook a program of "affirmative action" in the 1980s to recruit and admit minority students. The University of Maryland at College Park, for example, engaged in a wide variety of efforts to attract qualified minority students to its campus and created a special minority scholarship program, the Banneker Program, designed to make college more affordable for them. (This program would later be struck down by the Fourth Circuit Court of Appeals as unconstitutional "reverse discrimination.")

Affirmative action produced a backlash. Many white students who were not admitted to the college or graduate school of their choice blamed affirmative action. They felt cheated—why were minority students with lower test scores and grades being admitted when they were not? Of course, there was no way to prove that these white students would have been admitted in the absence of affirmative action—indeed, in many cases, they most certainly would not have been. But they still felt that race now worked unfairly to the disadvantage of whites.

In 1978 the Supreme Court considered a challenge to affirmative action in *Regents of the University of California v. Bakke.* In that case, Allan Bakke, a disappointed white applicant to the medical school of the University of California at Davis, sued the school for reserving 16 out of 100 places in the entering class for minority students, including African Americans, Chicanos, Asian Americans, and Native Americans. Bakke successfully showed that many minority applicants, though certainly qualified to go to medical school, "were admitted with grade point averages [and] Medical College Admissions Test scores significantly lower than Bakke's." He did not show, and could not show, that he would have been admitted absent the program, because many white applicants with scores lower than his were admitted.

The Court was deeply divided. Four justices thought that race-conscious admissions for the purposes of affirmative action and integration should not be subjected to strict scrutiny but to a lower level of examination. They found that the state's interests in correcting the historic underrepresentation of minorities in university life was surely important enough to justify the program. But four other justices would have imposed strict scrutiny and struck the program down as an unlawful use of race.

Justice Powell became the key justice in the case. He voted with the more conservative faction to find that the rigid numerical set-aside of 16 places was unconstitutional and therefore ordered Bakke admitted. But he allowed that an affirmative action plan that uses a minority's race or ethnicity as a softer "plus" factor was acceptable to promote educational "diversity," which he said was a goal of "paramount importance" in a university. Citing the so-called Harvard plan, Powell argued that it took race and ethnicity into account as one factor among many criteria that were not strictly meritocratic in nature, such as a student's home state or his or her parents' status as alumni.

The conservatives felt—and have since come to argue strenuously—that any use of race in the admissions process to help minority applicants violates equal protection. The liberals thought that this view twists and inverts equal protection to deny government the power to assist people who were victims of exclusion and discrimination for centuries. As Justice Marshall pointed out in *Bakke,* the same Congress that added the words *equal protection* to the Constitution in 1868 had voted by statute for the Freedmen's Bureau, whose explicit goal was to transfer resources to the recently freed black population. Marshall wrote that "it is inconceivable that the Fourteenth Amendment was intended to prohibit all race-conscious measures." Justice Blackmun's thoughts were especially cogent: "[In] order to get beyond racism, we must first take account of race."

But the explosive controversy over racial and ethnic affirmative action has never subsided, and the Supreme Court revisited the issue in 2003 in a pair of cases brought by white applicants disappointed by their rejection from the University of Michigan.

In *Gratz v. Bollinger,* the Court struck down the undergraduate admissions affirmative action plan at the University of Michigan, which automatically extended a bonus "20 points" to applicants from underrepresented minority groups on a 150-point selection index used by the admissions office to profile the strengths of those in the applicant pool. (An applicant was effectively guaranteed admission with a 100-point rating.) The Court found that this numerical race preference violated the equal protection rights of the white plaintiff, Jennifer Gratz, who graduated with a 3.8 grade point average (GPA) in high school but was denied admission at the University of Michigan at Ann Arbor and went on to study mathematics at the Dearborn campus instead. The Court reasoned that the numerical race preference departed from the individualized consideration that Justice Powell demanded from affirmative action plans in *Bakke* and which characterized the acceptable "Harvard Plan."

However, in *Gutter v. Bollinger,* which was handed down by the Court the same day, the majority upheld the University of Michigan Law School's affirmative action policy. The law school had never quantified a preference for minority applicants but simply considered race as a valid consideration among a host of factors, some of them "hard," such as LSAT scores and grades, and some of them "soft," for example, letters of recommendation and the geographic and college major diversity of the applicant pool. Significantly, the Court found that the law school, like other institutions of higher education across the country, does have a "compelling interest" in promoting educational "diversity," including the diversity achieved by assembling at least a "critical mass" of students belonging to traditionally underrepresented minority groups.

As you read these decisions, examine the underlying views of the justices about what the concept of equal protection means and what a university should be. Also, focus carefully on how the university considers the qualifications of college applicants—this is the same process that will affect you if and when you decide to apply to college!

JENNIFER GRATZ and PATRICK HAMACHER, Petitioners v. LEE BOLLINGER et al.

Supreme Court of the United States
Argued April 1, 2003.
Decided June 23, 2003.

Majority OPINION   Chief Justice REHNQUIST delivered the opinion of the Court.

We granted certiorari in this case to decide whether "the University of Michigan's use of racial preferences in undergraduate admissions violates the Equal Protection Clause of the Fourteenth Amendment." Because we find that the manner in which the University considers the race of applicants in its undergraduate admissions guidelines violates the [Constitution], we reverse that portion of the District Court's decision upholding the guidelines.

> **Equal Protection Clause**
> The clause contained in the Fourteenth Amendment requiring government to use only rational classifications among people and not draw lines on the basis of race, ethnicity, or religion without a "compelling" reason or on the basis of gender without an "important" reason.

I

A

Petitioners Jennifer Gratz and Patrick Hamacher both applied for admission to the University of Michigan's (University) College of Literature, Science, and the Arts (LSA) as residents of the State of Michigan. Both petitioners are Caucasian. Gratz, who applied for admission for the fall of 1995, was notified in January of that year that a final decision re-garding her admission had been delayed until April. This delay was based upon the University's determination that, although Gratz was "well qualified," she was "less compet-itive than the students who had been admitted on first review." Gratz was notified in April that the LSA was unable to offer her admission. She enrolled in the University of Michigan at Dearborn, from which she graduated in the spring of 1999.

Hamacher applied for admission to the LSA for the fall of 1997. A final decision as to his application was also postponed because, though his "academic credentials [were] in the qualified range, they [were] not at the level needed for first review admission." Hamacher's application was subsequently denied in April 1997, and he enrolled at Michigan State University....

B

The University has changed its admissions guidelines a number of times during the pe-riod relevant to this litigation, and we summarize the most significant of these changes briefly. The University's Office of Undergraduate Admissions (OUA) oversees the LSA ad-missions process. In order to promote consistency in the review of the large number of ap-plications received, the OUA uses written guidelines for each academic year. Admissions counselors make admissions decisions in accordance with these guidelines.

OUA considers a number of factors in making admissions decisions, including high school grades, standardized test scores, high school quality, curriculum strength, geogra-phy, alumni relationships, and leadership. OUA also considers race. During all periods rel-evant to this litigation, the University has considered African-Americans, Hispanics, and Native Americans to be "underrepresented minorities," and it is undisputed that the University admits "virtually every qualified ... applicant" from these groups.

During 1995 and 1996, OUA counselors evaluated applications according to grade point average combined with what were referred to as the "SCUGA" factors. These factors included the quality of an applicant's high school (S), the strength of an applicant's high school curriculum (C), an applicant's unusual circumstances (U), an applicant's geograph-ical residence (G), and an applicant's alumni relationships (A). After these scores were combined to produce an applicant's "GPA 2" score, the reviewing admissions counselors referenced a set of "Guidelines" tables, which listed GPA 2 ranges on the vertical axis, and American College Test/Scholastic Aptitude Test (ACT/SAT) scores on the horizontal axis. Each table was divided into cells that included one or more courses of action to be taken, including admit, reject, delay for additional information, or postpone for reconsideration.

In both years, applicants with the same GPA 2 score and ACT/SAT score were subject to different admissions outcomes based upon their racial or ethnic status. For example, as a Caucasian in-state applicant, Gratz's GPA 2 score and ACT score placed her within a cell calling for a postponed decision on her application. An in-state or out-of-state minority applicant with Gratz's scores would have fallen within a cell calling for admission....

Beginning with the 1998 academic year, the OUA dispensed with the Guidelines tables and the SCUGA point system in favor of a "selection index," on which an applicant could score a maximum of 150 points. This index was divided linearly into ranges generally call-ing for admissions dispositions as follows: 100-150 (admit); 95-99 (admit or postpone);

90-94 (postpone or admit); 75-89 (delay or postpone); 74 and below (delay or reject).

Each application received points based on high school grade point average, standardized test scores, academic quality of an applicant's high school, strength or weakness of high school curriculum, in-state residency, alumni relationship, personal essay, and personal achievement or leadership. Of particular significance here, under a "miscellaneous" category, an applicant was entitled to 20 points based upon his or her membership in an underrepresented racial or ethnic minority group. The University explained that the "development of the selection index for admissions in 1998 changed only the mechanics, not the substance of how race and ethnicity were considered in admissions."

In all application years from 1995 to 1998, the guidelines provided that qualified applicants from underrepresented minority groups be admitted as soon as possible in light of the University's belief that such applicants were more likely to enroll if promptly notified of their admission. Also from 1995 through 1998, the University carefully managed its rolling admissions system to permit consideration of certain applications submitted later in the academic year through the use of "protected seats." Specific groups—including athletes, foreign students, ROTC candidates, and underrepresented minorities—were "protected categories" eligible for these seats. A committee called the Enrollment Working Group (EWG) projected how many applicants from each of these protected categories the University was likely to receive after a given date and then paced admissions decisions to permit full consideration of expected applications from these groups. If this space was not filled by qualified candidates from the designated groups toward the end of the admissions season, it was then used to admit qualified candidates remaining in the applicant pool, including those on the waiting list....

II

B

... It is by now well established that "all racial classifications reviewable under the Equal Protection Clause must be strictly scrutinized." This "standard of review ... is not dependent on the race of those burdened or benefited by a particular classification." Thus, "any person, of whatever race, has the right to demand that any governmental actor subject to the Constitution justify any racial classification subjecting that person to unequal treatment under the strictest of judicial scrutiny."

To withstand our strict scrutiny analysis, respondents must demonstrate that the University's use of race in its current admission program employs "narrowly tailored measures that further compelling governmental interests." ... We find that the University's policy, which automatically distributes 20 points, or one-fifth of the points needed to guarantee admission, to every single "underrepresented minority" applicant solely because of race, is not narrowly tailored to achieve the interest in educational diversity that respondents claim justifies their program....

Justice Powell's opinion in *Bakke* emphasized the importance of considering each particular applicant as an individual, assessing all of the qualities that individual possesses, and in turn, evaluating that individual's ability to contribute to the unique setting of higher education. The admissions program Justice Powell described, however, did not contemplate that any single characteristic automatically ensured a specific and identifiable contribution to a university's diversity. Instead, under the approach Justice Powell described, each characteristic of a particular applicant was to be considered in assessing the applicant's entire application.

The current LSA policy does not provide such individualized consideration. The LSA's policy automatically distributes 20 points to every single applicant from an "underrepresented minority" group, as defined by the University. The only consideration that accompanies this distribution of points is a factual review of an application to determine whether an individual is a member of one of these minority groups. Moreover, unlike Justice Powell's example, where the race of a "particular black applicant" could be considered without being decisive, see *Bakke*, the LSA's automatic distribution of 20 points has the effect of making "the factor of race … decisive" for virtually every minimally qualified underrepresented minority applicant.…

Respondents contend that "[t]he volume of applications and the presentation of applicant information make it impractical for [LSA] to use the … admissions system" upheld by the Court today in *Grutter*. But the fact that the implementation of a program capable of providing individualized consideration might present administrative challenges does not render constitutional an otherwise problematic system. Nothing in Justice Powell's opinion in *Bakke* signaled that a university may employ whatever means it desires to achieve the stated goal of diversity without regard to the limits imposed by our strict scrutiny analysis.

We conclude, therefore, that because the University's use of race in its current freshman admissions policy is not narrowly tailored to achieve respondents' asserted compelling interest in diversity, the admissions policy violates the Equal Protection Clause of the Fourteenth Amendment.…

It is so ordered.

WHAT DO YOU Think?

Exercise 7.11. Jennifer Gratz graduated from the University of Michigan at Dearborn and went to work in the computer software industry. After winning her case in the Supreme Court, she returned to Michigan to become the executive director of the Michigan Civil Rights Initiative, a ballot initiative campaign working to eliminate all "racial preferences" in public education and employment in the State of Michigan. Its purpose was to eliminate not just the quota-like preferences that had been struck down by the Supreme Court in Jennifer's case but also the use of softer affirmative action standards that had been approved in *Grutter v. Bollinger* (case follows). The ballot measure passed by 58 percent to 42 percent on November 7, 2006, essentially requiring Michigan government to be "colorblind" in education and hiring. Do you think that Jennifer Gratz was discriminated against in the same way Linda Brown was or the children were in *Brown v. Board of Education* and *Griffin v. County School Board of Prince Edward County,* respectively? Why or why not?

The Court found that the undergraduate affirmative action plan depended on an unconstitutionally rigid and mechanical use of race to produce diversity in the freshman class. But the Court found in the next case that the law school's plan consciously promoted racial diversity with an admissions process sufficiently flexible as not to create an unlawful race quota. The conservative dissenters saw the "individualized" use of race as just a camouflaged form of the same reverse discrimination. What do you think?

....

BARBARA GRUTTER, Petitioner v. LEE BOLLINGER et al.

Supreme Court of the United States
Argued April 1, 2003.
Decided June 23, 2003.

Majority OPINION   Justice O'CONNOR delivered the opinion of the Court.

This case requires us to decide whether the use of race as a factor in student admissions by the University of Michigan Law School (Law School) is unlawful.

I

A

The Law School ranks among the Nation's top law schools. It receives more than 3,500 applications each year for a class of around 350 students. Seeking to "admit a group of students who individually and collectively are among the most capable," the Law School looks for individuals with "substantial promise for success in law school" and "a strong likelihood of succeeding in the practice of law and contributing in diverse ways to the well-being of others." More broadly, the Law School seeks "a mix of students with varying backgrounds

Barbara Grutter (left) and Jennifer Gratz talk to reporters outside the Supreme Court on April 1, 2003, the day that the Court heard arguments in their cases against the University of Michigan's admission procedures.

and experiences who will respect and learn from each other." In 1992, the dean of the Law School charged a faculty committee with crafting a written admissions policy to implement these goals....

The hallmark of that policy is its focus on academic ability coupled with a flexible assessment of applicants' talents, experiences, and potential "to contribute to the learning of those around them." The policy requires admissions officials to evaluate each applicant based on all the information available in the file, including a personal statement, letters of recommendation, and an essay describing the ways in which the applicant will contribute to the life and diversity of the Law School. In reviewing an applicant's file, admissions officials must consider the applicant's undergraduate grade point average (GPA) and Law School Admissions Test (LSAT) score because they are important (if imperfect) predictors of academic success in law school. The policy stresses that "no applicant should be admitted unless we expect that applicant to do well enough to graduate with no serious academic problems."

The policy makes clear, however, that even the highest possible score does not guarantee admission to the Law School. Nor does a low score automatically disqualify an applicant. Rather, the policy requires admissions officials to look beyond grades and test scores to other criteria that are important to the Law School's educational objectives. So-called "'soft' variables" such as "the enthusiasm of recommenders, the quality of the undergraduate institution, the quality of the applicant's essay, and the areas and difficulty of undergraduate course selection" are all brought to bear in assessing an "applicant's likely contributions to the intellectual and social life of the institution."

The policy aspires to "achieve that diversity which has the potential to enrich everyone's education and thus make a law school class stronger than the sum of its parts." The policy does not restrict the types of diversity contributions eligible for "substantial weight" in the admissions process, but instead recognizes "many possible bases for diversity admissions." The policy does, however, reaffirm the Law School's longstanding commitment to "one particular type of diversity," that is, "racial and ethnic diversity with special reference to the inclusion of students from groups which have been historically discriminated against, like African-Americans, Hispanics and Native Americans, who without this commitment might not be represented in our student body in meaningful numbers." By enrolling a "'critical mass' of [underrepresented] minority students," the Law School seeks to "ensure their ability to make unique contributions to the character of the Law School." ...

B

Petitioner Barbara Grutter is a white Michigan resident who applied to the Law School in 1996 with a 3.8 grade point average and 161 LSAT score. The Law School initially placed petitioner on a waiting list, but subsequently rejected her application.... Petitioner allege[s] that respondents discriminated against her on the basis of race in violation of the Fourteenth Amendment....

II

B

The Equal Protection Clause provides that no State shall "deny to any person within its jurisdiction the equal protection of the laws." Because the Fourteenth Amendment "protects *persons,* not *groups,*" all "governmental action based on race—a *group* classification long recognized as in most circumstances irrelevant and therefore prohibited—should be subjected to detailed judicial inquiry to ensure that the *personal* right to equal protection of the laws has not been infringed." We are a "free people whose institutions are founded upon the doctrine of equality." It follows from that principle that "government may treat people differently because of their race only for the most compelling reasons."

We have held that all racial classifications imposed by government "must be analyzed by a reviewing court under strict scrutiny." This means that such classifications are constitutional only if they are narrowly tailored to further compelling governmental interests....

III

A

With these principles in mind, we turn to the question whether the Law School's use of race is justified by a compelling state interest. Before this Court respondents assert only one justification for their use of race in the admissions process: obtaining "the educational benefits that flow from a diverse student body." ...

The Law School's educational judgment that such diversity is essential to its educational mission is one to which we defer. The Law School's assessment that diversity will, in fact, yield educational benefits is substantiated by respondents and their *amici....*

We have long recognized that, given the important purpose of public education and the expansive freedoms of speech and thought associated with the university environment, universities occupy a special niche in our constitutional tradition.... Our conclusion that the Law School has a compelling interest in a diverse student body is informed by our view that attaining a diverse student body is at the heart of the Law School's proper institutional mission...

As part of its goal of "assembling a class that is both exceptionally academically qualified and broadly diverse," the Law School seeks to "enroll a 'critical mass' of minority students." The Law School's interest is not simply "to assure within its student body some specified percentage of a particular group merely because of its race or ethnic origin." That would amount to outright racial balancing, which is patently unconstitutional. Rather, the Law School's concept of critical mass is defined by reference to the educational benefits that diversity is designed to produce.

These benefits are substantial. As the District Court emphasized, the Law School's admissions policy promotes "cross-racial understanding," helps to break down racial stereotypes, and "enables [students] to better understand persons of different races." These benefits are "important and laudable," because "classroom discussion is livelier, more spirited, and simply more enlightening and interesting" when the students have "the greatest possible variety of backgrounds." ...

These benefits are not theoretical but real, as major American businesses have made clear that the skills needed in today's increasingly global marketplace can only be developed through exposure to widely diverse people, cultures, ideas, and viewpoints.... Effective participation by members of all racial and ethnic groups in the civic life of our Nation is essential if the dream of one Nation, indivisible, is to be realized.

Moreover, universities, and in particular, law schools, represent the training ground for a large number of our Nation's leaders. Individuals with law degrees occupy roughly half the state governorships, more than half the seats in the United States Senate, and more than a third of the seats in the United States House of Representatives. The pattern is even more striking when it comes to highly selective law schools. A handful of these schools accounts for 25 of the 100 United States Senators, 74 United States Courts of Appeals judges, and nearly 200 of the more than 600 United States District Court judges.

In order to cultivate a set of leaders with legitimacy in the eyes of the citizenry, it is necessary that the path to leadership be visibly open to talented and qualified individuals of every race and ethnicity. All members of our heterogeneous society must have confidence in the openness and integrity of the educational institutions that provide this training....

B

... To be narrowly tailored, a race-conscious admissions program cannot use a quota system—it cannot "insulate each category of applicants with certain desired qualifications from competition with all other applicants." Instead, a university may consider race or ethnicity only as a "'plus' in a particular applicant's file," without "insulating the individual from comparison with all other candidates for the available seats." ...

We find that the Law School's admissions program bears the hallmarks of a narrowly tailored plan. As Justice Powell made clear in *Bakke,* truly individualized consideration demands that race be used in a flexible, nonmechanical way. It follows from this mandate that universities cannot establish quotas for members of certain racial groups or put members of those groups on separate admissions tracks. Nor can universities insulate applicants who belong to certain racial or ethnic groups from the competition for admission. Universities can, however, consider race or ethnicity more flexibly as a "plus" factor in the context of individualized consideration of each and every applicant.

We are satisfied that the Law School's admissions program, like the Harvard plan described by Justice Powell, does not operate as a quota. Properly understood, a "quota" is a program in which a certain fixed number or proportion of opportunities are "reserved exclusively for certain minority groups." ... In contrast, "a permissible goal requires only a good-faith effort ... to come within a range demarcated by the goal itself" and permits consideration of race as a "plus" factor in any given case while still ensuring that each candidate "competes with all other qualified applicants." ...

The Chief Justice believes that the Law School's policy conceals an attempt to achieve racial balancing, and cites admissions data to contend that the Law School discriminates among different groups within the critical mass. But, as the Chief Justice concedes, the number of underrepresented minority students who ultimately enroll in the Law School differs substantially from their representation in the applicant pool and varies considerably for each group from year to year....

Here, the Law School engages in a highly individualized, holistic review of each applicant's file, giving serious consideration to all the ways an applicant might contribute to a diverse educational environment. The Law School affords this individualized consideration to applicants of all races. There is no policy of automatic acceptance or rejection based on any single "soft" variable. Unlike the program at issue in *Gratz v Bollinger*, the Law School awards no mechanical, predetermined diversity "bonuses" based on race or ethnicity. Like the Harvard plan, the Law School's admissions policy "is flexible enough to consider all pertinent elements of diversity in light of the particular qualifications of each applicant, and to place them on the same footing for consideration, although not necessarily according them the same weight." ...

The Law School does not, however, limit in any way the broad range of qualities and experiences that may be considered valuable contributions to student body diversity. To the contrary, the 1992 policy makes clear "there are many possible bases for diversity admissions," and provides examples of admittees who have lived or traveled widely abroad, are fluent in several languages, have overcome personal adversity and family hardship, have exceptional records of extensive community service, and have had successful careers in other fields. The Law School seriously considers each "applicant's promise of making a notable contribution to the class by way of a particular strength, attainment, or characteristic—*e.g.,* an unusual intellectual achievement, employment experience, nonacademic performance, or personal background." All applicants have the opportunity to highlight their own potential diversity contributions through the submission of a personal statement, letters of recommendation, and an essay describing the ways in which the applicant will contribute to the life and diversity of the Law School....

We acknowledge that "there are serious problems of justice connected with the idea of preference itself." Narrow tailoring, therefore, requires that a race-conscious admissions program not unduly harm members of any racial group....

We are satisfied that the Law School's admissions program does not. Because the Law School considers "all pertinent elements of diversity," it can (and does) select nonminority applicants who have greater potential to enhance student body diversity over underrepresented minority applicants....

We are mindful, however, that "[a] core purpose of the Fourteenth Amendment was to do away with all governmentally imposed discrimination based on race." Accordingly, race-conscious admissions policies must be limited in time....

We take the Law School at its word that it would "like nothing better than to find a race-neutral admissions formula" and will terminate its race-conscious admissions program as soon as practicable. It has been 25 years since Justice Powell first approved the use of race to further an interest in student body diversity in the context of public higher education. Since that time, the number of minority applicants with high grades and test scores has indeed increased. We expect that 25 years from now, the use of racial preferences will no longer be necessary to further the interest approved today.

IV

In summary, the Equal Protection Clause does not prohibit the Law School's narrowly tailored use of race in admissions decisions to further a compelling interest in obtaining the educational benefits that flow from a diverse student body.... The judgment of the Court of Appeals for the Sixth Circuit, accordingly, is affirmed.

It is so ordered.

Dissenting VOICES

Chief Justice Rehnquist, joined by Justices Scalia, Kennedy, and Thomas, rejected the majority's distinction between the college and law school affirmative action plans in the *Grutter* case: he thought that both programs involved unlawful uses of race to distribute public goods. He wrote:

> Stripped of its "critical mass" veil, the Law School's program is revealed as a naked effort to achieve racial balancing.... [The] asserted justification for the Law School's use of race in the admissions process is "obtaining the educational benefits that flow from a diverse student body." ... From 1995 through 2000, the Law School admitted between 1,130 and 1,310 students. Of those, between 13 and 19 were Native American, between 91 and 108 were African-Americans, and between 47 and 56 were Hispanic. If the Law School is admitting between 91 and 108 African-Americans in order to achieve "critical mass," thereby preventing African-American students from feeling "isolated or like spokespersons for their race," one would think that a number of the same order of magnitude would be necessary to accomplish the same purpose for Hispanics and Native Americans. Similarly, even if all of the Native American applicants admitted in a given year matriculate, which the record demonstrates is not at all the case, how can this possibly constitute a "critical mass" of Native Americans in a class of over 350 students? In order for this pattern of admission to be consistent with the Law School's explanation of "critical mass," one would have to believe that the objectives of "critical mass" offered by respondents are achieved with only half the number of Hispanics and one-sixth the number of Native Americans as compared to African-Americans....

Chief Justice Rehnquist assailed the Law School's differing treatment of students in different minority groups. He pointed out that

> [I]n 2000, 12 Hispanics who scored between a 159-160 on the LSAT and earned a GPA of 3.00 or higher applied for admission and only 2 were admitted. Meanwhile, 12 African-Americans in the same range of qualifications applied for admission and all 12 were admitted. Likewise, that same year, 16 Hispanics who scored between a 151-153 on the LSAT and earned a 3.00 or higher applied for admission and only 1 of those applicants was admitted. Twenty-three similarly qualified African-Americans applied for admission and 14 were admitted.... [T]he Law School's disparate admissions practices with respect to these minority groups demonstrate that its alleged goal of "critical mass" is simply a sham.

After showing that the admission of minority students from different groups fluctuates with the number who apply, Chief Justice Rehnquist concluded,

> The Law School has offered no explanation for its actual admissions practices and, unexplained, we are bound to conclude that the Law School has managed its admissions program, not to achieve a "critical mass," but to extend offers of admission to members of selected minority groups in proportion to their statistical representation in the ap-

plicant pool. But this is precisely the type of racial balancing that the Court itself calls "patently unconstitutional."

Justice Kennedy filed his own dissenting opinion, in which he questioned whether the law school even had a compelling interest in having affirmative action. He wrote:

> The "educational benefit" that the University of Michigan seeks to achieve by racial discrimination consists, according to the Court, of "cross-racial understanding," and "better prepar[ation of] students for an increasingly diverse workforce and society," all of which is necessary not only for work, but also for good "citizenship." This is not, of course, an "educational benefit" on which students will be graded on their Law School transcript (Works and Plays Well with Others: B+) or tested by the bar examiners (Q: Describe in 500 words or less your cross-racial understanding). For it is a lesson of life rather than law—essentially the same lesson taught to (or rather learned by, for it cannot be "taught" in the usual sense) people three feet shorter and twenty years younger than the full-grown adults at the University of Michigan Law School, in institutions ranging from Boy Scout troops to public-school kindergartens. If properly considered an "educational benefit" at all, it is surely not one that is either uniquely relevant to law school or uniquely "teachable" in a formal educational setting.

Justice Thomas also filed his own impassioned dissenting opinion, which was joined by Justice Scalia. In it, he began with a long quotation from the great Frederick Douglass:

> Frederick Douglass, speaking to a group of abolitionists almost 140 years ago, delivered a message lost on today's majority:
> "In regard to the colored people, there is always more that is benevolent, I perceive, than just, manifested towards us. What I ask for the negro is not benevolence, not pity, not sympathy, but simply *justice*. The American people have always been anxious to know what they shall do with us.... I have had but one answer from the beginning. Do nothing with us! Your doing with us has already played the mischief with us. Do nothing with us! If the apples will not remain on the tree of their own strength, if they are worm-eaten at the core, if they are early ripe and disposed to fall, let them fall! ... And if the negro cannot stand on his own legs, let him fall also. All I ask is, give him a chance to stand on his own legs! Let him alone! ... Your interference is doing him positive injury."
> Like Douglass, I believe blacks can achieve in every avenue of American life without the meddling of university administrators. Because I wish to see all students succeed whatever their color, I share, in some respect, the sympathies of those who sponsor the type of discrimination advanced by the University of Michigan Law School (Law School). The Constitution does not, however, tolerate institutional devotion to the status quo in admissions policies when such devotion ripens into racial discrimination. Nor does the Constitution countenance the unprecedented deference the Court gives to the Law School, an approach inconsistent with the very concept of "strict scrutiny."

Justice Thomas likened affirmative action to racial discrimination:

> No one would argue that a university could set up a lower general admission standard and then impose heightened requirements only on black applicants. Similarly, a university may not maintain a high admission standard and grant exemptions to favored

races. The Law School, of its own choosing, and for its own purposes, maintains an exclusionary admissions system that it knows produces racially disproportionate results. Racial discrimination is not a permissible solution to the self-inflicted wounds of this elitist admissions policy.

He also pounced on Justice O'Connor's suggestion that affirmative action will be unnecessary in 25 years, transforming her prediction into a prospective decision:

> I agree with the Court's holding that racial discrimination in higher education admissions will be illegal in 25 years. I respectfully dissent from the remainder of the Court's opinion and the judgment, however, because I believe that the Law School's current use of race violates the Equal Protection Clause and that the Constitution means the same thing today as it will in 300 months.

Justice Thomas would have preferred to force the University of Michigan Law School to come up with race-neutral means of advancing diversity. He wrote:

> The Court will not even deign to make the Law School try other methods, preferring instead to grant a 25-year license to violate the Constitution. And the same Court that had the courage to order the desegregation of all public schools in the South now fears, on the basis of platitudes rather than principle, to force the Law School to abandon a decidedly imperfect admissions regime that provides the basis for racial discrimination....
>
> I believe what lies beneath the Court's decision today are the benighted notions that one can tell when racial discrimination benefits (rather than hurts) minority groups, and that racial discrimination is necessary to remedy general societal ills.... I must contest the notion that the Law School's discrimination benefits those admitted as a result of it. The Court spends considerable time discussing the impressive display of *amicus* support for the Law School in this case from all corners of society. But nowhere in any of the filings in this Court is any evidence that the purported "beneficiaries" of this racial discrimination prove themselves by performing at (or even near) the same level as those students who receive no preferences.

Justice Thomas argued that the "silence in this case" about how minority students fare under affirmative action

> is deafening to those of us who view higher education's purpose as imparting knowledge and skills to students, rather than a communal, rubber-stamp, credentialing process. The Law School is not looking for those students who, despite a lower LSAT score or undergraduate grade point average, will succeed in the study of law. The Law School seeks only a facade—it is sufficient that the class looks right, even if it does not perform right.
>
> The Law School tantalizes unprepared students with the promise of a University of Michigan degree and all of the opportunities that it offers. These overmatched students take the bait, only to find that they cannot succeed in the cauldron of competition. And this mismatch crisis is not restricted to elite institutions. Indeed, to cover the tracks of the aestheticists, this cruel farce of racial discrimination must continue—in selection for the Michigan Law Review, and in hiring at law firms and for judicial clerkships—until the "beneficiaries" are no longer tolerated. While these students may graduate with law degrees, there is no evidence that they have received a qualitatively better legal

education (or become better lawyers) than if they had gone to a less "elite" law school for which they were better prepared. And the aestheticists will never address the real problems facing "underrepresented minorities," instead continuing their social experiments on other people's children.

This system is particularly unfair, Justice Thomas thought, to minority students who would have been admitted without the boost of affirmative action. He wrote:

> It is uncontested that each year, the Law School admits a handful of blacks who would be admitted in the absence of racial discrimination. Who can differentiate between those who belong and those who do not? The majority of blacks are admitted to the Law School because of discrimination, and because of this policy all are tarred as undeserving. This problem of stigma does not depend on determinacy as to whether those stigmatized are actually the "beneficiaries" of racial discrimination. When blacks take positions in the highest places of government, industry, or academia, it is an open question today whether their skin color played a part in their advancement. The question itself is the stigma—because either racial discrimination did play a role, in which case the person may be deemed "otherwise unqualified," or it did not, in which case asking the question itself unfairly marks those blacks who would succeed without discrimination.

Justice Thomas returned to the notion of the twenty-five-year clock's ticking on affirmative action, with time apparently being up in 2028. He stated:

> While I agree that in 25 years the practices of the Law School will be illegal, they are, for the reasons I have given, illegal now. The majority does not and cannot rest its time limitation on any evidence that the gap in credentials between black and white students is shrinking or will be gone in that timeframe. In recent years there has been virtually no change, for example, in the proportion of law school applicants with LSAT scores of 165 and higher who are black. In 1993 blacks constituted 1.1% of law school applicants in that score range, though they represented 11.1% of all applicants. In 2000 the comparable numbers were 1.0% and 11.3%. No one can seriously contend, and the Court does not, that the racial gap in academic credentials will disappear in 25 years. Nor is the Court's holding that racial discrimination will be unconstitutional in 25 years made contingent on the gap closing in that time.
>
> Indeed, the very existence of racial discrimination of the type practiced by the Law School may impede the narrowing of the LSAT testing gap. An applicant's LSAT score can improve dramatically with preparation, but such preparation is a cost, and there must be sufficient benefits attached to an improved score to justify additional study. Whites scoring between 163 and 167 on the LSAT are routinely rejected by the Law School, and thus whites aspiring to admission at the Law School have every incentive to improve their score to levels above that range. Blacks, on the other hand, are nearly guaranteed admission if they score above 155. As admission prospects approach certainty, there is no incentive for the black applicant to continue to prepare for the LSAT once he is reasonably assured of achieving the requisite score. It is far from certain that the LSAT test-taker's behavior is responsive to the Law School's admissions policies. Nevertheless, the possibility remains that this racial discrimination will help fulfill the bigot's prophecy about black underperformance—just as it confirms the conspiracy theorist's belief that "institutional racism" is at fault for every racial disparity in our society.

WHAT DO YOU Think?

Exercise 7.12. In *Grutter,* the Court upheld the University of Michigan's claim that it needed to create a "critical mass" of students from different minority groups to foster real diversity on campus. When do students who belong to minority communities reach sufficient "critical mass" on campus to increase their comfort level and give them the sense that they will be seen by peers and professors as individuals and not as spokespeople for ethnic groups? Does Chief Justice Rehnquist succeed in demolishing the "critical mass" argument by showing that affirmative action is used to admit dramatically different numbers of African Americans versus Hispanics and Native Americans?

Exercise 7.13. The Court endorses the proposition that "classroom discussion is livelier, more spirited, and simply more enlightening and interesting" when there is more classroom diversity. Do you agree with this conclusion? Can you think of times when the dynamics of classroom discussion changed because of the presence of students who had a different family background or perspective?

Exercise 7.14. In *Grutter,* Justice O'Connor observed that "universities, and in particular, law schools, represent the training ground for a large number of our Nation's leaders" and pointed out that half of the nation's Governors and Senators are attorneys. Integrating law schools helps substantially to integrate the ranks of political leadership and government. For this reason, many law schools are determined to build a "pipeline" of qualified minority students from middle schools and high schools to college and law school. Are you someone, or do you know someone, who is thinking about going in that direction? Why or why not? If you are part of a Marshall-Brennan Project, talk to your Marshall-Brennan fellow about the things you can be doing now to sharpen your legal thinking and leadership skills. Ask him or her how you should start to plan your career if you think you may want to go to law school.

Exercise 7.15. Justice Thomas ridicules the majority's suggestion that affirmative action for college admissions is constitutional today but will be unconstitutional in 2028, twenty-five years after the decision was rendered. The meaning of the Constitution cannot change from one decade to the next, he argues. The majority apparently believes that the problems will be less severe then and the opportunities for race-neutral ways to guarantee diversity will be greater then. Who do you think makes a stronger case? Can you think of cases when the interpretation of Equal Protection (or other constitutional language) has indeed shifted over time? Hint: Think about school segregation; think about compulsory flag salutes.

Exercise 7.16. One of the key arguments Justice Thomas makes against affirmative action today is that it "stigmatizes" minority students by causing their fellow students and professors to assume that they were not admitted on the strength of their own intelligence and personal qualities. Do you think this is true? Does affirmative action stigmatize its intended beneficiaries?

Exercise 7.17. Several critics have observed that Justice Thomas himself likely benefited from early affirmative action efforts when he was admitted to Yale Law School in 1971. In his autobiography, *My Grandfather's Son,* Thomas blames Yale's affirmative action policy for devaluing his degree. "I'd graduated from one of America's top law schools, but racial preference had robbed my achievement of its true value." He said that he stored his Yale law degree in his basement with a 15-cent sticker from a cigar package pasted on it. Do you think that this personal experience influenced his constitutional analysis in the Michigan cases? Do you think that affirmative action has caused people to discount or devalue Justice Thomas's legal success and constitutional philosophy?

Further *Reading*

Bell, Derrick A. *Race, Racism, and American Law.* 5th ed. New York: Aspen, 2004.

Carson, Clayborne, et al., eds. *The Eyes on the Prize: Civil Rights Reader: Documents, Speeches, and Firsthand Accounts from the Black Freedom Struggle, 1954–1990.* New York: Penguin, 1991.

Kluger, Richard. *Simple Justice: The History of* Brown v. Board of Education *and Black America's Struggle for Equality.* Rev. and exp. ed. New York: Knopf, 2004.

Kozol, Jonathan. *Savage Inequalities: Children in America's Schools.* New York: Crown Publishing, 1991.

Lagemann, Ellen C., and LaMar P. Miller, eds. Brown v. Board of Education: *The Challenge for Today's Schools.* New York: Teachers College Press, 1996.

Martinez, Elizabeth Sutherland, ed. *Letters from Mississippi.* Brookline, Mass.: Zephyr Press, 2002.

Moses, Robert P., and Charles E. Cobb Jr. *Radical Equations: Math Literacy and Civil Rights.* Boston: Beacon Press, 2002.

Thomas, Clarence. *My Grandfather's Son: A Memoir.* New York: Harper, 2007.

THE OTHER LINES WE DRAW AT SCHOOL: Wealth, Gender, Citizenship, and Sexual Orientation

"We hold these truths to be self-evident, that all men are created equal..." DECLARATION OF INDEPENDENCE (JULY 4, 1776)

Because the guiding purpose behind passage of the equal protection clause in 1868 was to stamp out white supremacy, government classification along racial lines is presumed to be wrong and triggers the very close look we call "strict scrutiny." In this chapter we examine four other types of line drawing and how the courts approach them.

Wealth of the School District

Public schools are often places where young people feel the sting of inequality and difference. Sometimes a school will have the reputation of being "the rich kids' school" or of being "a ghetto school." Within schools, students sometimes have a sharply felt sense of those great unmentionables in American life—class and wealth.

Many students and teachers feel acutely uncomfortable talking about, even acknowledging, the way that class and wealth affect them; in many classrooms, it seems as if it is easier to talk about sex than about money! The last thing anyone decent ever wants to do is to embarrass someone else about his or her family's wealth or poverty.

But what about when the government itself sponsors a system of differential funding of public schools based on how wealthy or poor the local community tax base is? What about states where children who go to school in wealthy districts have 50 percent more money spent on their education than those in poor districts? Do the disparities that result in terms of teacher pay, school facilities, science equipment, arts electives, and athletic opportunities violate equal protection?

The Supreme Court confronted these questions in *San Antonio v. Rodriguez* (1973). It found that the equal protection clause does not compel states to set up school districts that will have equal amounts of money to spend on education. Children have no right to a public education that is equal, in terms of expenditures, to the education provided to other children in the state.

Gender

From time immemorial, girls have been treated differently than boys, often unfairly so. In various periods and places, girls have been excluded from classes, schools, or universities; confined to home economics–type classes or other subjects considered suitable for properly feminine students; belittled in class by teachers or classmates; sexually harassed; and shortchanged and discouraged on the athletics field.

This state of affairs has changed radically since the 1970s when the Supreme Court shifted equal protection jurisprudence in a feminist direction, subjecting sex-based distinctions to "intermediate scrutiny." This means that the government must now show (1) that it has an "important" interest in using a gender distinction and (2) that its gender classification along gender lines is substantially related to advancing its interest. Under this approach, the Court has knocked down a host of government policies that discriminated against women in the areas of Social Security benefits, government hiring, military and public benefits, and university admissions.

Moreover, in 1972 Congress passed Title IX, establishing the principle of equal treatment of boys and girls in all schools in America that receive federal funding—that is, nearly all of them. This law has caused a dramatic and historic equalization of educational opportunities for boys and girls, a process that is still unfolding.

In the case of *Jackson v. Birmingham Board of Education* (2005), the Court found that Title IX's mandate against discriminatory treatment of girls at school is so strong that it can protect even a grown man. Roderick Jackson was a girls' high school basketball coach who lost his coaching responsibilities and pay for insisting on the right of the girls on his team to fair treatment and equal resources from the school. The Court ruled that he had been unfairly treated and that such retaliation was illegal under Title IX.

Citizenship and Alienage

One form of line drawing that seems intuitively legitimate is between U.S. citizens and noncitizens. But noncitizens fall into different classes: permanent resident aliens ("green card holders"), college-age people on "student visas," undocumented ("illegal") aliens, or simply foreigners. Of these groups, permanent resident aliens have the most rights, and legislation excluding them from public benefits will generally trigger judicial strict scrutiny. Thus children of permanent resident aliens should generally be treated the same in public school as children who are citizens.

For most purposes, people who are in the United States illegally have no rights under the equal protection clause. However, in *Plyler v. Doe* (1982), the Supreme Court struck down a Texas law that denied a place in school to the children of illegal aliens. This decision has had a sweeping impact on the lives of many thousands of young people.

In *Ambach v. Norwick* (1979), the Court upheld a New York state law forbidding schools to employ as teachers any permanent resident aliens who could apply for full citizenship but decline to do so. The Court reasoned that teachers are role models whose decision not to become citizens sends the wrong message to students.

With the politics of immigration explosive once again in the twenty-first century, there are increasing efforts to draw lines between citizens and others. We will explore which classifications satisfy equal protection scrutiny, which do not, and why.

Sexual Orientation

We do not have a well-developed case law about gay and lesbian students, but everything we now know tells us that they may not be discriminated against by schools or other government authorities (with the exception of the military, which still has a policy of refusing to employ and also dismissing openly gay citizens).

In *Lawrence v. Texas* (2003), the Supreme Court struck down a law in Texas making sexual relations between gay people a crime and found that laws against homosexuals were based on prejudice and animosity, which can never be a "rational" basis for legislation under the equal protection clause.

Furthermore, as detailed in Chapter 9, Title IX's provisions against sex discrimination in schools prevent schools from allowing bullying or harassment of gay and lesbian young people at school.

Yet, even if gay students are protected against antigay legislation and government policy, they have no right to participate in private activities and associations sponsored by private groups that want to exclude them.

This point was decided in *Boy Scouts of America v. Dale* (2000), the famous case involving the Boy Scouts' decision to revoke the adult membership of a former Eagle Scout who had publicly revealed his homosexuality. New Jersey had found that the Boy Scouts' expulsion of James Dale violated the state's public accommodations law. But the Boy Scouts appealed to the Supreme Court, arguing that its members were a private association and therefore had a First Amendment right to decide with whom they would associate. The Supreme Court majority in this 5–4 decision agreed that the state of New Jersey had indeed violated the Boy Scouts' First Amendment rights by forcing them to include homosexuals in their group against their will.

P●INTS TO PONDER

What does equal protection mean when it comes to other rights asserted by students and parents in the public schools?

- Should public education be a fundamental right protected by the Constitution?
- Should states have to spend proportionately equal resources in local school districts?
- Should states be able to fund single-sex schools?
- Can states deny the children of undocumented workers—"illegal aliens"—the right to go to public school?
- Can states refuse to hire as public school teachers lawful resident aliens who are eligible to apply for United States citizenship but decline to do so?
- Can a state force private associations to accept gay members even if they want to express their opposition to homosexuality by excluding them?

Rich Schools, Poor Schools: The Court's Treatment of "Separate but Equal" School Financing

Schools can be segregated along *economic* lines as often as along racial ones. (Economic lines sometimes converge with racial lines.) How should the Supreme Court deal with constitutional challenges to public school systems in which certain schools receive more money and resources than others?

The 1973 Supreme Court case *San Antonio Independent School District v. Rodriguez* involved a challenge by Demetrio Rodriguez to Texas's system of funding public schools. A veteran of the U.S. armed forces who had grown up in a family of migrant farmers, Demetrio moved his family to live within the limits of the Edgewood School District, an overwhelmingly poor and working-class community whose student body was 90 percent Hispanic and 6 percent African American. The median family income there was $4,686 a year. Meantime, in the close-by Alamo Heights district, which served as a point of comparison in the litigation, the vast majority of students were white and the median family income was more than $8,000 a year, with a large number of professionals bringing middle-class stability to the community.

The state distributed aid to the various school districts through a rather complex formula, but local property taxes were the decisive factor. The bottom line was that per-pupil spending in Edgewood, where Demetrio sent his children, was $356 per year while in Alamo Heights it was nearly $600 a year—or more than two-thirds greater. Under this system, students in the poor district, which had far more pervasive and pressing need, received fewer educational services and opportunities than students in the wealthier district.

To make matters worse, the local tax rate was actually higher in Edgewood than in Alamo Heights, but because the property values were lower, less revenue was raised. Edgewood would have had to multiply its tax rate by a politically impossible factor of 18

Demetrio Rodriguez and other Mexican American parents challenged the property tax–based system of financing schools in Texas as a form of wealth discrimination that violated the fundamental right to education. The Court rejected their equal protection claim in 1973, holding that wealth-based classifications do not warrant any special scrutiny and that education is not a fundamental right under the equal protection clause.

to get close to what Alamo Heights raised—and that would have been literally impossible because it would have violated state law.

Invoking equal protection, Rodriguez and other Mexican American families sued over this state of pervasive inequality. But the Supreme Court held that wealth-based differences in the character of public schools (or any other public service) are *not* unconstitutional and that education is *not* a fundamental right. This holding is in deep tension with *Brown v. Board of Education* and helps to explain why we still see tremendous disparities in public schools in many parts of the country when it comes to teacher-student ratios, textbooks, science and art supplies, athletic equipment and facilities, cleanliness, and so on.

Many state supreme courts have responded to the conservatism of this decision by finding that there is a mandate in their own state constitutions for equal spending on schools. Thus in Texas itself, where the state supreme court interpreted the state constitution to compel equal spending, the gap between Edgewood and Alamo Heights has closed considerably. Nevertheless, there are still some funding differences as well as continuing dramatic differences in educational outcomes between the rich and poor areas.

WHAT DO YOU Think?

Exercise 8.1. Is the Supreme Court's decision in *Rodriguez* consistent with the *Brown* decision? Why or why not?

Exercise 8.2. Many state supreme courts have done what the U.S. Supreme Court was unwilling to do: They have found that under their *state* constitutions students have a right to equal rates of spending in each school district. Do you agree with this approach? What would you think about a rule in your state that there has to be an equal number of dollars spent per pupil in each school district and school? Is that fair? What happens if a local parents' group wants to donate extra money or supplies? Is it okay for certain local public schools to acquire more resources by seeking private funding or holding fundraisers, or both? Is there any viable argument that Texas should be forced to spend *more* money in the poor districts today than it spends in the more affluent communities?

Exercise 8.3. Should there be equal spending on public schools all across the United States? If people object to large disparities within the same county or state, what about large disparities across the nation? Are they any more justifiable?

Exercise 8.4. More than 90 percent of children in the United States go to public school, but many go to private schools that are funded by their families and by alumni contributions. Although some of these schools are relatively poor, many others are very wealthy and are able to give their students extraordinary resources and teacher attention. The Supreme Court in 1925 struck down an Oregon law that required all students to attend public schools rather than private ones. In *Pierce v. Society of Sisters,* the Court ruled that foreclosing alternatives to public school "unreasonably interferes with the liberty of parents and guardians to direct the upbringing and education of children under their control." Do you think that this decision was right, or should all students be required to go to public schools? What effect does the presence of private schools have on public schools? Should people have the right to send their children to any school they want, public or private, or do we lose something when families begin to sort themselves out according to wealth, religion, and race? Does the existence of private schools actually reduce the tax burden related to public schools by taking so many students away and providing for their education separately?

Exercise 8.5. In his dissent in the *Rodriguez* case, Justice Marshall argues that equal spending on education is necessary to equip poorer students to participate on an equal basis in politics with more affluent students as they enter adulthood. Do you think education is in fact critical to a person's ability to speak in public, participate effectively in voting, run for office, argue for particular public policies, and persuade fellow citizens? Make a list of five ways your education has prepared you to be a capable citizen. Does the quality of your education influence the development of these skills, such as eloquence and lucidity, or are these skills that people are born with or acquire outside of school?

FOR THE CLASS

School Vouchers: Pro or Con?   Some school systems have experimented with the policy of granting parents tax-financed "school vouchers" that they can redeem to pay tuition for their children at private schools. In Chapter 4 we saw the Court uphold the constitutionality of voucher plans against the charge that they violate the establishment clause.

The voucher idea, launched in 1955 in an essay penned by free-market economist Milton Friedman, has been adopted in Milwaukee, Wisconsin, and Cleveland, Ohio, as well as by the state of Florida. Proponents of vouchers say that every child, no matter how poor, should have the opportunity to attend the elite private schools typically reserved for children of the wealthy and that the voucher program will stir up beneficial competition among schools for parents' voucher dollars. Opponents say that vouchers will simply strip the public schools of their best students, further undermine public support for public schools, and benefit only a tiny percentage of less affluent families, because the vast majority still will not have enough money to send their children to the elite private schools. The rhetoric of proponents is "free choice for all"; the rhetoric of opponents is "don't destroy the public schools."

Pair up with one of your classmates and perform some research on all sides of the school voucher debate, then present a report to the class on your views. Are there ways that we could have vouchers without undermining public schools? Are there ways we could provide more choice and competition within the public schools?

Did the Clintons Make the Right Choice?   When Bill Clinton became president in 1993, he and his wife, Hillary, decided to send their daughter, Chelsea, to the private Sidwell Friends School in Washington, D.C., rather than to a public school. Sen.

Robert Dole, R-Kan., castigated the Clintons for sending Chelsea to private school while opposing school voucher programs that might allow poorer families as well to send their children to private school. In response, President Clinton told *Time* magazine that Chelsea "had always been in public schools," but the family chose Sidwell Friends because it is "an extraordinary school" and Chelsea would "have a measure of privacy there that she would not have otherwise." He said that voucher advocates want "to take funds now going to the public schools and give them to the private schools, when the public schools are already underfunded, which will hurt more children than the relatively small number they propose to help...."

Meanwhile, public school students and families in Washington expressed disappointment that the Clintons did not use the opportunity to show support for Washington's public schools and to get people who come to Washington for government purposes more invested in the city. What do you think? Did the Clintons make the right choice?

"Suspect" Classes and Gender-Based Segregation

Since *Brown* was decided in 1954, the Supreme Court has developed different tests for equal protection claims brought under the Fourteenth Amendment. If a law distinguishes among people based on race, the Court reviews the case using "strict scrutiny," because the Court views race as an inherently suspect, or discriminatory, classification. To pass a strict scrutiny test, the government must show that its racial classification advances a compelling public interest in an effective and necessary way.

If a law treats people differently according to their gender, the government must show that the law's classification advances an "important" public interest in a way that is substantially related to its purpose. This is "heightened" or "intermediate scrutiny."

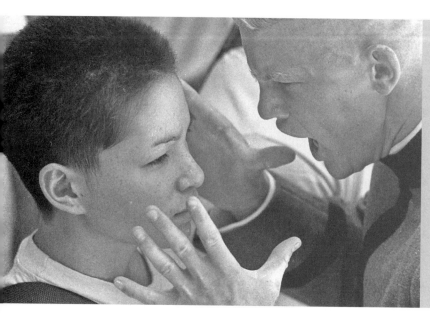

A male member of the Virginia Military Institute Cadre (right) yells at a female cadet during an initiation ceremony in August 1998. Women were admitted to VMI after the Supreme Court ruled in *United States v. Virginia* (1996) that excluding women from the state-funded institution violated the equal protection clause of the Fourteenth Amendment.

If a law differentiates between citizens based on physical disability, wealth, sexual orientation, or any number of other categories, the Court reviews the case using only "rational basis scrutiny." This test asks Is there any conceivable rational basis for this law other than pure prejudice and animosity or arbitrary action?

The nuances of Supreme Court equal protection analysis are complicated. But it is important that you be able to conceptualize the underlying notion that classifications based on race are the most difficult for the government to justify, whereas classifications based on sex or citizenship status are very suspicious but a little easier to justify. Classifications based on other categories, while still requiring some justification, are presumptively acceptable unless bigotry or animosity can be shown. If equal protection analysis were drawn on a continuum, it would look something like this:

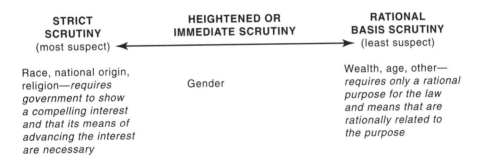

STRICT SCRUTINY (most suspect)	HEIGHTENED OR IMMEDIATE SCRUTINY	RATIONAL BASIS SCRUTINY (least suspect)
Race, national origin, religion—*requires government to show a compelling interest and that its means of advancing the interest are necessary*	Gender	Wealth, age, other—*requires only a rational purpose for the law and means that are rationally related to the purpose*

The Supreme Court has said that higher scrutiny is triggered when government draws lines that adversely affect a "discrete and insular minority." This is a group defined by some "immutable" (unchangeable) trait, a history of being the object of bias and discrimination, and political powerlessness in American society.

Why are race classifications more suspect than gender classifications? Is it because the history of race oppression in the United States is more severe or detrimental than the history of sex discrimination? Is it because women are the majority rather than a minority? Or is it because there are real differences between the sexes but not the races?

In *United States v. Virginia*, the Supreme Court heard arguments in January 1996 for and against the power of a state-funded military college to exclude women. Located in the Shenandoah Valley, the Virginia Military Institute (VMI) was the sole single-sex school left among Virginia's public institutions of higher learning. (Twenty years earlier a federal district court had ordered the University of Virginia at Charlottesville to admit women.) The VMI's distinctive mission is to produce "citizen-soldiers," individuals prepared for leadership in civilian life and in military service.

Using a harsh, marinelike, "adversative" method of training not available elsewhere in Virginia, VMI endeavors to instill physical and mental discipline in its cadets and impart to them a strong moral code. This model of education features physical rigor, mental stress, absence of privacy, stringent regulation of behavior, and indoctrination in "desirable values." The adversative method "dissects the young student" and makes him aware of his "limits and capabilities," so that he knows "how far he can go with his anger, ... how much he can take under stress ... exactly what he can do when he is physically exhausted."

Because of this intense specialized regimen, the alumni place high value on their VMI training, and VMI has the largest per-student endowment of all public undergraduate institutions in the nation. It also continues to evoke in its private and public rituals a romantic fascination with the Confederacy, Confederate general Stonewall Jackson, and the chivalric manners of the Old Dominion.

The United States sued Virginia and VMI, alleging that VMI's males-only admission policy violated the Fourteenth Amendment's equal protection clause. VMI received a favorable ruling from the district court. On review, the Fourth Circuit reversed and ordered Virginia to remedy the constitutional violation. In response, Virginia proposed a parallel program for women: Virginia Women's Institute for Leadership (VWIL), located at Mary Baldwin College, a private liberal arts school for women.

The Supreme Court rejected this attempt to create a parallel all-women's institution and instead insisted that VMI admit both men and women. Six justices made up the majority decision to find against Virginia in the VMI case: Justice Ruth Bader Ginsburg, who wrote the Court's opinion, and Justices Stevens, O'Connor, Kennedy, Souter, and Breyer. Chief Justice Rehnquist filed an opinion concurring in the judgment. Justice Scalia dissented. (Justice Thomas abstained from both the consideration and the decision of the case because his son was a student at VMI at the time.)

The Court used intermediate scrutiny to evaluate the constitutionality of this gender-based discrimination in *United States v. Virginia*. The Court asked whether: (1) Virginia's interest in having an all-male college to produce exemplary "citizen-soldiers" is "important" and (2) whether limiting the school to men is "substantially related" to achievement of Virginia's goal of producing citizen-soldiers.

Justice Ginsburg found that Virginia's arguments for a separate, all-female military college were unable to pass the test of intermediate scrutiny, which demands "an exceedingly persuasive justification." She rejected Virginia's argument for a separate women's military college based on three principles. First, Justice Ginsburg held that although gender-based classifications are not categorically prohibited, categorization by sex may not be used to create or reinforce the legal, social, or economic inferiority and inequality of women.

Second, Virginia failed to provide the Court with enough evidence that the exclusion of women was *substantially related* to the important state interest of VMI's adversative training method. In other words, the state had failed to offer enough proof that only an all-male setting would allow VMI's rigorous physical and mental conditioning program to operate. Why couldn't VMI continue to impose a tough set of academic and athletic protocols even with women participating along with men—the same way the armed forces do? Under orders from Congress, the United States military academies had been admitting women since 1975 without compromising troop readiness or unit cohesion.

Still, the Court was willing to allow the all-male policy to continue if the state could show that women were offered an alternative to VMI that would produce female graduates with opportunities "substantially equal" to those afforded male graduates of VMI.

But Virginia was unable to clear this final hurdle. The Supreme Court rejected Virginia's proposed all-female school because the disparities in geographic location and physical and mental training, and the inferior reputation of the institution itself, would not allow for educational results comparable to attending VMI. Therefore, the Court's conclusion that "separate" produced a result far from "equal" left VMI clinging to an unconstitutionally discriminatory policy.

Justice Scalia dissented from this analysis because he thought the school had met its burdens under intermediate scrutiny. He attacked the majority's view of the political vulnerability of women, pointing out that women constitute a majority of the electorate and have the power of the ballot to change educational policies they find disagreeable. Applying a weaker standard of scrutiny for Virginia's program, Justice Scalia concluded that VMI's program promoted the precise goal Virginia aspired to—the creation of leaders through a strict moral code—and that this goal clearly passed constitutional muster.

WHAT DO YOU **Think?**

Exercise 8.6. What is your opinion of the validity of sex-segregated schools? Can all-female schools ever help women in a constitutionally permissible way? Is there ever justification for all-male schools?

Exercise 8.7. What would you think of single-sex classes within your school? Would the subject matter of the class—math, science, English— influence your decision? Are all-girls and all-boys sex-education classes appropriate to prevent embarrassment on both sides?

Boys and Girls Equal: Title IX

In 1972 Congress adopted Title IX, which provides that: "No person in the United States shall, on the basis of sex, be excluded from participation in, be denied the benefit of, or be subjected to discrimination under any education program or activity receiving federal financial assistance." Under this provision, girls have reached parity, or come close to it, with respect to educational opportunities, including athletic opportunities, in America's schools and universities.

JUSTICES: A CLOSER LOOK

Beyond writing the Supreme Court's historic decision in *United States v. Virginia*, **JUSTICE RUTH BADER GINSBURG** (1933–) played an enormously important role in advocacy for women's rights before she was named to the Supreme Court by President Bill Clinton in 1993. While she was a law professor at Columbia University in the 1970s, she became the founding director of the Women's Rights Project at the American Civil Liberties Union (ACLU) and brought nine sex discrimination cases to the Court and gave the oral argument in six of them. No other person has had as great an influence on the transformation of our law to advance women's equality in American life.

HIGHLIGHTS

- In 1996 Justice Ginsburg wrote the opinion for a 7–1 majority invalidating the constitutionality of Virginia's all-male military college, the Virginia Military Institute, in *United States v. Virginia*.
- Although Justice Ginsburg and Justice Antonin Scalia have clashed over many of the most controversial issues to come before the Court, the two have been close friends since their days on the D.C. Circuit Court and share a common passion for the opera.
- Justice Ginsburg's daughter, Jane, is a law professor at Columbia.

The biggest terrain of conflict under this law has been athletics, where traditionally schools have invested far more money, personnel, and resources in boys' sports teams than those of girls. In order to prove that it has complied with Title IX in providing equal athletic opportunities, a school must show one of the following: (1) that the athletic opportunities offered to girls are "substantially proportionate" to the female enrollment at the school; or (2) that there has been a "continued expansion" of athletic opportunities for girls at the school; or (3) that the school has made a "full and effective" accommodation of the interests and abilities of girls at the school.

The federal government and courts have worked hard to equalize for boys and girls the chances for academic and athletic success at school. In the following case, the Supreme Court found that Title IX makes it illegal to retaliate against male teachers and coaches who complain of sex discrimination against girls by a school.

No one cared: *Jackson v. Birmingham Board of Education*

The plaintiff, Roderick Jackson, was a teacher and head coach of the girls' basketball team at Ensley High School in Birmingham, Alabama. From 1999 until May 2001, he was, by all accounts, an excellent coach leading a fine team. In 2001 six of seven graduating seniors on his team won college scholarships based, at least partially, on their basketball prowess.

But Jackson was disturbed from the beginning of his time coaching about the great advantages extended at the high school to the boys' team and the relative hardships imposed on the girls' team. "The girls were not allowed to use the new, regulation gym used by the boys' team," he said in a statement before the Supreme Court heard his case; "instead, the girls had to practice and play in the old gym with its wooden backboards, bent rims and no heat."

Even though the boys' team was transported by bus to away games, "the girls had to make their own arrangements to travel by car when their games were scheduled at different times from the boys' games." The girls lacked access to the ice machine and other amenities.

Ensley High School girls basketball coach Roderick Jackson was fired from his coaching position after he advocated for equal treatment for his team. He sued for damages under Title IX. The Supreme Court held that employees could sue their employers if they were dismissed for standing up for equal rights for female students.

Above all, there was financial discrimination imposed on the girls' team. As Jackson put it, "The girls were routinely denied any share of the money donated to the school's athletics program by the City of Birmingham—of the $8,000 donated one year, for example, the girls never saw a dime." Moreover, the boys' team kept the proceeds from admissions and concession sales during games, but the girls' team was not allowed to do so despite the fact that they had to pay for their own game referees. At one point Coach Jackson shelled out $700 of his own money to buy shoes for his team, most of which was never paid back to him.

Coach Jackson "went through the chain of command" to try to even things out between the boys and girls teams but "no one cared"—from the school's athletic director to the school's principal to the deputy superintendent of schools. On the contrary, for his passionate efforts to help his players, Jackson was fired as coach and lost the extra income he needed for his family (he and his wife have a son and a daughter). His reputation was tarnished, and he was even kept from other basketball coaching jobs.

Jackson sued under Title IX. He had no lawyer but eventually his case was taken up by the National Women's Law Center, which represented him. The question was whether school employees can sue for damages under Title IX if they lose their job for standing up for equal rights for female students. With Justice O'Connor writing the opinion, the Court said yes.

. . . .

RODERICK JACKSON, Petitioner v. BIRMINGHAM BOARD OF EDUCATION

Supreme Court of the United States
Argued November 30, 2004.
Decided March 29, 2005.

Majority OPINION   Justice O'CONNOR delivered the opinion of the Court.

Roderick Jackson, a teacher in the Birmingham, Alabama, public schools, brought suit against the Birmingham Board of Education alleging that the Board retaliated against him because he had complained about sex discrimination in the high school's athletic program. Jackson claimed that the Board's retaliation violated Title IX of the Education Amendments of 1972.... We consider here whether the private right of action implied by Title IX encompasses claims of retaliation. We hold that it does where the funding recipient retaliates against an individual because he has complained about sex discrimination.

> **Title IX**
> A section of the Education Amendments of 1972, which established the principle of equal treatment of boys and girls in all schools that receive federal funding.

I

… Jackson has been an employee of the Birmingham school district for over 10 years. In 1993, the Board hired Jackson to serve as a physical education teacher and girls' basketball coach. Jackson was transferred to Ensley High School in August 1999. At Ensley, he discovered that the girls' team was not receiving equal funding and equal access to athletic equipment and facilities. The lack of adequate funding, equipment, and facilities made it difficult for Jackson to do his job as the team's coach.

In December 2000, Jackson began complaining to his supervisors about the unequal treatment of the girls' basketball team, but to no avail. Jackson's complaints went unanswered, and the school failed to remedy the situation. Instead, Jackson began to receive negative work evaluations and ultimately was removed as the girls' coach in May 2001. Jackson is still employed by the Board as a teacher, but he no longer receives supplemental pay for coaching.

After the Board terminated Jackson's coaching duties, he filed suit in the United States District Court for the Northern District of Alabama. He alleged, among other things, that the Board violated Title IX by retaliating against him for protesting the discrimination against the girls' basketball team. The Board moved to dismiss on the ground that Title IX's private cause of action does not include claims of retaliation. The District Court granted the motion to dismiss....

We granted certiorari to resolve a conflict in the Circuits over whether Title IX's private right of action encompasses claims of retaliation for complaints about sex discrimination.

II

A

Title IX prohibits sex discrimination by recipients of federal education funding. The statute provides that "[n]o person in the United States shall, on the basis of sex, be excluded from participation in, be denied the benefits of, or be subjected to discrimination under any education program or activity receiving Federal financial assistance." ...

... Retaliation against a person because that person has complained of sex discrimination is another form of intentional sex discrimination encompassed by Title IX's private cause of action. Retaliation is, by definition, an intentional act. It is a form of "discrimination" because the complainant is being subjected to differential treatment. Moreover, retaliation is discrimination "on the basis of sex" because it is an intentional response to the nature of the complaint: an allegation of sex discrimination. We conclude that when a funding recipient retaliates against a person *because* he complains of sex discrimination, this constitutes intentional "discrimination" "on the basis of sex," in violation of Title IX....

Congress enacted Title IX not only to prevent the use of federal dollars to support discriminatory practices, but also "to provide individual citizens effective protection against those practices." We agree with the United States that this objective "would be difficult, if not impossible, to achieve if persons who complain about sex discrimination did not have effective protection against retaliation." If recipients were permitted to retaliate freely, individuals who witness discrimination would be loathe to report it, and all manner of Title IX violations might go unremedied as a result....

Title IX's enforcement scheme also depends on individual reporting because individuals and agencies may not bring suit under the statute unless the recipient has received "actual notice" of the discrimination. If recipients were able to avoid such notice by retaliating against all those who dare complain, the statute's enforcement scheme would be subverted. We should not assume that Congress left such a gap in its scheme.

Moreover, teachers and coaches such as Jackson are often in the best position to vindicate the rights of their students because they are better able to identify discrimination and bring it to the attention of administrators. Indeed, sometimes adult employees are "the only effective adversar[ies]" of discrimination in schools.

D

... To prevail on the merits, Jackson will have to prove that the Board retaliated against him *because* he complained of sex discrimination. The amended complaint alleges that the Board retaliated against Jackson for complaining to his supervisor, Ms. Evelyn Baugh, about sex discrimination at Ensley High School. At this stage of the proceedings, "[t]he issue is not whether a plaintiff will ultimately prevail but whether the claimant is entitled to offer evidence to support the claims." Accordingly, the judgment of the Court of Appeals for the Eleventh Circuit is reversed, and the case is remanded for further proceedings consistent with this opinion.

It is so ordered.

WHAT DO YOU **Think?**

Exercise 8.8. After the Court's ruling, the Birmingham School Board settled the case with Jackson, agreeing to ensure "equitable conditions" for all girls' teams in the city and to pay $50,000 to Jackson for his damages. Some people argued that Coach Jackson should not have been able to benefit from Title IX, since he was not discriminated against by the school on the basis of his own gender. But others thought that, as an assistant solicitor general put it, any "person who is victimized by retaliation because he complained about sex discrimination is a victim of sex discrimination." Do you agree?

Exercise 8.9. A number of universities have experienced controversy over Title IX as a number of male players and their coaches assert that budgets for men's sports have been cut to redirect money toward women's sports that fewer people play. Advocates for women's teams say that this is nonsense, since a college need only address the actual demand for women's sports in a "full and effective" way but not spend equal amounts of money on the male and female programs. They believe that less prominent male sports, such as wrestling or tennis, are indeed under-funded but blame that fact on excessive spending on the most expensive men's sports, for example, college football or basketball. Is it fair for a college to spend so much money on a single sport such as football?

Separating Citizens from Noncitizens under the Law

As we have seen, to legislate is to draw lines. One line we allow our government to draw is between citizens and noncitizens. When the nation began, there were very few distinctions between citizens and noncitizens. Indeed, noncitizens could vote in many states (so long as they were white male property owners). But anti-immigration sentiment became a powerful force in the twentieth century, and the Supreme Court often upheld discrimination against aliens, one vivid example being its permission in *Korematsu v. United States* (1944) for the relocation and internment of tens of thousands of Japanese resident aliens on the West Coast during World War II. (Since this order also applied to Japanese American citizens, it was an instance of racial and ethnic discrimination as well.)

But the Court's formal constitutional doctrine today bans prejudiced discrimination against permanent resident aliens. Citing the fact that the equal protection clause covers "persons" (not "citizens"), the modern Court, in fact, uses heightened scrutiny to test laws that disadvantage lawful aliens. It has often struck down laws that make it harder for resident aliens to own property, to get fishing and hunting licenses, and so on. Only when laws touch on an important "government function" does the Court routinely permit government to discriminate against noncitizens.

There are two ways to become an American citizen. The first is to be born here, even if it is to noncitizen parents, and this method of becoming a citizen is guaranteed explicitly by the Fourteenth Amendment. The other is to be "naturalized" by following the laws of the country. Generally, this means becoming a lawful permanent resident—a "green card holder"—and then taking a naturalization test in English, passing it, and being sworn in at a naturalization ceremony. The children outside of the United States but of naturalized parents can then become citizens through application.

Public school systems all over the United States routinely accept children of lawful permanent residents. But what about the children of "illegal aliens," or "undocumented workers," that is, children who are not U.S. citizens and whose parents are not lawfully in the country? Do they have an equal protection right to go to public school? In 1975 Texas passed a law withdrawing state funds for the education of such children and gave schools the power to deny them enrollment. In *Plyler v. Doe*, the Court struck this law down as a violation of equal protection. How did it reach this conclusion?

PLYLER v. DOE

Supreme Court of the United States
Argued December 1, 1981.
Decided June 15, 1982.

Majority OPINION   Justice BRENNAN delivered the opinion of the Court.

The question presented by these cases is whether, consistent with the Equal Protection Clause of the Fourteenth Amendment, Texas may deny to undocumented school-age children the free public education that it provides to children who are citizens of the United States or legally admitted aliens.

I

... In May 1975, the Texas Legislature revised its education laws to withhold from local school districts any state funds for the education of children who were not "legally admitted" into the United States. The 1975 revision also authorized local school districts to deny enrollment in their public schools to children not "legally admitted" to the country. These cases involve constitutional challenges to those provisions.

This is a class action on behalf of certain school-age children of Mexican origin residing in Smith County, Tex., who could not establish that they had been legally admitted into the United States. The action complained of the exclusion of plaintiff children from the public schools of the Tyler Independent School District....

> **Class Action**
> A lawsuit in which a large group of people with a common interest and complaint join together to sue.

II

The Fourteenth Amendment provides that "[n]o State shall ... deprive any person of life, liberty, or property, without due process of law; nor deny to *any person within its jurisdiction* the equal protection of the laws." Appellants argue at the outset that undocumented aliens, because of their immigration status, are not "persons within the jurisdiction" of the State of Texas, and that they therefore have no right to the equal protection of Texas law. We reject this argument. Whatever his status under the immigration laws, an alien is surely a "person" in any ordinary sense of that term. Aliens, even aliens whose presence in this country is unlawful, have long been recognized as "persons" guaranteed due process of law by the Fifth and Fourteenth Amendments. Indeed, we have clearly held that the Fifth Amendment protects aliens whose presence in this country is unlawful from invidious discrimination by the Federal Government....

> **Invidious Discrimination**
> Discrimination that is objectionable and offensive, usually involving prejudice and stereotyping.

... The more difficult question is whether the Equal Protection Clause has been violated by the refusal of the State of Texas to reimburse local school boards for the education of children who cannot demonstrate that their presence within the United States is lawful, or by the imposition by those school boards of the burden of tuition on those children. It is to this question that we now turn.

III

A

Sheer incapability or lax enforcement of the laws barring entry into this country, coupled with the failure to establish an effective bar to the employment of undocumented aliens, has resulted in the creation of a substantial "shadow population" of illegal migrants —numbering in the millions—within our borders. This situation raises the specter of a permanent caste of undocumented resident aliens, encouraged by some to remain here as a source of cheap labor, but nevertheless denied the benefits that our society makes available to citizens and lawful residents. The existence of such an underclass presents most difficult problems for a Nation that prides itself on adherence to principles of equality under law.

The children who are plaintiffs in these cases are special members of this underclass. Persuasive arguments support the view that a State may withhold its beneficence from those whose very presence within the United States is the product of their own unlawful

JUSTICES: A CLOSER LOOK

JUSTICE WILLIAM J. BRENNAN (1906–1997) was born in Newark, New Jersey, where his father was a popular local official in charge of public safety. Brennan attended Barringer High School and the Wharton School at the University of Pennsylvania. He went on to Harvard Law School. After a distinguished career as a labor lawyer, Brennan rose through the ranks of the New Jersey courts, landing on the New Jersey Supreme Court. President Dwight Eisenhower appointed him a justice of the U.S. Supreme Court in 1956, where he served until 1990.

HIGHLIGHTS

- Justice Brennan was a student of Justice Felix Frankfurter at Harvard Law School and later came to be both his colleague and frequent adversary on the Court.
- Unaware that President Eisenhower, a Republican, was considering nominating him to the Supreme Court, Brennan complained about having to travel to Washington, D.C., when Herbert Brownell mysteriously called him from the Attorney General's Office.
- Justice Brennan had a tremendous influence in promoting a progressive civil rights and civil liberties jurisprudence on the Court and was known as a great leader in forging consensus among his fellow justices.

conduct. These arguments do not apply with the same force to classifications imposing disabilities on the minor *children* of such illegal entrants. At the least, those who elect to enter our territory by stealth and in violation of our law should be prepared to bear the consequences, including, but not limited to, deportation. But the children of those illegal entrants are not comparably situated. Their "parents have the ability to conform their conduct to societal norms," and presumably the ability to remove themselves from the State's jurisdiction; but the children who are plaintiffs in these cases "can affect neither their parents' conduct nor their own status." ... Even if the State found it expedient to control the conduct of adults by acting against their children, legislation directing the onus of a parent's misconduct against his children does not comport with fundamental conceptions of justice.

> [V]isiting condemnation on the head of an infant is illogical and unjust. Moreover, imposing disabilities on the child is contrary to the basic concept of our system that legal burdens should bear some relationship to individual responsibility or wrongdoing. Obviously, no child is responsible for his birth and penalizing the child is an ineffectual—as well as unjust— way of deterring the parent....

... [This law] is directed against children, and imposes its discriminatory burden on the basis of a legal characteristic over which children can have little control. It is thus difficult to conceive of a rational justification for penalizing these children for their presence within the United States. Yet that appears to be precisely the effect of [the law].

Public education is not a "right" granted to individuals by the Constitution. But neither is it merely some governmental "benefit" indistinguishable from other forms of social welfare legislation. Both the importance of education in maintaining our basic institutions, and the lasting impact of its deprivation on the life of the child, mark the distinction. The "American people have always regarded education and [the] acquisition of knowledge as matters of supreme importance." We have recognized "the public schools as a most vital civic institution for the preservation of a democratic system of government" ... and as the primary vehicle for transmitting "the values on which our society rests." [A]s pointed out early in our history some degree of education is necessary to prepare citizens to participate effectively and intelligently in our open political system if we are to preserve freedom and independence. In addition, education provides the basic tools by which individuals might lead economically productive lives to the benefit of us all. In sum, education has a fundamental role in maintaining the fabric of our society. We cannot ignore the significant social costs borne by our Nation when select groups are denied the means to absorb the values and skills upon which our social order rests.

In addition to the pivotal role of education in sustaining our political and cultural heritage, denial of education to some isolated group of children poses an affront to one of the goals of the Equal Protection Clause: the abolition of governmental barriers presenting unreasonable obstacles to advancement on the basis of individual merit. Paradoxically, by depriving the children of any disfavored group of an education, we foreclose the means by which that group might raise the level of esteem in which it is held by the majority. But more directly, "education prepares individuals to be self-reliant and self-sufficient participants in society." Illiteracy is an enduring disability. The inability to read and write will handicap the individual deprived of a basic education each and every day of his life....

B

... [This law] imposes a lifetime hardship on a discrete class of children not accountable for their disabling status. The stigma of illiteracy will mark them for the rest of their lives. By denying these children a basic education, we deny them the ability to live within the structure of our civic institutions, and foreclose any realistic possibility that they will contribute in even the smallest way to the progress of our Nation....

V

... Apart from the asserted state prerogative to act against undocumented children solely on the basis of their undocumented status—an asserted prerogative that carries only minimal force in the circumstances of these cases—we discern three colorable state interests that might support [the provision].

First, appellants appear to suggest that the State may seek to protect itself from an influx of illegal immigrants. While a State might have an interest in mitigating the potentially harsh economic effects of sudden shifts in population, [this law] hardly offers an effective method of dealing with an urgent demographic or economic problem. There is no evidence in the record suggesting that illegal entrants impose any significant burden on the State's economy. To the contrary, the available evidence suggests that illegal aliens underutilize public services, while contributing their labor to the local economy and tax money to the state fisc. The dominant incentive for illegal entry into the State of Texas is the availability of employment; few if any illegal immigrants come to this country, or presumably to the State of Texas, in order to avail themselves of a free education. Thus, even making the doubtful assumption that the net impact of illegal aliens on the economy of the State is negative, we think it clear that "[c]harging tuition to undocumented children constitutes a ludicrously ineffectual attempt to stem the tide of illegal immigration," at least when compared with the alternative of prohibiting the employment of illegal aliens.

Second, appellants suggest that undocumented children are appropriately singled out for exclusion because of the special burdens they impose on the State's ability to provide high-quality public education. But the record in no way supports the claim that exclusion of undocumented children is likely to improve the overall quality of education in the State. [T]he State failed to offer any "credible supporting evidence that a proportionately small diminution of the funds spent on each child [which might result from devoting some state funds to the education of the excluded group] will have a grave impact on the quality of education." … [B]arring undocumented children from local schools would not necessarily improve the quality of education provided in those schools. Of course, even if improvement in the quality of education were a likely result of barring some *number* of children from the schools of the State, the State must support its selection of *this* group as the appropriate target for exclusion. In terms of educational cost and need, however, undocumented children are "basically indistinguishable" from legally resident alien children.

Finally, appellants suggest that undocumented children are appropriately singled out because their unlawful presence within the United States renders them less likely than other children to remain within the boundaries of the State, and to put their education to productive social or political use within the State. Even assuming that such an interest is legitimate, it is an interest that is most difficult to quantify. The State has no assurance that any child, citizen or not, will employ the education provided by the State within the confines of the State's borders. In any event, the record is clear that many of the undocumented children disabled by this classification will remain in this country indefinitely, and that some will become lawful residents or citizens of the United States. It is difficult to understand precisely what the State hopes to achieve by promoting the creation and perpetuation of a subclass of illiterates within our boundaries, surely adding to the problems and costs of unemployment, welfare, and crime. It is thus clear that whatever savings might be achieved by denying these children an education, they are wholly insubstantial in light of the costs involved to these children, the State, and the Nation.

VI

… Accordingly, the judgment of the Court of Appeals in each of these cases is *Affirmed*.

Dissenting VOICES

Chief Justice Burger dissented, focusing on the idea that the Court was engaged in policy-making rather than constitutional interpretation. He was joined in his opinion by Justices White, Rehnquist, and O'Connor.

If it were the Court's "business to set the Nation's social policy," Burger wrote,

> I would agree without hesitation that it is senseless for an enlightened society to deprive any children—including illegal aliens—of an elementary education. I fully agree that it would be folly—and wrong—to tolerate creation of a segment of society made up of illiterate persons, many having a limited or no command of our language.

But the Constitution, he pointed out, does not "vest in this Court the authority to strike down laws because they do not meet our standards of desirable social policy, 'wisdom,' or 'common sense.'" He objected that the majority had trespassed on "the assigned function of the political branches" by assuming a "policymaking role" simply because it disapproved of Congressional inaction.

Chief Justice Burger conceded that the

> failure of enforcement of the immigration laws over more than a decade and the inherent difficulty and expense of sealing our vast borders have combined to create a grave socioeconomic dilemma. It is a dilemma that has not yet even been fully assessed, let alone addressed. However, it is not the function of the Judiciary to provide "effective leadership" simply because the political branches of government fail to do so.

The real issue in the case, the chief justice emphasized, was not whether Congress had done a good job of addressing immigration policy, but whether Texas violated Equal Protection by discriminating against children unlawfully present in the country. Thus, the issue

> is whether, for purposes of allocating its finite resources, a state has a legitimate reason to differentiate between persons who are lawfully within the state and those who are unlawfully there. The distinction the State of Texas has drawn—based not only upon its own legitimate interests but on classifications established by the Federal Government in its immigration laws and policies—is not unconstitutional.

Chief Justice Burger was puzzled why the majority could see that education is not a "fundamental right" and "illegal aliens" are not a "suspect class" but then still find the Texas policy unconstitutional. All Texas needs to do to defend its law is pass "rational basis" scrutiny by showing that it has a rational purpose in excluding the children of undocumented aliens and that the exclusion is a reasonable means of advancing the purpose. Burger thought it evident that Texas could rationally seek to save its limited resources for children of lawful citizens and that excluding others is a logical way of going about it.

The fact that the penalized children lack "control" over their situation, Burger thought, is unfortunate but legally irrelevant. Even if they are "innocent" in a moral sense, since they have been brought to our country by their parents, Burger argued, they could still be deported, and "would deportation be any less a 'penalty' than denial of privileges provided to legal residents?" Burger rejected any comparison between the Texas law affecting these children and old laws discriminating against illegitimate children who are lawfully present in the country. The illegal "status" of children of undocumented aliens "is predicated upon the circumstances of their concededly illegal presence in this country, and is a direct result of Congress' obviously valid exercise of its 'broad constitutional powers' in the field of immigration and naturalization."

Chief Justice Burger concluded by restating his questions about the wisdom of the law and his certainty that this is not at all the issue:

> Denying a free education to illegal alien children is not a choice I would make were I a legislator. Apart from compassionate considerations, the long-range costs of excluding any children from the public schools may well outweigh the costs of educating them.

But that is not the issue; the fact that there are sound *policy* arguments against the Texas Legislature's choice does not render that choice an unconstitutional one.

WHAT DO YOU **Think?**

Exercise 8.10. The dissenters in *Plyler v. Doe* accuse the majority of abandoning legal analysis and making a policy judgment to allow the children of illegal aliens to enroll in school. Was this in fact an improper policy intervention by the Court? Go back and study the majority's arguments. Were they arguments about the meaning of equal protection, or were they practical and moral arguments about the soundness of the Texas law?

Exercise 8.11. Turn half of your class into the U.S. Congress and half into the Supreme Court. Imagine that a national clamor arises when it is learned that several dozen children of Mexican nationals are crossing the U.S. border every day into Texas (and returning home at night) to attend public schools in border communities. Some of the Texas schools apparently allow this practice, while others do not. In response, some members of Congress introduce a bill that states, "All funding from the United States Department of Education will be discontinued to any state that permits students to enroll in public school at any level if those students are aliens to the United States and living in other countries." For those of you in Congress, would you vote for or against this legislation? Now assume that it passes and goes to the Supreme Court. Is it constitutional under *Plyler*? Can the federal government punish Texas for allowing these students to come? Should Congress be able to control whatever it does with federal money? Have a conference on the case and discuss how it resembles, and differs from, the facts in *Plyler*.

Exercise 8.12. In the eighteenth and nineteenth centuries, many states gave noncitizens the right to vote at all levels of government. Today the practice of noncitizen voting survives in community school board elections in Chicago and New York and in municipal elections in a number of communities, including Takoma Park, Maryland.

Assume that there is an upcoming referendum in your community on the issue of granting noncitizen parents of children in public schools the right to vote in local school board elections. Divide the class in half; research the issue and hold a debate on the referendum. Should we vote yes or no?

One issue to consider is whether we want noncitizens involved in local government. Why or why not? Recall that permanent residents pay federal, state, and local taxes; are subject to the draft; and must obey all laws. But do we dilute the meaning of citizenship by giving permanent resident aliens (green card holders) the right to vote?

The Supreme Court uses heightened scrutiny to examine discrimination against aliens who are lawfully present in the country. The Court does not, however, use heightened scrutiny to test exclusions of aliens from "critical government functions," and the Court has considered teaching such a function. In *Ambach v. Norwick* (1979), the Court upheld New

York's ban on employing as teachers any aliens who have become eligible to apply for citizenship but decline to do so. Justice Powell reasoned that because "a teacher has an opportunity to influence the attitudes of students toward government, the political process, and a citizen's social responsibilities," a noncitizen teacher who fails to apply for citizenship sends a negative message to students. In his dissent, Justice Blackmun argued that New York's rule was "irrational. Is it better to employ a mediocre citizen teacher than an excellent resident alien teacher? Is it preferable to have a citizen who has never seen Spain or a Latin American country teach Spanish to eighth graders and to deny that opportunity to a resident alien who may have lived for 20 years in the culture of Spain or Latin America?" What is your response?

Exercise 8.13. Assume that you and your classmates are members of the appointments committee at your high school, which is looking for a new Spanish teacher. The choice has come down to two applicants. One is a forty-year-old Salvadoran immigrant fluent in both Spanish and English who has a master's degree in Spanish literature. She has lived and worked as a Spanish teacher in the United States for fifteen years, but she declines to apply for citizenship because she still owns property in El Salvador and plans to retire there in twenty years. The other applicant is a twenty-five-year-old recent college graduate and a U.S. citizen by birth who majored in Spanish in college and speaks it very well but with a strong North American accent. Unlike the first applicant, he is not certain that he wants to be a teacher for the rest of his career and may want to move into business. But he is a graduate of your school. Whom do you select and why?

Discrimination against Gays and Lesbians

The Supreme Court has never decided a case involving alleged equal protection violations by a public school or university against a gay or lesbian student; however, we know the general outline of the Court's thinking on the issue. In *Lawrence v. Texas* (2003), the Supreme Court struck down a law in Texas making homosexual sex a crime and found that laws targeting homosexuals based on prejudice and animosity can never be a "rational" basis for legislation under the equal protection clause.

This decision reinforced the Court's 1996 holding in *Romer v. Evans,* which struck down a Colorado state constitutional amendment forbidding local jurisdictions to grant civil rights protections to gays and lesbians. In that case the Court found that under equal protection government officials cannot discriminate against gays and lesbians by denying them equal treatment under law simply based on prejudice and hostility.

Although federal civil rights laws do not forbid discrimination on the basis of sexual orientation, many states have forbidden discrimination in places of public accommodation against gay citizens. The following case from New Jersey got its start when a young man named James Dale, an Eagle Scout, left home for college at Rutgers University. There he revealed to people that he was gay. He soon became copresident of the Rutgers University Lesbian/Gay Alliance. After his name appeared in a newspaper article relating to his work in that capacity, he received a letter from the Boy Scouts revoking his adult membership in the organization. When he asked why, he was told that homosexuals were not allowed as members. Dale sued for readmission under the state's public accommodations law, and

Eagle Scout James Dale was removed as an assistant scoutmaster in New Jersey after the Boy Scouts learned he was active in Rutgers University's Lesbian/Gay Alliance.

when the case went to the New Jersey Supreme Court, he won.

The Boy Scouts appealed to the United States Supreme Court, arguing that New Jersey was violating the First Amendment by forcing the Scouts to take gay members. They argued that being forced to take gay members offended the principles of the organization, which stood for "morally straight" conduct and against homosexuality. The Scouts invoked the Court's 1995 decision in *Hurley v. Irish American Gay, Lesbian and Bisexual Group of Boston, Inc.,* which had upheld the First Amendment right of the private organizers of the St. Patrick's Day parade in Boston to exclude a contingent of gay Irish Americans who had applied to march. In that decision Justice Souter found for the majority that private speakers could control their own messages by arranging or excluding particular elements of expression, much like a conductor putting together a symphony. The Boy Scouts argued that their overall message would be distorted and undermined by having to accept homosexual members. In a divided 5–4 opinion, the Supreme Court agreed with the Boy Scouts, finding that the group had a First Amendment right to exclude gays.

BOY SCOUTS OF AMERICA v. DALE

Supreme Court of the United States
Argued April 26, 2000.
Decided June 28, 2000.

Majority OPINION   Chief Justice REHNQUIST delivered the opinion of the Court.

Petitioners are the Boy Scouts of America and the Monmouth Council, a division of the Boy Scouts of America (collectively, Boy Scouts). The Boy Scouts is a private, not-for-profit organization engaged in instilling its system of values in young people. The Boy Scouts asserts that homosexual conduct is inconsistent with the values it seeks to instill. Respondent is James Dale, a former Eagle Scout whose adult membership in the Boy Scouts was revoked when the Boy Scouts learned that he is an avowed homosexual and gay rights activist. The New Jersey Supreme Court held that New Jersey's public accommodations law requires that the Boy Scouts readmit Dale. This case presents the question whether applying New Jersey's public accommodations law in this way violates the Boy Scouts' First Amendment right of expressive association. We hold that it does.

Public Accommodations Law
A law stipulating that a business must provide lodging, meal service, entertainment, or other services to all members of the public. In federal law, the Civil Rights Act of 1964 is the key example.

Expressive Association
A private organization or group, formal or informal, engaged in public expression of ideas and views.

I

James Dale entered Scouting in 1978 at the age of eight by joining Monmouth Council's Cub Scout Pack 142. Dale became a Boy Scout in 1981 and remained a Scout until he turned 18. By all accounts, Dale was an exemplary Scout. In 1988, he achieved the rank of Eagle Scout, one of Scouting's highest honors.

Dale applied for adult membership in the Boy Scouts in 1989. The Boy Scouts approved his application for the position of assistant scoutmaster of Troop 73. Around the same time, Dale left home to attend Rutgers University. After arriving at Rutgers, Dale first acknowledged to himself and others that he is gay. He quickly became involved with, and eventually became the copresident of, the Rutgers University Lesbian/Gay Alliance. In 1990, Dale attended a seminar addressing the psychological and health needs of lesbian and gay teenagers. A newspaper covering the event interviewed Dale about his advocacy of homosexual teenagers' need for gay role models. In early July 1990, the newspaper published the interview and Dale's photograph over a caption identifying him as the copresident of the Lesbian/Gay Alliance.

Later that month, Dale received a letter from Monmouth Council Executive James Kay revoking his adult membership. Dale wrote to Kay requesting the reason for Monmouth Council's decision. Kay responded by letter that the Boy Scouts "specifically forbid membership to homosexuals."

In 1992, Dale filed a complaint against the Boy Scouts in the New Jersey Superior Court. The complaint alleged that the Boy Scouts had violated New Jersey's public accommodations statute and its common law by revoking Dale's membership based solely on his sexual orientation. New Jersey's public accommodations statute prohibits, among other things, discrimination on the basis of sexual orientation in places of public accommodation. [Dale ultimately won his claim before the New Jersey Supreme Court. The Boy Scouts appealed to the United States Supreme Court on First Amendment grounds.]

II

In *Roberts v. United States Jaycees*, we observed that "implicit in the right to engage in activities protected by the First Amendment" is "a corresponding right to associate with others in pursuit of a wide variety of political, social, economic, educational, religious, and cultural ends." This right is crucial in preventing the majority from imposing its views on groups that would rather express other, perhaps unpopular, ideas. Government actions that may unconstitutionally burden this freedom may take many forms, one of which is "intrusion into the internal structure or affairs of an association" like a "regulation that forces the group to accept members it does not desire." Forcing a group to accept certain members may impair the ability of the group to express those views, and only those views, that it intends to express. Thus, "[f]reedom of association … plainly presupposes a freedom not to associate."

The forced inclusion of an unwanted person in a group infringes the group's freedom of expressive association if the presence of that person affects in a significant way the group's ability to advocate public or private viewpoints. But the freedom of expressive association, like many freedoms, is not absolute. We have held that the freedom could be overridden "by regulations adopted to serve compelling state interests, unrelated to the suppression of ideas, that cannot be achieved through means significantly less restrictive of associational freedoms."

To determine whether a group is protected by the First Amendment's expressive associational right, we must determine whether the group engages in "expressive association." The First Amendment's protection of expressive association is not reserved for advocacy groups. But to come within its ambit, a group must engage in some form of expression, whether it be public or private....

The general mission of the Boy Scouts is clear: "[T]o instill values in young people." The Boy Scouts seeks to instill these values by having its adult leaders spend time with the youth members, instructing and engaging them in activities like camping, archery, and fishing. During the time spent with the youth members, the scoutmasters and assistant scoutmasters inculcate them with the Boy Scouts' values—both expressly and by example. It seems indisputable that an association that seeks to transmit such a system of values engages in expressive activity.

Given that the Boy Scouts engages in expressive activity, we must determine whether the forced inclusion of Dale as an assistant scoutmaster would significantly affect the Boy Scouts' ability to advocate public or private viewpoints. This inquiry necessarily requires us first to explore, to a limited extent, the nature of the Boy Scouts' view of homosexuality.

The values the Boy Scouts seeks to instill are "based on" those listed in the Scout Oath and Law. The Boy Scouts explains that the Scout Oath and Law provide "a positive moral code for living; they are a list of 'do's' rather than 'don'ts.'" The Boy Scouts asserts that homosexual conduct is inconsistent with the values embodied in the Scout Oath and Law, particularly with the values represented by the terms "morally straight" and "clean."

Obviously, the Scout Oath and Law do not expressly mention sexuality or sexual orientation. And the terms "morally straight" and "clean" are by no means self-defining. Different people would attribute to those terms very different meanings. For example, some people may believe that engaging in homosexual conduct is not at odds with being "morally straight" and "clean." And others may believe that engaging in homosexual conduct is contrary to being "morally straight" and "clean." The Boy Scouts says it falls within the latter category.

The New Jersey Supreme Court analyzed the Boy Scouts' beliefs and found that the "exclusion of members solely on the basis of their sexual orientation is inconsistent with Boy Scouts' commitment to a diverse and 'representative' membership [and] contradicts Boy Scouts' overarching objective to reach 'all eligible youth.'" The court concluded that the exclusion of members like Dale "appears antithetical to the organization's goals and philosophy." But our cases reject this sort of inquiry; it is not the role of the courts to reject a group's expressed values because they disagree with those values or find them internally inconsistent.

The Boy Scouts asserts that it "teach[es] that homosexual conduct is not morally straight," and that it does "not want to promote homosexual conduct as a legitimate form of behavior." We accept the Boy Scouts' assertion. We need not inquire further to determine the nature of the Boy Scouts' expression with respect to homosexuality....

We must then determine whether Dale's presence as an assistant scoutmaster would significantly burden the Boy Scouts' desire to not "promote homosexual conduct as a legitimate form of behavior." As we give deference to an association's assertions regarding the nature of its expression, we must also give deference to an association's view of what would impair its expression. That is not to say that an expressive association can erect a shield against antidiscrimination laws simply by asserting that mere acceptance of a member from a particular group would impair its message. But here Dale, by his own admission, is one of a group of gay Scouts who have "become leaders in their community and are open and honest about their sexual orientation." Dale was the copresident of a gay and lesbian organization at college and remains a gay rights activist. Dale's presence in the Boy Scouts would, at the very least, force the organization to send a message, both to the youth members and the world, that the Boy Scouts accepts homosexual conduct as a legitimate form of behavior....

Here, we have found that the Boy Scouts believes that homosexual conduct is inconsistent with the values it seeks to instill in its youth members; it will not "promote homosexual conduct as a legitimate form of behavior." ... [T]he presence of Dale as an assistant scoutmaster would just as surely interfere with the Boy Scouts' choice not to propound a point of view contrary to its beliefs.

The New Jersey Supreme Court determined that the Boy Scouts' ability to disseminate its message was not significantly affected by the forced inclusion of Dale as an assistant scoutmaster because of the following findings:

> Boy Scout members do not associate for the purpose of disseminating the belief that homosexuality is immoral; Boy Scouts discourages its leaders from disseminating *any* views on sexual issues; and Boy Scouts includes sponsors and members who subscribe to different views in respect of homosexuality.

We disagree with the New Jersey Supreme Court's conclusion drawn from these findings.

First, associations do not have to associate for the "purpose" of disseminating a certain message in order to be entitled to the protections of the First Amendment. An association must merely engage in expressive activity that could be impaired in order to be entitled to protection....

Second, even if the Boy Scouts discourages Scout leaders from disseminating views on sexual issues—a fact that the Boy Scouts disputes with contrary evidence—the First Amendment protects the Boy Scouts' method of expression. If the Boy Scouts wishes Scout leaders to avoid questions of sexuality and teach only by example, this fact does not negate the sincerity of its belief discussed above.

Third, the First Amendment simply does not require that every member of a group agree on every issue in order for the group's policy to be "expressive association." The Boy

Scouts takes an official position with respect to homosexual conduct, and that is sufficient for First Amendment purposes. In this same vein, Dale makes much of the claim that the Boy Scouts does not revoke the membership of heterosexual Scout leaders that openly disagree with the Boy Scouts' policy on sexual orientation. But if this is true, it is irrelevant. The presence of an avowed homosexual and gay rights activist in an assistant scoutmaster's uniform sends a distinctly different message from the presence of a heterosexual assistant scoutmaster who is on record as disagreeing with Boy Scouts policy. The Boy Scouts has a First Amendment right to choose to send one message but not the other. The fact that the organization does not trumpet its views from the housetops, or that it tolerates dissent within its ranks, does not mean that its views receive no First Amendment protection.

Having determined that the Boy Scouts is an expressive association and that the forced inclusion of Dale would significantly affect its expression, we inquire whether the application of New Jersey's public accommodations law to require that the Boy Scouts accept Dale as an assistant scoutmaster runs afoul of the Scouts' freedom of expressive association. We conclude that it does.

State public accommodations laws were originally enacted to prevent discrimination in traditional places of public accommodation—like inns and trains. Over time, the public accommodations laws have expanded to cover more places. New Jersey's statutory definition of "[a] place of public accommodation" is extremely broad. The term is said to "include, but not be limited to," a list of over 50 types of places. Many on the list are what one would expect to be places where the public is invited. In this case, the New Jersey Supreme Court went a step further and applied its public accommodations law to a private entity without even attempting to tie the term "place" to a physical location. As the definition of "public accommodation" has expanded from clearly commercial entities, such as restaurants, bars, and hotels, to membership organizations such as the Boy Scouts, the potential for conflict between state public accommodations laws and the First Amendment rights of organizations has increased....

... We have already concluded that a state requirement that the Boy Scouts retain Dale as an assistant scoutmaster would significantly burden the organization's right to oppose or disfavor homosexual conduct. The state interests embodied in New Jersey's public accommodations law do not justify such a severe intrusion on the Boy Scouts' rights to freedom of expressive association. That being the case, we hold that the First Amendment prohibits the State from imposing such a requirement through the application of its public accommodations law....

The judgment of the New Jersey Supreme Court is reversed, and the case is remanded for further proceedings not inconsistent with this opinion.

Dissenting VOICES

Justice Stevens dissented and was joined by Justices Souter, Ginsburg and Breyer. He rejected the majority's assumption that "Dale's mere presence among the Boy Scouts will itself force the group to convey a message about homosexuality—even if Dale has no intention of doing so." He took issue with the majority's position that the presence of "an avowed homosexual and gay rights activist in an assistant scoutmaster's uniform" essentially forces "the organization to send a message, both to the youth members and the world, that the Boy Scouts accepts homosexual conduct as a legitimate form of behavior."

But this approach, Justice Stevens argued, misunderstands New Jersey's public accommodations law, which forbids discrimination against citizens on many different bases, including sexual orientation.

> The State of New Jersey has decided that people who are open and frank about their sexual orientation are entitled to equal access to employment as schoolteachers, police officers, librarians, athletic coaches, and a host of other jobs filled by citizens who serve as role models for children and adults alike.... Dozens of Scout units throughout the State are sponsored by public agencies, such as schools and fire departments, that employ such role models. BSA's affiliation with numerous public agencies that comply with New Jersey's law against discrimination cannot be understood to convey any particular message endorsing or condoning the activities of all these people.

Justice Stevens assailed the transformation of anti-gay prejudice into First Amendment associational freedom.

> Unfavorable opinions about homosexuals "have ancient roots." Like equally atavistic opinions about certain racial groups, those roots have been nourished by sectarian doctrine. Over the years, however, interaction with real people, rather than mere adherence to traditional ways of thinking about members of unfamiliar classes, have modified those opinions....
>
> That such prejudices are still prevalent and that they have caused serious and tangible harm to countless members of the class New Jersey seeks to protect are established matters of fact that neither the Boy Scouts nor the Court disputes. That harm can only be aggravated by the creation of a constitutional shield for a policy that is itself the product of a habitual way of thinking about strangers. As Justice Brandeis so wisely advised, "We must be ever on our guard, lest we erect our prejudices into legal principles."

FOR THE CLASS

Public Displays of Intolerance? Imagine that in May 2008 a high school in Bismarck, North Dakota, held its senior prom. A week prior, Principal Moffit received an anonymous letter indicating that several gay and lesbian couples were planning to attend, something that had never happened before. Principal Moffit read this letter aloud at a school assembly and announced that "any display of homosexual affection will upset many students, teachers, and parents and could create safety risks for the students involved. We want to remind everyone that we have a rule against public displays of affection here."

Nonetheless, two same-sex couples arrived together at the prom—John and Louis, and Elizabeth and Paula. Like other prom dates, the couples danced together, which caused much whispering at first. But as the night wore on, other students grew more comfortable with the same-sex couples, and some even invited the gay students to dance with them.

However, during the traditional last "slow dance" of the evening, Principal Moffit interrupted John and Louis and Elizabeth and Paula while they were dancing and escorted them brusquely out of the dance hall. He told them that they were violating rule twelve of the school code of conduct, which forbids "public displays of affection at school-sponsored events." He told the students that they had been photographed "making out" on the dance floor. They each admitted to "kissing" on the dance floor but protested that, as Elizabeth said, "Half of the people on the dance floor are making out." The principal said, "If you're caught speeding, it's no defense to say other people were doing it too." The next day Principal Moffit conducted hearings and suspended each student for seven days. He rejected the students' argument that no straight student was being suspended despite the fact that dozens had engaged in the same conduct. He also dismissed the argument that the school's usual punishment for first-offense public displays of affection was to issue a warning. Although Principal Moffit noted that no student had ever before been suspended for making out at school, he said there "were special circumstances, because I gave you specific warning and this type of contact could have been dangerous to you and others."

The four students appealed their suspensions to federal court, alleging that their disparate treatment violated their equal protection rights and also that they had a First Amendment right to kiss, like other students. The school says that it had authority to punish the gay students more harshly because they were "on special alert," "their conduct could provoke violence against them in a conservative community," and "homosexual sodomy is illegal in North Dakota anyway."

No federal court had ever ruled on these issues before, so it was a "case of first impression." Form a panel of three federal judges to hear the case and make other students into witnesses or lawyers for either side. The judges should rule on the equal protection and First Amendment claims.

Further **Reading**

Raskin, Jamin B. "Legal Aliens, Local Citizens: The Historical, Constitutional, and Theoretical Meanings of Alien Suffrage." *University of Pennsylvania Law Review* 141 (April 1993): 1391–1470.

Suggs, Welch. *A Place on the Team: The Triumph and Tragedy of Title IX.* Princeton, N.J.: Princeton University Press, 2006.

Whitman, Mark, ed. *The Irony of Desegregation Law, 1955–1995: Essays and Documents.* Princeton, N.J.: M. Wiener, 1998.

HARASSMENT IN THE HALLWAYS: Sexual Harassment, Bullying, and the Law

"No person in the United States shall, on the basis of sex, be excluded from participation in, be denied the benefits of, or be subjected to discrimination under any education program or activity receiving federal financial assistance." TITLE IX (20 U.S.C. § 1681)

"There were two or three boys touching me … and I'd tell them to stop but they wouldn't. This went on for months. Finally I was in one of my classes when all of them came back and backed me into a corner and started touching me all over.… After the class I told the principal, and he and the boys had a little talk. And after the talk was up, the boys came out laughing because they got no punishment." NAN STEIN AND LISA SJOSTROM, *FLIRTING OR HURTING? A TEACHER'S GUIDE ON STUDENT-TO-STUDENT SEXUAL HARASSMENT IN SCHOOLS (GRADES 6 THROUGH 12)*

For many adults, high school evokes images of cramming for calculus tests, going to yearbook meetings, cheering on the home team, enjoying school musicals, and pinning on corsages at senior proms. But there has always been a dark undertow to high school: the teasing, put-downs, ridicule, and hazing that students sometimes inflict on one another, as well as the abuse of power imposed on students by bad-apple teachers and administrators.

Sometimes these behaviors reach a point where they become illegal. This is the case with *sexual harassment,* which is defined as unwanted and unwelcome sexual advances and conduct that interfere with a student's education.

Sexual harassment is a serious problem in American schools. In 1993 the American Association of University Women released a study done by Louis Harris and Associates titled *Hostile Hallways: The AAUW Survey on Sexual Harassment in America's Schools,* which surveyed more than 1,600 American public high school students (grades eight through eleven). The findings were astonishing—85 percent of the girls and 76 percent of the boys reported experiencing some kind of sexual harassment, including unwanted sexual touching, grabbing, comments, and gestures. All told, four out of five students had, to one degree or another, faced sexual harassment. Such harassment can undermine a student's academic performance and ruin his or her sense of physical, emotional, and mental well-being.

While student-on-student harassment is most common, some students face sexual harassment from teachers, coaches, advisers, staff, and even principals.

Sexual harassment is illegal under Title IX of the Education Amendments of 1972, a federal law passed by Congress. Under Title IX, sexual harassment in any school receiving federal funds, whether the school is public or private, is considered a form of *illegal sex discrimination.* Thus any student, male or female, subjected to sexual harassment in any school program or activity—whether in class or on the sports field, on campus or off campus—can bring suit against the school system under Title IX. The cases in this chapter define when a school system is liable for such harassment.

Sexual harassment can take two different forms: quid pro quo sexual harassment and hostile environment sexual harassment.

Quid pro quo harassment occurs when a school employee, such as a teacher or staff member, tries to convince a student to submit to unwanted sexual advances as a condition for participating in a school program or extracurricular activity, as a means of getting ahead in some way (such as getting a better grade or a starting position on a team), or as a necessary way to avoid negative consequences (such as getting a bad grade or having rumors spread about him or her).

Hostile environment sexual harassment occurs when unwelcome hostile conduct of a sexual nature is so severe, persistent, and pervasive that it interferes with a student's ability to learn at school or creates an intimidating, threatening, or abusive academic environment. Such an environment might be created by teachers, administrators, other students, or some combination thereof. Examples of conduct that produces a hostile environment are leers; sexual banter and ridicule; use of pornography to embarrass and humiliate; unwanted touching, squeezing, or fondling; sexual graffiti; persistent negative sexual rumors; sexual "ratings" of students; sexual gestures and mooning; exhibitionist displays; and so on.

There is, of course, some ambiguity about when unwelcome juvenile sexual conduct actually crosses the line and creates a hostile learning environment. Obviously, a couple of bad jokes or a single unwelcome invitation to the movies does not translate into a Title IX violation. But the law considers severe, persistent, and pervasive sexual harassment a serious problem. The law assumes that judges and juries will be able to distinguish between an innocent (if undesired) love poem left at someone's desk and a pattern of sexually hostile and demeaning behavior that interferes with a student's education.

P⬤INTS TO PONDER

How can schools and courts tell the difference between innocent teasing or joking and illegal sexual harassment?

- If a teacher sexually pressures and harasses one of his or her students, should the school system be held legally and financially responsible even if the teacher's superiors were unaware of his or her conduct?
- Should school authorities be held responsible for student-on-student sexual harassment if they know about it and do nothing to stop it? What if they are totally unaware of what is going on?

When Teachers Harass Students

If a student brings a Title IX action alleging that he or she is being sexually harassed by a teacher and proves it, is the school automatically liable at that point for monetary damages? Or must the student first show that someone in authority at the school knew about the inappropriate behavior and failed to stop it? In the Texas case of *Gebser v. Lago Vista Independent School District* (1998), the Court found that a school district is liable for damages under Title IX for a teacher's sexual harassment of a student only if the teacher's superiors or other high-up officials in the school actually knew about it and chose to do nothing. Does this "deliberate indifference" standard leave young people at school too vulnerable to predatory adults? Does it give school officials incentive to stick their heads in the sand? See what you think by reading the majority and dissenting opinions.

GEBSER v. LAGO VISTA INDEPENDENT SCHOOL DISTRICT

Supreme Court of the United States
Argued March 25, 1998.
Decided June 22, 1998.

OPINION Justice O'CONNOR delivered the opinion of the Court.

The question in this case is when a school district may be held liable in damages in an implied right of action under Title IX of the Education Amendments for the sexual harassment of a student by one of the district's teachers. We conclude that damages may not be recovered in those circumstances unless an official of the school district who at a minimum has authority to institute corrective measures on the district's behalf has actual notice of, and is deliberately indifferent to, the teacher's misconduct.

I

In the spring of 1991, when petitioner Alida Star Gebser was an eighth-grade student at a middle school in respondent Lago Vista Independent School District (Lago Vista), she joined a high school book discussion group led by Frank Waldrop, a teacher at Lago Vista's high school. Lago Vista received federal funds at all pertinent times. During the book discussion sessions, Waldrop often made sexually suggestive comments to the students. Gebser entered high school in the fall and was assigned to classes taught by Waldrop in both semesters. Waldrop continued to make inappropriate remarks to the students, and he began to direct more of his suggestive comments toward Gebser, including during the substantial amount of time that the two were alone in his classroom. He initiated sexual contact with Gebser in the spring, when, while visiting her home ostensibly to give her a book, he kissed and fondled her. The two had sexual intercourse on a number of occasions during the remainder of the school year. Their relationship continued through the summer and into the following school year, and they often had intercourse during class time, although never on school property.

JUSTICES: A CLOSER LOOK

JUSTICE SANDRA DAY O'CONNOR (1930–), the first woman named to the U.S. Supreme Court, was born in El Paso, Texas. After graduating from high school at age sixteen, she attended Stanford University and majored in economics. She subsequently entered Stanford Law School, where she briefly dated fellow classmate William Rehnquist, made it onto the *Stanford Law Review*, and graduated third in her class of 102 students.

O'Connor settled in Arizona, where she became active in Republican politics. There she served as a state assistant attorney general and became the first woman in the United States to be a state senate majority leader. O'Connor was later appointed to the Arizona Court of Appeals. In August 1981, President Ronald Reagan nominated O'Connor to the Supreme Court, where she served as an associate justice until 2006.

HIGHLIGHTS

- Justice O'Connor grew up on a 198,000-acre ranch amid cattle and long stretches of uninhabited land in rural Arizona. Although her family would grow prosperous, there was no running water or electricity in her home for the first seven years of her life.
- Justice O'Connor was often the deciding vote in important cases on such controversial issues as affirmative action, abortion rights, school vouchers, and drug testing.

Gebser did not report the relationship to school officials, testifying that while she realized Waldrop's conduct was improper, she was uncertain how to react and she wanted to continue having him as a teacher. In October 1992, the parents of two other students complained to the high school principal about Waldrop's comments in class. The principal arranged a meeting, at which, according to the principal, Waldrop indicated that he did not believe he had made offensive remarks but apologized to the parents and said it would not happen again. The principal also advised Waldrop to be careful about his classroom comments and told the school guidance counselor about the meeting, but he did not report the parents' complaint to Lago Vista's superintendent, who was the district's Title IX coordinator. A couple of months later, in January 1993, a police officer discovered Waldrop and Gebser engaging in sexual intercourse and arrested Waldrop. Lago Vista terminated his employment, and subsequently, the Texas Education Agency revoked his teaching license. During this time, the district had not promulgated or distributed an official grievance procedure for lodging sexual harassment complaints; nor had it issued a formal anti-harassment policy....

III

... When a teacher's sexual harassment is imputed to a school district or when a school district is deemed to have "constructively" known of the teacher's harassment, by assumption the district had no actual knowledge of the teacher's conduct. Nor, of course, did the district have an opportunity to take action to end the harassment or to limit further harassment....

IV

... [W]e hold that a damages remedy will not lie under Title IX unless an official who at a minimum has authority to address the alleged discrimination and to institute corrective measures on the recipient's behalf has actual knowledge of discrimination in the recipient's programs and fails adequately to respond.

We think, moreover, that the response must amount to deliberate indifference to discrimination. The administrative enforcement scheme presupposes that an official who is advised of a Title IX violation refuses to take action to bring the recipient into compliance. The premise, in other words, is an official decision by the recipient not to remedy the violation. That framework finds a rough parallel in the standard of deliberate indifference. Under a lower standard, there would be a risk that the recipient would be liable in damages not for its own official decision but instead for its employees' independent actions....

V

... [W]e will not hold a school district liable in damages under Title IX for a teacher's sexual harassment of a student absent actual notice and deliberate indifference....

Dissenting VOICES

Justice Stevens, joined by Justices Souter, Ginsburg, and Breyer, dissented, maintaining that the school should be held responsible because the sexual harassment was a product of the teacher's authority over the student and, in turn, the school's delegation of authority to that teacher. He argued:

> This case presents a paradigmatic example of a tort that was made possible ... [and] was repeated over a prolonged period because of the powerful influence that Waldrop had over Gebser by reason of the authority that his employer, the school district, had delegated to him. As a secondary school teacher, Waldrop exercised even greater authority and control over his students than employers and supervisors exercise over their employees. His gross misuse of that authority allowed him to abuse his young student's trust.

Justice Stevens pointed out the irony of holding teachers responsible for preventing students from harassing other students in the classroom but not holding teachers responsible for harassing students themselves: "If petitioner had been the victim of sexually harassing conduct by other students during those classes, surely the teacher would have had ample authority to take corrective measures. The fact that he did not prevent his own harassment of petitioner is the consequence of his lack of will, not his lack of authority."

The dissenters finally observed that the majority's holding would create incentives for school authorities to keep themselves in the dark about sexual harassment: "As long as school boards can insulate themselves from knowledge about this sort of conduct, they can claim immunity from damages liability. Indeed, the rule that the Court adopts would preclude a damages remedy even if every teacher at the school knew about the harassment but did not have 'authority to institute corrective measures on the district's behalf.'"

WHAT DO YOU Think?

Exercise 9.1. What do you think of the dissenting justices' argument that the teacher is an authority figure within the school and therefore the school should be automatically (or "strictly") liable for his conduct? The majority believes that it is not fair to hold the school financially accountable, because school officials were not aware of the affair. Do you agree with the majority opinion (there must be actual knowledge and "deliberate indifference" before the school system becomes liable) or the dissenting opinion (the school must always be liable for the teacher's actions, even if there was no actual notice to administrators that a teacher was harassing a student or having an affair)? Why?

When Students Harass Students

If school systems are liable for their employees' sexual harassment of students when school authorities are aware of the offending behavior, what about when it occurs at the hands of fellow students?

One line of thinking contends that schools are absolutely responsible and liable for anything that happens inside their walls; an opposing line of thought maintains that schools cannot be, and should never be held, responsible for actions taken by students (as opposed to their own employees).

The Supreme Court has rejected both of these polar positions, ruling instead that under Title IX school systems will *sometimes* be liable for student-on-student sexual harassment. Under what conditions does the Court find schools responsible?

As in *Gebser*, the Court in *Davis v. Monroe County Board of Education* (1999) found that a Georgia school can be held liable only when it knows about the harassment and acts with "deliberate indifference" to its existence. The Court also found that in order for a plaintiff student to win her case, the harassment must be "severe, pervasive, and objectively offensive." The dissenters say that the decision opens the floodgates for litigation over trivial offenses. Do you agree?

LaShonda Davis (right) with her mother in May 1999. Davis was only ten years old when she suffered through five months of crude sexual taunts and advances in the 1992–1993 school year.

DAVIS v. MONROE COUNTY BOARD OF EDUCATION

Supreme Court of the United States
Argued January 12, 1999.
Decided May 24, 1999.

OPINION   Justice O'CONNOR delivered the opinion of the Court.

Petitioner brought suit against the Monroe County Board of Education and other defendants, alleging that her fifth-grade daughter had been the victim of sexual harassment by another student in her class. Among petitioner's claims was a claim for monetary and injunctive relief under Title IX. The District Court dismissed petitioner's Title IX claim on the ground that "student-on-student," or peer, harassment provides no ground for a private cause of action under the statute. The Court of Appeals for the Eleventh Circuit affirmed. We consider here whether a private damages action may lie against the school board in cases of student-on-student harassment. We conclude that it may, but only where the funding recipient acts with deliberate indifference to known acts of harassment in its programs or activities. Moreover, we conclude that such an action will lie only for harassment that is so severe, pervasive, and objectively offensive that it effectively bars the victim's access to an educational opportunity or benefit.

> **Injunctive Relief**
> A court order meant to force an organization or person either to do something or to stop doing it.

I

A

… According to petitioner's complaint, the harassment began in December 1992, when the classmate, G. F., attempted to touch LaShonda's breasts and genital area and made vulgar statements such as "I want to get in bed with you" and "I want to feel your boobs." Similar conduct allegedly occurred on or about January 4 and January 20, 1993. LaShonda reported each of these incidents to her mother and to her classroom teacher, Diane Fort. Petitioner, in turn, also contacted Fort, who allegedly assured petitioner that the school principal, Bill Querry, had been informed of the incidents. Petitioner contends that, notwithstanding these reports, no disciplinary action was taken against G. F.

G. F.'s conduct allegedly continued for many months. In early February, G. F. purportedly placed a door stop in his pants and proceeded to act in a sexually suggestive manner toward LaShonda during physical education class. LaShonda reported G. F.'s behavior to her physical education teacher, Whit Maples. Approximately one week later, G. F. again allegedly engaged in harassing behavior, this time while under the supervision of another classroom teacher, Joyce Pippen. Again, LaShonda allegedly reported the incident to the teacher, and again petitioner contacted the teacher to follow up.

Petitioner alleges that G. F. once more directed sexually harassing conduct toward LaShonda in physical education class in early March, and that LaShonda reported the incident to both Maples and Pippen. In mid-April 1993, G. F. allegedly rubbed his body against LaShonda in the school hallway in what LaShonda considered a sexually suggestive manner, and LaShonda again reported the matter to Fort.

The string of incidents finally ended in mid-May, when G. F. was charged with, and pleaded guilty to, sexual battery for his misconduct. The complaint alleges that LaShonda had suffered during the months of harassment, however; specifically, her previously high grades allegedly dropped as she became unable to concentrate on her studies, and, in April 1993, her father discovered that she had written a suicide note. The complaint further alleges that, at one point, LaShonda told petitioner that she "didn't know how much longer she could keep [G. F.] off her."

Nor was LaShonda G. F.'s only victim; it is alleged that other girls in the class fell prey to G. F.'s conduct. At one point, in fact, a group composed of LaShonda and other female students tried to speak with Principal Querry about G. F.'s behavior. According to the complaint, however, a teacher denied the students' request with the statement, "If [Querry] wants you, he'll call you."

Petitioner alleges that no disciplinary action was taken in response to G. F.'s behavior toward LaShonda. In addition to her conversations with Fort and Pippen, petitioner alleges that she spoke with Principal Querry in mid-May 1993. When petitioner inquired as to what action the school intended to take against G. F., Querry simply stated, "I guess I'll have to threaten him a little bit harder." Yet, petitioner alleges, at no point during the many months of his reported misconduct was G. F. disciplined for harassment. Indeed, Querry allegedly asked petitioner why LaShonda "was the only one complaining."

Nor, according to the complaint, was any effort made to separate G. F. and LaShonda. On the contrary, notwithstanding LaShonda's frequent complaints, only after more than three months of reported harassment was she even permitted to change her classroom seat so that she was no longer seated next to G. F. Moreover, petitioner alleges that, at the time of the events in question, the Monroe County Board of Education (Board) had not instructed its personnel on how to respond to peer sexual harassment and had not established a policy on the issue....

II

... [A]t issue here is the question whether a recipient of federal education funding may be liable for damages under Title IX under any circumstances for discrimination in the form of student-on-student sexual harassment.

A

... We disagree with respondents' assertion, however, that petitioner seeks to hold the Board liable for G. F.'s actions instead of its own. Here, petitioner attempts to hold the Board liable for its own decision to remain idle in the face of known student-on-student harassment in its schools. In *Gebser*, we concluded that a recipient of federal education funds may be liable in damages under Title IX where it is deliberately indifferent to known acts of sexual harassment by a teacher. In that case, a teacher had entered into a sexual relationship with an eighth grade student, and the student sought damages under Title IX for the teacher's misconduct....

Accordingly, we rejected the use of agency principles to impute liability to the district for the misconduct of its teachers. Likewise, we declined the invitation to impose liability under what amounted to a negligence standard—holding the district liable for its failure to react to teacher-student harassment of which it knew or *should have known*. Rather, we concluded that the district could be liable for damages only where the district itself intentionally acted in clear violation of Title IX by remaining deliberately indifferent to acts of teacher-student harassment of which it had actual knowledge.... [W]e concluded in *Gebser* that recipients could be liable in damages only where their own deliberate indifference effectively "cause[d]" the discrimination....

> **Liability**
> A legal obligation or responsibility. Liability is enforceable by a court in a civil or criminal trial.

We consider here whether the misconduct identified in *Gebser*—deliberate indifference to known acts of harassment—amounts to an intentional violation of Title IX, capable of supporting a private damages action, when the harasser is a student rather than a teacher. We conclude that, in certain limited circumstances, it does....

... The statute's plain language confines the scope of prohibited conduct based on the recipient's degree of control over the harasser and the environment in which the harassment occurs. If a funding recipient does not engage in harassment directly, it may not be liable for damages unless its deliberate indifference "subject[s]" its students to harassment. That is, the deliberate indifference must, at a minimum, "cause [students] to undergo" harassment or "make them liable or vulnerable" to it....

Where, as here, the misconduct occurs during school hours and on school grounds—the bulk of G. F.'s misconduct, in fact, took place in the classroom—the misconduct is taking place "under" an "operation" of the funding recipient. In these circumstances, the recipient retains substantial control over the context in which the harassment occurs. More importantly, however, in this setting the Board exercises significant control over the harasser. We have observed, for example, "that the nature of [the State's] power [over public schoolchildren] is custodial and tutelary, permitting a degree of supervision and control that could not be exercised over free adults." ...

While it remains to be seen whether petitioner can show that the Board's response to reports of G. F.'s misconduct was clearly unreasonable in light of the known circumstances, petitioner may be able to show that the Board "subject[ed]" LaShonda to discrimination by failing to respond in any way over a period of five months to complaints of G. F.'s in-school misconduct from LaShonda and other female students.

B

... Having previously determined that "sexual harassment" is "discrimination" in the school context under Title IX, we are constrained to conclude that student-on-student sexual harassment, if sufficiently severe, can likewise rise to the level of discrimination actionable under the statute....

The most obvious example of student-on-student sexual harassment capable of triggering a damages claim would thus involve the overt, physical deprivation of access to school resources. Consider, for example, a case in which male students physically threaten their female peers every day, successfully preventing the female students from using a particular school resource—an athletic field or a computer lab, for instance. District administrators are well aware of the daily ritual, yet they deliberately ignore requests for aid from the female students wishing to use the resource. The district's knowing refusal to take any action in response to such behavior would fly in the face of Title IX's core principles, and such deliberate indifference may appropriately be subject to claims for monetary damages. It is not necessary, however, to show physical exclusion to demonstrate that students have been deprived by the actions of another student or students of an educational opportunity on the basis of sex. Rather, a plaintiff must establish sexual harassment of students that is so severe, pervasive, and objectively offensive, and that so undermines and detracts from the victims' educational experience, that the victim-students are effectively denied equal access to an institution's resources and opportunities.

Whether gender-oriented conduct rises to the level of actionable "harassment" thus "depends on a constellation of surrounding circumstances, expectations, and relationships," including, but not limited to, the ages of the harasser and the victim and the number of individuals involved. [Courts, moreover, must bear in mind that schools are unlike the adult workplace and that children may regularly interact in a manner that would be unacceptable among adults. Indeed, at least early on, students are still learning how to interact appropriately with their peers. It is thus understandable that, in the school setting, students often engage in insults, banter, teasing, shoving, pushing, and gender-specific conduct that is upsetting to the students subjected to it. Damages are not available for simple acts of teasing and name-calling among school children, however, even where these comments target differences in gender. Rather, in the context of student-on-student harassment, damages are available only where the behavior is so severe, pervasive, and objectively offensive that it denies its victims the equal access to education that Title IX is designed to protect.]

The dissent fails to appreciate these very real limitations on a funding recipient's liability under Title IX. It is not enough to show, as the dissent would read this opinion to provide, that a student has been "teased," or "called offensive names[.]" Comparisons to an "overweight child who skips gym class because the other children tease her about her size," the student "who refuses to wear glasses to avoid the taunts of 'four-eyes,'" and "the child who refuses to go to school because the school bully calls him a 'scaredy-cat' at recess" are inapposite and misleading. Nor do we contemplate, much less hold, that a mere "decline in grades is enough to survive" a motion to dismiss. The drop-off in LaShonda's grades provides necessary evidence of a potential link between her education and G. F.'s misconduct, but petitioner's ability to state a cognizable claim here depends equally on the alleged persistence and severity of G. F.'s actions, not to mention the Board's alleged knowledge and deliberate indifference. We trust that the dissent's characterization of our opinion will not mislead courts to impose more sweeping liability than we read Title IX to require.

Moreover, the provision that the discrimination occur "under any education program or activity" suggests that the behavior be serious enough to have the systemic effect of denying the victim equal access to an educational program or activity. Although, in theory, a single instance of sufficiently severe one-on-one peer harassment could be said to have such an effect, we think it unlikely that Congress would have thought such behavior sufficient to rise to this level in light of the inevitability of student misconduct and the amount of litigation that would be invited by entertaining claims of official indifference to a single instance of one-on-one peer harassment. By limiting private damages actions to cases having a systemic effect on educational programs or activities, we reconcile the general principle that Title IX prohibits official indifference to known peer sexual harassment with the practical realities of responding to student behavior, realities that Congress could not have meant to be ignored....

The fact that it was a teacher who engaged in harassment in *Franklin* and *Gebser* is relevant. The relationship between the harasser and the victim necessarily affects the extent to which the misconduct can be said to breach Title IX's guarantee of equal access to educational benefits and to have a systemic effect on a program or activity. Peer harassment, in particular, is less likely to satisfy these requirements than is teacher-student harassment.

C

Applying this standard to the facts at issue here, we conclude that the Eleventh Circuit erred in dismissing petitioner's complaint. Petitioner alleges that her daughter was the victim of repeated acts of sexual harassment by G. F. over a 5-month period, and there are allegations in support of the conclusion that G. F.'s misconduct was severe, pervasive, and objectively offensive. The harassment was not only verbal; it included numerous acts of objectively offensive touching, and, indeed, G. F. ultimately pleaded guilty to criminal sexual misconduct. Moreover, the complaint alleges that there were multiple victims who were sufficiently disturbed by G. F.'s misconduct to seek an audience with the school principal. Further, petitioner contends that the harassment had a concrete, negative effect on her daughter's ability to receive an education. The complaint also suggests that petitioner may be able to show both actual knowledge and deliberate indifference on the part of the Board, which made no effort whatsoever either to investigate or to put an end to the harassment....

Dissenting VOICES

Justice Kennedy, joined by Chief Justice Rehnquist, Justice Scalia, and Justice Thomas, filed a sweeping dissent challenging every part of the majority decision.

Justice Kennedy pointed out that schools have an awesomely difficult task trying to control the behavior of "thousands of immature students" and that many schools "are already overwhelmed with disciplinary problems of all kinds." Thus, he contended, it will be no easy task to prevent peer-to-peer sexual harassment.

Moreover, Justice Kennedy maintained, the First Amendment weakens the ability of schools and universities to control sexually offensive speech, much of which is constitutionally protected.

More fundamentally, he questioned whether it makes sense to describe the messy and immature behavior of children as "sexual harassment." Children, he observed, "lack the capacity to exercise mature judgment. It should surprise no one, then, that the schools that are the primary locus of most children's social development are rife with inappropriate behavior by children who are just learning to interact with their peers." He quoted an educator on "the front lines of our schools" who described the situation this way: "The real world of school discipline is a rough-and-tumble place where students practice newly learned vulgarities, erupt with anger, tease and embarrass each other, share offensive notes, flirt, push and shove in the halls, grab and offend."

Justice Kennedy did not contest that "much of this 'dizzying array of immature or uncontrollable behaviors by students' is inappropriate, even 'objectively offensive' at times" or that "parents and schools have a moral and ethical responsibility to help students learn to interact with their peers in an appropriate manner....[M]uch of this inappropriate behavior is directed toward members of the opposite sex, as children in the throes of adolescence struggle to express their emerging sexual identities."

But he strongly doubted "whether it is either proper or useful to label this immature, childish behavior gender discrimination." Title IX was designed to prevent discrimination based on sex, he argued, not the separate problem of sexual harassment: "Nothing in Title IX suggests that Congress even contemplated this question, much less answered it in the affirmative in unambiguous terms...."

Justice Kennedy forecast that schools would have trouble

> identifying peer sexual harassment, [a problem] already evident in teachers' manuals designed to give guidance on the subject. For example, one teachers' manual on peer sexual harassment suggests that sexual harassment in kindergarten through third grade includes a boy being "put down" on the playground "because he wants to play house with the girls" or a girl being "put down because she shoots baskets better than the boys." Yet another manual suggests that one student saying to another, "You look nice," could be sexual harassment, depending on the "tone of voice," how the student looks at the other, and "who else is around." Blowing a kiss is also suspect. This confusion will likely be compounded once the sexual-harassment label is invested with the force of federal law, backed up by private damages suits.

Justice Kennedy also chided the majority for creating a standard for defining sexual harassment that offers no definite guidance. He wrote:

> The majority proclaims that "in the context of student-on-student harassment, damages are available only in the situation where the behavior is so serious, pervasive, and objectively offensive that it denies its victims the equal access to education that Title IX is designed to protect." The majority does not even purport to explain, however, what constitutes an actionable denial of "equal access to education." Is equal access denied when a girl who tires of being chased by the boys at recess refuses to go outside? When she cannot concentrate during class because she is worried about the recess activities? When she pretends to be sick one day so she can stay home from school? It appears the majority is content to let juries decide....
>
> The only real clue the majority gives schools about the dividing line between actionable harassment that denies a victim equal access to education and mere inappropriate teasing is a profoundly unsettling one: On the facts of this case, petitioner has stated a claim because she alleged, in the majority's words, "that the harassment had a concrete, negative effect on her daughter's ability to receive an education." In petitioner's words,

the effects that might have been visible to the school were that her daughter's grades "dropped" and her "ability to concentrate on her school work [was] affected." Almost all adolescents experience these problems at one time or another as they mature.

The bottom line, according to Justice Kennedy, is that the majority

seems oblivious to the fact that almost every child, at some point, has trouble in school because he or she is being teased by his or her peers. The girl who wants to skip recess because she is teased by the boys is no different from the overweight child who skips gym class because the other children tease her about her size in the locker room; or the child who risks flunking out because he refuses to wear glasses to avoid the taunts of "four-eyes"; or the child who refuses to go to school because the school bully calls him a "scaredy-cat" at recess. Most children respond to teasing in ways that detract from their ability to learn. The majority's test for actionable harassment will, as a result, sweep in almost all of the more innocuous conduct it acknowledges as a ubiquitous part of school life.

Justice Kennedy predicted an avalanche of lawsuits in the wake of the ruling:

There will be no shortage of plaintiffs to bring such complaints. Our schools are charged each day with educating millions of children. Of those millions of students, a large percentage will, at some point during their school careers, experience something they consider sexual harassment.... The cost of defending against peer sexual harassment suits alone could overwhelm many school districts, particularly since the majority's liability standards will allow almost any plaintiff to get to summary judgment, if not to a jury. In addition, there are no damages caps on the judicially implied private cause of action under Title IX. As a result, school liability in one peer sexual harassment suit could approach, or even exceed, the total federal funding of many school districts.

> **Summary Judgment**
> Resolution of a case by a judge without trial where all of the significant facts of the case are uncontested and one party is entitled to win as a matter of law.

Justice Kennedy accused the majority of trying

to put an end to student misbehavior by transforming Title IX into a Federal Student Civility Code. I fail to see how federal courts will administer school discipline better than the principals and teachers to whom the public has entrusted that task or how the majority's holding will help the vast majority of students, whose educational opportunities will be diminished by the diversion of school funds to litigation....

In the final analysis, this case is about federalism. Yet the majority's decision today says not one word about the federal balance. Preserving our federal system is a legitimate end in itself. It is, too, the means to other ends. It ensures that essential choices can be made by a government more proximate to the people than the vast apparatus of federal power. Defining the appropriate role of schools in teaching and supervising children who are beginning to explore their own sexuality and learning how to express it to others is one of the most complex and sensitive issues our schools face. Such decisions are best made by parents and by the teachers and school administrators who can counsel with them.

> **Federalism**
> The system of divided and allocated powers between the states and the federal government.

WHAT DO YOU **Think?**

Exercise 9.2. The majority holds that students suing over student-on-student sexual harassment must show that the harassment "is so severe, pervasive, and objectively offensive that it effectively bars the victim's access to an educational opportunity or benefit." Is this standard too tough to take care of many of the real sexual harassment problems that students face? Or is it too weak to prevent young people and their families from bringing federal court lawsuits over trivial issues such as unwanted love poetry, overly suggestive valentine cards, and the kind of sexual banter and horseplay that take place in school hallways all over America?

Exercise 9.3. Find out if there is a sexual harassment policy at your school. If there is, consider how well it implements the holdings of these cases and the rules of Title IX. If no policy is currently in place, gather some model school policies from the Internet and the Department of Education and draft one for your school.

Exercise 9.4. Justice Kennedy completes his dissent by insisting that the case is "about federalism," and that the majority's decision substitutes federal policy and federal courts for the power of local school boards and officials to deal with the sexual harassment problem through such methods as firing teachers and educating students about the problem. Yet, that is true more generally of Title IX's displacement of local power in favor of federal rules against sex discrimination that give students the right to sue school systems. Is there any reason to think local governments will do a better job of stopping sexual harassment if there is no federal law against it?

FOR THE **CLASS**

Sexual Harassment? Consider the following examples of potentially objectionable behavior and try to determine whether each one constitutes Title IX sexual harassment —either quid pro quo or hostile environment—under *Gebser* and *Monroe County*. Could the students in each case sue? What would be the strengths and weaknesses of each case? Pretend your class is a law firm advising the students in each case on what to do. What advice do you give them?

A. Andy Algebra, the math teacher at North High, calls Sally Senior every night to talk about their respective social lives and tries to engage her in phone sex. One night he asks her to meet him at the beach. Although Andy is by far her favorite teacher, Sally tells him that she thinks "the relationship is going in the wrong direction." He says, "Gee, I was planning to nominate you for the math award, but I guess you're not really my prize pupil after all." Sally is upset about the situation and receives a C+ on her next exam, the first time she has received below a B+ in the class. She tells her academic adviser, the assistant principal, about the situation, but he tells her to just "ignore his comments; he flatters all the pretty girls." A week later, Andy sends Sally an e-mail, saying: "I hope you meet me at the beach Friday night so we can discuss your poor grade on the last test. I know a way you can get your grades back up."

B. Albert Feinstein is slender and not athletically inclined. At gym, the other boys in the locker room tease him about being skinny and clumsy. Lately, they have taken to calling him "fag," "sissy," and "girl," and snapping their wet towels on his rear end. Several times when Albert has opened up his locker, he has found a bra or girl's panties with his name written on it. After another boy, forty pounds heavier than Albert, pounced on him on a wrestling mat and simulated sexual intercourse, Albert began to skip gym and complained about these events to his physical education teacher, who replied, "Come on, Albert, loosen up and take it like a man."

C. In a biology classroom discussion about the female reproductive system, Joe raised his hand and asked the teacher, "If girls are supposed to have mammary glands to feed their babies, why doesn't Mary have any?" The teacher immediately reprimanded Joe and demanded that he apologize to Mary, who was humiliated in front of her classmates; the teacher then sent Joe to the principal's office, where he was reprimanded again.

D. Every day when girls at Reading High enter school, players on the football team sit on the curb with scorecards and hold up numbers, one through ten, "grading" the girls on their looks and appearance. Many girls feel embarrassed and humiliated by having to pass this gauntlet, and they have begun to come to school late to avoid being rated in this way. After receiving a number of "tardy" notices, several of the girls were given detention and other forms of discipline. When they objected to their discipline on the ground that they could not enter the school because of the rating game, the principal told them, "That's simply a fall homecoming tradition, and it's certainly no excuse for blatantly violating the rules of the school." The girls were disciplined. Meanwhile, the members of the team also took to pasting head shots of girl students onto the nude bodies of women pictured in pornographic magazines and placing them in the boys' locker room. After a few weeks the coach took them down, but no one was disciplined.

The Rights of Gay and Lesbian Students against Harassment

Title IX's protections against sexual harassment apply to homosexual and heterosexual students alike. In 1996 an Ashland, Wisconsin, student named Jamie Nabozny received a $900,000 judgment against his school system for its failure to put an end to the violence Nabozny endured at the hands of classmates from grades seven through eleven. At one point Nabozny was beaten so badly that he was hospitalized. As the lethal attack against 21-year-old Matthew Shepard in Wyoming in October 1998 illustrates, gay bashing has, in some cases, led to murder.

Hostility toward gay, lesbian, bisexual, and transgendered students—and anyone who others mistakenly think may belong to one of these groups—can also take nonviolent forms. The ridicule, relentless teasing, and put-downs that can occur may also be grounds for successful lawsuits if they present sufficiently severe and pervasive problems for the victims and if the school knows about them and fails to respond. Many states and counties have passed specific laws and ordinances protecting students against harassment based on sexual orientation. California has such a law, as does Massachusetts, which also promotes the creation of gay and lesbian support groups in public high schools. The state now has well over 150 Gay/Straight Alliances on campus.

Many people think that passing laws to protect gays, lesbians, bisexuals and the trans-gendered against harassment encourages or promotes homosexuality. Do you agree? Do you believe that sexual orientation is innate or learned? How does this affect your position? Should gay and lesbian students have the right to form alliances on campus alongside other student clubs? Would it be viewpoint discrimination under the First Amendment to deny them the right to meet?

What can be done to prevent harassment of gay and lesbian students? Discuss with your classmates. (An interesting video on this issue, *It's Elementary,* is available from www.womedia.org.)

FOR THE CLASS

Bully For You: Columbine Revisited. Sexual harassment is a sexualized form of the student-on-student bullying that is all too common in schools. Many students learn habits of cruelty—the infliction of pain on persons with less power—at home or in their neighborhoods and bring these destructive behaviors to school.

America heard a wake-up call about bullying after the infamous mass killings at Columbine High School in Littleton, Colorado, by students Eric Harris and Dylan Klebold in April 1999. The two boys opened fire on teachers and fellow students, murdering over a dozen students and a teacher and wounding even more.

America mourned the slain and condemned the perpetrators of the massacre, but few people made the link between this explosion of gun violence and the problem of bullying. The next fall I received e-mails from a student at Columbine, who wrote that the school, in its recent back-to-school pep rally, had effectively banned mention of the deceased and the violence that took their lives the prior school year. My correspondent was convinced that the school had "learned nothing" and had specifically failed to confront the "bullying by jocks" that incensed Harris and Klebold and drove the boys over the brink.

A perceptive article in the *Washington Post* written on June 12, 1999, by Lorraine Adams and Dale Russakoff, and titled "Dissecting Columbine's Cult of the Athlete; In Search of Answers, Community Examines One Source of Killers' Rage," confirmed my correspondent's sentiments. The reporters wrote of Columbine High that "some parents and students believe a schoolwide indulgence of certain jocks—their criminal convictions, physical abuse, sexual and racial bullying—intensified the killers' feelings of powerlessness and galvanized their fantasies of revenge. Dozens of interviews and a review of court records suggest that Harris's and Klebold's rage began with injustices of jocks."

Friends of Harris and Klebold told the reporters that the boys grew increasingly angry and resentful over the bullying and the social system that tolerated it. "They just let the jocks get to them," one student said. "I think they were taunted to their limits."

Most of the boys' alleged taunters had graduated by the time Harris and Klebold unleashed their violence on the school, but six varsity athletes died in the attacks. No amount of bullying can ever excuse violence, and most bullied students never turn violent, much less kill anyone, in response. But this background may help us focus on the brutish conditions under which many students attend school and a few end up losing their minds.

Many school systems trying to solve the puzzle of juvenile violence, truancy, and academic dysfunction have developed antibullying rules and systemwide anitbullying programs. What is your school's policy on bullying? What can be done to end the social dynamics of bullying in our schools? What strategies work? Go online and find some resources that educators and young people have developed to stop bullying in their schools. Write a report on why bullying happens and how you think it can be stopped in your school and your community.

Further Reading

Adams, Lorraine, and Dale Russakoff. "Dissecting Columbine's Cult of the Athlete; In Search for Answers, Community Examines One Source of Killers' Rage," *Washington Post,* June 12, 1999.

American Association of University Women. *Hostile Hallways: The AAUW Survey on Sexual Harassment in America's Schools.* Washington, D.C.: AAUW Educational Foundation, 1993.

Department of Education, Office for Civil Rights. *Revised Sexual Harassment Guidance: Harassment of Students by School Employees, Other Students, or Third Parties.* Washington, D.C.: U.S. Government Printing Office, 2001.

Langelan, Martha. *Back Off: How to Confront and Stop Sexual Harassment and Harassers.* New York: Simon and Schuster, 1993.

Minnow, Martha. *Making All the Difference: Inclusion, Exclusion and American Law.* Ithaca, N.Y.: Cornell University Press, 1991.

Stein, Nan, and Lisa Sjostrom. *Flirting or Hurting? A Teacher's Guide on Student-to-Student Sexual Harassment in Schools.* Washington, D.C.: National Education Association, 1994.

On the Web

American Association of University Professors, www.aaup.org.

Gay, Lesbian and Straight Education Network, www.glsen.org.

Lambda Legal Defense, www.lambdalegal.org.

National Education Association, www.nea.org.

National Women's Law Center, www.nwlc.org.

NOW Legal Defense and Education Fund, www.legalmomentum.org.

A HEALTHY STUDENT BODY:
Disability, Privacy, Pregnancy, and Sexuality

"Leave all the afternoon for exercise and recreation, which are as necessary as reading. I will rather say more necessary because health is worth more than learning." THOMAS JEFFERSON

On any given day schools confront student health issues. Some students have physical disabilities, some have learning disabilities, some are pregnant, and some are sick. These students might need special accommodations or special help. They might feel exposed or embarrassed. These concerns raise both academic questions and serious legal issues.

For a long time, all students were assumed to be standard-issue, able-bodied children with no special learning challenges; for those who fell short of the norm, there was a thin safety net at best, but more often something like a tightrope. Schools simply ignored many student health problems. Our understanding of learning disabilities was meager, and many bright students with dyslexia were classified as "slow" and often forced out of school. Girls who became pregnant faced ridicule, shame, ostracism, and expulsion, not to mention criminal laws against abortion. Many visually or hearing-impaired students and students with mental health problems dropped out or were institutionalized. And students had to deal with the nightmare of schools refusing to keep their medical and educational records private. Sensitive information might be shared with other government agencies, employers, police, recruiters, teachers, and businesses.

In the 1970s, a disability rights movement arose to demand that children with different abilities and special challenges be educated and treated with dignity and respect. That movement has changed the landscape of public education—for everyone.

Today, students with serious health and learning disabilities enjoy meaningful legal protection. Section 504 of the Rehabilitation Act, passed in 1973, prevents discrimination on the basis of disability in programs receiving federal funds. The Americans with Disabilities Act (ADA), passed in 1990, blocks discrimination by both public and private schools on grounds of disability. It requires "reasonable accommodation" of student disabilities.

Perhaps the most dramatic improvement came in 1975 with the Individuals with Disabilities Education Act (IDEA), which was first enacted as the Education for All

Handicapped Children Act and amended in 1997. IDEA requires public schools to provide all disabled children with a special education and related services. Each disabled child's education must be free, appropriate, individualized, and conducted in the least restrictive appropriate setting.

Today, there are also more options for pregnant girls than there were in 1950, 1970, or even 1990. Many schools have special programs to keep pregnant students at school and engaged in their studies. Meantime, the Supreme Court has provided that women, including young women, have not only a right to bear children but also a right to choose a safe and legal abortion; however, states can condition exercise of this right on a parent's consent to the abortion or, in the absence of parental agreement, a judge's consent.

Finally, all students today enjoy the protections of the Family Educational Rights and Privacy Act of 1974 (FERPA), which establishes basic privacy protections for all students in their records maintained by school administrators.

These changes in the law do not mean that having a disability or medical problem at school is suddenly an easy thing to manage. Students with disabilities or illnesses still face many tough challenges in the process of learning and going through school. But we have at least arrived at a place where a student's personal struggles no longer have to be a ticket to unfair and cruel treatment at school.

POINTS TO PONDER

How far should schools go to provide "special services" to students with learning disabilities? Does it violate the Family Educational Rights and Privacy Act for teachers to practice "peer grading," in which students mark each other's exams and quizzes?

- Should girls younger than eighteen (considered "minors" under the law) be required to have the consent of one of their parents or a judge before obtaining an abortion?
- Should high schools make condoms available to sexually active teens as a way to cut teen pregnancy rates, or does this practice violate the rights of parents to control the upbringing of their children?

The Rights of the "Differently Abled" under the Individuals with Disabilities Education Act

Under IDEA, disabled students have a right to a free and appropriate special education and "related services." In *Irving Independent School District v. Tatro* (1984), the Supreme Court found that under the "related services" language a school district had to provide "clean intermittent catheterization"—an invasive medical substitute for urination—to an eight-year-old girl born with spina bifida, a congenital disorder that made it impossible for her to empty her own bladder. The Court found that providing this catheterization was not an impermissible "medical service" (and therefore something that must be performed by a doctor, such as surgery) under IDEA but simply a "school health service" easily rendered by a nurse.

Garret Frey sits in his Spanish class listening to his teacher, Valerie Neubauer, at Jefferson High School in Cedar Rapids, Iowa, on February 5, 1999.

In the following case the Court considers whether IDEA requires an Iowa school district to offer continuous one-on-one nursing services to a student in a motorized wheelchair who is dependent on a ventilator and communicates by working a computer with head movements. The school argues that it does not have a duty to provide nonstop nursing assistance to the student because of its heavy cost. But, as you can see, the majority establishes that it is Garret F.'s right under the statute to receive the nursing care in school regardless of the cost. Justices Thomas and Kennedy disagree. What do you think? As medical technology and knowledge advance, is it the responsibility of schools to keep up by providing students expensive care that they need in order to succeed in school?

CEDAR RAPIDS COMMUNITY SCHOOL DISTRICT v. GARRET F.

Supreme Court of the United States
Argued November 4, 1998.
Decided March 3, 1999.

Majority OPINION   Justice STEVENS delivered the opinion of the Court.

The Individuals with Disabilities Education Act (IDEA) ... was enacted, in part, "to assure that all children with disabilities have available to them ... a free appropriate public education which emphasizes special education and related services designed to meet their unique needs." Consistent with this purpose, the IDEA authorizes federal financial assistance to States that agree to provide disabled children with special education and "related services." The question presented in this case is whether the definition of "related services" requires a public school district in a participating State to provide a ventilator-dependent student with certain nursing services during school hours.

I

Respondent Garret F. is a friendly, creative, and intelligent young man. When Garret was four years old, his spinal column was severed in a motorcycle accident. Though paralyzed from the neck down, his mental capacities were unaffected. He is able to speak, to control his motorized wheelchair through use of a puff and suck straw, and to operate a computer with a device that responds to head movements. Garret is currently a student in the Cedar Rapids Community School District, he attends regular classes in a typical school program, and his academic performance has been a success. Garret is, however, ventilator dependent, and therefore requires a responsible individual nearby to attend to certain physical needs while he is in school.

... In 1993, Garret's mother requested the District to accept financial responsibility for the health care services that Garret requires during the schoolday. The District denied the request, believing that it was not legally obligated to provide continuous one-on-one nursing services....

[The administrative judge found that the IDEA required the school district to bear financial responsibility for all of the disputed services, including the disputed nursing services. The district and appeals courts agreed.]

II

The District contends that [the statute] does not require it to provide Garret with "continuous one-on-one nursing services" during the schoolday, even though Garret cannot remain in school without such care. However, the IDEA's definition of "related services," our decision in *Irving Independent School Dist. v. Tatro* and the overall statutory scheme all support the decision of the Court of Appeals ["that as a recipient of federal funds under the IDEA, Iowa has a statutory duty to provide all disabled children a 'free appropriate public education,' which includes 'related services.'"]

> **Statutory**
> Relating to a statement or provision of law in an act of Congress or a state legislature.

The text of the "related services" definition broadly encompasses those supportive services that "may be required to assist a child with a disability to benefit from special education." As a general matter, services that enable a disabled child to remain in school during the day provide the student with "the meaningful access to education that Congress envisioned." ...

... In *Tatro* we concluded that the Secretary of Education had reasonably determined that the term "medical services" referred only to services that must be performed by a physician, and not to school health services. Accordingly, we held that a specific form of health care (clean intermittent catheterization) that is often, though not always, performed by a nurse is not an excluded medical service. We referenced the likely cost of the services and the competence of school staff as justifications for drawing a line between physician and other services, but our endorsement of that line was unmistakable. It is thus settled that the phrase "medical services" in [the statute] does not embrace all forms of care that might loosely be described as "medical" in other contexts, such as a claim for an income tax deduction....

Instead, the District points to the combined and continuous character of the required care, and proposes a test under which the outcome in any particular case would "depend upon a series of factors, such as [1] whether the care is continuous or intermittent, [2] whether existing school health personnel can provide the service, [3] the cost of the service, and [4] the potential consequences if the service is not properly performed." ...

Finally, the District raises broader concerns about the financial burden that it must bear to provide the services that Garret needs to stay in school. The problem for the District in providing these services is not that its staff cannot be trained to deliver them; the problem, the District contends, is that the existing school health staff cannot meet all of their responsibilities and provide for Garret at the same time. Through its multifactor test, the District seeks to establish a kind of undue-burden exemption primarily based on the cost of the requested services. The first two factors can be seen as examples of cost-based distinctions: Intermittent care is often less expensive than continuous care, and the use of existing personnel is cheaper than hiring additional employees. The third factor—the cost of the service—would then encompass the first two. The relevance of the fourth factor is likewise related to cost because extra care may be necessary if potential consequences are especially serious.

The District may have legitimate financial concerns, but our role in this dispute is to interpret existing law. Defining "related services" in a manner that *accommodates* the cost concerns Congress may have had is altogether different from using cost *itself* as the definition. Given that [the statute] does not employ cost in its definition of "related services" or excluded "medical services," accepting the District's cost-based standard as the sole test for determining the scope of the provision would require us to engage in judicial lawmaking without any guidance from Congress. It would also create some tension with the purposes of the IDEA. The statute may not require public schools to maximize the potential of disabled students commensurate with the opportunities provided to other children, and the potential financial burdens imposed on participating States may be relevant to arriving at a sensible construction of the IDEA. But Congress intended "to open the door of public education" to all qualified children and "require[d] participating States to educate handicapped children with nonhandicapped children whenever possible."

This case is about whether meaningful access to the public schools will be assured, not the level of education that a school must finance once access is attained. It is undisputed that the services at issue must be provided if Garret is to remain in school. Under the statute, our precedent, and the purposes of the IDEA, the District must fund such "related services" in order to help guarantee that students like Garret are integrated into the public schools.

The judgment of the Court of Appeals is accordingly
Affirmed.

Dissenting VOICES

Justice Thomas, joined by Justice Kennedy, dissented, arguing that continuous nursing care
is too burdensome and costly an obligation to impose on school districts trying to comply
with IDEA. Justice Thomas maintained that "a school nurse cannot provide the services
that respondent requires, and continue to perform her normal duties." Because Garret "requires continuous, one-on-one care throughout the entire schoolday, all agree that the district must hire an additional employee to attend solely to respondent. This will cost a minimum of $18,000 per year. Although the majority recognizes this fact, it nonetheless
concludes that the 'more extensive' nature of the services that respondent needs is irrelevant to the question whether those services fall under the medical services exclusion." This
approach, he urged, interferes with federalism and "blindsides unwary States with fiscal obligations that they could not have anticipated."

WHAT DO YOU **Think?**

Exercise 10.1. Assume a sixth-grade student with dyslexia suffers from anxiety and
low-level depression because of her reading problems. Is she entitled to psychological
counseling (along with her reading tutoring) under IDEA? Regulations issued by the U.S.
Department of Education establish that psychological counseling is a necessary "related
service" if it becomes essential to a learning-disabled child's ability to receive a quality education. Should psychological counseling be covered for *all* students who are feeling upset
or depressed, even those who have no other diagnosed learning or physical disability? Why
or why not?

Peer Grading and the Right to Privacy

Many teachers conduct tests and quizzes by having their students grade each other's papers
and then either shout out the grades or turn them in to the teacher. In the following case,
the Falvo family, which lives outside Tulsa, Oklahoma, objected to the practice. One of the
Falvo children, who had a learning disability, felt humiliated by having his grades calcu-
lated by a fellow student and then read aloud in front of the class. After the school refused
to stop the practice or at least grant a special exemption for the Falvo children, the family
sued, alleging that "peer grading" violates the Family Educational Rights and Privacy Act,
which requires student "education records" to be kept confidential if they "are maintained
by an educational agency or institution or by a person acting for such agency or institution." The question in this case became whether grades on a classroom quiz or test were
such an institutional "record." The Court says no and that such a reading would distort the
law. What is its reasoning?

· ·

OWASSO INDEPENDENT SCHOOL DIST. NO. I-011 v. FALVO

Supreme Court of the United States
Argued November 27, 2001.
Decided February 19, 2002.

Majority

OPINION   Justice KENNEDY delivered the opinion of the Court.

Teachers sometimes ask students to score each other's tests, papers, and assignments as the teacher explains the correct answers to the entire class. Respondent contends this practice, which the parties refer to as peer grading, violates the Family Educational Rights and Privacy Act of 1974 (FERPA or Act)....

I

Under FERPA, schools and educational agencies receiving federal financial assistance must comply with certain conditions. One condition specified in the Act is that sensitive information about students may not be released without parental consent. The Act states that federal funds are to be withheld from school districts that have "a policy or practice of permitting the release of education records (or personally identifiable information contained therein ...) of students without the written consent of their parents." The phrase "education records" is defined, under the Act, as "records, files, documents, and other materials" containing information directly related to a student, which "are maintained by an educational agency or institution or by a person acting for such agency or institution." The definition of education records contains an exception for "records of instructional, supervisory, and administrative personnel ... which are in the sole possession of the maker thereof...." The precise question for us is whether peer-graded classroom work and assignments are education records.

Three of respondent Kristja J. Falvo's children are enrolled in Owasso Independent School District No. I-011, in a suburb of Tulsa, Oklahoma. The children's teachers, like many teachers in this country, use peer grading. In a typical case, the students exchange papers with each other and score them according to the teacher's instructions, then return the work to the student who prepared it. The teacher may ask the students to report their own scores. In this case it appears the student could either call out the score or walk to the teacher's desk and reveal it in confidence, though by that stage, of course, the score was known at least to the one other student who did the grading. Both the grading and the system of calling out the scores are in contention here.

Respondent claimed the peer grading embarrassed her children. She asked the school district to adopt a uniform policy banning peer grading and requiring teachers either to grade assignments themselves or at least to forbid students from grading papers other than their own. The school district declined to do so, and respondent brought a class action ... against the school district, Superintendent Dale Johnson, Assistant Superintendent Lynn Johnson, and Principal Rick Thomas (petitioners). Respondent alleged the school district's grading policy violated FERPA....

... [We find] no violation of the Act....

Kristja Falvo and her husband Jim filed suit against their school district to stop the practice of peer grading in their children's classrooms. Their child with a learning disability had felt humiliated by having his grades announced in front of the class.

II

… The parties appear to agree that if an assignment becomes an education record the moment a peer grades it, then the grading, or at least the practice of asking students to call out their grades in class, would be an impermissible release. Without deciding the point, we assume for the purposes of our analysis that they are correct. The parties disagree, however, whether peer-graded assignments constitute education records at all. The papers do contain information directly related to a student, but they are records under the Act only when and if they "are maintained by an educational agency or institution or by a person acting for such agency or institution."

Petitioners … contend the definition covers only institutional records—namely, those materials retained in a permanent file as a matter of course. They argue that records "maintained by an educational agency or institution" generally would include final course grades, student grade point averages, standardized test scores, attendance records, counseling records, and records of disciplinary actions—but not student homework or classroom work.

Respondent … contends student-graded assignments fall within the definition of education records.… Grade books and the grades within, the court concluded, are "maintained" by a teacher and so are covered by FERPA. The Court of Appeals recognized that teachers do not maintain the grades on individual student assignments until they have recorded the result in the grade books. It reasoned, however, that if Congress forbids teachers to disclose students' grades once written in a grade book, it makes no sense to permit the disclosure immediately beforehand. The court thus held that student graders maintain the grades until they are reported to the teacher.

The Court of Appeals' logic does not withstand scrutiny. Its interpretation, furthermore, would effect a drastic alteration of the existing allocation of responsibilities between States and the National Government in the operation of the Nation's schools. We would hesitate before interpreting the statute to effect such a substantial change in the balance of federalism unless that is the manifest purpose of the legislation. This principle guides our decision.

Two statutory indicators tell us that the Court of Appeals erred in concluding that an assignment satisfies the definition of education records as soon as it is graded by another student. First, the student papers are not, at that stage, "maintained" within the meaning of [the Act]. The ordinary meaning of the word "maintain" is "to keep in existence or continuance; preserve; retain." ... Even assuming the teacher's grade book is an education record ... the score on a student-graded assignment is not "contained therein" until the teacher records it. The teacher does not maintain the grade while students correct their peers' assignments or call out their own marks. Nor do the student graders maintain the grades within the meaning of [the Act]. The word "maintain" suggests FERPA records will be kept in a filing cabinet in a records room at the school or on a permanent secure database, perhaps even after the student is no longer enrolled. The student graders only handle assignments for a few moments as the teacher calls out the answers. It is fanciful to say they maintain the papers in the same way the registrar maintains a student's folder in a permanent file.

The Court of Appeals was further mistaken in concluding that each student grader is "a person acting for" an educational institution for purposes of [the Act]. The phrase "acting for" connotes agents of the school, such as teachers, administrators, and other school employees. Just as it does not accord with our usual understanding to say students are "acting for" an educational institution when they follow their teacher's direction to take a quiz, it is equally awkward to say students are "acting for" an educational institution when they follow their teacher's direction to score it. Correcting a classmate's work can be as much a part of the assignment as taking the test itself. It is a way to teach material again in a new context, and it helps show students how to assist and respect fellow pupils. By explaining the answers to the class as the students correct the papers, the teacher not only reinforces the lesson but also discovers whether the students have understood the material and are ready to move on. We do not think FERPA prohibits these educational techniques. We also must not lose sight of the fact that the phrase "by a person acting for [an educational] institution" modifies "maintain." Even if one were to agree students are acting for the teacher when they correct the assignment, that is different from saying they are acting for the educational institution in maintaining it....

FERPA also requires recipients of federal funds to provide parents with a hearing at which they may contest the accuracy of their child's education records. The hearings must be conducted "in accordance with regulations of the Secretary," which in turn require adjudication by a disinterested official and the opportunity for parents to be represented by an attorney. It is doubtful Congress would have provided parents with this elaborate procedural machinery to challenge the accuracy of the grade on every spelling test and art project the child completes.

Respondent's construction of the term "education records" to cover student homework or classroom work would impose substantial burdens on teachers across the country. It would force all instructors to take time, which otherwise could be spent teaching and in preparation, to correct an assortment of daily student assignments. Respondent's view would make it much more difficult for teachers to give students immediate guidance. The interpretation respondent urges would force teachers to abandon other customary practices, such as group grading of team assignments. Indeed, the logical consequences of respondent's view are all but unbounded....

We doubt Congress meant to intervene in this drastic fashion with traditional state functions. Under the Court of Appeals' interpretation of FERPA, the federal power would exercise minute control over specific teaching methods and instructional dynamics in classrooms throughout the country. The Congress is not likely to have mandated this result, and we do not interpret the statute to require it.

For these reasons, even assuming a teacher's grade book is an education record, the Court of Appeals erred, for in all events the grades on students' papers would not be covered under FERPA at least until the teacher has collected them and recorded them in his or her grade book. We limit our holding to this narrow point, and do not decide the broader question whether the grades on individual student assignments, once they are turned in to teachers, are protected by the Act.

The judgment of the Court of Appeals is reversed....

WHAT DO YOU Think?

Exercise 10.2. Assume your school uses "peer grading" in most classes. The *Falvo* decision has just come down upholding the practice. A student group still wants to debate whether it is a good idea for teachers to have their students grade each other's work. Form two teams to prepare to debate the issue at a schoolwide assembly. Have a group of students ask questions as if they were teachers and administrators.

Exercise 10.3. Write an op-ed for your local or school newspaper about the practice of peer grading. Is it an effective teaching tactic that could lead to better peer collaboration, or it is a tool for lazy teachers that violates student privacy?

Exercise 10.4. Under the No Child Left Behind Act of 2002, Congress required public high schools to give identifying information about their students to the United States Department of Defense for recruiting purposes. Parents have the right to "opt out" of this arrangement by writing a letter to the school asking for their children's information to be kept confidential. Although very few people are aware that families can opt out of the recruiting, peace groups have organized young people and their parents to submit opt-out letters. Do you want your information (name, address, phone number, grade) to be shared with the military recruiters? Why or why not? Should military recruiters be given free access to cafeterias, sports fields, and locker rooms to recruit high school students on campus?

Three Trimesters: Pregnant at School

Every year millions of American teenagers engage in sexual relations. Consider this 2006 statistic from the Alan Guttmacher Institute in New York: Each year nearly 750,000 U.S. teenage girls become pregnant. The good news is that this number is down sharply from nearly 1 million a year in 2000 and is at a thirty-year low. Nonetheless, when girls in high school get pregnant, and far too many do, they face a serious crisis. Beyond having to decide whether to become a teen mother or to have an abortion, they are often shamed and belittled. And sometimes they experience discriminatory official reactions at school.

In the following 1990 case, Arlene Pfeiffer was dismissed from the National Honor Society in Marion Center Area High School in Marion, Pennsylvania, after the honor society learned she was pregnant. A model student with fine grades and activities, Pfeiffer was also president of the student council. The honor society said she was being dismissed because of her premarital sexual conduct. Pfeiffer claimed that this was sex discrimination, because boys who engaged in premarital sex were not expelled from the honor society. Which way does the Third Circuit Court of Appeals rule on Pfeiffer's appeal from her expulsion from the honor society? Why?

PFEIFFER v. MARION CENTER AREA SCHOOL DISTRICT

United States Court of Appeals for the Third Circuit
Decided October 30, 1990.

OPINION ALDISERT, Circuit Judge....

Majority

II

The appellant, Arlene Pfeiffer, was a member of the class of 1984 at the Marion Center Area High School in Marion, Indiana County, Pennsylvania. She was a good student who earned high grades and participated in a wide variety of school organizations, including serving as president of the student council. Based on her record, she was elected to her high school's chapter of the National Honor Society (NHS) in 1981. The local chapter was governed by a faculty council composed of Robert L. Stewart, the principal of the high school, and Theda Lightcap, Jane Smith, Judith Skubis, and George Krivonick, all teachers at the Marion Center Area High School.

During the spring of 1983, Pfeiffer, who was unmarried, discovered that she was pregnant. She informed her school guidance counselor and principal and indicated that she wanted to rear her child but that she also wanted to finish high school. Principal Stewart told her that he saw no problem in her plan to continue school and graduate.

The handbook for the National Honor Society requires that students be selected for membership on the basis of scholarship, service, leadership and character. The constitution of the local chapter followed that of the national organization, requiring admission and maintenance be based on the same qualities....

Upon learning of Pfeiffer's pregnancy, Judith Skubis, a teacher and member of the faculty council, brought the matter to the attention of the other council members in the spring of 1983. That fall, when school resumed, the council scheduled a meeting for November 4, 1983, and Pfeiffer was invited to attend. The council members explained to her that her NHS membership was in question because premarital sex appeared to be contrary to the qualities of leadership and character essential for membership. When asked if her sexual activity leading to her pregnancy had been voluntary, the plaintiff answered in the affirmative. The council deferred further action.

On November 8, 1983, Pfeiffer's father, Delmont Pfeiffer, telephoned Principal Stewart requesting a prompt decision because an induction ceremony for seniors was scheduled for the next day and Arlene wanted to attend. The council met on the morning of November 9, 1983, and by secret ballot unanimously voted to dismiss her from the NHS chapter. By letter the council advised her:

> By action of the faculty council, you have been dismissed from the National Honor Society for the following reason:
> Failure to uphold the high standards of leadership and character required for admission and maintenance of membership. It is the opinion of the faculty council that a member must consistently set a positive example for others and, as outlined in the selection guidelines, always uphold all of the high standards of moral conduct.

On November 30, 1983, the council met with her parents, who requested that the subject be placed on the agenda of the school board meeting scheduled for December 12, 1983. Pfeiffer and her parents appeared at the meeting with counsel....

At the discussion, the board was asked to review the decision of the faculty council. On December 19, 1983, the board and the council met to consider the matter further and on January 16, 1984, the school board adopted a resolution unanimously affirming the action of the faculty council.

After graduation from high school, with honors, Pfeiffer elected not to go to college and began working with the Holiday Inn of Indiana, where she is presently a sales manager. She is married, but not to the father of the child conceived while she was in school.

III

Arlene Pfeiffer filed suit alleging discrimination in her dismissal from the local chapter of the NHS.... The complaint included claims of gender discrimination....

IV

At the onset of the case, the question arose whether Title IX applied because the School District did not receive federal funds for the operation of its chapter of the NHS, while it did receive federal funds for its school lunch program....

Title IX of the Education Amendment of 1972 provides, in part, as follows:

No person in the United States shall, on the basis of sex, be excluded from participation in, be denied the benefits of, or be subjected to discrimination under any education program or activity receiving Federal financial assistance.

Regulations promulgated pursuant to Title IX specifically apply its prohibition against gender discrimination to discrimination on the basis of pregnancy, parental status, and marital status.

A recipient shall not apply any rule concerning a student's actual or potential parental, family, or marital status which treats students differently on the basis of sex....

(b)(1) A recipient shall not discriminate against any student or exclude any student from its education program or activity, including any class or extracurricular activity, on the basis of such student's pregnancy, childbirth, false pregnancy, termination of pregnancy or recovery therefrom unless the student requests voluntarily to participate in a separate portion of the program or activity of the recipient....

VI

... [T]he appellant's entire argument before us rests upon her allegation that she was dismissed from the chapter because of her condition of pregnancy. Unfortunately for her theory, however, the district court found that the plaintiff was not dismissed for her pregnancy but because the council thought she had failed to uphold the standards already discussed as evidenced by Plaintiff's Exhibit 1 (the letter directed to her) and Plaintiff's Exhibit 3 (the resolution of the School Board dated January 16, 1984.)

... Supporting this finding is the stated reason given by the council for her dismissal: Failure to uphold the standards of leadership and character required for admission and maintenance of membership. Moreover, the finding is supported by the testimony of the faculty council members before the district court, each of whom testified at trial. Each faculty council member specifically denied that his or her dismissal vote was based anywhere on Pfeiffer's sex, on her pregnancy, or on her failure to marry after she had engaged in premarital sexual activity.

This factual finding is bolstered by the district court's reasoning that

> [f]aced with the task of educating hundreds of young people, and with constant demand by the public that the schools instill attributes of good character as part of the educational process, the Council and the Board can scarcely be criticized for taking the action which was taken.

Indeed, the Supreme Court has given us express guidance in matters relating to student conduct in public schools:

> The process of educating our youth for citizenship in public schools is not confined to books, the curriculum, and the civics class; schools must teach by example the shared values of a civilized social order. Consciously or otherwise, teachers—and indeed the older students—demonstrate the appropriate form of ... conduct and deportment in and out of class. Inescapably, like parents, they are role models. The schools, as instruments of the state, may determine that the essential lessons of civil, mature conduct cannot be conveyed in a school that tolerates lewd, indecent, or offensive speech and conduct....

The judgment of the District Court is upheld.

WHAT DO YOU Think?

Exercise 10.5. In 1985 the Seventh Circuit Court of Appeals found in *Wort v. Vierling* that a school district's dismissal of a pregnant student from the National Honor Society *did* violate both Title IX and Equal Protection. The division between the Seventh and Third Circuit Courts of Appeal over the issue—a so-called "circuit split"—means that the law governing expulsions from the National Honor Society for being pregnant differs from region to region. A circuit split on a substantial issue will often provide the Supreme Court impetus to take up the issue to resolve the split within the federal judiciary's appeals courts.

Imagine, therefore, that the Supreme Court takes a case in which a pregnant high school senior, who is an outstanding student and community leader, gets dismissed from the honor society at Cape Cod High School. The honor society admits that it has dismissed pregnant girls in the past only because it cannot, and does not want to, investigate the sexual lives of its students, whether female or male. The honor society says it would exclude any student member who admitted to having premarital sex, but as of yet no one had come forward to turn himself or herself in.

The student claims that this policy is a violation of her equal protection rights because, under the honor society's practice, only girls (who get pregnant) will be punished. Return to Chapter 8 [see p. 215] and retrieve the standard for challenges to alleged governmental sex discrimination. Is this sex discrimination? If not, the case is over. If it is, the government can win only if it can show an "important interest"—an "exceedingly persuasive justification"—for its policy and that its means are "substantially related" to the interest.

Take oral arguments from lawyers on behalf of both the school and the girl. Other students should act as Supreme Court justices who must decide whether the society's dismissal of a pregnant student violates the equal protection clause or Title IX's ban on sex discrimination in schools. The justices should discuss the problem and then state their opinions and reasoning.

Some people place the blame for our still-too-high rates of teen pregnancy on the sexual images that saturate the media; others attribute teen pregnancy to an appalling lack of proper sexual education and knowledge about contraception. Very likely, these two factors go hand in hand to create a large number of unplanned pregnancies. Yet, the number is dropping substantially now. Why? Many school systems have sought to promote abstinence or sex education; some have gone so far as to distribute contraceptives—specifically, condoms—to students when they ask for them.

In the next case the Supreme Judicial Court of Massachusetts held that a school program for voluntary distribution of condoms to male or female students who request them, without parental notification, did not violate the family's or student's privacy interests. The court determined that because the program was wholly voluntary and parents could instruct their children on whether or not to participate, there was no unlawful coercion or pressure for students to use the contraceptive services.

CURTIS v. SCHOOL COMMITTEE OF FALMOUTH

Supreme Judicial Court of Massachusetts
Argued March 7, 1995.
Decided July 17, 1995.

Majority OPINION   Opinion: LIACOS, C.J.

The plaintiffs, students and parents of students in the Falmouth public school system, appealed from a grant of summary judgment in favor of the defendants, the school committee of Falmouth (school committee) and three individual defendants. We granted the school committee's application for direct appellate review. We affirm....

> **Direct Appellate Review**
> When a case is appealed directly from trial to an appellate court or body without making other stops.

The plaintiffs … argue before this court, that the condom-availability program, as it stands, violates their right to familial privacy and their guaranteed liberties as parents in the control of the education and upbringing of their children, protected by the Fourteenth Amendment to the United States Constitution.… The plaintiffs ask us to reverse the judge's entry of summary judgment for the defendants and to enjoin the school committee from continuing to make condoms available to students without the inclusion of a provision which would permit parents to opt out of the program and without a system of parental notification of their child's requests for a condom.

Enjoin
To stop or restrain by injunction.

… "On January 2, 1992, following an authorizing vote of the FSC [Falmouth school committee], the Superintendent of Schools issued a memorandum to the teaching staff of grades 7 through 12, detailing the condom availability program. At Lawrence Junior High School, students could request free condoms from the school nurse. Prior to receiving them, students would be counseled. The nurse was also instructed to give students pamphlets on AIDS/HIV and other sexually transmitted diseases. At Falmouth High School, students could request free condoms from the school nurse, or students could purchase them for $.75 from the condom vending machines located in the lower level boys' and girls' restrooms. Counseling by trained faculty members would be provided to students who requested it, and informational pamphlets were available in the [school] nurse's office. The Superintendent's memorandum instructed the staff to reserve their own opinions regarding condom availability in order to respect students' privacy. The memorandum also indicates that the Superintendent's presentation of the condom availability to the student body would stress abstinence as the only certain method for avoiding sexually transmitted diseases. The condom availability program took effect on January 2, 1992.

"The FSC condom program does not provide for an 'opt out' for students' parents whereby the parents have the option of excluding their student child from the availability of condoms. Nor is there a parental notification provision in the FSC program by which parents would be notified of their children's requests for condoms." …

The [lower court] judge concluded that the plaintiffs had failed to meet the threshold requirement for each of their claims because they were unable to demonstrate that the condom-availability program placed a coercive burden on their rights.… [T]hey argue [that] the State was required to prove the existence of a compelling State interest in maintaining the condom-availability program.

… [T]he condom-availability program in Falmouth is in all respects voluntary and in no way intrudes into the realm of constitutionally protected rights. Because no threshold demonstration of a coercive burden has been made, nor could have been made on these facts, the defendants properly were granted summary judgment.…

We discern no coercive burden on the plaintiffs' parental liberties in this case. No classroom participation is required of students. Condoms are available to students who request them and, in the high school, may be obtained from vending machines. The students are not required to seek out and accept the condoms, read the literature accompanying them, or participate in counseling regarding their use. In other words, the students are free to decline to participate in the program. No penalty or disciplinary action ensues if a student does not participate in the program. For their part, the plaintiff parents are free to instruct their children not to participate. The program does not supplant the parents' role as advisor in the moral and religious development of their children. Although exposure to condom vending machines and to the program itself may offend the moral and religious sensibilities of the plaintiffs, mere exposure to programs offered at school does not amount to unconstitutional interference with parental liberties without the existence of some compulsory aspect to the program....

Judgment affirmed.

WHAT DO YOU Think?

Exercise 10.6. In an older case from New York state, an appeals court struck down a similar condom distribution program that also had no parental notification requirement or opt-out option. Two courts came to opposite conclusions on the same issue. Which case had the better outcome? Why?

Exercise 10.7. Do you think that public high schools should participate in condom and birth control pill distribution programs? What about middle schools? After a sudden rise in teen pregnancy rates in Portland, Maine, the King Middle School in fall 2007 embarked on a policy of distributing both condoms and birth control pills to sexually active middle school students who visit the school health center. Although the students, who might be as young as eleven, must receive parental permission to go to the center, the services they receive remain confidential. Is this an effective way to deal with the persistent problem of teen pregnancy or a subtle promotion of teen sex?

FOR THE CLASS

Condoms and Consent. Imagine that you and your classmates are members of the school board in a district that sees 15 percent of its female students drop out before graduation as a result of pregnancy. How should the school district tackle the problem of teenage pregnancy? Do you favor condom distribution? Abstinence education? General Educational Development (GED) programs? Discuss the issue and your options with your classmates and see if you can develop an approach that you believe will actually remedy the problem.

Abortion and the Privacy Rights of Teenagers

Few constitutional issues in our time have been as politically controversial as that of abortion. Some people see abortion as a medical procedure essential to a woman's reproductive autonomy, equality in society, and personal control over her own body. Others see the procedure as the unjustified taking of human life and think that the Supreme Court has essentially finger-painted on the Constitution by reading into it a right of abortion that does not exist.

In 1973, in *Roe v. Wade*, the Supreme Court upheld the fundamental right of a woman to choose an abortion in consultation with her doctor. In *Roe*, the Court derived the right to an abortion from the basic right to privacy. The right to privacy is founded in the liberty interest protected in the Fourteenth Amendment: "[N]or shall any state deprive any person of life, liberty, or property...."

The controversy over abortion has never subsided, and the Supreme Court has dealt with repeated attempts by states to restrict a woman's abortion options. In the following 1992 decision, *Planned Parenthood of Southeastern Pennsylvania v. Casey*, the Court reaffirmed the essential "core" right of a woman to make a decision about terminating a pregnancy before the fetus would be independently viable outside her womb. But the Court also found that this right could be restricted by the states so long as they do not impose an "undue burden" on the woman's basic right to choose. An "undue burden" is any burden that places a "substantial obstacle in the path" of a woman seeking an abortion.

As controversial as abortion rights have been, even more explosive has been the issue of whether girls under 18 should have abortion rights. The *Casey* decision specifically allowed the states to tighten regulation of abortion when teenagers under 18 (or other minor females) seek to have one. The Court upheld the rule in the Pennsylvania Abortion Control Act that unless there is a medical emergency, pregnant females under the age of 18 in the state must obtain the "informed consent" of either one of their parents to get an abortion. The law also provides: "In the case of a pregnancy that is the result of incest, where the father is a party to the incestuous act, the pregnant woman need only obtain the consent of her mother."

If the young woman cannot get one of her parents to agree to letting her have an abortion or she is simply too afraid or too ashamed to ask them, she may go to court and seek the permission of a judge in Pennsylvania, who will have a hearing on whether she will be granted a right to have one. At the hearing, the judge will allow an abortion if the court determines that the pregnant woman is mature and capable of giving informed consent, and has, in fact, given her consent.

If the judge determines that the pregnant woman is immature and thus incapable of giving informed consent or if she does not even claim to be mature enough to make her own decision, then the judge will determine whether the performance of an abortion is in the young woman's best interests; that is, if the judge finds the young woman is not mature enough to make her own decision, the judge himself or herself will decide whether it is best for her to have an abortion or have a baby.

The Supreme Court upheld this "parental consent" regulation with a "judicial bypass" option but struck down a similar "spousal notification" regulation that would have required married adult women in Pennsylvania to prove that they had notified their husbands before having an abortion.

Read the Court's analysis of the two different provisions. Why does it uphold the "parental consent" provisions but reject the "spousal notification" provisions?

. . . .

PLANNED PARENTHOOD OF SOUTHEASTERN PENNSYLVANIA v. CASEY

Supreme Court of the United States
Argued April 22, 1992.
Decided June 29, 1992.

Majority OPINION   Justice O'CONNOR, Justice KENNEDY, and Justice SOUTER announced the judgment of the Court and delivered the opinion of the Court with respect to [these] parts....

C

Section 3209 of Pennsylvania's abortion law provides, except in cases of medical emergency, that no physician shall perform an abortion on a married woman without receiving a signed statement from the woman that she has notified her spouse that she is about to undergo an abortion. The woman has the option of providing an alternative signed statement certifying that her husband is not the man who impregnated her; that her husband could not be located; that the pregnancy is the result of spousal sexual assault which she has reported; or that the woman believes that notifying her husband will cause him or someone else to inflict bodily injury upon her. A physician who performs an abortion on a married woman without receiving the appropriate signed statement will have his or her license revoked, and is liable to the husband for damages....

... In well-functioning marriages, spouses discuss important intimate decisions such as whether to bear a child. But there are millions of women in this country who are the victims of regular physical and psychological abuse at the hands of their husbands. Should these women become pregnant, they may have very good reasons for not wishing to inform their husbands of their decision to obtain an abortion. Many may have justifiable fears of physical abuse, but may be no less fearful of the consequences of reporting prior abuse to the Commonwealth of Pennsylvania. Many may have a reasonable fear that notifying their husbands will provoke further instances of child abuse; these women are not exempt from [the] notification requirement. Many may fear devastating forms of psychological abuse from their husbands, including verbal harassment, threats of future violence, the destruction of possessions, physical confinement to the home, the withdrawal of financial support, or the disclosure of the abortion to family and friends.... [B]ut women who are the victims of the abuse are not exempt from [the] notification requirement.... [V]ictims of spousal sexual assault are extremely reluctant to report the abuse to the government; hence, a great many spousal rape victims will not be exempt from the notification requirement imposed by [the proposed law].

The spousal notification requirement is thus likely to prevent a significant number of women from obtaining an abortion....

... [For] a large fraction of [these] cases, [the spousal notification requirement] will operate as a substantial obstacle to a woman's choice to undergo an abortion. It is an undue burden, and therefore invalid.

This conclusion is in no way inconsistent with our decisions upholding parental notification or consent requirements. Those enactments, and our judgment that they are constitutional, are based on the quite reasonable assumption that minors will benefit from consultation with their parents and that children will often not realize that their parents have their best interests at heart. We cannot adopt a parallel assumption about adult women....

D

We next consider the parental consent provision. Except in a medical emergency, an unemancipated young woman under 18 may not obtain an abortion unless she and one of her parents (or guardian) provides informed consent as defined above. If neither a parent nor a guardian provides consent, a court may authorize the performance of an abortion upon a determination that the young woman is mature and capable of giving informed consent and has in fact given her informed consent, or that an abortion would be in her best interests.

We ... reaffirm today, that a State may require a minor seeking an abortion to obtain the consent of a parent or guardian, provided that there is an adequate judicial bypass procedure. Under these precedents, in our view, the one-parent consent requirement and judicial bypass procedure are constitutional....

Dissenting VOICES

Justice Blackmun, who wrote the Supreme Court's landmark opinion protecting a woman's right to choose an abortion in *Roe v. Wade* (1973), dissented from the Court's decision to uphold the parental consent rule. He took the position that the government could certainly promote parental involvement in a young woman's decision but only in a way that does not nullify her basic right to choose. "While the State has an interest in encouraging parental involvement in the minor's abortion decision," he wrote, "[the law] is not narrowly drawn to serve that interest." Unlike a parental consent law, a parental *notification* law would properly assure that the parents have been consulted by the minor without requiring her to obtain their written consent, which sets up a potential obstacle to her exercising the right to choose.

Each year, hundreds of thousands of American girls and young women between the ages of twelve and nineteen become pregnant. Studies show that most young women in this situation will approach one of their parents, usually their mother, to discuss their situation. But many young women do not, citing fear, embarrassment, and anxiety. Some are in abusive or dysfunctional families and are afraid that their pregnancy will further complicate family dynamics or even provoke violence.

As of June 2008, thirty-five states required some form of parental involvement in the teen's abortion decision—whether it was simple notice that the procedure was to take place or a requirement of consent (backed up by the "judicial bypass" option if consent was not forthcoming). The arguments for such laws focus on keeping parents closely connected to the lives of their children. Proponents of these laws say that children need help and support during times of crisis and that the parental involvement laws promote family decision making and protect parental rights. Many parents say that if they are asked to consent to any other form of surgery for their minor children, why not abortion? They consider it a matter of their fundamental right to raise their children and set family values. In cases where abuse is a real danger, the minor can find her way to a judge in family court to authorize the procedure.

Opponents of mandatory parental involvement argue that although most young women facing an unwanted pregnancy will of their own accord talk to one or both parents, the laws traumatize and endanger precisely those young women who come from the most difficult family situations. They also argue that the laws turn many young women into criminals or outlaws who go to other states or jurisdictions to seek an abortion. The whole legal machinery here, they claim, delays the ability to get an abortion, increasing both the cost and the risk of the procedure. In addition, they cite the embarrassment young women experience going before a judge (and a bailiff and a court reporter and anyone else who might be in the courtroom) to ask for the right to have an abortion. Some judges lecture

JUSTICES: A CLOSER LOOK

JUSTICE HARRY A. BLACKMUN (1908–1999) was born in Nashville, Illinois, and raised in St. Paul, Minnesota. Although he wanted to be a doctor rather than a lawyer, he went to Harvard Law School in 1929. He clerked on the Eighth Circuit Court of Appeals, practiced privately, and then took the place of his former employer and mentor, Judge John B. Sanborn, on the Eighth Circuit. In 1970 President Richard Nixon appointed Blackmun to the Supreme Court after Nixon's two prior choices, both southern conservatives, were rejected by the Senate. Blackmun remained until his retirement in 1994.

HIGHLIGHTS

- Blackmun began a long-lasting friendship with fellow future Supreme Court justice Warren Burger in kindergarten and was even the best man at Burger's wedding. On the Court, the two were initially called "the Minnesota twins," but then their opinions began to diverge and their relationship cooled.
- In private practice Blackmun was resident general counsel for the Mayo Clinic, a prestigious research hospital in Minnesota. He described those ten years as "the happiest years of [my] professional experience."
- Though he regretted not going to medical school, Justice Blackmun had more of an impact on the field of medicine than most doctors because of his famous opinion in *Roe v. Wade*, upholding the right of a woman to choose abortion in consultation with her doctor. This was the opinion of which Justice Blackmun was most proud.

Abortion continues to be one of the most controversial issues in America today. Here, protesters gather in front of the Supreme Court building on the day the Court issued its opinion in *Gonzales v. Carhart*. In a 5-4 decision, the Court decided to uphold a ban on late-term abortion, a procedure commonly referred to as partial-birth abortion.

and upbraid the young women, and many have found them not mature enough to get an abortion.

WHAT DO YOU **Think?**

Exercise 10.8. Currently, more than thirty-five states require some type of parental involvement in a minor's decision to have an abortion. Do "parental consent" requirements that force young women to obtain the consent of their parents or a judge for an abortion violate their right to privacy, or is the Court correct in allowing states to assume that women and girls under eighteen are simply not mature enough to make their own decision without help from a parent or a judge?

Exercise 10.9. Although the *Casey* Court upheld the *parental* consent provision in the Pennsylvania law, it struck down the *spousal* notification provision that required women to attest that they had either notified their husbands of their plans to get an abortion or could not find them or had another compelling reason not to notify him. Why do you think the Court treated the two provisions differently? One factor cited by Justice O'Connor was the high incidence of domestic violence and abuse by husbands of their wives, a problem often exacerbated by the decision of whether or not to proceed with a pregnancy. Does this argument sufficiently distinguish the two kinds of provisions? Do pregnant teenagers themselves ever face domestic violence because of their predicament? On the other hand, if minors cannot obtain other kinds of surgery and medical procedures without parental consent, is there any reason—from a constitutional perspective—to treat abortion differently?

Exercise 10.10. If you are a judge who determines that a girl is *not* mature enough to decide for herself whether to have an abortion, under what conditions would it ever be in her "best interests" to go ahead and have the child?

FOR THE CLASS

Legislative Decision Making. Turn your class into a state legislature. In the wake of the Supreme Court's decision in *Casey*, which upheld parental consent laws, your state is considering whether to require every female age eighteen and younger seeking an abortion to obtain the signature of one of her parents or, if her parents refuse, the consent of a state trial court judge before she is permitted to proceed. Would you vote for or against such a law? Make an inventory of all of the arguments available on both sides of the issue. Have a debate and discussion. Take testimony from classmates. Write the law the way that you think is most fair.

Role Play: What Factors Are Most Important in a Court's Decision to Allow an Abortion? Assume you are on a panel of three judges in a state with abortion judicial bypass proceedings for pregnant minors. A fifteen-year-old high school sophomore, Sally, appears before you seeking your permission to have an abortion. She says she cannot get her parents' support because her father left the family long ago and has not been heard from and her mother is a violently abusive alcoholic. You are charged with determining whether Sally is (1) mature enough to make her own decision and (2) if not, whether abortion or childbirth would be in her "best interests." Sally's boyfriend, Robert, also fifteen, very badly wants Sally to have the baby and promises in a letter to "help pay for diapers and stuff." He is Sally's classmate and comes from a supportive family of financial means to back up his promises; his parents write a letter to the judge saying that they will "share in the expenses of raising Robert's child." But, at the hearing on her petition for an abortion, Sally says, "I feel way too young to have a baby, and I wouldn't know how to take care of it. I'm overwhelmed right now." Sally says that her home situation is "pretty bad and I wouldn't want to bring a baby into it, but I would never give my child up for adoption." She says that she considers herself "a religious person; I definitely believe in God, and I will raise my children in a religious way when I get married and have kids." Sally's aunt, who is strongly opposed to abortion on religious grounds, told her she could help with babysitting on "most weekends" if Sally had the baby. But Sally testifies, "I just don't have a good support system. I think I may regret it one day, but I really want an abortion." Sally's math teacher comes to support Sally's petition at the hearing and says, "Sally is a very promising math student but has not proven to be very mature at all in making judgments about her future. I hope she will not have to drop out to have this baby." As a judge, what do you do? Do you grant her the right to have an abortion? Do you find that she is not mature enough to decide on her own and substitute your own judgment for hers? If so, what is your decision? Go around the panel of three judges and state your opinion. Would your decision be different if her boyfriend was poor or didn't want to support the child?

Further **Reading**

Schimmel, David, Louis Fischer, and Leslie R. Stellman. *School Law: What Every Educator Should Know.* Boston: Pearson/Allyn and Bacon Publishers, 2008.

On the **Web**

Planned Parenthood website for teens, www.teenwire.com.
National Dissemination Center for Children with Disabilities, www.nichcy.org.
American Civil Liberties Union teen website www.aclu.org/standup.
Summary of the Individuals with Disabilities Education Act, http://idea.ed.gov.

SUPREME COURT CONFIRMATION EXERCISE: YOU BE THE JUDGE

"[The President] shall appoint ... Judges of the supreme Court." ARTICLE II, SECTION 2

"The Judges, both of the supreme and inferior courts, shall hold their Offices during good behaviour...." ARTICLE III, SECTION 1

Article II of the Constitution gives the president the power to appoint Supreme Court justices (and other federal judges) with "the Advice and Consent of the Senate." This means that the president's candidates for the Supreme Court have to receive a majority favorable vote in the Senate before they are able to take office.

Historically, the Senate has taken its duties seriously and has closely scrutinized presidential nominees to the Court. Indeed, over the centuries judicial nominees have generated heated controversy, and many have been rejected by the Senate. Because Supreme Court justices have life tenure, Senate confirmation hearings are the single occasion upon which Congress can carefully probe the viewpoints of Supreme Court nominees. It is also the only opportunity the public and press have to witness and indirectly participate in a dialogue with nominees about justice, the Constitution, and the Court.

This public educational function has become increasingly important since the 1939 confirmation hearing of Felix Frankfurter, the first nominee to appear before the Senate, and infinitely more important since the 1981 confirmation hearing of Sandra Day O'Connor, which was the first to be shown on television and broadcast on radio. Today Supreme Court confirmation hearings draw intense public interest and media scrutiny.

In the following exercise, students will assume the roles of key actors in a mock U.S. Supreme Court confirmation hearing before the U.S. Senate's Committee on the Judiciary.

Select three students to play the roles of the U.S. Supreme Court justice nominees, nine students to be the Senate Committee on the Judiciary (with the teacher acting as the committee chair), three students to be television commentators, one student to act as the president of the United States, and three students to serve as counsel to the three Supreme Court nominees. In this exercise we are assuming that there are suddenly three vacancies on the Supreme Court. In fact, this scenario is highly unlikely; vacancies almost always occur one at a time. However, as several of the justices as of 2008 are in their seventies or eighties, we can expect a number of departures and nominations on the near horizon.

The confirmation process for U.S. Supreme Court judicial nominees typically involves the following four-part sequence: First, the White House and the Federal Bureau of Investigation undertake several background checks on individuals identified by the president as potential nominees;[1] second, the president makes his or her selection based on the outcome of these checks and on ideological and political grounds; third, a confirmation hearing to judge the fitness of the president's nominee (or, in our case, nominees) is conducted by the Senate Judiciary Committee; and fourth, the full Senate votes on whether to confirm the president's choice.

Start by having the student who is playing the president spend some time with his or her nominees to elicit background information. The president should then write and present a speech in a mock press conference introducing the nominees and trumpeting their virtues as potential justices. What are the outstanding qualities and experiences that qualify these persons to sit on the most important court in the land? What are the considerations and characteristics that the president cites as having informed his or her decision? The members of the media should ask questions about the president's choices and raise any issues of controversy surrounding the nominees. How does the president respond? (Note that the nominees should not make comments on their views at this time but instead should wait to do so at the Senate Judiciary Committee hearings.)

Next, move on to the Senate Judiciary Committee hearing process. The nominees should fill out the Questionnaire for Judicial Nominees, which is a mixture of the actual questions nominees answer and some questions designed for teaching purposes, and distribute copies of their answers to every member of the Senate Judiciary Committee (and other students as well) for their consideration.

QUESTIONNAIRE FOR JUDICIAL NOMINEES

1. Full name
2. Date and place of birth
3. Education
4. Marital status
5. Health: The physical and mental requirements of this position require you to prove that you are currently capable and do not foresee any likelihood of mental or emotional instability. Please disclose all information concerning this issue and provide the date of your last physical examination.
6. Memberships: List all organizations to which you belong and the positions you hold in each.
7. Public service: Provide your record of public service over the past five years.
8. Net worth: Provide a complete, current financial net worth statement.
9. Have you to your knowledge ever been under investigation for a possible violation of a civil or criminal statute? Have you ever been arrested or charged with a crime?
10. Please advise the committee on any unfavorable information that may influence public or congressional response to your nomination.
11. What is your judicial philosophy? Do you believe in "judicial activism," the idea that federal courts should actively intervene to enforce people's rights, or do you think that the Court should generally defer to the political branches of government?
12. What do you think are the best Supreme Court decisions involving the rights of students and young people? What do you think are the worst?

As this is a hypothetical exercise, please feel free to use whatever credentials you would like, real or imagined. Remember, however, to stay in character during your hearing. Once the nominees' answers have been shared, the confirmation hearing can begin.

The committee should consider one nominee at a time. Each nominee should make an opening statement thanking the president and the committee and describing his or her views and commitment to the Supreme Court. The students on the Senate Judiciary Committee should take turns posing two or three questions each to the nominee. The chair of the committee should call on senators in order of seniority (perhaps by age?), always making sure that order and protocol prevail throughout the proceedings. The nominees' counsels should be seated next to them during the hearings and be prepared to aid the nominees as necessary.

Senators may ask any questions they want, but the nominees always have the option of choosing not to answer. In fact, many nominees refuse to answer questions about their views of specific cases that will come before the Court, saying that such pointed answers would be inappropriate. Notwithstanding these objections, most nominees do their best to address the concerns of the senators. Oftentimes, senators will try to pin nominees down on their specific commitments and beliefs. The following are sample questions that the senators might ask. Feel free to change them or make up your own:

1. What are your qualifications to serve on the U.S. Supreme Court?
2. What aspects of law do you find the most intriguing?
3. What do you think are the greatest Supreme Court cases of all time?
4. Do you think that minors and students have constitutional rights? Are those rights equal to the rights of adults, or are they of less weight?
5. Do you think that it is unconstitutional for public universities to use race as a factor in admissions, even if it is to promote diversity in the incoming class? Does affirmative action violate equal protection?
6. What are the most important qualities that a Supreme Court justice should have?
7. What would you do if the law compels one answer but your heart tells you it is not fair?

When all of the senators have finished asking questions, the nominee should offer his or her closing thoughts. At this point the chair of the Senate Judiciary Committee should thank the nominee and excuse him or her.

Now bring out the next nominee and repeat the process.

When all the nominees have had their hearings, the committee should take a break, and the three television reporters and commentators should simulate a talk show and discuss how the nominees fared. What were their strengths and weaknesses as candidates? How did they handle hot issues and controversial questions? How will the senators react to their testimony?

The committee should then reconvene and discuss the legal philosophies and positions of the nominees and then vote on whether to confirm each of them. Now the classroom exercise is at an end. Of course, the nomination process is not yet complete. Normally, the names of the nominees who have passed the committee process are sent to the full Senate for a final vote. If you have a large class, have those students who were not selected to play any of the previous roles act as the full Senate and put the issue to them for a final vote. Which nominee or nominees did the class select?

The Supreme Court nominees (now justices, perhaps!) should discuss their experience—what they found difficult about the process, what they enjoyed, and what they learned. Would they do anything differently next time? What about the other actors? What did they learn? Do you think you would ever like to be a justice on the Supreme Court?

WHAT DO YOU Think?

Exercise A.1. Write a one-page essay on any or all of the following questions: What is the most important thing people should know about the Constitution? How do you think learning about constitutional rights and responsibilities has changed your thinking about citizenship? Do you think there is a difference between young people who are constitutionally literate and those who are not? How would you convince a fellow teenager that it is important to study constitutional law? Is it important? Read your essay aloud.

Exercise A.2. Write a letter to a current Supreme Court justice detailing which of his or her decisions or opinions you admire and why.

Exercise A.3. What causes Supreme Court justices to think differently from one another about the meaning of constitutional language? How would you explain the existence of majority and dissenting opinions to a younger brother or sister? Can you think of analogies to other subjects, such as English, chemistry, or history?

Note

1. This text is modeled after material furnished by the U.S. Senate Judiciary Committee. The first background check requires the nominee to complete numerous questionnaires that cover issues ranging from the nominee's address, education, and marital status to health conditions, legal activities, and ethical beliefs. The second background check is a computerized search for a nominee's criminal record or involvement in potentially embarrassing activities. The final background check is made by the FBI and includes a compilation of detailed interviews with current and previous employers and employees, family members, friends, colleagues, and neighbors. The FBI's background check is made available only to the Senate Judiciary Committee chair and the ranking minority member when the confirmation hearing exposes damaging information about the nominee.

APPENDIX B

CONSTITUTION OF THE UNITED STATES

WE THE PEOPLE of the United States, in Order to form a more perfect Union, establish Justice, insure domestic Tranquility, provide for the common defence, promote the general Welfare, and secure the Blessings of Liberty to ourselves and our Posterity, do ordain and establish this Constitution for the United States of America.

Article I

SECTION 1. All legislative Powers herein granted shall be vested in a Congress of the United States, which shall consist of a Senate and House of Representatives.

SECTION 2. The House of Representatives shall be composed of Members chosen every second Year by the People of the several States, and the Electors in each State shall have the Qualifications requisite for Electors of the most numerous Branch of the State Legislature.

No Person shall be a Representative who shall not have attained to the Age of twenty five Years, and been seven Years a Citizen of the United States, and who shall not, when elected, be an Inhabitant of that State in which he shall be chosen.

[Representatives and direct Taxes shall be apportioned among the several States which may be included within this Union, according to their respective Numbers, which shall be determined by adding to the whole Number of free Persons, including those bound to Service for a Term of Years, and excluding Indians not taxed, three fifths of all other Persons.][1] The actual Enumeration shall be made within three Years after the first Meeting of the Congress of the United States, and within every subsequent Term of ten Years, in such Manner as they shall by Law direct. The Number of Representatives shall not exceed one for every thirty Thousand, but each State shall have at Least one Representative; and until such enumeration shall be made, the State of New Hampshire shall be entitled to chuse three, Massachusetts eight, Rhode-Island and Providence Plantations one, Connecticut five, New-York six, New Jersey four, Pennsylvania eight, Delaware one, Maryland six, Virginia ten, North Carolina five, South Carolina five, and Georgia three.

When vacancies happen in the Representation from any State, the Executive Authority thereof shall issue Writs of Election to fill such Vacancies.

The House of Representatives shall chuse their Speaker and other Officers; and shall have the sole Power of Impeachment.

Section 3. The Senate of the United States shall be composed of two Senators from each State, [chosen by the Legislature thereof,][2] for six Years; and each Senator shall have one Vote.

Immediately after they shall be assembled in Consequence of the first Election, they shall be divided as equally as may be into three Classes. The Seats of the Senators of the first Class shall be vacated at the Expiration of the second Year, of the second Class at the Expiration of the fourth Year, and of the third Class at the Expiration of the sixth Year, so that one third may be chosen every second Year; [and if Vacancies happen by Resignation, or otherwise, during the Recess of the Legislature of any State, the Executive thereof may make temporary Appointments until the next Meeting of the Legislature, which shall then fill such Vacancies.][3]

No Person shall be a Senator who shall not have attained to the Age of thirty Years, and been nine Years a Citizen of the United States, and who shall not, when elected, be an Inhabitant of that State for which he shall be chosen.

The Vice President of the United States shall be President of the Senate, but shall have no Vote, unless they be equally divided.

The Senate shall chuse their other Officers, and also a President pro tempore, in the Absence of the Vice President, or when he shall exercise the Office of President of the United States.

The Senate shall have the sole Power to try all Impeachments. When sitting for that Purpose, they shall be on Oath or Affirmation. When the President of the United States is tried, the Chief Justice shall preside: And no Person shall be convicted without the Concurrence of two thirds of the Members present.

Judgment in Cases of Impeachment shall not extend further than to removal from Office, and disqualification to hold and enjoy any Office of honor, Trust or Profit under the United States: but the Party convicted shall nevertheless be liable and subject to Indictment, Trial, Judgment and Punishment, according to Law.

Section 4. The Times, Places and Manner of holding Elections for Senators and Representatives, shall be prescribed in each State by the Legislature thereof; but the Congress may at any time by Law make or alter such Regulations, except as to the Places of chusing Senators.

The Congress shall assemble at least once in every Year, and such Meeting shall [be on the first Monday in December],[4] unless they shall by Law appoint a different Day.

Section 5. Each House shall be the Judge of the Elections, Returns and Qualifications of its own Members, and a Majority of each shall constitute a Quorum to do Business; but a smaller Number may adjourn from day to day, and may be authorized to compel the Attendance of absent Members, in such Manner, and under such Penalties as each House may provide.

Each House may determine the Rules of its Proceedings, punish its Members for disorderly Behaviour, and, with the Concurrence of two thirds, expel a Member.

Each House shall keep a Journal of its Proceedings, and from time to time publish the same, excepting such Parts as may in their Judgment require Secrecy; and the Yeas and Nays of the Members of either House on any question shall, at the Desire of one fifth of those Present, be entered on the Journal.

Neither House, during the Session of Congress, shall, without the Consent of the other, adjourn for more than three days, nor to any other Place than that in which the two Houses shall be sitting.

SECTION 6. The Senators and Representatives shall receive a Compensation for their Services, to be ascertained by Law, and paid out of the Treasury of the United States. They shall in all Cases, except Treason, Felony and Breach of the Peace, be privileged from Arrest during their Attendance at the Session of their respective Houses, and in going to and returning from the same; and for any Speech or Debate in either House, they shall not be questioned in any other Place.

No Senator or Representative shall, during the Time for which he was elected, be appointed to any civil Office under the Authority of the United States, which shall have been created, or the Emoluments whereof shall have been encreased during such time; and no Person holding any Office under the United States, shall be a Member of either House during his Continuance in Office.

SECTION 7. All Bills for raising Revenue shall originate in the House of Representatives; but the Senate may propose or concur with Amendments as on other Bills.

Every Bill which shall have passed the House of Representatives and the Senate, shall, before it become a Law, be presented to the President of the United States; If he approve he shall sign it, but if not he shall return it, with his Objections to that House in which it shall have originated, who shall enter the Objections at large on their Journal, and proceed to reconsider it. If after such Reconsideration two thirds of that House shall agree to pass the Bill, it shall be sent, together with the Objections, to the other House, by which it shall likewise be reconsidered, and if approved by two thirds of that House, it shall become a Law. But in all such Cases the Votes of both Houses shall be determined by yeas and Nays, and the Names of the Persons voting for and against the Bill shall be entered on the Journal of each House respectively. If any Bill shall not be returned by the President within ten Days (Sundays excepted) after it shall have been presented to him, the Same shall be a Law, in like Manner as if he had signed it, unless the Congress by their Adjournment prevent its Return, in which Case it shall not be a Law.

Every Order, Resolution, or Vote to which the Concurrence of the Senate and House of Representatives may be necessary (except on a question of Adjournment) shall be presented to the President of the United States; and before the Same shall take Effect, shall be approved by him, or being disapproved by him, shall be repassed by two thirds of the Senate and House of Representatives, according to the Rules and Limitations prescribed in the Case of a Bill.

SECTION 8. The Congress shall have Power To lay and collect Taxes, Duties, Imposts and Excises, to pay the Debts and provide for the common Defence and general Welfare of the United States; but all Duties, Imposts and Excises shall be uniform throughout the United States;

To borrow Money on the credit of the United States;

To regulate Commerce with foreign Nations, and among the several States, and with the Indian Tribes;

To establish an uniform Rule of Naturalization, and uniform Laws on the subject of Bankruptcies throughout the United States;

To coin Money, regulate the Value thereof, and of foreign Coin, and fix the Standard of Weights and Measures;

To provide for the Punishment of counterfeiting the Securities and current Coin of the United States;

To establish Post Offices and post Roads;

To promote the Progress of Science and useful Arts, by securing for limited Times to Authors and Inventors the exclusive Right to their respective Writings and Discoveries;

To constitute Tribunals inferior to the supreme Court;

To define and punish Piracies and Felonies committed on the high Seas, and Offences against the Law of Nations;

To declare War, grant Letters of Marque and Reprisal, and make Rules concerning Captures on Land and Water;

To raise and support Armies, but no Appropriation of Money to that Use shall be for a longer Term than two Years;

To provide and maintain a Navy;

To make Rules for the Government and Regulation of the land and naval Forces;

To provide for calling forth the Militia to execute the Laws of the Union, suppress Insurrections and repel Invasions;

To provide for organizing, arming, and disciplining, the Militia, and for governing such Part of them as may be employed in the Service of the United States, reserving to the States respectively, the Appointment of the Officers, and the Authority of training the Militia according to the discipline prescribed by Congress;

To exercise exclusive Legislation in all Cases whatsoever, over such District (not exceeding ten Miles square) as may, by Cession of particular States, and the Acceptance of Congress, become the Seat of the Government of the United States, and to exercise like Authority over all Places purchased by the Consent of the Legislature of the State in which the Same shall be, for the Erection of Forts, Magazines, Arsenals, dock-Yards, and other needful Buildings;—And

To make all Laws which shall be necessary and proper for carrying into Execution the foregoing Powers, and all other Powers vested by this Constitution in the Government of the United States, or in any Department or Officer thereof.

SECTION 9. The Migration or Importation of such Persons as any of the States now existing shall think proper to admit, shall not be prohibited by the Congress prior to the Year one thousand eight hundred and eight, but a Tax or duty may be imposed on such Importation, not exceeding ten dollars for each Person.

The Privilege of the Writ of Habeas Corpus shall not be suspended, unless when in Cases of Rebellion or Invasion the public Safety may require it.

No Bill of Attainder or ex post facto Law shall be passed.

No Capitation, or other direct, Tax shall be laid, unless in Proportion to the Census or Enumeration herein before directed to be taken.[5]

No Tax or Duty shall be laid on Articles exported from any State.

No Preference shall be given by any Regulation of Commerce or Revenue to the Ports of one State over those of another; nor shall Vessels bound to, or from, one State, be obliged to enter, clear, or pay Duties in another.

No Money shall be drawn from the Treasury, but in Consequence of Appropriations made by Law; and a regular Statement and Account of the Receipts and Expenditures of all public Money shall be published from time to time.

No Title of Nobility shall be granted by the United States: And no Person holding any Office of Profit or Trust under them, shall, without the Consent of the Congress, accept of any present, Emolument, Office, or Title, of any kind whatever, from any King, Prince, or foreign State.

SECTION 10. No State shall enter into any Treaty, Alliance, or Confederation; grant Letters of Marque and Reprisal; coin Money; emit Bills of Credit; make any Thing but gold and silver Coin a Tender in Payment of Debts; pass any Bill of Attainder, ex post facto Law, or Law impairing the Obligation of Contracts, or grant any Title of Nobility.

No State shall, without the Consent of the Congress, lay any Imposts or Duties on Imports or Exports, except what may be absolutely necessary for executing its inspection Laws: and the net Produce of all Duties and Imposts, laid by any State on Imports or Exports, shall be for the Use of the Treasury of the United States; and all such Laws shall be subject to the Revision and Controul of the Congress.

No State shall, without the Consent of Congress, lay any Duty of Tonnage, keep Troops, or Ships of War in time of Peace, enter into any Agreement or Compact with another State, or with a foreign Power, or engage in War, unless actually invaded, or in such imminent Danger as will not admit of delay.

Article II

SECTION 1. The executive Power shall be vested in a President of the United States of America. He shall hold his Office during the Term of four Years, and, together with the Vice President, chosen for the same Term, be elected, as follows

Each State shall appoint, in such Manner as the Legislature thereof may direct, a Number of Electors, equal to the whole Number of Senators and Representatives to which the State may be entitled in the Congress: but no Senator or Representative, or Person holding an Office of Trust or Profit under the United States, shall be appointed an Elector.

[The Electors shall meet in their respective States, and vote by Ballot for two Persons, of whom one at least shall not be an Inhabitant of the same State with themselves. And they shall make a List of all the Persons voted for, and of the Number of Votes for each; which List they shall sign and certify, and transmit sealed to the Seat of the Government of the United States, directed to the President of the Senate. The President of the Senate shall, in the Presence of the Senate and House of Representatives, open all the Certificates, and the Votes shall then be counted. The Person having the greatest Number of Votes shall be the President, if such Number be a Majority of the whole Number of Electors appointed; and if there be more than one who have such Majority, and have an equal Number of Votes, then the House of Representatives shall immediately chuse by Ballot one of them for President; and if no Person have a Majority, then from the five highest on the list the said House shall in like Manner chuse the President. But in chusing the President, the Votes shall be taken by States, the Representation from each State having one Vote; A quorum for this Purpose shall consist of a Member or Members from two thirds of the States, and a Majority of all the States shall be necessary to a Choice. In every Case, after the Choice of the President, the Person having the greatest Number of Votes of the Electors shall be the Vice President. But if there should remain two or more who have equal Votes, the Senate shall chuse from them by Ballot the Vice President.][6]

The Congress may determine the Time of chusing the Electors, and the Day on which they shall give their Votes; which Day shall be the same throughout the United States.

No Person except a natural born Citizen, or a Citizen of the United States, at the time of the Adoption of this Constitution, shall be eligible to the Office of President; neither shall any Person be eligible to that Office who shall not have attained to the Age of thirty five Years, and been fourteen Years a Resident within the United States.

In Case of the Removal of the President from Office, or of his Death, Resignation, or Inability to discharge the Powers and Duties of the said Office, the Same shall devolve on the Vice President, and the Congress may by Law provide for the Case of Removal, Death, Resignation or Inability, both of the President and Vice President, declaring what Officer shall then act as President, and such Officer shall act accordingly, until the Disability be removed, or a President shall be elected.[7]

The President shall, at stated Times, receive for his Services, a Compensation, which shall neither be encreased nor diminished during the Period for which he shall have been elected, and he shall not receive within that Period any other Emolument from the United States, or any of them.

Before he enter on the Execution of his Office, he shall take the following Oath or Affirmation:—"I do solemnly swear (or affirm) that I will faithfully execute the Office of President of the United States, and will to the best of my Ability, preserve, protect and defend the Constitution of the United States."

SECTION 2. The President shall be Commander in Chief of the Army and Navy of the United States, and of the Militia of the several States, when called into the actual Service of the United States; he may require the Opinion, in writing, of the principal Officer in each of the executive Departments, upon any Subject relating to the Duties of their respective

Offices, and he shall have Power to grant Reprieves and Pardons for Offences against the United States, except in Cases of Impeachment.

He shall have Power, by and with the Advice and Consent of the Senate, to make Treaties, provided two thirds of the Senators present concur; and he shall nominate, and by and with the Advice and Consent of the Senate, shall appoint Ambassadors, other public Ministers and Consuls, Judges of the supreme Court, and all other Officers of the United States, whose Appointments are not herein otherwise provided for, and which shall be established by Law: but the Congress may by Law vest the Appointment of such inferior Officers, as they think proper, in the President alone, in the Courts of Law, or in the Heads of Departments.

The President shall have Power to fill up all Vacancies that may happen during the Recess of the Senate, by granting Commissions which shall expire at the End of their next Session.

SECTION 3. He shall from time to time give to the Congress Information of the State of the Union, and recommend to their Consideration such Measures as he shall judge necessary and expedient; he may, on extraordinary Occasions, convene both Houses, or either of them, and in Case of Disagreement between them, with Respect to the Time of Adjournment, he may adjourn them to such Time as he shall think proper; he shall receive Ambassadors and other public Ministers; he shall take Care that the Laws be faithfully executed, and shall Commission all the Officers of the United States.

SECTION 4. The President, Vice President and all civil Officers of the United States, shall be removed from Office on Impeachment for, and Conviction of, Treason, Bribery, or other high Crimes and Misdemeanors.

Article III

SECTION 1. The judicial Power of the United States, shall be vested in one supreme Court, and in such inferior Courts as the Congress may from time to time ordain and establish. The Judges, both of the supreme and inferior Courts, shall hold their Offices during good Behaviour, and shall, at stated Times, receive for their Services, a Compensation, which shall not be diminished during their Continuance in Office.

SECTION 2. The judicial Power shall extend to all Cases, in Law and Equity, arising under this Constitution, the Laws of the United States, and Treaties made, or which shall be made, under their Authority;—to all Cases affecting Ambassadors, other public Ministers and Consuls;—to all Cases of admiralty and maritime Jurisdiction;—to Controversies to which the United States shall be a Party;—to Controversies between two or more States;—between a State and Citizens of another State;—between Citizens of different States;—between Citizens of the same State claiming Lands under Grants of different States, and between a State, or the Citizens thereof, and foreign States, Citizens or Subjects.[8]

In all Cases affecting Ambassadors, other public Ministers and Consuls, and those in which a State shall be Party, the supreme Court shall have original Jurisdiction. In all the other Cases before mentioned, the supreme Court shall have appellate Jurisdiction, both as to Law and Fact, with such Exceptions, and under such Regulations as the Congress shall make.

The Trial of all Crimes, except in Cases of Impeachment, shall be by Jury; and such Trial shall be held in the State where the said Crimes shall have been committed; but when not committed within any State, the Trial shall be at such Place or Places as the Congress may by Law have directed.

SECTION 3. Treason against the United States, shall consist only in levying War against them, or in adhering to their Enemies, giving them Aid and Comfort. No Person shall be convicted of Treason unless on the Testimony of two Witnesses to the same overt Act, or on Confession in open Court.

The Congress shall have Power to declare the Punishment of Treason, but no Attainder of Treason shall work Corruption of Blood, or Forfeiture except during the Life of the Person attainted.

Article IV

SECTION 1. Full Faith and Credit shall be given in each State to the public Acts, Records, and judicial Proceedings of every other State. And the Congress may by general Laws prescribe the Manner in which such Acts, Records and Proceedings shall be proved, and the Effect thereof.

SECTION 2. The Citizens of each State shall be entitled to all Privileges and Immunities of Citizens in the several States.

A Person charged in any State with Treason, Felony, or other Crime, who shall flee from Justice, and be found in another State, shall on Demand of the executive Authority of the State from which he fled, be delivered up, to be removed to the State having Jurisdiction of the Crime.

[No Person held to Service or Labour in one State, under the Laws thereof, escaping into another, shall, in Consequence of any Law or Regulation therein, be discharged from such Service or Labour, but shall be delivered up on Claim of the Party to whom such Service or Labour may be due.][9]

SECTION 3. New States may be admitted by the Congress into this Union; but no new State shall be formed or erected within the Jurisdiction of any other State; nor any State be formed by the Junction of two or more States, or Parts of States, without the Consent of the Legislatures of the States concerned as well as of the Congress.

The Congress shall have Power to dispose of and make all needful Rules and Regulations respecting the Territory or other Property belonging to the United States; and nothing in this Constitution shall be so construed as to Prejudice any Claims of the United States, or of any particular State.

SECTION 4. The United States shall guarantee to every State in this Union a Republican Form of Government, and shall protect each of them against Invasion; and on Application of the Legislature, or of the Executive (when the Legislature cannot be convened) against domestic Violence.

Article V

The Congress, whenever two thirds of both Houses shall deem it necessary, shall propose Amendments to this Constitution, or, on the Application of the Legislatures of two thirds of the several States, shall call a Convention for proposing Amendments, which, in either Case, shall be valid to all Intents and Purposes, as Part of this Constitution, when ratified by the Legislatures of three fourths of the several States, or by Conventions in three fourths thereof, as the one or the other Mode of Ratification may be proposed by the Congress; Provided [that no Amendment which may be made prior to the Year One thousand eight hundred and eight shall in any Manner affect the first and fourth Clauses in the Ninth Section of the first Article; and][10] that no State, without its Consent, shall be deprived of its equal Suffrage in the Senate.

Article VI

All Debts contracted and Engagements entered into, before the Adoption of this Constitution, shall be as valid against the United States under this Constitution, as under the Confederation.

This Constitution, and the Laws of the United States which shall be made in Pursuance thereof; and all Treaties made, or which shall be made, under the Authority of the United States, shall be the supreme Law of the Land; and the Judges in every State shall be bound thereby, any Thing in the Constitution or Laws of any State to the Contrary notwithstanding.

The Senators and Representatives before mentioned, and the Members of the several State Legislatures, and all executive and judicial Officers, both of the United States and of the several States, shall be bound by Oath or Affirmation, to support this Constitution; but no religious Test shall ever be required as a Qualification to any Office or public Trust under the United States.

Article VII

The Ratification of the Conventions of nine States, shall be sufficient for the Establishment of this Constitution between the States so ratifying the Same.

Done in Convention by the Unanimous Consent of the States present the Seventeenth Day of September in the Year of our Lord one thousand seven hundred and Eighty seven and of the Independence of the United States of America the Twelfth. IN WITNESS whereof We have hereunto subscribed our Names,

George Washington,
President and deputy from Virginia.

NEW HAMPSHIRE:	John Langdon, Nicholas Gilman.
MASSACHUSETTS:	Nathaniel Gorham, Rufus King.
CONNECTICUT:	William Samuel Johnson, Roger Sherman.
NEW YORK:	Alexander Hamilton.
NEW JERSEY:	William Livingston, David Brearley, William Paterson, Jonathan Dayton.
PENNSYLVANIA:	Benjamin Franklin, Thomas Mifflin, Robert Morris, George Clymer, Thomas FitzSimons, Jared Ingersoll, James Wilson, Gouverneur Morris.
DELAWARE:	George Read, Gunning Bedford Jr., John Dickinson, Richard Bassett, Jacob Broom.
MARYLAND:	James McHenry, Daniel of St. Thomas Jenifer, Daniel Carroll.
VIRGINIA:	John Blair, James Madison Jr.

NORTH CAROLINA:	William Blount, Richard Dobbs Spaight, Hugh Williamson.
SOUTH CAROLINA:	John Rutledge, Charles Cotesworth Pinckney, Charles Pinckney, Pierce Butler.
GEORGIA:	William Few, Abraham Baldwin.

[The language of the original Constitution, not including the Amendments, was adopted by a convention of the states on September 17, 1787, and was subsequently ratified by the states on the following dates: Delaware, December 7, 1787; Pennsylvania, December 12, 1787; New Jersey, December 18, 1787; Georgia, January 2, 1788; Connecticut, January 9, 1788; Massachusetts, February 6, 1788; Maryland, April 28, 1788; South Carolina, May 23, 1788; New Hampshire, June 21, 1788.

Ratification was completed on June 21, 1788.

The Constitution subsequently was ratified by Virginia, June 25, 1788; New York, July 26, 1788; North Carolina, November 21, 1789; Rhode Island, May 29, 1790; and Vermont, January 10, 1791.]

Amendments

AMENDMENT I   *(First ten amendments ratified December 15, 1791.)*

Congress shall make no law respecting an establishment of religion, or prohibiting the free exercise thereof; or abridging the freedom of speech, or of the press; or the right of the people peaceably to assemble, and to petition the Government for a redress of grievances.

AMENDMENT II

A well regulated Militia, being necessary to the security of a free State, the right of the people to keep and bear Arms, shall not be infringed.

AMENDMENT III

No Soldier shall, in time of peace be quartered in any house, without the consent of the Owner, nor in time of war, but in a manner to be prescribed by law.

AMENDMENT IV

The right of the people to be secure in their persons, houses, papers, and effects, against unreasonable searches and seizures, shall not be violated, and no Warrants shall issue, but upon probable cause, supported by Oath or affirmation, and particularly describing the place to be searched, and the persons or things to be seized.

AMENDMENT V

No person shall be held to answer for a capital, or otherwise infamous crime, unless on a presentment or indictment of a Grand Jury, except in cases arising in the land or naval forces, or in the Militia, when in actual service in time of War or public danger; nor shall any person be subject for the same offence to be twice put in jeopardy of life or limb; nor shall be compelled in any criminal case to be a witness against himself, nor be deprived of life, liberty, or property, without due process of law; nor shall private property be taken for public use, without just compensation.

AMENDMENT VI

In all criminal prosecutions, the accused shall enjoy the right to a speedy and public trial, by an impartial jury of the State and district wherein the crime shall have been committed, which district shall have been previously ascertained by law, and to be informed of the nature and cause of the accusation; to be confronted with the witnesses against him; to have compulsory process for obtaining witnesses in his favor, and to have the Assistance of Counsel for his defence.

AMENDMENT VII

In Suits at common law, where the value in controversy shall exceed twenty dollars, the right of trial by jury shall be preserved, and no fact tried by a jury, shall be otherwise re-examined in any Court of the United States, than according to the rules of the common law.

AMENDMENT VIII

Excessive bail shall not be required, nor excessive fines imposed, nor cruel and unusual punishments inflicted.

AMENDMENT IX

The enumeration in the Constitution, of certain rights, shall not be construed to deny or disparage others retained by the people.

AMENDMENT X

The powers not delegated to the United States by the Constitution, nor prohibited by it to the States, are reserved to the States respectively, or to the people.

AMENDMENT XI *(Ratified February 7, 1795)*

The Judicial power of the United States shall not be construed to extend to any suit in law or equity, commenced or prosecuted against one of the United States by Citizens of another State, or by Citizens or Subjects of any Foreign State.

AMENDMENT XII *(Ratified June 15, 1804)*

The Electors shall meet in their respective states and vote by ballot for President and Vice-President, one of whom, at least, shall not be an inhabitant of the same state with themselves; they shall name in their ballots the person voted for as President, and in distinct bal-lots the person voted for as Vice-President, and they shall make distinct lists of all persons voted for as President, and of all persons voted for as Vice-President, and of the number of votes for each, which lists they shall sign and certify, and transmit sealed to the seat of the government of the United States, directed to the President of the Senate;—The President of the Senate shall, in the presence of the Senate and House of Representatives, open all the certificates and the votes shall then be counted;—The person having the greatest number of votes for President, shall be the President, if such number be a majority of the whole number of Electors appointed; and if no person have such majority, then from the persons having the highest numbers not exceeding three on the list of those voted for as President, the House of Representatives shall choose immediately, by ballot, the President. But in choosing the President, the votes shall be taken by states, the representation from each state having one vote; a quorum for this purpose shall consist of a member or members from two-thirds of the states, and a majority of all the states shall be necessary to a choice. [And if the House of Representatives shall not choose a President whenever the right of choice shall devolve upon them, before the fourth day of March next following, then the Vice-President shall act as President, as in the case of the death or other constitutional disabil-ity of the President.—][11] The person having the greatest number of votes as Vice-President, shall be the Vice-President, if such number be a majority of the whole number of Electors appointed, and if no person have a majority, then from the two highest num-bers on the list, the Senate shall choose the Vice-President; a quorum for the purpose shall consist of two-thirds of the whole number of Senators, and a majority of the whole num-ber shall be necessary to a choice. But no person constitutionally ineligible to the office of President shall be eligible to that of Vice-President of the United States.

AMENDMENT XIII   *(Ratified December 6, 1865)*

- *SECTION 1.* Neither slavery nor involuntary servitude, except as a punishment for crime whereof the party shall have been duly convicted, shall exist within the United States, or any place subject to their jurisdiction.
- *SECTION 2.* Congress shall have power to enforce this article by appropriate legislation.

AMENDMENT XIV   *(Ratified July 9, 1868)*

- *SECTION 1.* All persons born or naturalized in the United States, and subject to the jurisdiction thereof, are citizens of the United States and of the State wherein they re-side. No State shall make or enforce any law which shall abridge the privileges or im-munities of citizens of the United States; nor shall any State deprive any person of life, liberty, or property, without due process of law; nor deny to any person within its ju-risdiction the equal protection of the laws.
- *SECTION 2.* Representatives shall be apportioned among the several States according to their respective numbers, counting the whole number of persons in each State, ex-cluding Indians not taxed. But when the right to vote at any election for the choice of electors for President and Vice President of the United States, Representatives in Congress, the Executive and Judicial officers of a State, or the members of the Legislature thereof, is denied to any of the male inhabitants of such State, being twenty-one years of age,[12] and citizens of the United States, or in any way abridged,

except for participation in rebellion, or other crime, the basis of representation therein shall be reduced in the proportion which the number of such male citizens shall bear to the whole number of male citizens twenty-one years of age in such State.

- *SECTION 3.* No person shall be a Senator or Representative in Congress, or elector of President and Vice President, or hold any office, civil or military, under the United States, or under any State, who, having previously taken an oath, as a member of Congress, or as an officer of the United States, or as a member of any State legislature, or as an executive or judicial officer of any State, to support the Constitution of the United States, shall have engaged in insurrection or rebellion against the same, or given aid or comfort to the enemies thereof. But Congress may by a vote of two-thirds of each House, remove such disability.

- *SECTION 4.* The validity of the public debt of the United States, authorized by law, including debts incurred for payment of pensions and bounties for services in suppressing insurrection or rebellion, shall not be questioned. But neither the United States nor any State shall assume or pay any debt or obligation incurred in aid of insurrection or rebellion against the United States, or any claim for the loss or emancipation of any slave; but all such debts, obligations and claims shall be held illegal and void.

- *SECTION 5.* The Congress shall have power to enforce, by appropriate legislation, the provisions of this article.

AMENDMENT XV　*(Ratified February 3, 1870)*

- *SECTION 1.* The right of citizens of the United States to vote shall not be denied or abridged by the United States or by any State on account of race, color, or previous condition of servitude.

- *SECTION 2.* The Congress shall have power to enforce this article by appropriate legislation.

AMENDMENT XVI　*(Ratified February 3, 1913)*

The Congress shall have power to lay and collect taxes on incomes, from whatever source derived, without apportionment among the several States, and without regard to any census or enumeration.

AMENDMENT XVII　*(Ratified April 8, 1913)*

The Senate of the United States shall be composed of two Senators from each State, elected by the people thereof, for six years; and each Senator shall have one vote. The electors in each State shall have the qualifications requisite for electors of the most numerous branch of the State legislatures.

When vacancies happen in the representation of any State in the Senate, the executive authority of such State shall issue writs of election to fill such vacancies: *Provided,* That the legislature of any State may empower the executive thereof to make temporary appointments until the people fill the vacancies by election as the legislature may direct.

This amendment shall not be so construed as to affect the election or term of any Senator chosen before it becomes valid as part of the Constitution.

AMENDMENT XVIII *(Ratified January 16, 1919)*[13]

- *SECTION 1.* After one year from the ratification of this article the manufacture, sale, or transportation of intoxicating liquors within, the importation thereof into, or the exportation thereof from the United States and all territory subject to the jurisdiction thereof for beverage purposes is hereby prohibited.
- *SECTION 2.* The Congress and the several States shall have concurrent power to enforce this article by appropriate legislation.
- *SECTION 3.* This article shall be inoperative unless it shall have been ratified as an amendment to the Constitution by the legislatures of the several States, as provided in the Constitution, within seven years from the date of the submission hereof to the States by the Congress.

AMENDMENT XIX *Ratified August 18, 1920)*

The right of citizens of the United States to vote shall not be denied or abridged by the United States or by any State on account of sex.

Congress shall have power to enforce this article by appropriate legislation.

AMENDMENT XX *(Ratified January 23, 1933)*

- *SECTION 1.* The terms of the President and Vice President shall end at noon on the 20th day of January, and the terms of Senators and Representatives at noon on the 3d day of January, of the years in which such terms would have ended if this article had not been ratified; and the terms of their successors shall then begin.
- *SECTION 2.* The Congress shall assemble at least once in every year, and such meeting shall begin at noon on the 3d day of January, unless they shall by law appoint a different day.
- *SECTION 3.*[14] If, at the time fixed for the beginning of the term of the President, the President elect shall have died, the Vice President elect shall become President. If a President shall not have been chosen before the time fixed for the beginning of his term, or if the President elect shall have failed to qualify, then the Vice President elect shall act as President until a President shall have qualified; and the Congress may by law provide for the case wherein neither a President elect nor a Vice President elect shall have qualified, declaring who shall then act as President, or the manner in which one who is to act shall be selected, and such person shall act accordingly until a President or Vice President shall have qualified.
- *SECTION 4.* The Congress may by law provide for the case of the death of any of the persons from whom the House of Representatives may choose a President whenever the right of choice shall have devolved upon them, and for the case of the death of any of the persons from whom the Senate may choose a Vice President whenever the right of choice shall have devolved upon them.
- *SECTION 5.* Sections 1 and 2 shall take effect on the 15th day of October following the ratification of this article.
- *SECTION 6.* This article shall be inoperative unless it shall have been ratified as an amendment to the Constitution by the legislatures of three-fourths of the several States within seven years from the date of its submission.

AMENDMENT XXI *(Ratified December 5, 1933)*

- *SECTION 1.* The eighteenth article of amendment to the Constitution of the United States is hereby repealed.
- *SECTION 2.* The transportation or importation into any State, Territory, or possession of the United States for delivery or use therein of intoxicating liquors, in violation of the laws thereof, is hereby prohibited.
- *SECTION 3.* This article shall be inoperative unless it shall have been ratified as an amendment to the Constitution by conventions in the several States, as provided in the Constitution, within seven years from the date of the submission hereof to the States by the Congress.

AMENDMENT XXII *(Ratified February 27, 1951)*

- *SECTION 1.* No person shall be elected to the office of the President more than twice, and no person who has held the office of President, or acted as President, for more than two years of a term to which some other person was elected President shall be elected to the office of the President more than once. But this Article shall not apply to any person holding the office of President when this Article was proposed by the Congress, and shall not prevent any person who may be holding the office of President, or acting as President, during the term within which this Article becomes operative from holding the office of President or acting as President during the remainder of such term.
- *SECTION 2.* This article shall be inoperative unless it shall have been ratified as an amendment to the Constitution by the legislatures of three-fourths of the several States within seven years from the date of its submission to the States by the Congress.

AMENDMENT XXIII *(Ratified March 29, 1961)*

- *SECTION 1.* The District constituting the seat of Government of the United States shall appoint in such manner as the Congress may direct:

    A number of electors of President and Vice President equal to the whole number of Senators and Representatives in Congress to which the District would be entitled if it were a State, but in no event more than the least populous State; they shall be in addition to those appointed by the States, but they shall be considered, for the purposes of the election of President and Vice President, to be electors appointed by a State; and they shall meet in the District and perform such duties as provided by the twelfth article of amendment.
- *SECTION 2.* The Congress shall have power to enforce this article by appropriate legislation.

AMENDMENT XXIV *(Ratified January 23, 1964)*

- *SECTION 1.* The right of citizens of the United States to vote in any primary or other election for President or Vice President, for electors for President or Vice President, or for Senator or Representative in Congress, shall not be denied or abridged by the United States or any State by reason of failure to pay any poll tax or other tax.

- *SECTION 2.* The Congress shall have power to enforce this article by appropriate legislation.

AMENDMENT XXV *(Ratified February 10, 1967)*
- *SECTION 1.* In case of the removal of the President from office or of his death or resignation, the Vice President shall become President.
- *SECTION 2.* Whenever there is a vacancy in the office of the Vice President, the President shall nominate a Vice President who shall take office upon confirmation by a majority vote of both Houses of Congress.
- *SECTION 3.* Whenever the President transmits to the President pro tempore of the Senate and the Speaker of the House of Representatives his written declaration that he is unable to discharge the powers and duties of his office, and until he transmits to them a written declaration to the contrary, such powers and duties shall be discharged by the Vice President as Acting President.
- *SECTION 4.* Whenever the Vice President and a majority of either the principal officers of the executive departments or of such other body as Congress may by law provide, transmit to the President pro tempore of the Senate and the Speaker of the House of Representatives their written declaration that the President is unable to discharge the powers and duties of his office, the Vice President shall immediately assume the powers and duties of the office as Acting President.

Thereafter, when the President transmits to the President pro tempore of the Senate and the Speaker of the House of Representatives his written declaration that no inability exists, he shall resume the powers and duties of his office unless the Vice President and a majority of either the principal officers of the executive department or of such other body as Congress may by law provide, transmit within four days to the President pro tempore of the Senate and the Speaker of the House of Representatives their written declaration that the President is unable to discharge the powers and duties of his office. Thereupon Congress shall decide the issue, assembling within forty-eight hours for that purpose if not in session. If the Congress, within twenty-one days after receipt of the latter written declaration, or, if Congress is not in session, within twenty-one days after Congress is required to assemble, determines by two-thirds vote of both Houses that the President is unable to discharge the powers and duties of his office, the Vice President shall continue to discharge the same as Acting President; otherwise, the President shall resume the powers and duties of his office.

AMENDMENT XXVI *(Ratified July 1, 1971)*
- *SECTION 1.* The right of citizens of the United States, who are eighteen years of age or older, to vote shall not be denied or abridged by the United States or by any State on account of age.
- *SECTION 2.* The Congress shall have power to enforce this article by appropriate legislation.

AMENDMENT XXVII *(Ratified May 7, 1992)*

No law varying the compensation for the services of the Senators and Representatives shall take effect, until an election of Representatives shall have intervened.

Notes

1. The part in brackets was changed by section 2 of the Fourteenth Amendment.
2. The part in brackets was changed by the first paragraph of the Seventeenth Amendment.
3. The part in brackets was changed by the second paragraph of the Seventeenth Amendment.
4. The part in brackets was changed by section 2 of the Twentieth Amendment.
5. The Sixteenth Amendment gave Congress the power to tax incomes.
6. The material in brackets has been superseded by the Twelfth Amendment.
7. This provision has been affected by the Twenty-fifth Amendment.
8. These clauses were affected by the Eleventh Amendment.
9. This paragraph has been superseded by the Thirteenth Amendment.
10. Obsolete.
11. The part in brackets has been superseded by section 3 of the Twentieth Amendment.
12. See the Nineteenth and Twenty-sixth Amendments.
13. This Amendment was repealed by section 1 of the Twenty-first Amendment.
14. See the Twenty-fifth Amendment.

Source: U.S. Congress, House, Committee on the Judiciary, *The Constitution of the United States of America, as Amended,* 100th Cong., 1st sess., 1987, H Doc 100-94.

APPENDIX C

GLOSSARY

AD HOC. Created for a singular and temporary purpose.

ADVISORY OPINION. An opinion issued by a court in which it states how it would rule on a legal matter that is not actually ripe for decision; significantly, the Supreme Court and other federal courts do not issue advisory opinions.

AFFIRMATIVE ACTION. Deliberate efforts by universities and employers to recruit and attract women and members of racial and ethnic minority groups as students or employees.

ALIEN. A person who lives within the borders of a country but is not a citizen. Legal aliens are lawfully present, illegal aliens unlawfully so.

AMICUS CURIAE. A "friend of the court" who is not a direct party to a case but files a brief to offer advice and useful information to the court. The plural is "Amici Curiae," for friends of the court.

ANTIMISCEGENATION STATUTE. A law that forbids people of different races to marry or have children. In *Loving v. Virginia* (1967), the Supreme Court ruled state antimiscegenation laws unconstitutional.

APPELLANT. The party that appeals a lower court's decision. This party is usually seeking reversal of the lower court's decision. *See also* PETITIONER.

APPELLEE. The party that responds to an appeal. This party is generally seeking affirmance of a lower court's decision. *See also* RESPONDENT.

ARGUENDO. For the sake of argument.

ATTORNEY GENERAL, U.S. Head of the Department of Justice; appointed by the president. Responsibilities include representing the United States in legal matters, standing before the Supreme Court in cases where the United States is a party, and counseling the president and others within the executive branch as needed. Each state also has its own attorney general.

BILL OF RIGHTS. The first ten amendments of the Constitution guaranteeing citizens basic constitutional rights and liberties.

CASE-OR-CONTROVERSY REQUIREMENT. The constitutional requirement that cases before the federal courts must involve an actual, and not hypothetical, dispute between parties.

CASTE. A rigid social class or stratum; characteristic of a stratified class-bound society.

CERTIORARI. *See* WRIT OF CERTIORARI.

CIVIL ACTION. A lawsuit undertaken to protect an individual's private legal rights. Also known as a civil suit.

CLASS ACTION. A lawsuit in which a large group of people with a common interest and complaint join together to sue.

COMMERCIAL SPEECH. Expression that proposes a sale or other commercial transaction. Commercial speech receives less constitutional protection than does political speech.

COMMON LAW. Body of law that develops over time from the judgments of courts; contrasted with statutory law, which is written by legislatures.

COMPLAINT. The document that a plaintiff serves upon a defendant and submits to court. It details a "cause of action," meaning the alleged legal injury in a case; the facts that give rise to it; and the relief or damages sought.

CONCURRING OPINION. Opinion written by a justice or judge that agrees with the judgment of the majority in a case but that offers a separate explanation or process of reasoning for arriving there.

CONSTITUTIONAL INJURY. Harm caused by violation of an individual's constitutional rights that gives rise to standing to sue.

CONSTRUCTIVE KNOWLEDGE. Knowledge that a reasonable person in the same circumstances would have.

CONTRABAND. Goods that are illegal to obtain, possess, or distribute.

CORPORAL PUNISHMENT. The use of hitting, spanking, and other forms of physical correction to discipline children.

CRIMINAL PROSECUTION. Process by which the government charges a person with a criminal violation and brings him or her to trial.

DAMAGES. The costs of an accident or civil injury; the money sought by an injured party to pay for the costs of such an injury.

DE FACTO. A state of affairs that exists as a matter of fact, rather than law, without official compulsion behind it.

DE MINIMIS. A trivial or insignificant thing that a court may choose to overlook in deciding an issue.

DECLARATIVE RELIEF. A binding declaration by a court defining the rights and duties of parties in a case. Also known as declaratory relief.

DEFENDANT. Person or party that is sued in a civil case or prosecuted in a criminal case.

DELIBERATE INDIFFERENCE. Ignoring something on purpose.

DESIGNATED PUBLIC FORUM. Public property that the government opens up for free speech purposes. Unlike traditional public forums—streets, sidewalks, parks—this is property that the government does not have to use for expressive purposes but chooses to in any event.

DIRECT APPELLATE REVIEW. When a case is appealed directly from trial to an appellate court or body without making other stops.

DISCLAIMER. A statement that one disclaims or refuses responsibility for some liability, eventuality, or risk.

DISSENTING OPINION. Opinion written by a justice or judge that disagrees with the ruling of the majority opinion in a case. One can dissent without filing a dissenting opinion.

DOUBLE JEOPARDY. The prosecution of an individual twice for the same criminal offense. This practice is outlawed by the Fifth Amendment to the Constitution.

DUE PROCESS CLAUSE. Clause in the Fifth and Fourteenth Amendments declaring that no person may be deprived of life, liberty, or property without due process of law; interpreted to mean that every individual is entitled to a fair trial with significant protections, such as the right to be heard, to call witnesses, to cross-examine witnesses, and so forth.

EMPIRICAL. Based on experience or observation.

ENJOIN. To stop or restrain by injunction.

EQUAL PROTECTION CLAUSE. The clause contained in the Fourteenth Amendment requiring government to use only rational classifications among people and not draw lines on the basis of race, ethnicity, or religion without a "compelling" reason or on the basis of gender without an "important" reason.

EQUITABLE REMEDY. When a court enforces a right in a way that does not involve the awarding of money damages, as when it orders someone to stop committing an unlawful act.

ESTABLISHMENT CLAUSE. The religion clause in the First Amendment that prohibits both federal and state governments from formally establishing, coercing, or endorsing a religion or religion in general.

EXCLUSIONARY RULE. The rule under the Fourth Amendment in which evidence obtained unlawfully, in violation of a suspect's rights, may be suppressed and excluded in court.

EXPRESSIVE ASSOCIATION. A private organization or group, formal or informal, engaged in public expression of ideas and views.

EXPRESSIVE CONDUCT. Actions that do not literally involve speaking or writing but that nonetheless send a message. Picketing a store, wearing a political button, and painting a picture are all examples of expressive conduct.

FEDERALISM. The system of divided and allocated powers between the states and the federal government.

FREE EXERCISE CLAUSE. The religion clause in the First Amendment guaranteeing people the right to worship and believe as they please (or not at all) against deliberate interference by government.

GENERAL COUNSEL. The top lawyer in a government or private legal department.

GRAND JURY. A body of citizens that sits to review relevant evidence and testimony to determine whether a person should be formally charged with a crime.

HOLDING. A court's decision on a matter of law in a case.

ILLEGAL. Action or conduct in violation of municipal, state, or federal law.

IN LOCO PARENTIS. Literally, "in the place of a parent." Teachers and school authorities act *in loco parentis* in the school domain when there is no direct supervision by a parent or guardian.

INJUNCTION. An order from a court commanding or preventing an action.

INJUNCTIVE RELIEF. A court order meant to force an organization or person either to do something or to stop doing it.

INJURY. The violation of another party's legal rights or its legally protected interests. If the government puts you in prison without a trial, it has violated your due process rights and you have been injured by its actions.

INVIDIOUS DISCRIMINATION. Discrimination that is objectionable and offensive, usually involving prejudice and stereotyping.

JUDICIAL RESTRAINT. The theory and practice whereby judges defer to the political branches and strive not to invalidate democratically chosen public policies and laws.

JUDICIAL REVIEW. The constitutional power of a court to examine laws and policies made by other branches of government and to invalidate them if they are unconstitutional or unlawful.

JURISDICTION. A court's power to hear a case; also, territory over which a government exercises authority.

JURISPRUDENCE. The fundamental and linked principles of a body of law or legal system.

LEGISLATIVE HISTORY. The specific legislative background and events leading to passage of a statute, including hearings, committee reports, floor statements, and debates. Legislative history is sometimes used by a court as an aid in interpreting a statute or a constitutional provision.

LIABILITY. A legal obligation or responsibility. Liability is enforceable by a court in a civil or criminal trial.

LITIGATE. To sue or seek a resolution to a conflict in the courts.

MAGISTRATE. A judicial officer similar to a judge but with lesser and circumscribed authority.

MAJORITY OPINION. Opinion written by a justice or judge indicating the court's ruling in a case and offering an explanation for that ruling.

MANDAMUS. Latin for "we command." Usually, a writ of mandamus is issued from a court to force another court or government official to undertake a specific action.

MEDIATOR. A neutral party that helps to bring opposing sides to agreement by suggesting solutions and fostering productive negotiations.

MOOT. Descriptive of a case that is no longer fit for judicial resolution because an actual controversy no longer exists.

MOTION. An oral or written request for a court to rule on an issue or to compel a party in a case to do something.

NARROWLY TAILORED. A government policy that is closely linked to its objective and so restricts only as much liberty as is necessary to achieve it.

NONSECULAR. Religious.

NOTICE. Adequate warning, a "head's up."

ONEROUS. Difficult or burdensome.

ORDINANCE. Local law enacted by a city, suburb, town, municipality, or other local entity.

OVERBROAD. A law that sweeps too far by proscribing conduct or speech that is constitutionally protected.

PER CURIAM. By the court as a whole, rather than by a single author. It generally indicates the majority or plurality opinion (if not the unanimous opinion of the court), but there can still be concurring or dissenting opinions.

PETITIONER. Party that presents a petition to a court in an effort to seek appeal of a judgment. *See also* APPELLANT.

PLAINTIFF. Party that brings an original civil suit in a state or federal court.

PLURALITY OPINION. An opinion that does not receive support from enough justices (or judges) to constitute a majority on a court but receives more votes than any other opinion. Such an opinion will usually state the "judgment of the court" and may be accompanied by other opinions concurring in the judgment or dissenting from it.

POLITICAL QUESTION. Doctrine that compels federal courts to avoid deciding cases involving the discretionary powers of the executive or legislative branch.

PRECEDENT. Prior case law.

PRELIMINARY INJUNCTION. A temporary court order for a party to a case to do something or to stop doing something. The injunction lasts until the case has been fully decided on its merits.

PRESUMPTION. When something is assumed or probable (rather than proven).

PRIOR RESTRAINT. The restriction of speech before it is actually expressed or published; advance censorship.

PROBABLE CAUSE. Sufficient reason to believe that a person has committed, or is committing, a crime or that a place contains evidence connected with a crime.

PROMULGATE. To put a law or regulation into effect; to make known.

PROSCRIBE. To prohibit or ban.

PUBLIC ACCOMMODATIONS LAW. A law stating that a business must provide lodging, meal service, entertainment, or other services to all members of the public. In federal law, the Civil Rights Act of 1964 is the key example.

QUID PRO QUO. Something for something else; this for that. Quid pro quo campaign contributions ("I will give your campaign $1,000 if you vote for the farm bill") are illegal bribes.

RATIONAL BASIS REVIEW. The standard by which a court will uphold a nondiscriminatory law, under equal protection or due process, if it bears a reasonable relationship to the attainment of a legitimate public objective.

REASONABLE SUSPICION. The level of suspicion required for school officials to search a student's belongings or person; this is a weaker standard than probable cause.

RECORD. The facts and evidence assembled by a trial court in a case.

RELIEF. The monetary benefit or other restitution a court in a civil suit grants to a party that has suffered damages or injury.

REMAND. To send back to a lower court for further proceedings.

RESPONDEAT SUPERIOR. Doctrine that allows an employer (or superior) to be held liable for an employee's actions committed in the course of employment.

RESPONDENT. Party that answers to a petition for review in court. *See also* APPELLEE.

RESTITUTION. Making a person or persons whole, usually by giving them their money back.

RIPENESS. Doctrine requiring that an actual live case or controversy—as opposed to a hypothetical or potential controversy—be present for a case to be heard. A case will not be heard unless it is ripe for a court's consideration.

SECULAR. Not related to religion.

SEIZURE. Under the Fourth Amendment, government confiscation of property or arrest of a person.

SELF-INCRIMINATION. To say something that implicates you in a crime. The privilege against self-incrimination, as one high school senior put it, is the right "not to have to tell on yourself."

SEPARATION OF POWERS. The constitutional doctrine establishing that each of the three branches of government—legislative, executive, and judicial—is essentially independent and exercises unique powers.

SETTLEMENT AGREEMENT. Resolution of a legal dispute outside of court.

SEXUAL HARASSMENT. Sexually-related conduct, sometimes accompanied by promises or threats, that (1) creates a hostile learning or workplace environment and/or (2) involves express or implied conditions in which rejection of, or submission to, the conduct will affect an individual's employment or academic status (quid pro quo harassment).

SOLICITOR GENERAL. Attorney in the Department of Justice who represents the government in cases that go before the U.S. Supreme Court.

STANDING. The doctrine requiring that an individual show he or she suffered a direct and concrete injury that is traceable to the government and that can be redressed through court-ordered relief before the person's constitutional case against the government may be heard.

STATE ACTION. Action undertaken by a government agency or actor, whether federal, state, or local. State action is required to bring a constitutional case against the government.

STATUTE. A law passed by Congress or a state legislature.

STATUTORY. Relating to a statement or provision of law in an act of Congress or a state legislature.

STRICT SCRUTINY. The legal standard applied to suspect classifications, such as race, under equal protection and to burdens on fundamental rights, such as reproductive freedom or free speech, under due process or the First Amendment in which the government must show the court that it has used the least restrictive means to advance a compelling state interest.

SUMMARY JUDGMENT. Resolution of a case by a judge without trial where all of the significant facts of the case are uncontested and one party is entitled to win as a matter of law.

SUPPRESSION HEARING. A court hearing to determine whether a particular piece of evidence may be admitted and used at trial or will be "suppressed" because it was obtained unlawfully.

TITLE IX. A section of the Education Amendments of 1972, now known as the Patsy T. Mink Equal Opportunity in Education Act, which was enacted by Congress as a federal law on June 23, 1972. It provides that: "No person in the United States shall, on the basis of sex, be excluded from participation in, be denied the benefits of, or be subjected to discrimination under any education program or activity receiving Federal financial assistance." The legislation has had its chief effect on assuring fair and proportionate spending on boys' and girls' athletic and sports programs, but it actually applies to all educational activities, facilities, and programs.

TORT. A civil wrong. If you drive recklessly and knock down your neighbor's mailbox, he or she can sue you for committing a tort.

TRADITIONAL PUBLIC FORUM. A public place traditionally open to citizen communication, expression, and assembly: specifically, streets, sidewalks, and parks.

UNCONSTITUTIONAL. Descriptive of actions that are in violation of the commands or guarantees of the Constitution.

UNITED STATES CIRCUIT COURTS OF APPEAL. Body of courts consisting of thirteen federal circuits, including the Court of Appeals for the District of Columbia and the Court of Appeals for the Federal Circuit. These appellate courts hear cases that have been appealed from the United States District Courts.

UNITED STATES DISTRICT COURTS. Body of trial courts in which cases involving federal lawsuits are first tried.

UNITED STATES SUPREME COURT. Highest court in the United States. The Supreme Court is made up of a chief justice and eight associate justices and is charged with ruling on appeals from the United States Circuit Courts of Appeal and from state supreme courts. The Court also functions as a trial court in certain cases, including those that occur between states or those that involve ambassadors.

VAGUENESS. A law is unconstitutionally vague under due process if it is so ambiguous as not to give people notice of what is forbidden and what is allowed.

VERDICT. A jury's decision in a case or, in a nonjury trial, a judge's decision.

VIEWPOINT NEUTRALITY. The First Amendment requirement that government may not suppress or censor speech based on the point of view taken.

WARRANT. A writ or an order authorizing an officer to conduct a search of a place or to execute an arrest.

WRIT. A court's written order commanding someone to do, or refrain from doing, something.

WRIT OF CERTIORARI. A writ issued by the U.S. Supreme Court to a lower court directing the lower court to deliver the case for review. *Certiorari* is Latin and means "to be more fully informed."

APPENDIX D

BIBLIOGRAPHY

Abraham, Henry J., and Barbara A. Perry. *Freedom and the Court: Civil Rights and Liberties in the United States.* 7th ed. New York: Oxford University Press, 1998.

Adams, Lorraine, and Dale Russakoff. "Dissecting Columbine's Cult of the Athlete; In Search for Answers, Community Examines One Source of Killers' Rage," *Washington Post,* June 12, 1999.

American Association of University Women. *Hostile Hallways: The AAUW Survey on Sexual Harassment in America's Schools.* Washington, D.C.: AAUW Educational Foundation, 1993.

Arbetman, Lee, and Edward O'Brien. *Street Law: A Course in Practical Law.* 5th ed. St. Paul, Minn.: West Publishing, 1994.

Axelrod, Alan. *Minority Rights in America.* Washington, D.C.: CQ Press, 2002.

Ball, Howard. *The Bakke Case: Race, Education, and Affirmative Action.* Lawrence: University Press of Kansas, 2000.

Bell, Derrick A. *Race, Racism, and American Law.* 5th ed. New York: Aspen, 2004.

Biskupic, Joan, and Elder Witt. *Guide to the U.S. Supreme Court.* 3d ed. Washington, D.C.: Congressional Quarterly, 1997.

Bollinger, Lee C., and Geofrey R. Stone, eds. *Eternally Vigilant: Free Speech in the Modern Era.* Chicago: University of Chicago Press, 2002.

Bosmajian, Haig. *The Freedom Not to Speak.* New York: New York University Press, 1999.

Bosworth, Matthew H. *Courts as Catalysts: State Supreme Courts and Public School Finance Equity.* Albany: State University of New York Press, 2001.

Branch, Taylor. *At Canaan's Edge: America in the King Years, 1965–68.* New York: Simon and Schuster, 2007.

———. *Parting the Waters: America in the King Years 1954–63.* New York: Simon and Schuster, 1989.

Carson, Clayborne, ed. *Eyes on the Prize: Civil Rights Reader: Documents, Speeches, and Firsthand Accounts from the Black Freedom Struggle, 1954–1990.* New York: Viking, 1991.

Chin, Gabriel Jack. *Affirmative Action and the Constitution.* New York: Garland, 1998.

Clark, Charles S. "Charter Schools," *CQ Researcher,* December 20, 2002, 1033–1056.

Cole, David. *No Equal Justice: Race and Class in the American Criminal Justice System.* New York: New Press, 1999.

Cortner, Richard C. *Civil Rights and Public Accommodations: The Heart of Atlanta and McClung Cases.* Lawrence: University Press of Kansas, 2001.

Cushman, Clare, ed. *Supreme Court Decisions and Women's Rights.* Washington, D.C.: CQ Press, 2001.

———. *The Supreme Court Justices: Illustrated Biographies, 1789–1995.* 2d ed. Washington, D.C.: Congressional Quarterly, 1995.

Department of Education, Office for Civil Rights. *Revised Sexual Harassment Guidance: Harassment of Students by School Employees, Other Students, or Third Parties.* Washington, D.C.: U.S. Government Printing Office, 2001.

Devine, John. *Maximum Security: The Culture of Violence in Inner-City Schools.* Chicago: University of Chicago Press, 1996.

Douglas, Davison. *Reading, Writing, and Race: The Desegregation of the Charlotte Schools.* Chapel Hill: University of North Carolina, 1995.

———. *School Busing: Constitutional and Political Developments.* New York: Garland, 1997.

Epps, Garrett. *To an Unknown God: Religious Freedom on Trial.* New York: St. Martin's Press, 2001.

Finkelman, Paul, ed. *Religion and American Law: An Encyclopedia.* New York: Garland, 2000.

Finkelman, Paul, and Melvin I. Urofsky. *Landmark Decisions of the United States Supreme Court.* Washington, D.C.: CQ Press, 2003.

Fish, Stanley. *There's No Such Thing as Free Speech, and It's a Good Thing Too.* New York: Oxford University Press, 1994.

Foersel, Herbert N. *Free Expression and Censorship in America: An Encyclopedia.* Westport, Conn.: Greenwood, 1997.

Freyer, Tony. *The Little Rock Crisis: A Constitutional Interpretation.* Westport, Conn.: Greenwood, 1984.

Friendly, Fred W. *Minnesota Rag: The Dramatic Story of the Landmark Supreme Case That Gave New Meaning to Freedom of the Press.* New York: Random House, 1981.

Garcia, Alfredo. *The Sixth Amendment in Modern American Jurisprudence: A Critical Perspective.* Westport, Conn.: Greenwood, 1992.

Greenburg, Jan Crawford. *Supreme Conflict: The Inside Story of the Struggle for Control of the United States Supreme Court.* New York: Penguin Press, 2007.

Hall, Kermit. *The Oxford Companion to the Supreme Court of the United States.* New York: Oxford University Press, 1992.

Heins, Marjorie. *Not in Front of the Children: "Indecency," Censorship, and the Innocence of Youth.* New York: Hill and Wang, 2001.

Hentoff, Nat. *Free Speech for Me—But Not for Thee: How the American Left and Right Relentlessly Censor Each Other.* New York: HarperCollins, 1992.

Heumann, Milton, Thomas Church, and David Redlawsk, eds. *Hate Speech on Campus: Cases, Case Studies, and Commentary.* Boston: Northeastern University Press, 1997.

Hyman, Irwin A., and James H. Wise, eds. *Corporal Punishment in American Education: Readings in History, Practice, and Alternatives.* Philadelphia: Temple University Press, 1979.

Johnson, John W. *The Struggle for Student Rights:* Tinker v. Des Moines *and the 1960s.* Lawrence: University Press of Kansas, 1997.

Jost, Kenneth. "Affirmative Action," *CQ Researcher,* September 21, 2001, 737–759.

———. "School Vouchers Showdown," *CQ Researcher,* February 15, 2002, 121–144.

———. "Single-Sex Education," *CQ Researcher,* July 12, 2002, 569–592.

———, ed. *The Supreme Court A to Z.* 2d ed. Washington, D.C.: Congressional Quarterly, 1998.

Kalven, Harry. *A Worthy Tradition: Freedom of Speech in America.* New York: Harper and Row, 1988.

Kennedy, Randall. *Nigger: The Strange Career of a Troublesome Word.* New York: Pantheon, 2002.

Kluger, Richard. *Simple Justice: The History of* Brown v. Board of Education *and Black America's Struggle for Equality.* Rev. and exp. ed. New York: Knopf, 2004.

Kousser, J. Morgan. "Separate but *Not* Equal: The Supreme Court's First Decision on Racial Discrimination in Schools." *Journal of Southern History* 17 (1980).

Kozol, Jonathan. *Savage Inequalities: Children in America's Schools.* New York: Crown Publishing, 1991.

LaFave, Wayne R. *Search and Seizure: A Treatise on the Fourth Amendment.* 4th ed. St. Paul, Minn.: Thomson/West, 2004.

Lagemann, Ellen C., and LaMar P. Miller, eds. Brown v. Board of Education: *The Challenge for Today's Schools.* New York: Teachers College Press, 1996.

Landsberg, Brian K. *Enforcing Civil Rights: Race, Discrimination, and the Department of Justice.* Lawrence: University Press of Kansas, 1997.

Langelan, Martha. *Back Off: How to Confront and Stop Sexual Harassment and Harassers.* New York: Simon and Schuster, 1993.

Lantieri, Linda, and Janet Patti. *Waging Peace in Our Schools.* Boston: Beacon Press, 1998.

Larson, Edward J. *Trial and Error: The American Controversy over Creation and Evolution.* 3d ed. New York: Oxford University Press, 2003.

Leonard, Arthur S., ed. *Homosexuality and the Constitution.* New York: Garland, 1997.

Levy, Leonard W. *Origins of the Fifth Amendment.* New York: Oxford University Press, 1968.

———. *The Establishment Clause: Religion and the First Amendment.* 2d ed. Chapel Hill: University of North Carolina Press, 1994.

Lewis, Anthony. *Gideon's Trumpet.* New York: Random House, 1964.

———. *Make No Law: The Sullivan Case and the First Amendment.* New York: Random House, 1991.

Lin, Ann Chih, ed. *Immigration.* Washington, D.C.: CQ Press, 2002.

Lofgren, Charles A. *The Plessy Case: A Legal-Historical Interpretation.* New York: Oxford University Press, 1987.

Manfredi, Christopher P. *The Supreme Court and Juvenile Justice.* Lawrence: University Press of Kansas, 1998.

Manwaring, David. *Render Unto Caesar: The Flag-Salute Controversy.* Chicago: University of Chicago Press, 1962.

Marshall, Patrick. "Homework Debate," *CQ Researcher,* December 6, 2002, 993–1012.

———. "Religion in Schools," *CQ Researcher,* January 12, 2001, 1–24.

Martinez, Elizabeth Sutherland, ed. *Letters from Mississippi.* Brookline, Mass.: Zephyr Press, 2002.

Masci, David. "Evolution and Creationism," *CQ Researcher,* August 12, 1997, 745–768.

———. "Preventing Teen Drug Use," *CQ Researcher,* March 15, 2002, 217–240.

Metcalf, George R. *From Little Rock to Boston: A History of School Desegregation.* Westport, Conn.: Greenwood, 1983.

Minnow, Martha. *Making All the Difference: Inclusion, Exclusion and American Law.* Ithaca, N.Y.: Cornell University Press, 1991.

Moses, Robert P., and Charles E. Cobb Jr. *Radical Equations: Math Literacy and Civil Rights.* Boston: Beacon Press, 2002.

Murdoch, Joyce, and Deb Price. *Courting Justice: Gay Men and Lesbians v. The Supreme Court.* New York: Basic Books, 2001.

Patterson, James T. Brown v. Board of Education: *A Civil Rights Milestone and Its Troubled Legacy.* New York: Oxford University Press, 2001.

Raskin, Jamin B. "Legal Aliens, Local Citizens: The Historical, Constitutional, and Theoretical Meanings of Alien Suffrage." *University of Pennsylvania Law Review* 141 (April 1993): 1391–1470.

Ravitch, Frank S. *School Prayer and Discrimination: The Civil Rights of Religious Minorities and Dissenters.* Boston: Northeastern University Press, 1999.

Schwartz, Bernard. *Swann's Way: The School Busing Case and the Supreme Court.* New York: Oxford University Press, 1986.

Shiell, Timothy C. *Campus Hate Speech on Trial.* Lawrence: University Press of Kansas, 1998.

Sitkoff, Harvard. *The Struggle for Black Equality, 1954–1992.* Rev. ed. New York: Hill and Wang, 1993.

Stein, Nan, and Lisa Sjostrom. *Flirting or Hurting? A Teacher's Guide on Student-to-Student Sexual Harassment in Schools (Grades 6 through 12).* Washington, D.C.: National Education Association, 1994.

Stewart, David O. *The Summer of 1787: The Men Who Invented the Constitution.* New York: Simon and Schuster, 2007.

Strum, Phillippa. *Women in the Barracks: The VMI Case and Equal Rights.* Lawrence: University Press of Kansas, 2002.

Suggs, Welch. *A Place on the Team: The Triumph and Tragedy of Title IX.* Princeton, N.J.: Princeton University Press, 2006.

Thomas, Clarence. *My Grandfather's Son: A Memoir.* New York: Harper, 2007.

Toobin, Jeffrey. *The Nine: Inside the Secret World of the Supreme Court.* New York: Doubleday, 2007.

Turow, Scott. *One L: The Turbulent True Story of a First Year at Harvard Law School.* Reissued ed. New York: Farrar, Straus, and Giroux, 1988.

Tushnet, Mark V. *The NAACP's Legal Strategy Against Segregated Education, 1925–1950.* Chapel Hill: University of North Carolina Press, 1987.

Tyack, David B. "The Perils of Pluralism: The Background of the Pierce Case." *American Historical Review* 74 (October 1968): 74–98.

Wallenstein, Peter. "Race, Marriage, and the Supreme Court: From *Pace v. Alabama* to *Loving v. Virginia.*" *Journal of Supreme Court History* 65 (1998).

Wheeler, Stanton, and Leonard S. Cottrell Jr. *Juvenile Delinquency: Its Prevention and Control.* New York: Russell Sage Foundation, 1966.

Whitman, Mark, ed. *The Irony of Desegregation Law, 1955–1995: Essays and Documents.* Princeton, N.J.: M. Wiener, 1998.

Wilkinson, J. Harvie. *From* Brown *to* Bakke: *The Supreme Court and School Integration, 1954–1978.* New York: Oxford University Press, 1979.

Williams, Juan. *Eyes on the Prize: America's Civil Rights Years 1954–1965.* New York: Penguin, 1988.

Wills, Garry. *Under God: Religion and American Politics.* New York: Simon and Schuster, 1990.

Yudof, Mark G., David L. Kirp, and Betsy Levin. *Educational Policy and the Law.* 3d ed. St. Paul, Minn.: West Publishing, 1992.

THE MARSHALL-BRENNAN CONSTITUTIONAL LITERACY PROJECT

If *We the Students* does not seem like an ordinary textbook, it is probably because the materials in it are constantly being revised and improved by high school students and teachers, law students, and law professors all over America.

They volunteer their ideas because *We the Students* is the textbook for the Marshall-Brennan Constitutional Literacy Project, whose aims are to uplift constitutional understanding, advance democratic values, and promote young people's engagement in politics and government.

The Program and Its Origins

The Marshall-Brennan Project sends law students who have demonstrated their excellence in constitutional law into public high school classrooms to share their knowledge and passion with high school students. It involves the students in moot court competitions, essay contests, field trips, voter registration drives, and service learning projects. The Project began in 1999, when Mrs. Thurgood Marshall and Mrs. William Brennan came to American University's Washington College of Law (WCL) and invoked the memory of their husbands to bless the new initiative to put gifted law students—the Marshall-Brennan fellows—into public high schools to spread constitutional values. Both Justice Marshall and Justice Brennan were champions of teaching the Constitution, especially the Bill of Rights, to all Americans.

Marshall-Brennan Expands: Boston to Berkeley

Today, the Marshall-Brennan Project is thriving from coast to coast. More than a thousand Marshall-Brennan fellows have served in the nation's schools, and thousands of high school students have studied with them. In this chain of learning, lives are being transformed.

In the nation's capital, the project at WCL is run by Professor Steve Wermiel, Justice Brennan's biographer. The program has been bolstered by adjunct professor and former Marshall-Brennan fellow Maryam Ahranjani, who coteaches the seminar for fellows, and by the support of Dean Claudio Grossman, a renowned human rights lawyer whose own work involves spreading ideas of human dignity and freedom. Since 2006, former Marshall-Brennan fellows in the District of Columbia have also worked with Professor Ahranjani on the Youth Services Center Project, in which students teach our companion

At the U.S. District Court in Washington, D.C., (left to right) Treay Montgomery of Wilson High School and Elizabeth Dollmeyer of School Without Walls receive congratulations from Judges Louis F. Oberdorfer and Emmet G. Sullivan after winning the William H. Karchmer Spring 2008 High School Moot Court competition.

text, *Youth Justice in America,* to detained and incarcerated young people at the Youth Services Center.

The WCL Marshall-Brennan Project has been joined by Marshall-Brennan fellows from Howard University School of Law, where Professor Carmia Caesar launched the Marshall-Brennan Project in 2004. Each year these two law schools now place more than fifty Marshall-Brennan fellows into eighteen public high schools and junior high schools in Washington, D.C., and Montgomery County, Maryland. The annual Moot Court, Essay, and Creative Arts competitions are much-celebrated affairs that routinely draw United States Court of Appeals judges, including such luminaries as Judge Emmett Sullivan, Judge Paul Friedman, Judge Reggie Walton, Judge Gerald Bruce Lee, and Judge Louis Oberdorfer.

In 2001 Professors Beth Wilson and Traci Overton brought the Marshall-Brennan Project to Rutgers University School of Law's Camden campus in New Jersey. Since then, it has mobilized the talent and energy of Rutgers law students to teach in high schools in Camden, one of the poorest urban areas in the country. Today, Adjunct Professor William Ryan, himself a former Marshall-Brennan fellow, teaches the seminar at Rutgers.

Just across the Delaware River from Camden, another Marshall-Brennan chapter is flourishing in Philadelphia, the birthplace of the Constitution. There, Roger Dennis, the dean of Drexel University College of Law, and Marshall-Brennan dynamo Gwen Stern have given the Constitution a new birth of freedom locally by sending dozens of students from Drexel and the University of Pennsylvania Law School into public schools across the city. This project has produced dramatic and tantalizing successes that are helping to close the gap between the city's great universities and its public schools. The moot court competitions have teased out new talents in local high school students; in 2006, for instance, Jawanna Davis, a University City High School senior, went all the way to the finals of the National High School Moot Court Competition and so dazzled the judges with her precocious appellate talents that the *Philadelphia Inquirer* wrote a front-page article about her courtroom oratory and described her as a human "Stradivarius." The Marshall-Brennan Project will soon be unveiling an annual moot court competition for all of its chapters nationwide, taking place in Philadelphia.

In Boston, at the Northeastern University School of Law, Adjunct Professor Roy Karp has galvanized support across Massachusetts for an ambitious program of civic literacy education and has made the Marshall-Brennan Project a leader in both classroom teaching and education through moot courts and mock trials.

The Marshall-Brennan Project continues to spread: to Tempe, Arizona, at the Sandra Day O'Connor College of Law at Arizona State University (ASU), with a project launched by former WCL Marshall-Brennan fellow Carmen Forrest Corbin and run by K Royal, the pro bono coordinator at ASU; to the University of Louisville Louis D. Brandeis School of Law in Kentucky, where Professor Laura Rothstein has put together a first-class initiative; and to the University of California, Berkeley School of Law—Boalt Hall, where the program's director, Professor Jennifer Elrod, and the dean of students, Victoria Ortiz, have quickly made the program a dynamic force in the community and the Marshall-Brennan fellowship a highly coveted honor among law students who seek to teach constitutional values to young people in the community.

The most far-flung Marshall-Brennan Project has developed on the island of Palau, where four classes are being taught in two high schools. Because there is no law school there, the program is run by volunteer attorneys from the Palau Bar in the main city of Koror. It has achieved instant prominence in Palau and has been educating people about constitutional change, including an anticipated national referendum on whether to pass a series of proposed Constitutional amendments. The aforementioned Carmen Forrest Corbin launched this project under the name of Constitutional Literacy International and is planning to expand it to other countries as well.

In all of these projects, the law student fellows find that the way to learn something most deeply is to teach it to other people. Many fellows are now going on to splendid teaching careers in law schools, colleges, or high schools. They have found a passionate lifelong commitment to their students, to public schools, and to the communities where they study. The Marshall-Brennan fellows are helping young Americans wake up to their democratic citizenship, their intellectual potential and, in countless cases, their ability to go to college and succeed.

For More Information

If you are interested in bringing the Marshall-Brennan Constitutional Literacy Project to your community, please contact me at raskin@wcl.american.edu, Tabitha Acosta at tacosta@wcl.american.edu, or Gwen Stern at gstern@drexel.edu; we will see what we can do to help you. For more information, please visit our Web site at www.wcl.american.edu/marshallbrennan.

PHOTO CREDITS

Preface

x AP Images; xi AP Images; xii AP Images; xiii Marshall-Brennan Program.

1. "WE THE PEOPLE": Our Constitution and Courts

3 Library of Congress; 7 National Archives; 9 Ken Heinen; 11 Collection of the Supreme Court of the United States.

2. VOICES AND CHOICES:
The First Amendment and Student Speech

15 Collection of the Supreme Court of the United States; 17 Bill Pierce; 19 Collection of the Supreme Court of the United States; 22 The Granger Collection, New York; 24 Collection of the Supreme Court of the United States; 30 Reuters/Tami Chappell; 36 Library of Congress; 40 Collection of the Supreme Court of the United States; 41 Chris Pyle; 43 Brian Wallace/Juneau Empire/ZUMA Press; 54 AP Images; 56 Steven Aden.

3. FREEDOM OF THE STUDENT PRESS:
All the News the School Sees Fit to Print

64 AP Images; 66 Collection of the Supreme Court of the United States.

4. THE WALL OF SEPARATION BETWEEN
CHURCH AND SCHOOL

80 AP Images/*Delta Democratic Times*/Bill Johnson; 81 Collection of the Supreme Court of the United States; 83 Collection of the Supreme Court of the United States; 88 Daniel Weisman; 103 AP Images/Rick Bowmer; 107 Reuters/Tami Chappell; 112 AP Images/*The Gazette*/ Buzz Orr; 114 Reuters/Susan Ragan; 124 Library of Congress; 127 AP Images.

5. THE FOURTH AMENDMENT:
Searching the Student Body

140 AP Images; 141 AP Images/Susan Walsh; 142 Supreme Court Historical Society; 148 Brownsburg Community School Corporation; 152 AP Images/*The Decatur Daily*/Emily Saunders.

6. THE CONSTITUTION AND STUDENT DISCIPLINE:
"Due Process" and "Cruel and Unusual
Punishment" at School

169 *Miami Herald*, 1976; 170 Collection of the Supreme Court of the United States.

7. EQUAL PROTECTION AGAINST RACE
DISCRIMINATION: From Segregation to
Multicultural Democracy

178 Library of Congress; 179 Library of Congress; 181 Library of Congress; 183 AP Images; 184 Collection of the Supreme Court of the United States; 192 AP Images/Brian Bohannon; 203 AP Images/Susan Walsh.

8. THE OTHER LINES WE DRAW AT SCHOOL:
Wealth, Gender, Citizenship, and Sexual Orientation

217 Institute of Texan Culture; 220 AP Images/Steve Helber; 223 Supreme Court Historical Society; 224 AP Images/Jay Reeves; 230 Library of Congress; 236 AP Images/Stuart Ramson.

9. HARASSMENT IN THE HALLWAYS:
Sexual Harassment, Bullying, and the Law

246 Collection of the Supreme Court of the United States; 248 Alan Weiner.

10. A HEALTHY STUDENT BODY:
Disability, Privacy, Pregnancy, and Sexuality

262 AP Images/*The Cedar Rapids Gazette*/David Lee Hartlage; 267 AP Images/Dennis Cook; 279 Collection of the Supreme Court of the United States; 280 Scott J. Ferrell/Congressional Quarterly.

APPENDIX E: The Marshall-Brennan
Constitutional Literacy Project

321 Hilary Schwab.

INDEX

Italic page numbers indicate illustrations.

Abington School District v. Schempp (1963), 86–87
Abortion, 275–281
Abstinence programs, 273
Acton, James, *140*
Adams, Lorraine, 258
Advertising and U.S. flag, 20
Advisory opinions, 4
Affirmative action, 197–213
African Americans. *See* Race
Aguillard, Don, *127*
Alan Guttmacher Institute on number of teen
  pregnancies, 269
Alaska's legalization of marijuana possession and
  use, 52
Aliens
    illegal aliens in public school, 215, 228–235
    permanent residents as teachers, 215–216,
      234–235
Alito, Samuel A., Jr., *11*, 191–194
*Allegheny County v. American Civil Liberties Union of
  Greater Pittsburgh Chapter* (1989), 113
Ambach v. Norwick (1979), 215–216, 234–235
Amendments to the Constitution, 3, 21. *See also
    specific amendment (e.g., First Amendment)*
Americans with Disabilities Act (ADA), 260
Amicus curiae, defined, 193
Amish, exemption from compulsory school
  attendance, 120–125
Antimiscegenation statutes, 189
Appellants, 10
    defined, 156
Appellate courts, federal and state, 8–10
Appellees, 10
    defined, 153
Ardizzone, Kris, 71
Assembly, right to peaceful, 14
Athletics
    school prayer at events, *80,* 87, 93–99
    sex discrimination in, 215, 223–227

Bakke, Alan, 198
Barthes, Roland, 35
Bellamy, Francis, 114
Bethel School District No. 403 v. Fraser (1986), 36,
    37–40, 64
Beussink, Brandon, 73
Beussink v. Woodland R-IV School District (1998), 73
Bible readings, 86–87
Bill of Rights
    definition, 2
    incorporation, 6–8
Black, Hugo L.
    on desegregation and state-supported private
      schools, 186–187
    on government aid to private religious schools,
      100–101
    profile, *81*
    on protest speech, 27–28
    on reaction and resistance to desegregation,
      184–185
    on school prayer, 81–83
Blackmun, Harry
    on affirmative action in admissions, 198
    on Christmas nativity displays, 113
    on due process and discipline in schools, 163–164
    on library selection policies, 54
    on parental consent for teenage abortion, 278
    on permanent resident alien teachers, 235
    profile, *279*
    on school-sponsored newspapers and yearbooks,
      68–69
Blair High School, Silver Spring, Md., 70–72
Blue jeans, ban on, 33–34
*Board of Education, Island Trees Union Free School
    District #26 v. Pico* (1982), 53–55
*Board of Education of Independent School District #92
    of Pottawatomie County v. Earls* (2002). *See
    Pottawatomie County v. Earls* (2002)
Bob Jones University, 189

"BONG HiTS FOR JESUS" case (*Morse v. Frederick*)
   (2007), 43–52
Books, objectionable, 53
Boyd, Graham, *141*
Boy Scouts of America v. Dale (2000), 216, 235–241
Brennan, William J.
   on corporal punishment in schools, 172–173
   on library selection policies, 54–55
   profile, *230*
   on public school for illegal aliens, 228–232
   on reaction and resistance to desegregation,
      184–185
   on reasonable suspicion for searching students'
      property, 136–137
   on religious symbols displays, 113
   on school-sponsored newspapers and yearbooks,
      68–69
   on symbolic speech, 20
Breyer, Stephen G., *11*
   on Boy Scouts and homosexuals, 240–241
   on race as factor in school assignments, 194–196
   on school vouchers, 106–107
   on sex-based segregation, 222–223
   on sexual harassment of students by teachers, 247
Briefing a case, 11–12
Brown, Amanda, 73
Brown, Henry Billings, 179, *179*
Brown v. Allen (1953), 11
Brown v. Board of Education of Topeka, Kansas (1954)
   excerpt, 180–182
   historical importance, 30, 178–179
   reaction and resistance to, 183–187
Brown v. Gilmore (2001), 84
Bryan, William Jennings, 126–127
Bullying, 258–259
Burger, Warren E.
   on Christmas nativity displays, 112
   on free exercise of religion, 120–123
   on gender discrimination, 40
   profile, *36*
   on public school for illegal aliens, 232–234
   on sexual innuendo, 37–40
Burton, Harold H., 102, 184–185
Busing policies, 187

California v. Acevedo (1991), 137
Case-or-controversy requirement, 4
Cedar Rapids Community School District v. Garret F.
   (1999), 262–265
Center Moriches Union Free School District, 57
Ceremonial deism, 80, 112–113
Chicago, City of v. Morales (1999), 131, 164–167
Chief justice, 5
Christmas nativity displays, 111–114, *112*
Circuit Courts of Appeal, U.S., 9
Citizenship rights and illegal aliens, 215–216, 227–228
City of. See name of city
Civil suits, 10

Clark, Tom C., 184–185
Class action, defined, 229
Cleveland voucher program. *See Zelman v.*
   Simmons-Harris (2002)
Clinton, Bill, 5, 219–220
Clinton, Chelsea, 219–220
Coercion test for establishment of religion, 80
Columbine High School, 81, 111, 258–259
Columbus, Ohio. *See Goss v. Lopez* (1975)
Commercial speech
   flag cases, 20–21
   soft drink sponsorships in schools, 29
Common law, 10
Commonwealth of. See name of commonwealth
Concurring opinions, 10
Condoms, distribution of, 273–275
Confederate flag cases, 30–32
Congress, 3
Constitution of the United States. *See also* Appendix
   B, 287
   description, 2, *7*
   government branches, 4–5
   interpretation of, 4
   scope of, 4
   state law, 6
Cooper v. Aaron (1958), 184–185
Coronado High School, El Paso, Texas, 33. *See also*
   Karr v. Schmidt (1972)
Corporal punishment, 169–175
Courts. *See also* Bill of Rights; Constitution of the
   United States
   briefing a case, 11–12
   federal and state, 8–10
   majority and dissenting opinions, 10–11
Creation story versus evolution theory, 126–129
Criminal prosecutions, 10
Curtis v. School Committee of Falmouth (1995),
   273–275

Dade County, Florida. *See Ingraham v. Wright* (1977)
Dale, James, *236*
Darrow, Clarence, 126–127
Darwinism versus creation story, 126–129
Davis, LaShonda, *248*
Davis v. Monroe County Board of Education (1999),
   248–255
Declarative relief, defined, 141
Defendants, 12
Des Moines School District. *See Tinker v. Des Moines*
   School District (1969)
Direct appellate review, defined, 273
Discipline. *See also* Corporal punishment
   due process rights, 159–164
   suspensions, 159–164
"Dissecting Columbine's Cult of the Athlete" (Adams
   & Russakoff), 258
Dissenting opinions, 10–11
District Courts, U.S., 9

Diversity in schools, 198
"Dixie," as school song, 30
Doe v. See name of opposing party
Dole, Robert, 219–220
Double jeopardy, 2
Douglas, William O.
    on free exercise of religion, 124–125
    profile, *124*
    on reaction and resistance to desegregation,
       184–185
Dred Scott case (1857), 179
Dress codes, 41–43. *See also* Uniform policies
Driving, legal age for, 176
Drugs, legalized use of, 52
Drug-sniffing dogs, use of, *152,* 152–155
Drug testing, 131, 139–147
Due process
    discipline and punishment, 159–164
    due process clause, defined, 161
    in Fourteenth Amendment, 6
    loitering with no apparent purpose, 164–168
    suspensions, 159–164
    vague laws, 168

Earls, Lindsay, *141*
Eckford, Elizabeth, 183
Eckhardt, Christopher, 23
Economic segregation and school financing, 214–215
Editorial policies, 70
Education, U.S. Department of, 6
Education Amendments. *See* Title IX of the Education
    Amendments (1972)
Edward v. Aguillard (1987), 128
Eighth Amendment
    corporal punishment, 169–174
    excessive physical force, 174–175
    text of, 158
Eisenhower, Dwight D., 114–115, 183
Elk Grove Unified School District v. Newdow (2004),
    118–119
Employment Division v. Smith (1990), 126
Endorsement test for establishment of religion, 80
Engel v. Vitale (1962), 80, 81–84
Enjoin, defined, 274
Epperson v. Arkansas (1968), 127–128
Equal Access Act, 57
Equal protection
    aliens, rights of, 215–216, 228–234
    antimiscegenation statutes, 189
    Brown v. Board of Education (1954), 180–182
    desegregation and state-supported private schools,
       185–187
    economic segregation, 217–220
    equal protection clause, defined, 199
    for gays and lesbians, 216, 235–242
    for noncitizens, 227–228
    pregnant student dismissal, 272–273
    race as factor in school assignments, 189–196

resistance to desegregation, 183–187
reverse discrimination, 197–213
school funding inequalities, 214–215
segregated schools, 178–182
sex-based segregation, 215, 221–223
tests for, 220–221
Title IX. *See* Title IX of the Education
    Amendments (1972)
Establishment of religion
    Bible readings, 86–87
    Christmas nativity displays, 111–114
    coercion test for, 80
    endorsement test for, 80
    establishment clause, defined, 89
    evolution theory versus creation story, 126–129
    freedom from, 14, 78–79, 80–86
    government aid to private religious schools,
       100–102
    school prayer, 80–84, 86–99
    school vouchers, 102–107
    Ten Commandments, display of, 107–111
    words "under God" in Pledge of Allegiance,
       114–119
Everson v. Board of Education of the Township of Ewing
    (1947), 100–102
Evolution theory versus creation story, 126–129
Exclusionary rule, 132
Executive branch, 5
Exercise of religious freedom. *See* Free exercise
    of religion
Expressive association, defined, 237
Expressive conduct, 14–22
    cable channel censorship, 70–72
    censureship of symbolic speech, 20
    flag desecration, 20–21
    flag salute, 14, 15–20
    Jehovah's Witnesses, 15–16
Extracurricular activities and drug testing, 139–148

Facts, of cases, 10, 12
Falvo, Jim & Kristja, *267*
Family Educational Rights and Privacy Act (FERPA),
    261, 265–269
Faubus, Orval, 183
Federal courts, 8–10
Federalism
    definition, 2, 255
    Supreme Court versus local school districts, 6
Federalist No. 49, 3
Fifth Amendment
    due process clause, 161
    self-incrimination, prohibition against, 159
Fighting words, 14
First Amendment. *See also* Expressive conduct; Press,
    freedom of
    dress codes, 14, 42–43
    establishment of religion clause, 14, 78–79, 80–86.
       See also Establishment of religion

First Amendment (cont.)
  flag desecration, 20–21
  flag salute during Pledge of Allegiance, 14, 15–20
  free exercise of religion clause, 78–79, 80–86,
      119–126
  hair length, 14, 33–36
  library selection policies, 53–56
  protest speech, 22–28
  racial harassment and intimidation, 30–32
  Supreme Court building activity and, 9
  Ten Commandments and, 107–111
  text of, 14, 78
  uniform policies, 32
  viewpoint neutrality and religious speech, 56–62
  vulgar or profane language, 14, 36–41, 54, 56
Flag cases. *See also* Pledge of Allegiance
  advertising, 20–21
  Confederate, 30–32
  flag desecration, 20–21
  semioticians on, 31
Flag Protection Act, 17
Fortas, Abe, 13, *24*, 24–27
Founders, *3*
Fourteenth Amendment, 6, 158, 176. *See also* Due
  process; Equal protection
Fourth Amendment, 130–131. *See also* Searches and
  seizures
Frankfurter, Felix
  on government aid to private religious
      schools, 102
  profile, *19*
  on reaction and resistance to desegregation,
      184–185
  on salute during Pledge of Allegiance, 19–20
Fraser, Matthew, 36–38, *38*
Frederick, Joseph, 52
Frederick, Morse v. (2007), 44–51
Free exercise clause, defined, 82
Free exercise of religion, 14, 78–79, 80–86, 119–126
Free speech, limits of, 43–52
Frey, Garrett, *262*, 262–265
Friedman, Milton, 219

Gainous, Philip, 72
Gangs and loitering regulations, 131, 164–168
Garcia v. Miera (1987), 174–175
Gault, In re (1967), 159
Gays and lesbians
  Boy Scouts, membership in, 216, 235–241
  equal protection, 216, 235–242
  harassment of, 257–258
  participation in Boston St. Patrick's Day
      parade, 236
  public displays of affection, 241–242
Gay/Straight Alliances, 257
Gebser v. Lago Vista Independent School District
  (1998), 245–247

Gender discrimination, 40, 215, 221–223. *See also*
  Sexual harassment
Ginsburg, Ruth Bader, *xii*, *11*
  on Boy Scouts and homosexuals, 240–241
  on drug testing and extracurricular activities,
      146–147
  on free speech rights of religiously oriented group,
      60–61
  on loitering with no apparent purpose, 165–166
  profile, *223*
  on race as factor in school assignments,
      194–196
  on school vouchers, 106–107
  on sex-based segregation, 222–223
  on sexual harassment of students by
      teachers, 247
Gonzales v. Carhart (2007), *280*
Good News Club v. Milford Central School (2001), *56*,
  57–61
  debate issues, 61–62
  excerpt, 57–60
Goss v. Lopez (1975), 159–163
Govers, Paula, 70–71
Graduation ceremonies, school prayer at, 87–93
Gratz, Jennifer, 202, *203*
Gratz v. Bollinger (2003), 190, 198–203
Green card holders, 228
Grievances, right to petition for redress of, 14
*Griffin v. County School Board of Prince Edward
  County* (1964), 185–187
Grutter, Barbara, *203*
Grutter v. Bollinger (2003), 190, 199, 203–211, 212

Hair length cases, 33–36
Hall v. Tawney (1980), 174
Harlan, John Marshall (1833-1911), 181, *181*
Harlan, John Marshall, II (1899-1971), 184–185
Harris, Eric, 258
Harvard Plan on race and ethnicity for
  admissions, 199
Hazelwood School District v. Kuhlmeier (1988)
  cable channel censorship, 72
  excerpt, 65–69
  regulation of student expression found
      reasonable, 27–28, 63
  scope of, 69
Hearing-impaired students, 260
Heightened scrutiny, 220, 234
Henery, Adam, 41
Hitler, Adolph, 15
Holdings, of cases, 12
Holmes v. Montgomery (2003), 151–152
Homosexuality. *See* Gays and lesbians
Hostile environment sexual harassment, 244
Hostile Hallways (Louis Harris and Associates
  study), 243
Huckleberry Finn (Twain), 55

Hurley v. Irish American Gay, Lesbian and Bisexual Group of Boston, Inc. (1995), 236

Illegal aliens, public school for, 215, 228–235
Illness, 260
Impeachment, 5
Important interest test, 273
Incorporation doctrine, 6, 8, 14
Indecent speech, 36–41
Individuals with Disabilities Education Act (IDEA), 260, 261–265
Ingraham v. Wright (1977), 169–173
Injunctive relief, defined, 141, 249
Injury and case-or-controversy requirement, 4
In loco parentis, 48, 174
In re. See name of party
Intermediate scrutiny, 220, 223. *See also* Heightened scrutiny
Internet homepages, 73–76
Interracial dating and marriages, 189
Invidious discrimination, defined, 229
Irving Independent School District v. Tatro (1984), 261
Island Trees Union Free School District #26, New York, 53
Issue(s), of cases, 12

Jackson, Robert H., 11, 15, *15,* 16–19, 102
Jackson, Roderick, *224*
Jackson v. Birmingham Board of Education (2005), 215, 224–227
Japanese Americans and resident aliens, WWII internment of, 228
Jefferson, Thomas, 2
Jehovah's Witnesses, 15–16
Jim Crow laws, *178*
Jocks, privileges for, 258
Johnson, Austin, *192*
Johnson, Gregory, 17, *17*
Judicial branch, 5, *8,* 8–10
Judicial bypass, 276
Judicial review, 3
Jurisprudence, defined, 105

Kameny, Frank, 70–71
Karr, Chesley, 33
Karr v. Schmidt (1972), 34–35
Kennedy, Anthony M., *11*
   on affirmative action, 208–209
   coercion test for religious establishment, 80
   on nursing care in school for physically disabled students, 264–265
   on parental consent for teenage abortion, 277–278
   on peer grading, 266–269
   on prayer at ceremonial events, 87–92
   on race as factor in school assignments, 196
   on religious symbols displays, 113

   on sex-based segregation, 222–223
   on sexual harassment of students by students, 253–255
   on viewpoint-oriented school publications, 57
Kennedy, Randall, 55
Kennedy, Robert F., 23
Kentucky statute on Ten Commandments. *See Stone v. Graham* (1980)
Killion v. Franklin Regional School District (2001), 74–76
King, Coretta Scott, 23
Klebold, Dylan, 258
Korematsu v. United States (1944), 228
Ku Klux Klan, 183

Lamb's Chapel v. Center Moriches Union Free School District (1993), 57
Latasha W., In re (1998), 155–156
Lawrence v. Texas (2003), 216, 235
Learning disabilities, 260
Lee v. Weisman (1992), 87–93
Legislative branch, 4–5. *See also* Congress
Lemon v. Kurtzman (1971), 80
Lesbians. *See* Gays and lesbians
Lewd speech, 36–41
Liability, defined, 251
Library selection policies, 53–56
Lincoln, Abraham, 3
Litigate, defined, 94
Little Rock, Arkansas. *See Cooper v. Aaron* (1958)
"Little Rock Nine," *183*
Lloyd, Christopher, 70
Locke, John, 2
Locker searches, *152,* 152–155
Loitering, 131, 164–168
Louisiana. *See Edward v. Aguillard* (1987)
Loving v. Virginia (1967), 189
Lynch v. Donnelly (1984), 111–113

Madison, James, 3
Magnet schools, 187
Majority opinions, definition, 10
Marbury v. Madison (1803), 3, 9
Marshall, John, 3
Marshall, Thurgood
   on affirmative action in admissions, 198
   on corporal punishment in schools, 172–173
   on economic segregation, 219
   on library selection policies, 54
   profile, *40*
   on racial desegregation and municipal boundary lines, 187
   on reasonable suspicion for searching students' property, 136–137
   on religious symbols displays, 113
   on school-sponsored newspapers and yearbooks, 68–69

Marshall-Brennan Constitutional Literacy Project, xv, 12
McCulloch v. Maryland (1819), 9
Melton, Rod, 30–31
Melton v. Young (1972), 30–31
Meredith v. Jefferson County Board of Education (2007), 190
Metal detectors, 155–157
Metzger v. Osbeck (1988), 175
Military recruiters and No Child Left Behind Act, 269
Miller, William E., 30
Milliken v. Bradley (1974), 187
Minersville School District v. Gobitis (1940), 11, 15
Missouri v. Jenkins (1995), 187
Moments of silence, 84
Montgomery County (Md.) Board of Education, 71–72
Moore, Roy, 110
Moot cases and case-or-controversy requirement, 4
Morgan, Lewis R., 34–35
Morse v. Frederick (2007), 44–51
Mueller v. Allen (1983), 103

Nabozzy, Jamie, 257
National Committee for a Sane Nuclear Policy, 23
Naturalized citizens, 228
Nazism, 15
Newdow, Michael, *114,* 115, 118
Newdow v. U.S. Congress (2002), 21, 115–118
New Jersey v. T. L. O. (1984), 131, 132–137
Nigger (Kennedy), 55
No Child Left Behind Act (2002), 269
Noncitizens, voting by, 227, 234–235

Obscenity, 13
O'Connor, Sandra Day, *x*
    on affirmative action, 203–208
    on drug testing and extracurricular activities participation, 146–147
    endorsement of religion test, 80
    on parental consent for teenage abortion, 277–278
    profile, *246*
    on public school for illegal aliens, 232–234
    on religious symbols displays, 112–113
    on sex-based segregation, 222–223
    on sex discrimination in athletics, 225–227
    on sexual harassment of students by students, 249–253
    on sexual harassment of students by teachers, 245–247
    on words "under God" in Pledge of Allegiance, 118–119
Offensive speech, 36–41
Ordinances, 10
Owasso Independent School District No. I-011 v. Falvo (2002), 265–269

Paine, Thomas, 2
Paper Chase, The (film), 12

Parental approval for teenage abortion, 276, 277–280
Parents Involved in Community Schools v. Seattle School District No. 1 (2007), 190, 191–196, *192*
Parents of New York United (PONYU), 53
Parties, in cases, 12
Peer grading, 265–269
Pennsylvania, Commonwealth of v. Cass (1998), 153–155
Per curiam, defined, 108
Permanent resident aliens, 215–216, 228
Petitioners, definition of, 10
Pfeiffer v. Marion Center Area School District (1990), 270–272
Physical disabilities, 260, 261
Pierce v. Society of Sisters (1925), 218–219
Plaintiffs, 10, 12
Planned Parenthood of Southeastern Pennsylvania v. Casey (1992), 276, 277–280
Pledge of Allegiance
    flag salute, 14, 15–20
    "under God" phrase in, 80, 114–119
Plessy v. Ferguson (1896), 179
Plyler v. Doe (1982), 215, 228–234
Political questions, 4
Poorman, Yancy, 73
Pottawatomie County v. Earls (2002), 131, 140–147
Powell, Lewis F., Jr.
    on affirmative action in admissions, 198
    on corporal punishment in schools, 169–172, 173
    on due process and discipline in schools, 159–160, 163–164
    on permanent resident alien teachers, 235
    profile, *170*
Prayer. *See* School prayer
Precedents, 4
Pregnancy, 260, 261, 269–281. *See also* Abortion
    abstinence or sex education programs, 273
    condom distribution programs, 273–275
    dismissal of pregnant students, 270–273
President, school choice of, 219–220
Press, freedom of, 63–77
    cable channel censorship, 70–72
    Internet homepages, 73–76
    school-sponsored activities, 64–70
Privacy. *See also* Searches and seizures
    medical and educational records, 260, 265–269
    parental consent for teenage abortion, 276
    student rights, 132–139
Private schools
    desegregation and state-supported, 185–187
    government aid to religion-based, 100–102
    public school attendance laws, 218–219
    state action requirement, 8
Probable cause
    defined, 154
    Fourth Amendment, 130–131
    searching cars, 137
Procedure of cases, 10, 11–12

Property taxes and school financing, 214–215
Protest speech, 22–28
Public accommodations law, defined, 237
Pyle, Jeffrey & Jonathan, *41,* 41–43
Pyle v. South Hadley School Committee (1996), 42–43

Quid pro quo and sexual harassment, 244

Race
    admissions policies, 197–213
    Brown v. Board of Education. See Brown v. Board of
        Education of Topeka, Kansas (1954)
    busing policies, 187
    Dred Scott case (1857), 179
    equal protection, 177
    interracial dating and marriages, 189
    Jim Crow laws, *178*
    "Little Rock Nine," *183*
    magnet schools, 187
    postponing desegregation due to hostility,
        184–185
    protests, discipline for, 159
    school assignments based on, 189–196
    segregated schools, 178–179
    special schools based on, 188
    state-supported private schools, 185–187
    strict scrutiny, 220–221
    white flight and desegregation across county
        lines, 187
Racist symbols and free speech, 31–32
Rational basis test or scrutiny, 176, 221
Rationale for cases, 12
Reasonable suspicion. *See also* Probable cause
    defined, 133
    searching students' property, 132–139
Reasoning for cases, 12
Regents of University of California v. Bakke (1978), 198
Rehabilitation Act, Section 504 (1973), 260
Rehnquist, William H., x
    on affirmative action, 199–202, 208–209
    on Boy Scouts and homosexuals, 236–240
    on due process and discipline in schools, 163–164
    on library selection policies, 55
    on loitering with no apparent purpose, 167
    on public school for illegal aliens, 232–234
    on religious symbols displays, 113
    on school vouchers, 104–106
    on sex-based segregation, 222–223
    on sexual harassment of students by students,
        253–255
    on solemnizing speakers at football games, 98–99
    on Ten Commandments statutes, 109
    on words "under God" in Pledge of Allegiance,
        118–119
Related services, for special education, 261, 262–265
Relief, 10
Religion
    Bible readings, 86–87

cable channel censorship, 71–72
    ceremonial deism, 80, 112–113
    ceremonial events, 86–99
    Christmas nativity displays, 111–114, *112*
    display of religious symbols, 111–114
    establishment clause. *See* Establishment of religion
    evolution theory versus creation story, 126–129
    free exercise clause. *See* Free exercise of religion
    government aid to private religious schools,
        100–102
    school prayer, 80–84, 86–89
    school vouchers, 102–107
    Ten Commandments statutes, 107–111
    viewpoint neutrality, 56–62
    words "under God" in Pledge of Allegiance,
        114–119
Renfrow, Doe v. (1980), 149–150
Reverse discrimination, 197–213
Reynolds, Robert, *64*
Ripeness doctrine, 4
Roberts, John G., Jr., *11*
    on free speech and power to discipline, 44–48
    on race-based public school assignments, 191–194
Rodriguez, Demetrio, *217*
Roe v. Wade (1973), 276, 279
Romer v. Evans (1996), 235
*Rosenberger v. Rector and Visitors of the University of
    Virginia* (1995), 57, 71
Rumspringa, 125–126
Russakoff, Dale, 258
Rutledge, Wiley B., 102

St. Charles High School, Mo., 41
San Antonio Independent School District v. Rodriguez
    (1973), 214–215, 217–218
Santa Fe Independent School District v. Doe (2000), *80,*
    94–99
Scabs, 28–29
Scalia, Antonin, *11*
    on affirmative action, 208–211
    on establishment clause test, 80
    on loitering, 167
    on prayer at ceremonial events, 92–93
    on race as factor in school assignments, 191–194
    on religious symbols displays, 113
    on sex-based segregation, 222, 223
    on sexual harassment of students by students,
        253–255
    on solemnizing speakers at football games, 98–99
Schaeffer, Judith, 71
Schempp family, 86
School assignments, race as factor in, 189–196
School districts, Supreme Court versus decisions by, 6
School districts, wealth of, 214–215
School prayer, 80–84, 86–89
    at athletic games, *80*
    at ceremonial events, 87–93
    establishment clause, 81–84

School publications, viewpoint-oriented, 57
School-sponsored newspapers and yearbooks, 65–69
    cable channel censorship and, 72
School vouchers, 102–107, *103*, 219
Scopes, John T., 126–127
Scopes Monkey Trial, 126–127
Searches and seizures
    drug-sniffing dogs, use of, 152–155
    drug testing of students, 139–148
    exclusionary rule, 132
    Fourth Amendment protections, 130–131
    locker searches, *152,*152–155
    metal detectors, 155–157
    privacy versus government intrusion, 138–139
    probable cause, 137
    reasonable suspicion, 132–139
    strip searches, 149–152
    student privacy rights, 132–139
    of students' property, 132–139
Section 504, Rehabilitation Act (1973), 260
Self-incrimination, prohibition against, 159
Separate but equal doctrine
    racially segregated schools, *179*
    school financing, 217–220
Separation of powers, 2
Sex-based segregation, 215
Sex discrimination in athletics, 215, 223–227
Sex education programs, 273
Sexist symbols, free speech and, 33
Sexual harassment. *See also* Bullying
    of gay and lesbian students, 257–258
    hostile environment, 244
    quid pro quo, 244
    statistics, 243
    of students by students, 248–256
    of students by teachers, 245–248
Sexual innuendo, 36–41
Slavery, 178–179
Smith, Sharon, *141*
Soft drink sponsorships in schools, 29
Solemnizing speakers at football games, 93–99
Souter, David H., *11*
    on drug testing and extracurricular activities
        participation, 146–147
    on free speech rights of religiously oriented group,
        60–61
    on loitering with no apparent purpose, 165–166
    on parental consent for teenage abortion, 277–278
    on race as factor in school assignments, 194–196
    on school vouchers, 106–107
    on sex-based segregation, 222–223
    on sexual harassment of students by teachers, 247
South Hadley School Committee, Pyle v. (1996), 42–43
Speech, freedom of, 14. *See also* First Amendment
Spina bifida and school health services, 261
Spock, Benjamin, 23
Sports events. *See* Athletics

Stallworth, Deborah, *192*
Standing, 4
State action requirement, 8
State courts, 9–10
States government, 8
State supreme courts, 9–10
Statutes, 9
    defined, 101
Statutory, defined, 263
Stevens, John Paul, *11*
    on Boy Scouts and homosexuals, 240–241
    on corporal punishment in schools, 172–173
    on drug testing and extracurricular activities
        participation, 146–147
    on flag burning, 20
    on free speech and power to discipline, 49–51
    on library selection policies, 54–55
    on loitering with no apparent purpose, 165–166
    on nursing care in school for physically disabled
        students, 262–264
    on race as factor in school assignments, 194–196
    on reasonable suspicion for searching students'
        property, 136–137
    on religious symbols displays, 113
    on school vouchers, 106–107
    on sex-based segregation, 222–223
    on sexual harassment of students by teachers, 247
    on solemnizing speakers at football games, 94–98
Stewart, Potter
    profile, *83*
    on school prayer, 83–84
Stone v. Graham (1980), 108–109
Strict scrutiny
    defined, 191
    overview, 220–221
    permanent resident aliens and, 215
    racial discrimination and, 220
Strip searches, 149–152
Student Free Expression Act (Mass.), 42
Student group meetings, viewpoint-oriented, 57
Substantially related test, 222, 273
Summary discipline and due process, 159
Summary judgment, defined, 255
Suppression hearing, defined, 154
Supremacy clause and state enforcement of national
    judicial orders, 183
Supreme Court, U.S., 3, 9
    building, *9*
    hearing arguments, 31
    justices (2003), *11*
Supreme courts, state, 9–10
Suspension from school and due process, 159–164
Suspicion. *See also* Probable cause; Reasonable
    suspicion
Swann v. Charlotte-Mecklenburg Board of Education
    (1971), 187
Sweatt v. Painter (1950), 197

Taft, William Howard, 9
Teacher strikes, student opinion on, 28–29
Ten Commandments
    public display of, *107*
    statutes on, 108–109
    versions of, 109–111
Tennessee, Scopes Monkey trial, 126–127
Terry v. Ohio (1968), 131
Texas v. Johnson (1989), 17, 20
Thomas, Clarence, *xi, 11*
    on affirmative action, 208–211, 212, 213
    on drug testing and extracurricular activities
        participation, 140–146
    on free speech and power to discipline students,
        48–49
    on free speech rights of religiously oriented group,
        57–60
    on loitering, 167, 168
    on nursing care in school for physically disabled
        students, 264–265
    profile, *142*
    on race as factor in school assignments, 191–194
    on sex-based segregation, 222
    on sexual harassment of students by students,
        253–255
    on solemnizing speakers at football games, 98–99
    on words "under God" in Pledge of Allegiance,
        118–119
Thomas ex rel. Thomas v. Roberts (2003), 151
Tinker, John, *22,* 22–23
Tinker, Mary Beth, *xvii, 22,* 22–23, *29*
Tinker v. Des Moines School District (1969)
    excerpt, 23–27
    Hazelwood compared to, 66–69
    official school-sponsored activities, 64
    student right to free speech that does not interfere
        with school functioning, 22, 63
Title IX of the Education Amendments (1972)
    athletics, sex discrimination in, 215, 223–227
    defined, 225
    pregnant student dismissal, 272–273
    sexual harassment, 244, 248
    text of, 243
Topeka, Kansas. *See Brown v. Board of Education of
    Topeka, Kansas* (1954)
Torts, 10
Trial courts, federal and state, 9–10

Unconstitutional laws or policies, 3
Underground newspapers, 72–73. *See also* Internet
    homepages
Uniform policies, 32. *See also* Dress codes
    boys' hair length, 33–36
United States v. See name of opposing party
University of Virginia, 57, 71

Vagueness, 168
Vernonia School District v. Acton (1995), 131, 139–140
Vietnam War and protest speech, *22,* 23, 68
Viewpoint neutrality
    library selection policies, 53–56
    viewpoint neutrality and religious speech, 56–62
    vulgar or profane language, 57
Virginia; United States v. (1996), 222–223
Virginia Military Institute, 221–223
Virginia Women's Institute for Leadership, 222
Visually impaired students, 260
Vonnegut, Kurt, Jr., *54*
Voting by noncitizens, 227, 234–235
Vouchers. *See* School vouchers
Vulgar language, 36–41, 54–56

Wallace v. Jaffree (1985), 84
War on Drugs, 52
Warren, Earl
    profile, *184*
    on reaction and resistance to desegregation,
        184–185
    reaction to *Brown* decision, 183
    on segregated schools, 180–182
Weisman family, *88*
West v. Derby Unified School District No. 260 (2000),
    31
West Virginia State Board of Education v. Barnette
    (1943), 11, 15–20, 114
White, Byron R.
    on corporal punishment in schools, 172–173
    on due process and discipline in schools, 160–163
    profile, *66*
    on public school for illegal aliens, 232–234
    on reasonable suspicion for searching students'
        property, 132–136
    on religious symbols displays, 113
    on school-sponsored newspapers and yearbooks,
        65–67, 69
White flight and desegregation across county lines, 187
Whittaker, Charles E., 184–185
Widmar v. Vincent (1981), 57
Wisconsin v. Yoder (1972), 120–125
*Witters v. Washington Department of Services for the
    Blind* (1986), 103
Women. *See* Sex-based segregation; Sexual harassment
Wood, Barbara, 70
Wort v. Vierling (1985), 272
Wright, Willie, *169*
Writ of certiorari, 31

Zelman v. Simmons-Harris (2002), 103–107
Zobrest v. Catalina Foothills School District (1993), 103